Larry Watkin

A Memoir of an American Man of Letters

Pulp Hero Press
The Most Dangerous Books on Earth
www.PulpHeroPress.com

Although every precaution has been taken to verify the accuracy of the information contained herein, no responsibility is assumed for any errors or omissions, and no liability is assumed for damages that may result from the use of this information.

The views expressed in this book are those of the author and do not necessarily reflect the views of Pulp Hero Press.

Pulp Hero Press publishes its books in a variety of print and electronic formats. Some content that appears in one format may not appear in another.

Editor: Bob McLain
Layout: Artisanal Text
ISBN 978-1-68390-127-3
Printed in the United States of America
Pulp Hero Press | www.PulpHeroPress.com
Address queries to bob@pulpheropress.com

Larry Watkin

A Memoir

1

A grandson, reading a story about "the olden days," commiserated with me when I told him that I too had managed to live through those primitive times before World War I when nobody had ever heard of television and not a single member of our family owned a car.

We didn't have a car, but we had a well-sprung, two-seated carriage with a fringe on top, and my father, who prided himself on having beautiful horses, would bring out his finest team. He'd let me hold the reins steady as he helped my mother up the step into the back seat. It was an act of pure gallantry, for my mother was so nimble and self-reliant that she could have climbed a tree unaided, long skirts and all, if it had been the lady-like thing to do. She was a beautiful woman whose mere presence brightened the world for us. My father adored her, as he did my younger sister Glenevieve and my older sister Elsie, who sat on either side of my mother, pretty as flowers in their colored dresses.

My father took over the reins. I sat erect on the seat, fascinated by the supple power in the glossy hips of those two great horses. Why couldn't I have had legs like that? Every morning I climbed the fence that led to the abandoned racetrack on Humpy Upton's place, but my skinny legs would barely take me once around that old oval. Those horses could have done it in nothing flat. They had been stabled too long and wanted to run, but my father kept them well under control. He held the reins in his left hand, the whip in his right, and though the braided tassel flicked over their backs like a trout fly, he never touched them with it. It was all part of the show. We pranced past the gang of loiterers outside the post office. I knew they were saying to themselves: "Here comes Ed. Watkin with a fine, matched pair of bays, taking his family out for a Sunday afternoon drive through Forest Park. Man, I'll bet those horses can step!"

They could, too.

We rode through the downtown area, went past the foundry, crossed the long bridge, drove by the knitting mill, and were soon in the peripheries where a sign read: Incorporated Village of Camden. Early on I learned that Camden, Oneida County, in New York State, was a village, which is bigger than a hamlet, smaller than a town, and nowhere near as large as a city. What impressed it on my mind was that the painter painstakingly labeled it the *Villtage* of Camden and had to paint the signs all over again after some purist objected to the misspelling. I rather liked it myself. It showed a certain flair for independence. I always ate in a country hotel if the legend "Dinning Room" was posted above a doorway. I knew I'd get food that was beyond the ordinary, hadn't come out of a can, and had been prepared by an individualist.

To enter Forest Park you passed under a grilled ironwork arch that warned all motor vehicles to stay out. The early chug-a-lugs were more buggies than automobiles with noisy, under-powered motors that scared the horses. The park was a preserve of fine old trees—birch, poplar, pine, with sugar maples predominating. No hunting was allowed, so birds and little forest creatures were everywhere. Hoofbeats were muffled on the smooth dirt roads, which turned and twisted just enough to vary the view around each bend. There were stopping points like the rustic gazebo, the swimming hole with its bank of clay, which would mold into shapes that hardened in the sun. And there was a big pavilion with picnic tables, a structure large enough to house a number of people in case of a sudden shower. My favorite stop I called the babbling brook, where the clear spring water, diverted through a culvert under the road, talked with a cut-throat gurgle bubbling up into a pool on the other side before wandering off through a meadow to join the big river. I was the only one that got down, but my father allowed me several minutes to enjoy it and to chunk in a·farewell pebble before I clambered into my seat again.

The horses were restive; they knew to the second when I had regained my perch and started the moment my father gave the slightest tug on the reins. Once I slipped and fell under the wagon; they started ahead and the back wheel ran over my right foreleg. To everyone's surprise the bone was not broken. The dirt road was so soft and springy from tree roots that the wheel merely pressed the leg down and bruised it a little.

The bays had their favorite part of the park, too, a long stretch of road, straight as an arrow with perfect visibility on all sides. The maintenance force, who seemed to know what this stretch would be used for, ran their scrapers along the gutters to remove any brambles and sent the steam roller over the center to pack down the spongy loam. My father would shout "Hang on!" and give the big fellows their heads, but he tightened the reins and brought them smoothly into unison if their running got ragged. It was exhilarating. That pair could fly!

I've been told that the roads in our part of Camden were macadamized in 1910. I know that they were dirt when I was a little boy, and I was born in 1901. My mother told me that Father built our big rambling five-bedroom house in 1902 at a cost of two thousand dollars. The fine end of the house that held the parlor faced on Oswego Street, one of the main arteries into the village; the porch, sitting room, dining room, and woodshed, all the living area, looked out upon a street then named Watkin's Addition, later Fayette St. We reserved and never sold two double lots in back for a huge garden between us and our nearest neighbor, and two more on the other side, which gave a long driveway into the red horse barn, to the side of which was a big exercise yard enclosed by high wooden fences connected to a cow barn.

Behind the cow barn the land he owned stretched off to the west in a strip a few hundred yards wide and possibly three miles long, all the way to a smaller country road leading into a scrubbier part of town. My father had been born on a farm, and he liked some things about it, especially the livestock. He was as adept at curing a sick animal as a veterinarian. But he didn't like the backbreaking work of clearing the stony land, and he didn't enjoy the insularity, for he liked to be around people. So now he had in effect a small farm, most of it in flat tillable land, and yet he and his family were villagers. Right in the middle of the tract was a 35-acre pasture, its borders outlined by a beautiful river. That's where I spent most of my free time while growing up.

Not from any thought of death, but because he believed in preparing for any contingency, my father had made an early will. In it I was surprised to find, when he died unexpectedly in 1913, that the pasture had been left to me. My mother and I used it to good advantage from the time that I was twelve until I went away to college.

About those dirt highways. In addition to the other vehicles a two-wheeled racing gig was stored in the horse barn. If my father had a fast trotter, he would race him at the county fair in Rome. He had only to bring that gig out to exercise his trotter and Dan Crimmins, a tavern keeper living a good two miles distant, would magically appear with a similar horse and gig to inquire, "Care for a little brush, Ed?"

"Suits me," my father would answer, and away they'd go, the horses kicking up rounded, delicate balls of earth behind them. They made a strange pair, Ed Watkin, the teetotaler, and Dan Crimmins, the barkeep. After the race they would tell great stories, cronies for a day.

2

Because my father was by nature a reticent man and because I was too young when he died to care about anybody's past, I know very little concerning his life before he married my mother. It was no secret that he had been previously married and that he loved the children his first wife left him before she died. There were three of them, a young man named George and his two sisters, Anna and Elizabeth. All three were personable and old enough to marry, but none ever did. There was no constraint between the new family and the old; they accepted my mother gracefully, and we three younger children thought of them as full relatives, not as half-brother and half-sisters. To visit Anna and Lizzie in their apartment in Syracuse was a treat. I think they did dressmaking. Anna was tall, darkly handsome, and stylishly dressed. She was always the gentle and refined great lady, slightly aloof but kind, with a genuine patrician quality, not affected, that never varied over her 95 years. Tuberculosis condemned her to invalidism in later life, but it never touched her spirit. Lizzie, in awe of her sister, was a tomboy, who'd wrestle with you or hug you to death. She had a tiny secretive laugh like a gurgle, but when she laughed her eyes were merry. Both idolized George, as other women wished to do. But George preferred freedom, periodically striking out for the West. He wore a wide belt and moccasins, moving so quietly that no cake would fall when he walked through the room. He could turn his hand to anything. If he found me in the tool shed making skis from two-barrel staves, he'd build me a bobsled, the biggest and best on the hill. He inhibited my skill with tools, but made me some lovely playthings.

For a long period he farmed it with my father until the repetitious work bored them both. Before I was born my father had dabbled in real estate and in cattle buying. He did so again with just enough farming to provision both barns, often empty of stock before he brought carloads of horses from Colorado to train and sell. He could train any horse, working him in a wide circle with ropes and gadgets and infinite patience, and that bored me. I liked it best when he would take me along on a tour of all the farms that the big long-legged road could reach in one day, or sometimes two. That horse would cover twice as many miles as any other horse he ever had, and without tiring. We would drive through beautiful farmland, my father with one leg in the buggy, the other on the step, singing in a low voice a hymn that went well with the cadence of the hoof beats:

> How *tee*-jus and *tasteless* the hours
> When *Jee*-sus no *lon*-ger I see;
> Sweet *pros*-pects, sweet *birds* and sweet *flow'rs*
> Have all lost their sweetness for me.

> The mid-summer *sun* shines but dim
> The *fields* strive in *vain* to look *gay*,
> But *when* I am *hap*-py in him
> Dee-*cem*-ber's as *pleas*-ant as *May*.

My father would make small talk with the farmer and buy any calves the man wanted to part with. On the following Saturday they would all drive in with their calves to the stock pens in the railroad yard. My father would pay them and shake hands. He had usually made a friend, too. He'd ship some calves off for veal, and sort out a few to take home to be fattened for baby beef. He never shouted or swore, and he'd find some excuse not to accompany another cowman into the Erwin House or the Crimmins bar, but he wasn't pious about it. He was quietly religious, always took communion, and sat stoically through the most ponderous sermons, nibbling a tiny piece of orange peel he had dried on the shelf above our kitchen stove. If I fidgeted, he would slip me a shred. The spicy flavor helped me daydream about pleasant things not connected with hellfire or heavy-handed theology. I never listened to a sermon that didn't bore me. The first one I enjoyed was in Syracuse. A friend, a devout Christian Scientist, begged me to attend a service with him. The preacher was developing the theme that in pursuit of your Christian duty no harm, nor error, could befall you. He was seized with a coughing fit and couldn't go on. A drink of water did not help. He asked a devout elder to whack him on the back. That didn't help either. Error had him finally in its grip. I enjoyed that.

At the Methodist Church in Camden I learned to sit with glazed eyes with what I hoped was a sanctified look on my face, while I entertained lustful thoughts for the girl two pews below. I usually saved those for later, because my mother sat in the choir and if I caught a glimpse of severity on her face, I was sure she could read my mind.

She was the soprano and often sang solos. She had a fine voice but kept me tense with anxiety on Easter Sunday, singing: "Let Mount Zion rejoice, let the daughters of Judah be glad. Rejoice! Rejoice!

Re—*Joice!*" I didn't see how anybody could sing that high, but she always made it with a squeak to spare.

I liked it better when I pumped the organ. I was then in the organ loft behind a screen and had to push this large wooden handle up and down to fill the bellows that supplied the air for the music. Once while daydreaming I forgot to pump in time. As the music quavered, the organist, Mr. Swanson, whispered my name loudly, and I pumped like a demon to save the organ from its death rattle. I was shamed for that, especially as I received a small honorarium. My mother didn't. City choirs were paid, but she would have been shocked to take money for the Lord's work.

Though my mother was intemperate in religion, my father was not. He confined worship to Sundays, seldom attending Thursday night prayer meeting or Tuesday night testimonial gatherings during which all present were enjoined to rise and relate any small crisis during the week in which religion had sustained them. The testimonies were always begun by Miss Spencer, a Pecksniffian little woman with a pencil-line mustache, who would rise briskly and rattle off the same set speech: "I've been serving the Lord for thirty years, and the way grows brighter every day." She looked sixty, but religion kept her young; she never admitted to a day over thirty.

Across the street, only two houses down from ours, lived Tam Miller, the village atheist. He, too, was a psalm singer; whenever he felt the urge he would poke his head out of an upstairs window and bellow a hymn at a passing stranger or at nobody. He had a strong, tuneful voice and he sang hymns not in parody or derision. The blasphemy was only in his professional atheism. I loved to hear him sing and sometimes on my way home from school would stand in the yard below and sing with him. He might render, "Blest be the tie that binds," or "Shall we gather at the river," or "Yield not to temptation," or "Sweet hour of prayer," and infrequently, because it was more mocking than the rest: "Jesus loves me; this I know, for the Bible tells me so." When a group of church people visited him with the request to stop it, he would say, "Why, bless your hearts, I'm not making fun of them; I like the old hymns, and I never argue about religion unless I'm in a bar and some good Christian who can't hold his liquor starts throwing the Bible at me."

For many years during my boyhood, evangelism swept America. Not only were the local preachers extra diligent in soul saving, but itinerate evangelists, spurred on by the success of Billy Sunday, who had won renown for his antics, would come to town, pitch a big circus tent on an empty lot beside a church, and turn the aisles into "sawdust trails," which penitents were invited to "hit." One, I recall, made a lasso of clothesline, which he would heave out into the audience while singing, "Throw out the lifeline; throw out the lifeline; someone is drifting today," and haul in imaginary sinners. Those who accepted the invitation to come forward would walk up front, shake the evangelist's hand, and be saved. The evangelist left town quickly before the saved had time to think it over and become "backsliders."

Catholics and Episcopalians held their usual dignified services, but the other denominations went all out, especially the Methodists, our persuasion, as might be expected. John Wesley founded Methodism. Horace Walpole, who went to hear him preach, accused him of enthusiasm and said he talked through his nose. At least once a year the Methodist Church invited Evangelist Miller, who happened to be Tam's brother, in to revive us.

Tam, who never went to church, was on hand. Dressed in his Sunday best, he marched down and occupied the exact middle of the otherwise empty front pew. He took part in the whole service, causing no disruption, except to smile and nod and whisper, "Amen, brother," whenever Evangelist Miller scored a point against the devil. Then came the invitation to come forward. A hush fell over the congregation. Reverend Miller exhorted all those who had not yet accepted Jesus to rise, come forward, and kneel at the altar. Such an easy thing to do, yet how much it meant. Their souls would be among the saved on the Day of Judgment. The organ muted its tones; the choir began singing very quietly the song that traditionally was reserved to this occasion:

> Just as I am without one plea
> But that thy blood was shed for me
> and that thou bidd'st me come to thee
> O Lamb of God, I come, I come...

> Just as I am and waiting not
> To rid my soul of one dark blot
> To thee, whose blood can cleanse each spot,
> O Lamb of God, I come, I come...

At this point the personal workers were sent forth. Never more than six in number, these were old reliables who knew all the miscreants in the audience, and would whisper personal invitations to come and walk with them down the aisle. Often that's all it took. Knowing he would not be alone, a neurotic might burst into tears and take the proffered hand. His surrender could impel another, sick of being poked in the ribs by his wife's elbow, to join the leader. So it happened today. Sinner after sinner caved in until a whole squad had assembled in the center aisle.

Brother Short, working the side aisle, was unable to flush a bird worth bagging; so he resolved to try for really big game. He hurried down to Tam Miller's pew, and bent over him, whispering the standard overture. The whole church froze into silence; Brother Short's words could be clearly heard: "Won't you come forward, brother? Won't you start leading the good life today?"

Tam's answer shattered the sacred silence: "Not today, brother. No thank you, not today!"

I was only eight at the time, and I found Tam Miller's defiance of the church worrisome. I had always accepted community thinking in the past. Everybody else hated Tam Miller, but I secretly admired him. After breakfast and morning prayers I asked my father if Tam Miller would go to hell. He told me it wasn't up to us to judge him. He himself couldn't help liking the cross-grained old coot, but after yesterday, things didn't look too promising. My father had to sympathize with the evangelist. It had to be sheer torture to try to preach with your own brother sneering in your face. Something terrible had occurred in that family to engender such hate. It should be a lesson to all of us not to hate anybody. Everybody hated Tam; wanted him kicked out of town. That was wrong. We shouldn't condone what he did, but we shouldn't hate him either. Hate the sin but not the sinner. Whoever said that said it all.

That was like my father, I thought. My mother wouldn't have such qualms. She'd hate the sinner, too, for if you excuse such people, you'll soon be down to their level. She would hate Tam, all right—unless he was sick. If he were sick she'd march right down to his house and nurse him back to health. Then she would come back home and hate him again. I didn't know whether to side with my father or my mother. I was like Milton. That stern moralist couldn't help admiring Lucifer. But I hadn't heard of Milton then.

My father gave me another bad moment—when his honesty was questioned. I had heard someone say that a cow buyer is always a liar, but I knew that my father wasn't. Or was he?

I was with him in the bank. He had spent some time with the banker at the cashier's window cashing a bunch of checks. He carried the bills across to the wall table to count them again, but he picked them up before he put them into his wallet and started back to the window, saying to the banker, "Looks like you made a little mistake."

"Sorry, Ed," the banker said firmly. "No mistakes can be rectified after you leave the window"

My father was taken aback; he gesticulated with the bills. "But it's all right here. I haven't put any of it in my pocket. We can at least count it again, can't we?"

"Not after you leave the window."

I could see my father getting angry, and I knew he was counting to ten before he spoke out loud. He was hurt but trying very hard to speak slowly and reasonable. "I've always considered myself a very honest man. To the best of my knowledge I have never cheated any man out of a penny as long as I've lived."

"That's not the point, Ed."

"What is the point?"

"It's a rule we have here, and we can't break it for anybody. All transactions are final once you leave the window."

"Couldn't you make an exception...you've known me for a long time."

"A rule's no rule at all if you start making exceptions."

"Very well," said my father a trifle sadly. He peeled off the top bill and showed it to the banker. "You gave me ten dollars too much. I tried to give it back to you, but if you won't break your rule, I guess I'll have to keep it." He folded the bill in with the others and put them in his wallet.

The banker's face turned red. He tried to speak, but he choked. He tried again, but no words came. He was still gasping for air and clearing his throat when my father shut the door on the outside. I looked back through the plate glass window, concerned.

My father grinned. "Don't worry...he'll be all right...though it may take him quite a little time to recover."

3

My mother was of German-Swiss descent, christened Caroline Harriet Winterberger, the daughter of Ulrich Winterberger and his wife Margrette, whose maiden surname was Stritch. Ulrich was a wood carver. While they were young he and his wife left for America via London. It took them six weeks in a sailing vessel. Arrived in New York, Ulrich was sick enough to go to a hospital and had to sell his precious carving tools to pay the bills. Cured, he left the big city and took the first job offered, working in a tannery in Gaines, Pennsylvania. He must have improved his position for he sired 11 children, two dying in infancy, nine surviving. Caroline was born in 1871 at English Center, Pennsylvania. All the children were considered educated and substantial citizens, poor to begin with, but not impoverished. At five years of age, Caroline was legally adopted by John and Eliza Covert because she was such a beautiful, bright child. Both families lived then at Pine Creek, Pennsylvania. Though her real parents did not try to get rid of her, the entreaties of the Coverts to adopt "the pale, sweet-faced child," as the preacher then described her, prevailed. She loved her new parents, but her blood brothers and sisters always treated her as part of the original family. Later she confided in me that she could never quite forgive the Winterbergers for letting her go, though she never let them know it.

When she was 11 years old the Coverts moved to Wellsboro, Pennsylvania, where she received a remarkable grounding in grammar, spelling, punctuation, composition, and reading from a couple of brilliant teachers and from Swinton's 3rd and 4th readers. Published in 1882 and 1883, they would be far too advanced for many of our flunking high school students today. Neither contains any Dick and Jane twaddle, nor any hint of "social studies." No behaviorist psychologist was given a chance to water it down with confused prattle about cooperation, nor were the pedagogical hacks from schools of education allowed to profane its pages with cute little tales like "A Trip to the Zoo" to bore the kid with puerile fables hiding profound sociological messages.

Rather, the young readers were challenged to understand and enjoy Dickens, Hawthorne, the Brothers Grimm, the Talmud, the New

Testament, Bayard Taylor, Addison, Defoe, Whittier, Holmes, Bryant, and Byron. Both volumes were crammed with American history, from the landing of the Pilgrims to Yorktown. For diversion an editor might toss in a nicely written, terse little essay under the heading: useful knowledge about tea, the steam engine, silk, our foodstuffs, or the air we breathe, all of which I found interesting and instructive today.

Along with composition a child learned to read aloud. Four aids were stressed but not to the point of artificiality: articulation, inflection, pauses, and emphases. No phony tricks of elocution were proposed, such as those I was taught in elocution class in high school. We were told to pause, take three steps forward, and throw out an art, the palm upward as if asking for a match. Also we were made to learn the fine gradation of vowel sounds in pronouncing this sentence: "Little Mary married Harry at half past two in the Presbyterian church." We sounded like adenoidal Eliza Doolittles before the philologists took her in hand. My mother's teachers knew better than that. Old girlfriends of Mother's, writing to my sister Glenevieve to ask about my mother's health, said that she was by far the prettiest girl in Wellsboro, had the most irresistible smile, and a voice like an angel's. She used that voice to read to us three children for an hour before bedtime. We didn't care what it was. To please my sisters she would read from one of the Elsie books, or from *Treasure Island* to please me. She made it all delightful. I can remember being outraged when that cruel stepfather made Elsie Dinsmore sit on a piano stool until she fainted because she refused to practice on the Sabbath.

I have often been amazed that my mother, whose formal education ended in grammar school, spoke grammatically, whereas my children with degrees from fine universities did not. Maybe I should not have thought it remarkable. My mother wanted to learn. I have her report card from the Wellsboro elementary school. She got all As in deportment, reading, spelling, writing, drawing, arithmetic, geography, grammar, and composition. Her readers were stimulating and her teachers skilled and confident.

If she were alive today, my mother's eyebrow might have shot up to hear a broadcaster remark, "The Russians aren't like we Americans," or to ponder the president's statement: "Hopefully, the play we have set up will halt inflation before mid-summer." She might very well wonder what in the world that adverb "Hopefully" could modify.

The Coverts were restless people and moved frequently. Besides the father and mother, there was a foster sister Stella, and two foster brothers, Charles and George, all older than Mother. The whole family moved to North Bay, New York, and then to Camden when

Caroline was 18. Undoubtedly my father had his eye on her then, but again the Coverts moved, this time for keeps, to Rochester.

Caroline worked in the Eastman Kodak plant and sang in the South Rochester Baptist choir. It is known that she rode a bicycle to work, one with a large front wheel, and instead of an underskirt wore pantaloons. One day the support holding up the pantaloons snapped, letting the voluminous cloth drop like a tent in folds about her feet. While people sniggered she folded them neatly, tucked them under her arm, and walked on in to work. She never panicked.

On June 15, 1897, she married George Edward Watkin. Before going back to Camden to live, the couple went to Niagara Falls for a honeymoon. She was 26 and he 45, but the difference in their ages was never a cause of disagreement. Children know if their parents quarrel and they didn't. They made no show of affection in public or even in front of us children, but I discovered that my father hated to be away from home and never ceased to marvel that Carrie Covert was really his. Many years later my mother said that Papa was an early riser, and that he had to call to her, but did so in some amusing way. Sometimes he would quietly sing this little song:

> I have passed by one, I have passed by two
> I have passed by many a smiling lass because I wanted you.

She got me up by tickling my feet. Still asleep, I would climb them away from her up the wall and awaken in such a grotesque position it made her laugh. Her laugh was so infectious I would laugh, too. She'd say, "Huckleberry pancakes for breakfast," which kept me from dawdling.

She was a great cook, and I don't think she ever tired of practicing her art. She never measured things. It was almost impossible to follow one of her recipes because she would describe all condiments as just a little "pinch" of this and that. She used little seasoning, but her dishes tasted wonderful. There were no supermarkets then with frozen dinners, crammed full of all kinds of sodium derivatives to give the product "shelf life" that would kill a heart patient. She made her own butter, all of us kids begging to have a go at the churn, and she made her own bread, huge top-heavy loaves that burst out over their tins like mushrooms. It didn't have to be refrigerated; it stayed moist and sweet for days in a tin breadbox. You couldn't find such bread anywhere today for love or money. All the vegetables came from our huge garden, even the red raspberries and blackberries whose bushes surrounded the gardens. Sweet corn was golden bantam. My mother said it was no good if it didn't go into the pot 20 minutes after it was picked. We ate young peas fresh from crisp

pods, and carrots and wax beans and spinach and lettuce. The thing
I liked best were the greens made from the tender beet tops only half
matured with little marble-sized beets left on the stalks. If I wanted
to chew on something, I would pull a carrot, shuck off the outer layer
of red, and eat just the pale yellow heart raw. Usually we had a few
rows of potatoes in the garden. The big potatoes in the vegetable
cellar bins in the fall were left to ripen in some other field; these
were the ones for summer use. I'd dig a few hills when the potatoes
were like little balls; she'd scrape or peel them, leaving them round,
and; after they were boiled, cover them with a cream sauce with a big
blob of butter on top. We corned our own beef, smoked our own
ham, collected our own fresh eggs, drank the milk from a cow or two
we kept for that purpose. After straining the milk my mother would
set it down in big round pans on the cool cellar floor. The cream on
top rose thick as shoe leather. It went into the ice cream freezer
I used to turn on Sunday mornings before church.

We had a refrigerator in the woodshed, too. When the iceman
came with a big block to fill the galvanized top, all the kids in the
neighborhood would gather round his wagon for chips of ice to suck.
If I went to the river and came back with a mess of trout, Mother
would make me clean and wash them, then she'd fry them in butter.
They came out of cold water and were real fish, not those tasteless,
logy things fed on liver that go by the name of trout in California. If
I brought back frogs' legs, she would skin them, dip them in a batter,
and fry them in deep fat. After haying, the field would be dotted with
white mushrooms. They came up in the shape of small Indian clubs,
covered with brown fluffy scales, sealed with white rings around the
bottom of the ellipse. They were just as edible as those fully grown,
which opened like an umbrella. One of those big ones would almost
fill a medium size skillet and when covered with flour and fried in
butter tasted a lot like beef steak. The small pink mushrooms, the
kind bought in stores, could always be found in the cropped grass of
our pasture. Sometimes stupid people would pick toadstools instead
and be deathly sick from the poison, but the smell of the real mush-
room was so different I could tell them with my eyes bandaged.

There was one particular dish my mother made for Sunday
dinners we called chicken biscuits. She would fill the bottom of
a huge tureen with pieces of fried chicken, then top them with two
rows of baking powder biscuits and smother the lot with chicken
gravy. I can still smell the steamy fragrance when the lid was lifted.

I wished many times that I had learned how to cook. During my
year of teaching at Syracuse, I shared an apartment with Matthew

Rosa, another freshman English teacher, and we both had friends who would visit us for a weekend, bringing steaks or other supplies, which we had to cook for them. One most unusual friend of Matt's was George De Mille, a scholar, high-church Episcopalian, and raconteur. His taffy-colored hair stood straight up, and he wore thick glasses. If you asked him a question, he would bend his head forward, peer through his thick spectacles at his feet, listen intently, then answer. And you never knew what was coming out.

While apologizing for my bad cookery, I would describe my mother's effortless art at the stove until George said, "Watkin, either stop talking about your mother's cooking or invite us home for dinner." So I did. Mother liked having extra guests. Matt couldn't come, but George drove me to Camden and charmed my whole family. I expected something unusual, but he surprised even me. Mother passed him the chicken biscuits. George lifted the top, took one look, and burst into tears. Smiling at my mother through wet eyes, he explained: "I always weep at the sight of anything supremely beautiful." He stuffed himself, too. After that, if anyone exclaimed over something she had cooked, she said: "That is a nice compliment, but it isn't quite up to the one George De Mille paid me."

Our mother was little and quick, and when she was working at that big wood-burning cook stove, her movements were deft and sure. She never minded if my father brought two or even three buyers home with him for dinner. She seemed to like the big, clumsy, bashful men, who relished her dinners and never refused to send their plates back when she offered them more. She treated them like gentlemen and they responded. Several men who my father had befriended were not above cheating his widow when he died, but not these fellows. They did us innumerable favors and would never accept pay. In the early 1900s good cooking was a woman's most prized accomplishment. If you had a friend you invited the whole family over to dinner. Societies of any sort indulged in frequent picnics and innumerable suppers. A church supper meant a stunning variety of good things to eat, because each woman tried to outdo the rest by bringing her best dish. Often the recipe for her specialty was a closely guarded secret, which passed on to a friend only if she left town or died. Other women often tried to duplicate the dish by guessing its ingredients but invariably failed. My mother made such a comestible, and I don't think she kept it a secret, but nobody else could make it, not in our village, at least. She called it pressed meat. It was a variety of meats blended together, and though she put it into deep tins and you could cut out slices, it didn't have the slightest resemblance to meat loaf. It was a very fine texture. It had body but was almost soft enough to spread, and I have never tasted anything more delectable. You didn't want a lot of it. It was too rich. It tasted like the finest cuts of chicken and veal and beef and pork, yet no particular flavor stood out. It had its own flavor and to add catsup or even a more delicate and savory sauce would be sacrilege.

In 1950 we were far away from Camden, in Paris. Our leader, who wanted the best, had our party put up at the Georges Cinq. If he wanted the best, I told him, we should bed down at the Ritz, which was not only posh but also French. No, he insisted, a friend who had traveled all over the world said for swank go to the Georges Cinq.

We were dining there. The maître d' insisted that we try a bit of the pâté maison. I asked him if it was the goose or the goose's liver that was fat. "Non, non!" he said. "Ziss is not like zat. You will nevaire taste ziss anywhere else in zee world."

I tried it. I couldn't believe it. I was the one who should burst into tears. How those clever Frenchmen hit upon it I don't know. It was the same; it was identical—my mother's old pressed meat.

4

My mother was no stranger to grief; she just appeared to be. For the sake of her family she always presented the world with a smiling face. Her sorrow she suffered in silence.

She had four children: Elsie Louise Watkin, born April 15, 1898; Lamoyne Watkin, born January 11, 1900; Lawrence Edward Watkin, born December 9, 1901; and Glenevieve Ruth Watkin, born December 11, 1904. (My mother coined the name, adding the "l" to Genevieve to make it more liquid.)

I was a full-grown boy before somebody happened to mention that I just missed having a brother to play catch with. When I asked my mother about it she related the tragedy calmly. Lamoyne was crawling around the floor quite happily where she was working when he suddenly was taken with convulsions and choked to death. Neither my mother nor the doctor who worked on him could understand why until an autopsy revealed a collar button lodged in his windpipe. It must have fallen off the bureau and he had spied it and put it in his mouth. She showed me his baby picture. Lamoyne was far more handsome than the rest of us children, with my mother's dark blue eyes and curly hair. "When you came along soon after his death, you can be sure you were welcome," she told me, and did not allude to the matter again. I had completely forgotten about it and I fear I took it for granted that she had, too, when some years after her death my sister Glenevieve found in a scrap of diary my mother kept spasmodically:

> January 11, 1952. My dear little Lamoyne's birthday, and he never lived till his second birthday. He was a beautiful little fellow. One comfort when a child goes, you know he is safe in the arms of Jesus.

Her effects bore evidence of her deep and abiding love for us all. She kept every letter and snapshot any of us had ever sent her, but she was intelligent enough to know that love worn on the sleeve can become a burden to the one loved and even retard his growth.

I was lucky enough to have known both a grandfather and a grandmother: John Watkin, my father's father, and Eliza Maria Van Huesen Covert, my mother's foster mother. Grandpa Watkin lived with us first, a cocky old man in his nineties when I first knew him. All I have been able to learn about him was that he was born in 1814 in Montgomeryshire, Wales, just across the English border, and that he came to America in 1839 and married a Higby from Vermont, a highly educated woman for those days. Little of her erudition rubbed off on John, and when he bought a farm a few miles above Camden he was a hard worker and eager to learn from her how to run it. She even taught him how to cut wheat with a cradle. When she died he came to live with us. He was 90 and I was barely 3, but I remember visiting him every day in the small back room that looked out on the slate roof over the woodshed. He called me the "little chummy." Though he never went to church, he'd get out a boiled shirt, as one with a starched white bosom was called, and dress for the Sabbath at 6 pm, on Saturday night. Sunday night at 6 pm, the Sabbath was over for him, and he'd go back to his regular clothing. He warned me repeatedly never to spell my name with an "s." "It's Watkin, not Watkins, and don't you forget it. That's another breed of cat."

Then suddenly he was gone and Grandma Covert took me over. She always smelled faintly of lavender, because her handkerchiefs were saturated with the fragrance, a nice, old-lady's smell. I remember perfectly the haven of her lap while she taught me my letters. When I recited the alphabet for her, I ended it with a conclusion of my own: "r,s,t,u,v,w,x,y-o-u, Grandma." She taught me to read.

My parents seldom reprimanded me, but upon those rare occasions when they did, Grandma, who never interfered in family discipline, would rise and leave the room, her nose in the air, her features frozen in disapproval. She could not stay and watch a perfect child brutally browbeaten by two unfeeling parents. Then suddenly she disappeared, too. But I have no recollection of their funerals. I can only guess that my parents thought it best for me not to witness the grisly aspects of a funeral, and entrusted me to a relative for an out-of-town visit. They must have believed that I was so young I would soon forget about them if I was told that they had gone away. Anyway, I did, for my young life was too active for me to sit and repine. Every year widened my world. First there was school, which was pleasant enough, though nothing stands out for me until I reached the third grade.

There a prize was given at the end of the year—the Liberty Bell, a small bronze medal, to the kid with the best overall grades. My mother was so anxious for me to win it that I studied hard. I was definitely a contender and was coming down the home stretch when I almost lost it through a woman's perfidy. The girl whose desk was across from mine double-dared me to come sit beside her and kiss her. Though she wasn't very toothsome, I couldn't be thought a coward; so I did it on the spot. The teacher caught us at it. The girl, who saw that we were in for it before I did, shrank back in seeming horror, protecting herself from a rapist. The teacher asked why I did it. I looked at the girl, waiting for her to take her share of the blame, but she looked away. I had to sit on the podium facing the class and stay after school. Since I wouldn't snitch, the teacher told me that my disgraceful performance may have cost me the Liberty Bell. I worked doubly hard and at the end of the term won it and gave it to my mother. In the fourth grade I remember falling in love with the radiant blonde whose desk was in front of mine. Her golden tresses fell upon my desk, so I dipped their ends in my inkwell and learned another truth, that women like heels who treat them rough, for she sat next to me at sleigh rides and blushingly repaired with me to the closet at parties where "spin the platter" was played.

I fell in love pretty regularly after that, but none of these attachments was lasting. Only in television does the man return in later life to find his childhood sweetheart twice as desirable as before. I remember meeting two such beauties fully matured. One had buck teeth and the other needed a shave worse than I did.

It was not until the 9th grade that I had a truly remarkable teacher, a tall enthusiastic woman named Elizabeth Dorrance, called by one and all Queen Bess. There is probably one such teacher in every school. She taught me everything I needed to know about grammar and punctuation and the shape of an English sentence. She also confirmed my love of Shakespeare, for I had read all of his plays and sonnets before I reached her class. There were two books in our library I read sprawled on our living room floor on stormy days, Shakespeare and a ten-volume set, beautifully engraved, called *Great Men and Famous Women*. From that I learned Greek and Roman history.

Another delight of my boyhood was to go visiting relatives and have them visit us in return. This meant a train ride for the whole family, for my father spent less time farming and more buying and selling. He would buy a farm and the machinery to run it, then keep his eye open for a young fellow ambitious enough to own it eventually by making it produce bumper crops. With the extra incentive in mind the tenant would take better care of the machinery, too. This way they both profited. My father kept faith with them and they became our friends. Long after the deal had been concluded they would bring my mother prime cuts when they butchered or made sausage. I was surprised to learn that my father owned the butcher shop though he never worked in it. From his dealing in stock and real estate he never seemed to lack for money or the time to take a trip with us. By far the best of these and the trip that has remained most vividly in my mind was the one that he and Mother and I made to New York City, including the train ride to Albany, the excursion down the Hudson on a day boat, and the eighteen warships I counted lined up above New York. It was the Hudson-Fulton Exposition of 1909, when I was eight. My father got tickets for the Old Hippodrome. The whole stage was transformed into a lake, and two lovers in a tiny boat sank beneath the surface. Because they did not reappear, a small child behind us started crying, but I thought there could be nothing more wonderful than dying for love. From the window of our hotel room I was enthralled by an only slightly lesser marvel on an adjacent rooftop: the brightly lit, larger-than-life figure of Old Dutch Cleanser chasing dirt. I still buy the odd can of it loyally, instead of Comet. The Empire State Building didn't exist then, but the Flatiron Building was wonder enough for me. Had I but known it, the father of the girl I married had an office there.

We had no relatives to visit in New York, but Mother's foster brother, Uncle Charley, persuaded her to bring the family for the Shriner's Convention in Rochester. There were marching bands and men in funny hats, but nothing to what we saw in a refreshment palace in which we were sipping sodas. At the next table a man and a woman drunk on beer were urging their pet bantam rooster to empty the mug ordered for him. He was already staggering as he paraded around the top of the table, crowing repeatedly. Glenevieve and I laughed without restraint, Elsie frowned, and mother would have called the police save for Uncle Charley. The man loudly ordered another round and spilled a fistful of silver on the table. Glenevieve and I stepped on coins that rolled our way, but Mother wouldn't let us keep them.

Though our mother had no wish to visit her real parent—indeed none of us children ever saw them—all of her Winterburger brothers and sisters considered her part of the family, and we exchanged visits with the families of her two favorite sisters, Aunt Lena in Elmira, New York, and Aunt Flora not far from there in the country. Aunt Lena was married to Uncle Dan Stevens. Aunt Lena was blonde, next to my mother the prettiest of the Winterburger girls, very good-natured and so credulous that I would tell her outrageous lies to entertain her. She had two children, both slightly younger than we were. Esther was a daredevil, who in spite of wearing a cast for a broken collarbone climbed the big pine tree in the middle of our pasture. Emil was quietly mischievous. Fascinated by the design made by the paper punch I used when collecting on my newspaper route, he left a lovely perforation in the tip of our cat's ear. Uncle Dan played the guitar, and was beloved by all children as a singer of crazy songs. He sang two that became "standards" with us. I sang them to my children; they in turn sang them to theirs, and now my grandson is singing them to my great granddaughter. Nobody has ever explained what may amuse children and what leaves them cold, but kids certainly like these:

> Next winter, last summer
> The year before last
> A man with a hammer
> Was breaking his fast;
> Some cast-iron cakes
> He was trying to eat;
> He dropped them and knocked
> All the corns off his feet.
> He went to the doctor
> And stated his case
> While tears from his eyes
> Burned holes in his face
> He filled them up
> With some sawdust and tar
> And with a baseball match
> He lit a cigar.
> He went up to bed
> And his candle he lit
> He got his revolver
> And soon loaded it;
> I'll stand it no longer
> He savagely said
> So he blew out the candle
> And went back to bed.

The other one, sung to a similarly humdrum little tune, was called "The Skinniest Man":

> The skinniest man I ever saw
> He lived in Hoboken
> And when you hear how skinny he was
> You'll think I am a-jokin.
> Through chimneys he would often crawl
> Through sieves he'd go a-sliding
> And when the landlord called for the rent
> In the gas pipe he was hiding.
> He never went out on a windy night

He never went out alone
For all the dogs they followed him
They thought he was a bone.
One night when he was sleeping
The candle burning dimly
A skeeter grabbed him by the neck
And pulled him up the chimney.

I made a better rhyme of it because I thought the word was chimbley.

The other prize sister, Aunt Flora, was much like Aunt Lena and married to a farmer, Uncle Grant Thurber. Thereafter, if I read a story about a farm, I visualized it as happening on the Thurber farm, no matter how the writer had described it. Their farm had an orchard.

My father always bought a barrel of apples from Uncle Grant. They would arrive months later just as the cold struck Camden. It took three barrels of apples to last us through the winter, a barrel of greenings and two barrels of Northern Spies, the world's best apple. On our various pastures we had early apples only, two with standout names: "sheep-nose" and "seek-no-further."

I once made a side trip alone to play with the many sons of Aunt Margaret at Corning. I stayed a week, but when I came home I could remember the names of only three. By contrast, Elsie visited them for just one day and brought back this report: Aunt Margaret married a Catholic so they had a lot of children—James, age 26; Jane 21; Herbert 19; Robert 13; Raymond 10; Edward 7; and Bernice, only 2, but tall for her age. She gave exact descriptions of several even to the color of their eyes. I should have been impressed that she had secured such a wealth of factual observation in her quiet, unobtrusive way, but I wasn't. She was so much more mature than I, far beyond the three years difference in our ages. When Glen and I had laughed at the drunken rooster and Elsie did not, it never occurred to me that I was lacking in sensitivity at the affront to the dignity of the tiny animal, which kept Elsie from laughing. I thought she lacked a sense of humor and that it was a bore to remember all the names of cousins we would never see again. She was reticent like my father and easy to tease. She worried about me at all times like a second mother and called me Lawrence, as some grown-up might have done. I resented that, too. So I teased her to make my younger sister laugh.

For example, she had to give a high-school class oration and practiced it aloud in her room, but I could hear what she was saying. If she asked me a question, I answered with a passage from her oration: "The birds were our first musicians. Andrew Carnegie said, "I'd rather shoot an angel than a bird." Or at the table I might remark, "When the white searchlight of science beat upon the birds, not even the crow was found to be entirely black."

She should have hated me, but excused me instead and adored me.

While she was still in high school, she fell desperately in love with another student named Walter Ammann, and he with her. They never kissed openly or acted lover-like in front of the family, yet they missed no chance to be together. You can imagine how vulnerable she would have been about that. But I liked Walter, who was strong and affable and quiet. He let me ride on the back of his motorcycle. So, thank God, I never kidded her about Walter. They were engaged when he joined the Navy, but he met his death from World War I, and the double wedding of Elsie to Walter and Elsie's best girlfriend to Milton Eastham never came off. She would borrow our small son, Parke, to spend a weekend with her to lift her loneliness. She became the embodiment of the old-maid schoolteacher, but when her girl-friend died, she married Milton Eastham on September 2, 1940. They lived in harmony until she died of cancer in 1945.

I never really knew my older sister until I received this letter a short time ago. I was amazed that overmodest Elsie was capable of such forceful action. Glenevieve wrote:

> Yes, she was very happily married to Milt. Elsie was quiet and smart in business like Papa, but a loving and devoted sister. You may recall that I was fired from my first teaching job along with the entire high-school faculty. The real reason was that two of our young high-school teachers were sleeping with two high-school seniors. When Elsie heard that I was fired she was furious. She said not to take it lying down, but I was timid and crushed, as I had worked like a dog. She hopped the Watertown train and came to town with fire in her eyes. She wrote me a *great* speech and made me memorize it. I went to a special meeting of the board. Elsie was right. Only one of the board members even knew my name. When I had finished they offered me a new contract and a $300 raise. Elsie said to tear it up and walk out.

> Not me. I took it and taught there thirty-two years, thanks to Sis. She was more unselfish than most girls and would give you her shirt.

Because I wanted to know more about Elsie, Glenevieve searched her attic and discovered the diaries of Elsie and of my mother. Both were recorded in little three-by-five inch notebooks, but neither was kept day by day. Instead, they served as reminders of some important date or event, rather than being diaries in the ordinary sense, as if one or the other, about to take a trip, had started out with a fresh little notebook to deal with that occasion.

One notebook that Elsie used had some fact of general interest for me. She had jotted down a few books that appealed to a teenage girl in the second decade of the 20th century. She labels *Philippa at Halcyon* as "great." She also liked *Tanglewood Tales; The Spy; John Halifax, Gentleman;* and *Rebecca of Sunnybrook Farm.* She remarks about the prevalence of childhood diseases, pink eye and measles, which we all had in full measure, though escaping typhoid and scarlet fever.

The most complete entry describes the death of my father. She was 15 years old at the time. She didn't write a word of it until a month after it happened. It begins:

> Oh dear, I can't ever say "papa" again. My dear, dear papa went to heaven July 18, 1913. He was taken sick July 8 and didn't have a doctor for two days. Anna, George, and I were camping in the Adirondacks. Mama wrote to me about it, but I didn't get the mail until it started. Lizzie was in Syracuse and Mama phoned her and Lizzie telegraphed us. Papa was never sick, not to be sick in bed. I knew it must be something awful. I never felt so sick in my life as I did coming down on that old train. When we got there they said he was better, and he seemed to stay that way until Tuesday night. When the doctor came next morning, he wouldn't let us call Mama though she wanted to see him. We thought he seemed worse, but that awful doctor said he wasn't. I will never feel as well as though I was there when Papa was first taken.

(Elsie, as long as I can remember, felt responsible not only for me, but for everybody in the family. She wasn't bossy with my parents. She didn't think that she knew more than they did, but she had a compulsion to be on hand for every emergency, in case there was something she could do.)

To continue:

> The plagued old doctor finally said his heart was getting weaker. We sent for Edith Watkin, Papa's niece, a trained nurse. We would have had her before, but Papa didn't want anyone—only Mama. The doctor said it would harm him if it annoyed him.
>
> He had a chill about 8 o'clock and I ran around to the neighbors and with Andrew Smith's and Mr. Knapp's help I got seven water bags.

Papa seemed to know he couldn't stay with us, because when I went into the room he said, "If Edith could only have been here. She has more experience. I kissed him then and said goodnight, and he said good*bye*. That goodbye was to last for a long time. He never said another word to me. Oh, dear Papa! We had Doctor Ford from Utica the day I came home and we had him and Doctor Stewart from Syracuse. The day after he was taken with this chill Ford said he hadn't given up hope, *but I had*. He said it was just like bleeding to death, his bowels ran so and he vomited so much that the moisture of his blood was all gone. If he had only drunk hot water before, he might have lived. He never could drink cold water without its distressing him. He didn't keep a thing on his stomach from Tuesday till Saturday. The Thursday after he had a chill I just stayed at the neighbors. I couldn't seem to stay at home until just about night. ... I had given up hope more than the rest and I knew if I went in to face him I would probably cry. I told Mama I would come in if he wanted me, but she said he was in a daze most of the time and didn't know whether I came or not, but I was afraid he'd think I didn't want to see him. That morning when Glenevieve went in, he told her there was an east wind blowing and to put on her coat when she went outdoors. Dear old Papa was always taking care of us and seeing that we didn't catch cold.

Aunt Mary [his only sister] came that night, but he never knew her. Friday morning at two different times Glenevieve and Lawrence went in. Mama told him that they were there, and just was able to say "yes." He didn't when I went in. He didn't seem to understand them. Lawrence was there until about 8 o'clock, then he and Mr. Fifield went after the cows. I asked him not to, but he did. Glen was with Perdita [another neighbor]. Papa went to heaven at just half past eight. Lawrence came back about two minutes too late. Perhaps it was all for the best. Papa lay there with that awful death stare for half an hour. He panted for breath so you could hear him at the foot of the stairs. About 15 minutes before the last he choked, and at the very last also I got Mrs. Flagg. She came over to help bear Mama up. Mr. Maunder, our good pastor, was up just as he died.

We had a funeral Monday, July 21, at 3 pm. Reverend Maunder's text was: "He was a good man, full of the Holy Ghost and of faith." The house was full downstairs and the stairs also. The piazza was crowded until it cracked, and many stood out on the lawn. Everybody was good to us and just stacked us with everything to eat.

At the funeral there were 26 pieces of flowers. The choir sent a beautiful piece of red roses. Mr. Ezra Williams and Mr. Wilder sent a large wreath with AT REST on it. F. Kelsey sent a big piece of roses. Mr. Snow sent cream roses. The church sent a lovely pillow, the Missionary Society a piece of carnations. We had a large pillow with FATHER on it and also a piece of palm with cream roses. The Cemetery Association sent a large anchor and the Van Allens four-dozen loose pink and white carnations.

Here she concludes the death of our father and does not refer to it again.

Only Elsie would have remembered the funeral so exactly that she could quote the text of the funeral sermon. I would give a lot to know how the Reverend Maunder associated my father with the Holy Ghost. At least 18 years later when I was taking summer courses at Columbia University under Professor Chandler, a Jewish student leaned over and whispered to me, "What is the Holy Ghost?" Try to explain that in a few whispered words to a seeker after truth. The best I could do was, "A holy spirit who partakes of the nature of both God the Father and Christ the Son."

That didn't satisfy him at all; so I added after class the tiny bit more I had learned. The Jews recognize only God the father, the one God appearing in the Old Testament. The New Testament adds the tripartite nature of Christ, the Son of God as the Redeemer, with the Holy Ghost as a spirit who supposedly enlightens us regarding the other two, by partaking of both their natures. The Holy Ghost caused a split between the Eastern and Western Christian churches, the Eastern holding that the Holy Spirit preceded only from God the Father; the Western holding that it proceeded from Father *and* Son. The schism was typical of all religionists. Before you believe, you don't ask, "What does the Holy Ghost do for mankind?" but rather, "What is the date of its commission?" It was ironically divisive too because both sides believed that the Holy Ghost could not be grasped by the human intellect, but only through divine revelation. The idea of God in three persons also exists in the Hindu religion: Brahma the creator, Vishnu the Preserver, and Shiva the Destroyer. Whatever is created must die, though there can be one death, once saved by Vishnu. I told him to read Emerson's poem "Brahma," which threw Emerson's countrymen into a tempest of confusion:

They reckon ill who leave me out
When me they fly I am the wings
I am the doubter and the doubt
And I the hymn the Brahmin sings.

Emerson is using Hinduism as a way of saying that God is found in everything. My Jewish friend understood that, and we both agreed that Emerson would have small use for the caste system. I wondered if the Reverend Maunder thought of the Holy Ghost as a leveler, interpreting the goodness of God in terms of simple kindness and love.

In trying to assess my feelings about the death of my father, I know I did not suffer the way Elsie did. I was only eleven, and I'm sure that made some difference. I remember not so much being a part of it as observing it. I cried, but more in pity for my father than for the loss to me. It was a dirty shame that he had to die just when things seemed to be running smoothly for him, for I know he was happy.

I hated the doctors; they had let him down. I thought they just stood around and looked wise and didn't *do* anything. I had overheard one of them saying only two days ago: "Get better? Of course he'll get better. He's strong as an ox. Why, you couldn't kill him with a club!" I don't know whom he was talking to, but that's what he said. They didn't seem to know what he had, but I believe toward the end they called it cholera morbus. If so, they really weren't to blame because medicine was not far enough advanced in 1913 to deal with the excessive dehydration that destroyed his kidneys and heart. Today he would have been given one of the wonder drugs and fed intravenously to bring moisture into his bloodstream.

I was proud of the way everybody rallied to help our family. They all loved my father. Dan Crimmins sent his finest, oldest bottle of cherry brandy. The neighbors offered to cook, clean, run errands, take us children off my mother's hands, prepare their guest room if it was needed, sit up all night—anything.I missed him more as I grew older. I wish my wife could have known him, and I wish he had been alive when any of my children was born. I often heard someone say, "Ed Watkin didn't have a mean bone in his body," or "Ed Watkin didn't have an enemy in the world." There was a good reason why, though you don't hear it mentioned too much today: he lived by the Golden Rule.

5

The death of a father works great changes within a family. Mother was determined that it should not destroy ours. There were three of us to send to college, and we were land poor. If she could sell some of our possessions we would be all right, but it wouldn't be easy. Neither Elsie nor I thought we had to go to college, but my mother did. It was the dearest wish of my father's heart and she was determined to see it carried out.

It permitted small time for grieving. In the bits and pieces that she left behind as a diary she makes no allusion to his passing until a year after he died:

> Sunday, June 14, 1914. Children's Day and I was in charge of the program. All went well.
>
> Tomorrow is my anniversary, and bitter tears will fall when I think of the living husband who was my friend, my lover, and guide and comforter always. Oh, Edward, come back!
>
> Monday, June 15. Seventeen years ago today I was married to one of God's noblemen. This is a sad day, for I must spend it alone.

I had aspired to be a farmer and told my father so, but he never encouraged me in that ambition. He wanted me to go away to college and do something bigger than that. He expected me to do my chores faithfully but no more. He had no objection to my brother George teaching me how to milk a cow. Possibly because it was so frowned upon I wanted to learn it all and do things beyond my strength. Years later I learned that I was being watched for any incipient tuberculosis, for both my father and George had gone to Estes Park, Colorado, to ward off the disease. When my father caught our good-natured tenant-farmer standing aside while I drove the team that pulled the plow, he put a stop to it. I still remember the sensation when the plow cut deep and turned over a furrow. An engineer in a lumberyard let me drive a steam locomotive, and the feel of smoothness and reserve power was similar though not in the same degree. If I had hit a big rock and had the plow handles yanked from my hands, I might have been more quickly disenchanted.

I never regretted my decision, reached in college, to become a teacher rather than a farmer, with the secret hope that I might write books as well as discuss them, but I have always envied the farmer the immediacy of the satisfaction he gets from seeing the result of a day's work well done.

For ready money, my mother sold a building lot and one of the farms, while I took over alone what my father had started to do with the pasture. Every spring he would buy a few scrawny cows that still gave milk but would never be a fine dairy stock. Good pasturage would help fatten them. He secured an equal number of young calves to run with them and suck on them whenever they pleased or the cows permitted. But to be sure that all calves were being fed, the whole herd had to be rounded up and brought into the old slaughter-house perched on top of the embankment on the village side of the river. The lower half of the slaughterhouse was empty, the upper half was a usable stable with stanchions and a feeding trough on either side that would just accommodate the eight cows and eight calves. At first a handful of bran in the trough would lure the cows into the stanchions, so that I could lock them in. I soon learned which calves had already nursed themselves full outside, and which had to be given more. Sometimes a cow had to be coaxed into letting a calf suck, but usually they were placid enough. I had to be sure that every cow had been sucked clean, for if milk remained in her bag she would soon go dry. From this "stripping" I usually got a quarter of a milk pail to take home. At first the job was time-consuming and irksome, for the stock usually hid in the woodlot across the river, and in the course of a hard day's rain the river would rise enough so I had to rope and half drag a calf through the forty-foot expanse of deep-ening water, but once the herd learned the routine the job was easy.

I thought I knew everything there was to know about livestock until a high school teacher, a reputed tartar, had me stand to read a passage from a book aloud. When I came to the word *teat*, I pro-nounced it *teet*. The teacher exploded. "Mr. Watkin," she snapped, "the word is *tit*! It always has been and always will be *tit*! Now read it again." I read it again her way, though Webster's gives my nasty-nice pronunciation first billing; and for some time thereafter I was known to my friends as *teetyman*.

Fattening calves for market occupied my summer vacations, for with the war in Europe heating up, beef made real money. But my mother could never have made it at the start without the help of friends and of my brother George. He was the one who got in touch with my father's old cattlemen friends who secured the cows and calves we needed anew each summer. I know that in the beginning at least they did it as a favor. George taught me how to fix fence and ride the hay rake and even build a load of hay when it was time to cut the clover that grew on spare lots. George would forego his trips west to lend a hand. He became the man of the house, though I thought I was. Eventually, he owned and ran the Camden greenhouse.

Other business acquaintances helped a struggling widow. The family lawyer, George Skinner, would take care of the deeds if my mother sold land, and forget to send the bill.

Camden was patriotic. It would have a parade on Washington's Birthday or at any other time it found an excuse. The Fourth of July was celebrated on the village green with speeches honoring the flag and with the band playing heroic airs through the afternoon. All of us teenagers put huge cannon-crackers under tin cans that would send them high above the telephone wires. Yet there wasn't much talk about the war. War fever was less intense than in the big cities, even though we had enlistment rallies. These affairs took place in the Opra House, as the movie theater was called, and all of us kids hoped that the fighting would last long enough to let us get into it. One of the earliest meetings almost put an end to my patriotism. They were conducted by local politicians, speakers from both political parties trying to outdo the opposition. At last it came time for a particularly gross character, grown fat from eating out of the public trough, to harangue us. He came racing out of the wings to center stage. There he stopped and shook his fist at us, shouting: "My fellow Americans, I would to God that I could see my blood running down the trenches in Flanders Fields!" Those were his exact words, and in spite of my youth and jingoism, I could not miss the fact that he wanted to see his blood coursing down a muddy ditch in France—while he sang the "Marseillaise," no doubt.

The war was never discussed in our house, possibly because of Elsie, but more likely because it was too far away. My father, when he was alive, got out the team and surrey to take old people to the polls to vote, but none of us at that time had any great interest in national or international issues. When Chautauqua came to town and pitched its tent on the baseball field, we trooped down to listen because a United States senator was billed to address us. We agreed that this senator with his smooth gray hair and gray suit and soothing voice was most imposing, but when he talked on and on and on and never said a thing, I and my buddies nodded to each other, and slipped out quietly and sat on the grass at the back of the tent for a game of mumble-ty-peg. The voice of Warren Gamaliel Harding droned on.

When he became president in 1920, the whole nation yawned, and when much much later it learned that this dolt had performed the sexual act with a secretary in the White House closet, we were amazed that such wonders would have taken place, all in the name of normalcy.

First and last I did a lot of work in my teens aiding and abetting my mother in her schemes to get rich. One was to raise chickens. She bought a 100-egg Prairie State incubator and built a henhouse, a structure mounted on a cement base roughly 30 feet long skirting our garden, near the horse barn. It had three separate rooms, all leading to outdoor yards fenced with hogwire to keep the baby chicks from straying. When all those fuzzy little bundles hatched at one time, we had a job keeping the late arrivals, pecking their way out of their shells, from being smothered by the masses of chicks climbing over them. There was the problem of keeping them warm and seeing that they all had water to drink, even if it meant using an eyedropper. A few died but too many of them lived to please me, for my mother had a second henhouse built to accommodate the older hens out behind the cowshed. This was a double decker, which made it easier to back a wagon up to clean out the droppings. All were White Leghorns, supposed to be the best layers, but they were also more nervous than Rhode Island Reds, a heavier hen that I much preferred. But Reds laid brown eggs, and people thought white eggs were better. They weren't, only prettier. The least little disturbance would drive the white leghorns to hysteria. They'd cackle shrilly and beat up a dust with their wings, which made me despise them. I think we made a little money, but not much. Eggs sold in New York for $1 a dozen during World War I.

Before our furnace was converted to coal, it burned big chunks of wood. We hired a man-of-all-work, half Indian, to work with me in our woodlot that covered the whole south end of the pasture. I learned how to bring down trees by notching them low down and chopping above the notch to fell them. Some were too big to reach around, so I must have been in my later teens when I did this work. Cutting them into chunks, which in turn could be split into stove wood for the kitchen, meant a lot of work with a crosscut saw. The woodsman tutored me until I could make the saw sing. The trick was not to push the saw but to pull it.

We drove wedges in the top crack to keep the blocks from binding. Another skill was splitting the block, usually a straight grain beech. You didn't bring the axe straight down. You turned the edge ever so slightly as it hit the block a few inches from the side. That would send the stove wood chunk flying. When you hit a knot that wouldn't split, you saved the whole big jagged piece to stoke the furnace.

I liked this work best. It was clean, didn't stink up your clothes, taxed your judgment to choose the trees that might thin out the grove without denuding it, demanded skill to drop it without ripping off the limbs from fine young trees, and improved your wind by pulling that crosscut, for we had no power tools. Even constructing a woodpile that wouldn't topple was an art, a kind of dry masonry.

6

Though my mother was grateful for any help I could give her, she was in no way a demanding taskmistress who robbed me of my youth. Quite the opposite. If she thought something was becoming a drudgery, she sent me out to play. I played much harder than I worked, in a more beautiful and diverse natural setting than most kids have today, with no restrictions or supervision. I did many wild and foolish things but committed no depredations. There were no cops dogging my footsteps, and small need for them. I played with boys with all kinds of different backgrounds, but almost all parents made their kids understand that the number-one rule was to accept responsibility.

For example, the editor of the local paper had an outdoor privy on the bank of the river that flowed behind all the downtown stores. It was too much of a target to go unnoticed. On Halloween, a gang of us kids toppled it into the river. Deprived of his editorial wee-wee, the owner challenged us to meet with him. I was one of those who did so. We were surprised to learn that the backhouse had destroyed an Old Town canoe valued at $32 beached below. It took us some time to raise that much money; so we formed a Castle on the Rhine Club, and gave a movie benefit to pay for our crime. We cleared enough over the $32 to make a small gift to the volunteer fire department. This donation was probably wasted, for I had seen the fire department in action. A small frame house on Second Street was threatened by a brisk blaze in the kitchen, well in the rear of the structure. I arrived with a sizable crowd of gawkers out in front. A helmeted fireman wearing a heavy rubber coat drew a line with his axe along the edge of the sidewalk. No onlooker was to cross that line. Then he went to work. There were four windows across the front of the house, two on each side of the entrance door. Heroically he attacked them with his axe. Now we had a clearer view of the furniture in the living room on the right, the dining room on the left. A man offered to help carry out the furniture, but the fireman answered curtly: "Too dangerous!" There hadn't been a sign of flame until he had created the draft with his axe, but now the flames licked their way into the room. At last another fireman had hitched a hose to the nearest hydrant and together the two firemen directed a powerful stream through the windows, knocking the chairs at the table back into the path of the fire. The flames disregarded the water and leaped through the windows to seize upon the roof. In an instant the dry shingles caught fire and the flames had won. The paper reported that despite the valiant efforts of the volunteer fire department, between fire damage and water damage the building was a total loss.

It's a wonder that our old slaughterhouse did not suffer a similar fate. It stood alone·at the end of the plateau of level land on this side of the river, the top half or stable an extension of the field, the lower half, where the old slaughter house had been, dropped down to take advantage of the slant that led to the river. The building was a weather-beaten gray, but it was stoutly built, the shingled roof was tight, and it did not sag anywhere. The lower room was the headquarters for our teenage gang. There we smoked, not tobacco, but dried corn silk cigarettes and smoke-wood stogies. Smoke wood was the root system of an elm tree, partly washed away by the rampaging river in the spring. Appropriately the stream was called Mad River. In dry weather you could snap off any length of the porous brittle root you pleased, light the end, and have a cigar that bit the tongue unmercifully but put out a prodigious amount of smoke with each puff. The nearest human habitation was three hundred yards away, but the lady of the house came running one afternoon, for the smoke was issuing from every crack and crevice. She gave us a pretty fair tongue-lashing and went her way.

Mad River was a quiet enough stream in summer so that my brother George and I could span it with a footbridge made of two long skinny trees with all the limbs cut off, laid end to end, all four ends resting on cross-pieces nailed to pairs of sturdy stages driven deep into the riverbed. Along the whole length of the tree-frame, we nailed a number of foot-long crosspieces that would support wide boards, eight to ten feet long, which supplied the footpath. Then we rigged a long rope or wire to hang onto if your balance was faulty, though we scorned to use it. The cakes of ice tearing down the river at high speed when an ice jam broke in the spring would carry our bridge away. We made a new one each year.

Our pasture was the first wide, level land the river encountered during the spring freshets, and it often left its old channel to carve another path through the soft sod. When it did it might leave a deep crater or two that became frog ponds. The whole upper section of our pasture was pockmarked with these cavities, hollowed out by plunging blocks of ice. Though the river was replete with ice jams, it never froze smoothly enough for us to skate on. We had to go across town to Fish Creek for that, except for the magical year when a sudden rain on the snow pack, followed by a quick freeze, left a crust so thick that we could skate anywhere across the fields. Our snows were always so deep that drifts would cover the fences. Walter Ammann skated twelve miles to visit my sister Elsie. The wonder lasted a full week.

Mad River created only one new riverbed that it continued to use year around—not to replace but in addition to its old channel. The new branch headed straight for a forty-foot high bank, where it scooped out a pool and felled a big tree whose base dammed the pool. A nearby spring ran into it, assuring its permanence. The run-off water came out at right angles through reeds and willows until the river water discovered a new outlet, bypassing the pond entirely. So there it remained, a pool larger than the others, but still just another frog pond. Or so I thought until the day that I cast a fish line in it and landed a fine, fat trout. We seldom caught trout this far downstream, but that pool was chock full of them with no way for them to get out. I told my mother and not another soul. I had my own privately stocked pool. She need only tell me what day and how many she wanted and I'd get them to her well before dinner. That pool furnished us with mess after mess of those speckled beauties, until I had caught the very last one. Trout and small-mouth black bass bring your heart into your mouth. When you sneak up like a shadow and drop the bait into the still water and your line zings out and races crazily around the pool until you set the hook and heave that beauty free from the water, his curved tail slapping it and his body writhing in ten different directions at once trying to dislodge that hook and you're almost afraid to grab him he's so furious. That's a fish worth catching.

What you expected to catch in Mad River were whitefish, good enough eating but as dull to catch as a slice of limp bacon. To enliven the sport I salvaged the longer pieces of copper wire the streetlamp man left behind whenever he came around to put a new carbon in the streetlight. Attaching one end of a three-foot length of wire to a stiff cane pole, I made a slip noose on the other end for a fish snare. There was one deep hole in the river where you could see suckers and whitefish headed downstream side by side but barely moving their fins as they poked along the bottom. I eased the noose down where the whitefish could have a good look at it. He was jittery at first, and then swam close to the noose to investigate it. I moved it away, slipping it over the head of a sucker. I didn't want the sucker; they were bony and mushy at this season of the year. I removed it and with extreme care looped it over the head of the whitefish, stopped when the snare was across his gills, gave a yank and pulled him out. I got another one the same way, then stopped. I never told anybody about it, not even my mother, and I didn't try it again. It was too predictable. After the trout, it was too tame.

Guns were more exciting. I don't know where he got it, but one day. Fatty Root appeared looking for me. He led me to a hollow log in the pasture and pulled out an ancient gun, a 45-90 Sharps rifle. Each of us fired it that afternoon, but seldom thereafter. It was too hard to find cartridges. When we shot it we made sure that there were no cows or fishermen about, and we tried to use a hill as a backstop, for there was no telling how far a stray bullet from that gun would travel. It kicked so hard it usually spun us around. First I had a sling-shot, then a bow and arrow, then a crossbow George made me that worked. If a stone or an arrow was aimed at a chipmunk the creature was perfectly safe. The .45-90 was so lethal we dared not aim it at anything. The solution arrived that Christmas when both Fatty and I got .22 rifles. Mine was a Remington with an octagon barrel, a clip gun that took short, long, or long-rifle cartridges. To make sure that I learned how to handle my gun safely, my mother turned me over to the choirmaster, who liked to go woodchuck hunting Saturdays. The farmers hated woodchucks, which would slip into a field of clover or oats to build a burrow. When the grain was cut by a mower drawn by a farm team, many a horse broke a leg by stepping into the open mouth of the burrow hidden by the crop. My companion would take the short shots with his shotgun; I'd take the long shots with my rifle. After killing the quarry, we would hang the woodchuck on a stake, so the farmer could trap the others in the burrow and close the tunnel. The old man taught me to be always conscious of where the muzzle of my rife was pointing and how to place it when I crawled under a fence. Many hunters shot themselves in the leg so doing. In turn, I passed this information along to Fatty. I lived with that gun, winter and summer. In the winter we put a snowball in the ring fastened to the side of the slaughterhouse to tether a carriage horse. We'd move a long way off before we tried to explode it. Also we sat on the top of the bank that looked down forty feet to the river. We threw in a chip and as it passed, tossed about by the current, we knocked it out of the water. It taught us not to overshoot when sighting downhill. Any athletic boy could outrun me, but none could outshoot me. During deer season George took me with him far out in the country where he practiced with his .30-30 at distant objects on a desolate hill. Both he and the choirmaster assured my mother that I could be trusted with a gun.

She never knew that Fatty and I thought nothing of shooting the ashes off the end of the corn silk cigarettes we held in our mouths at 17 feet distant. If parents knew what boys really did!

A game I played by myself was to ride a huge block of ice downstream toward an ice jam. I had cut a long pole and driven a spike in the end of it. When I thought it was getting too close to the jam I poled it nearer and vaulted off to safety. Thirty years later I would probably have been killed, but teenaged kids are sure-footed and haven't enough sense to be afraid.

Usually with my gun but sometimes without it I prowled for miles up the river in the summertime, barefoot and bareheaded. I risked no danger from poisonous snakes or venomous spiders that far north. Sometimes I would see a big black snake sunning himself on a warm riverside stone, and once I beheld a very large pure white snake descending from our hayloft, where he must have spent the winter in hibernation or in hunting mice. Somebody told me it was a milk snake, but my knowledge of reptiles was restricted to garter snakes that could be carried in a boy's pocket to school and shown to girls as an expression of esteem when the teacher wasn't looking. I never used that ploy. If I fingered anything larger than a fish worm, I experienced Emily Dickinson's "zero at the bone." Yet I would have trod on vipers to go barefooted. Before I grew a defensive callous on the bottom of my feet I hobbled on gravel paths and feared to walk among thistles. But as they hardened I disregarded such irritations for the sensuous pleasure of running my toes through patches of cool moss in forest glades and wading without encumbrances. I knew every blackberry and huckleberry patch. I was continuously nibbling on something, a wintergreen berry or one of its new leaves or the tender end of a timothy spear. I even liked to pucker my mouth with a chokecherry. In the fall I would climb a beech tree for a pocketful of the tiny nuts or stop to crush a nut or two from a butternut tree, which has the sweetest meat inside the hardest shell. It takes two heavy stones to crack it. If I saw a muskrat swimming in a pool or foraging for provender, I promised to trap him when winter came.

On such an expedition my heart jumped to witness a covey of full-grown ruffed grouse roosting on the branches of a tamarack tree. You seldom saw a grouse up close except in early summer when you might stumble upon a mother bird in a wood warning her downy chicks to take cover. While they scamper under a bush or hide in a clump of grass, she will try to lead you away from them by affecting a zig-zag limp, pretending that she is easier game, for like a true mother she would die for her children. All young boys are unfeeling hunters, but one who would take advantage of her then should be finger-printed. In the fall the full-grown grouse whir up in front of you with a noisy beating of wings so that you'll be lucky to get off one good shot with a twelve-gauge shotgun before they are lost in the heavy timber. In the north we call them partridges, the same name Southerners give to their quail, but grouse are three times bigger. I told my mother I would be late for supper the next night, but not to worry. I would have a surprise for her.

On the following evening I returned to the same spot, though this time the grouse were roosting in a spruce, silhouetted against the setting sun. By crawling deliberately on my belly I drew very near without disturbing them. I hoped that the sound of my gun, using short cartridges, would not be loud enough to flush them all. If you fired birdshot straight on, the feathers covering the breastbone sometimes deflected the shot if none of the little pellets hit the bird in the head. I hoped a bullet might be different. I drew a bead on the bird's head low down and shot. The bird tumbled off the limb. The others were alarmed, but not enough to make them depart. They soon settled down again, and I got another. This time they took off, sailing away in a wide, high arc and landing I knew not where.

I snatched up my all but decapitated birds and ran all the way home. My mother was delighted, but asked me not to do it again. It was dark and she worried.

That was the biggest game I brought home, though I used my rifle to kill bullfrogs. Before that I caught them with a piece of red flannel on a big fishhook, which meant I still had to kill them before I cut off and skinned their legs. I didn't enjoy killing anything, but it didn't stop me from doing so. Man the hunter does not become man the philosopher until well past middle age.

7

Nothing could estrange any member of our family from another as long as we lived, but college separated us, though all three of us children attended Syracuse University because it was a strongly Methodist university only sixty miles from Camden. Elsie went in 1918, I in 1920, Glenevieve in 1923. I planned to enter Syracuse in the fall of 1919, but we lacked the money. Both my mother and I worked that winter in Conant's furniture factory. I ran a homemade machine which one of the supervisors invented. They were making a chair with a six-inch-wide back panel, and no existing machine would sand the concave side of the panel smooth. So the inventor came up with a contrivance that clamped the panel curved-side uppermost under a wide sanding belt. I had a curved wooden sander the size of a flatiron covered with graphite, which I applied to the fabric side of the revolving belt and, by learning the right amount of pressure, could smooth the panel free of any saw cuts. I did one after another of these hour after hour, day after day, from fall until spring. The factory work was deadly dull. My mother operated a punch. Any moron could have done our jobs. The only interesting things were the stalagmites the workers constructed. Since the men couldn't smoke they chewed tobacco, and beside every machine except my mother's and mine a stalagmite of the dust that filled the air mingled with the tobacco juice spat in one place all day long to form a cone a foot or more high. They were gnomish. I hated to see them removed.

On May 4, 1920, my mother quit to be remarried to a preacher, the Revered Albert Loucks. I quit to plant two acres of sweet corn, from which I hoped to make enough money to enter college in the fall. I knew the owner and bosses of the canning factory, for I had worked there as a bean boy. When they canned green beans they hired women and young girls to cut off the ends of each bean. My job was to see that every woman had a fresh basket of uncut beans by the time she had finished the prepared basket. I also became adept at bandaging cut fingers, and I helped Jim Lambie, a great story-teller, to round up all the under-age kids and herd them into the loft when management had been tipped off that a state inspector was coming. The inspector, who probably received something more than the fine cigar, spent all his time in the front office admiring the new machine the factory had just purchased. When the coast was clear Jim cut his current story short and put the youngsters back to work again. I told the powers in charge that I wished to buy from them the finest seed corn they had, because I was going to raise a crop of corn so perfect that they would want to buy it all back from me at so much an ear, which I would leave up to their well-known reputation for fair dealing. All I asked was that they did not buy any seed corn from any farmer until they had inspected my corn. They promised to take a first look at my crop, since all their workers said I was the best bean boy they had ever had. They expected great things from me.

Because the corn was my own idea I remember every step. I hired the two-acre lot plowed. It was stony, but stones would hold the heat on cold nights. One of my father's old friends gave me a horse outright. He was named Frank and couldn't work fast for he was 26 years old. But he was steady. I hitched Frank to the farm wagon and removed the old, well-rotted cow manure piled up outside the cow barn and spread it over the land. The plow took it under. It was stinking work, but it didn't smell as nauseating as some commercial fertilizers. Frank was sweating terribly, so I asked my brother for the only help I allowed anyone to give me. He got out the electric horse clippers and cut off Frank's thick coat of shaggy curly hair. He looked terrible and his ribs showed, but he was a different horse from then on. At the same time two of my buddies, Spin and Vernon Lewis, came over for a free haircut, and George obligingly all but shaved their heads.

After the plowing, I cultivated that patch until it was smooth. Then I marked it for planting. I sawed off a four by four a little over nine feet long, put the piece in a vice, and bored holes three feet apart, shaved the ends of three heavy branches and drove them in, cut them off at the same distance from the beam, and had my marker. I held the marker steady and Frank plodded across the field in a straight line. Then I marked it the long way and had my checkerboard of hills three feet apart.

The dean of the college at Washington and Lee University had the habit of breaking off in the middle of his lecture to add some bit of information worth remembering. He would stop and say, "Young gentlemen, do you know the most efficacious fertilizer in the world? The most efficacious fertilizer in the world is dove dung."

I'm sure that a close second was hen manure. We had piles of that, too. I dug a hole several inches deep at each cross mark over the whole field. It took forever, so it seemed. Then I carried a scuttle of the stuff up and down the rows, tossing in half a scoop-shaped trow-elful under every hill. After coating the seed corn with ashes and creosote to discourage the crows I was ready to plant, carrying the seed in a sack tied around my middle to leave my hands free to use the hoe. First I covered the hen manure with dirt, then put in four kernels, covered them with dirt and tamped it down. Now I could only wait, hoping for a gentle rain, and lie in wait for crows with my father's old twelve-gauge shotgun. I bagged several and used them for scarecrows, which discouraged the rest. The rains came, some not so gentle, but they washed away no hill of corn. Every seed must have germinated, for soon the plot was covered with the wavy light green shoots that lopped over into leafy plants before they formed stalks and began their upward climb. I had to hold myself back until they were about eight inches tall before I gave them their next feeding. I'm sure that no other farmer in the county had the time or the material to do what I did next. Inasmuch as our furnace burned wood I had to shovel out the ashes regularly to insure a draft before I stoked the furnace. I had barrel after barrel of wood ashes, almost pure nitrogen. Very carefully I threw a scoopful of ashes around every hill and when I had done several rows I stopped and hoed in each hill, at the same time pulling or chopping all weeds.

"Corn knee high the Fourth of July," was the saying in upstate New York and mine was higher than that. Very little hoeing was needed thereafter, for Old Frank and I lived in that cornfield with the cultivator all summer. You can rip out a row with a skittish horse, but Frank was so deliberate you could snag a weed with the last curved side blade and steer the cultivator back into the middle of the row without skipping too much. If you did, Frank was willing to stop and let you pull the cultivator back a foot or two. I let him rest frequently in the shade and made sure that he had enough fresh water to drink, but not too much, and I kept the flies off him and scratched him where he itched. I treated him with the consideration due a fine old gentleman, and he was not ungrateful. If the barn was stifling hot at night, I turned him loose in the pasture. He liked that. When I came for him in the morning I had only to whistle and he would leave the little grove at the foot of the hill, plod up the road, and nuzzle me at the gate. I slipped a halter over him knowing it was a work of supererogation. I tried walking him down the side of the road with no halter and he tagged along after me. My mother saw us heading for the barn and came out of the house. I stopped and Frank stopped. She was smiling and pleased. "I thought you said you had no way with horses."

"I haven't. Elsie is the horse fancier in this family. They'll do anything for her."

"That one seems to have taken to you."

"Frank's not a horse. He's a fugitive from a glue factory, aren't you, Frank?"

My mother laughed loudly, but Frank paid no attention to her, and followed me into the barn.

The corn turned out better than expected. The ears were large with even rows of kernels that covered the rounded ends. I invited the canning factory people up to have a look and to take their samples at random. They were so greatly impressed that they paid me the high price of two cents an ear.

Frank and I worked long hours to deliver it; for since the factory stayed open after hours, I delivered right up to the time they closed. When it was all over I had a check for $600.00. I don't know which was more tired, the boy or the horse.

My system was so run down that I developed a carbuncle on the back of my neck. Again, it was a friend of the family who cared for it. We and the Van Allens had interchanged visits. I played with Roy, the son, a year or two older than I, and my sisters played with Dorrit, whom I worshipped from afar. Evidently Dr. Van Allen, a dentist, had observed my devotion, for when he was working on my teeth he would put as much as possible of his burly hand into my mouth and ask me with a serious face if my intentions toward his daughter were honorable. I gagged and made animal noises trying to assure him that they were. He would remove just enough of the hand to let me get half a sentence out then would cut it off by depressing my tongue and making me repeat my honorable motives and my circumspect regard.

Mrs. Van Allen was the loveliest lady that I had ever met. On afternoons she would sit in a rocker on their veranda that faced the shopping area, watching people come and go. Whenever I spied her I always straddled the porch rail for a chat. She most nearly represented the word lady of any woman I have ever known. Plato talked of the absolute and eternal reality, which the world can only reflect, but Mrs. Van Allen in the matter of gentility is the prototype by which I have always judged other women. She alone deserved Dryden's saying that "the noblewoman is she whose noble mind is filled with inborn worth, un-borrowed from her kind."

It was she who noticed the boil on the back of my neck and insisted that I must come down that evening and let Dr. Van Allen treat it for me. She said that he was more than a dentist in dealing with this particular affliction. She was so persistent that I would not be imposing on him, that he would be flattered to demonstrate his skill, that at last I promised. Dr. Van Allen was ready for me with all kinds of tools laid out on a towel on a kitchen table. After he had lanced and drained and poulticed it, I asked him, "How do you happen to be such an authority on boils?"

"I've had them myself," he chuckled, "all the way from Dan to Beersheba. "As a matter of fact..." His face wrinkled into a wicked grin. "I had one right in Beersheba."

I laughed loudly, but Mrs. Van Allen only smiled and said gently, "Now, William..."

Dr. Van Allen made me come for another treatment and a fresh bandage every night that week. I knew he wouldn't let me pay him, but they both knew that I was humbly grateful.

Only one misfortune rose out of the sweet corn growing. I didn't know what to do with Frank. I tried to give him away but couldn't find anyone who wanted to feed him all winter for the little work he could do. Nor could I impose upon George or my mother to keep him fed, watered, stabled, and currycombed. Tight as money was, I had decided to pay some well-disposed youngster—maybe the boy who inherited my paper route—to take care of him in the big stable with the window in our horse barn and to give him a sugar cube and take him for a walk once a week. The boy agreed, but since the time was growing short before I had to leave for college, I decided to give Frank a few days of freedom in the pasture during the Indian summer we were enjoying. Twice I visited and petted him and told him I'd see him soon during my vacations or on the long weekends when I would slip back home to see my mother and my sister Glen. After both such visits he stood at the gate staring at me reproachfully.

Near the end of the week the wind sprang up, the sky grew black as night; thunder roared and lightning flashed and a rain came down torrentially enough to be considered a cloudburst. I wanted to retrieve Frank, but my mother wouldn't let me. It rained all night, beating on the tin roof of the porch so noisily I couldn't sleep for thinking of Frank. I stuck my head under the covers, and then I couldn't breathe. At daylight I slipped out of bed and down the hall, stepping around the board that always squeaked.

I had made it out without waking anybody, for the rain still beat against the house in noisy gusts. I had no coat or hat that would shed rain, but donned the old blue jacket I wore around the barn, put on my shoes and socks and was on the point of taking them off again when my mother appeared, carrying the long rubber coat and rubber hat my father had worn. It was too big for me and much too long, but the hat fitted well enough. The coat didn't have buttons but was outfitted with the same kind of clamps they put on overshoes.

Thrusting a glass of milk into my hand, my mother pulled her robe more snugly around her and went into the woodshed to bring back the knee-high jackboots I wore on the manure pile. I slipped them on; the coat now covered the tops of my boots. I didn't see how a drop of water could wet me. I kissed my mother for her kindness. Not until I had children of my own could I understand how a parent knew when a child was not in bed.

The rain beat against me harmlessly, but the wind was so strong that when I leaned into it, it would bear me up. After a gust when it relaxed its push against me, I'd stumble and almost fall.

Frank was not at the gate. I opened it with difficulty and walked down the stony path that had so recently been a hard-packed dirt road. All the earth had been washed away. It was a pile of stones with two gullies instead of wheel tracks. I glanced down to the right where Frank made his bed in the little grove, but there was no sign of him. I looked left at the wide expanse of raging river. The foot-bridge was gone; then I saw him, half in and half out of the water. He must have climbed the road in the storm, tried to return to his grove, lost his footing, fell over the bank, and broke his neck. He was so obviously dead; there was nothing I could do. I went back home and told my mother.

"As soon as this storm lets up we'll get Charley Clark and his team to haul him out of there. You can dig a grave for him down at the bottom of the hill." She threw her arms around me, and then I couldn't keep back the tears.

It came off hot and sunny. The earth steamed. I took a pick and a long-handled shovel and went to the pasture, wearing my heaviest work shoes.

Frank was gone. Dead bodies bloated, I knew. It would help him float. I walked down as far as Conant's dam, our old swimming hole, but there was no sign of Frank. I had never been farther down the river than that, and went no farther now. In a way it was a relief to have him disposed of, but it's never pleasant to lose a true friend.

8

Though nothing could break the bonds that tied my mother to me, one subject, religion, could never be resolved between us. She was a very intelligent woman, but believed in the literal interpretation of the Bible. Charles William Eliot, at age 91, addressed the incoming class at Harvard in 1925 and said in his cracked voice, "Though I have reached the age when I would be thinking about going there, I have never read a description of heaven that was even passable." Everyone chuckled. If my mother had heard him, she would not have smiled. She believed the streets of gold, the heavenly choir, just as she believed in a devil and a fiery hell. Since the Middle Ages the devil had been a sort of comic figure, but he was not a figure of folklore to her. Possibly the fundamentalists are right; if you want to have an organized religion you must accept it all. When I was a small boy I wanted to believe and as I grew older I at least wanted to be thought a Christian and a churchgoer to please my mother. But when I told her my doubts, she was so horrified and so determined to drive them out of my mind by heavier and heavier doses of religion that she not only kept those doubts alive but made me question everything. If I tried to argue, she told me to read the Bible. I did, assiduously. I approved of Jesus and his teaching. I admired him intensely, but I simply couldn't swallow all the folklore. Then I discovered that she had a secret ambition for me; from the time I was a little boy she had wanted me to become a preacher. That was the very last thing I would have chosen. I could not have conducted a communion service, handing a man or woman a square of bread, saying that this represents the body of Christ, which he sacrificed for you, followed by a sip of grape juice, saying that this was his precious blood which he had shed for us, and we all must drink his blood to be saved. When I was sixteen, she told me that she had prayed and God had told her that if I listened, I would hear Him tell me, "Go ye forth into all the world and preach my gospel." She begged me to open my heart and listen.

I listened as hard as I could in high seriousness for three nights in a row and never heard a thing. I even prayed, or tried to. I so much wanted to make my mother happy. God kept his silence, and from that day till this I have never believed any religion. I told my mother how I felt and said that I had learned many fine things from her and from my father that should make me a halfway decent man. But I could not be a shining evangel and that was all there was to it.

After that she was not quite so combative, but she didn't drop the matter either. Upon several occasions we were visited by her favorite brother, an uncle I adored, despite him being a preacher. He didn't talk about religion all day long; he seldom mentioned it, though he had attained national recognition as a sort of self-appointed missionary to Alaska. In Anchorage he started the first radio church for those too far inland to have a church or a preacher. He had printed a little cardboard folder stating the name of the member in good standing of the Northland Radio Church, Anchorage, Alaska. Inside was a picture of him standing before a radio broadcasting box, Station KFQD. Across the page was a little verse by Whittier and on the back, alone on the white page, a picture of Jesus that showed a bearded man with strong but kindly features, the best representation of the man I have ever seen, for most of them are so sappy and mollycoddle you couldn't imagine the character depicted as having enough fire to drive the money changers out of the temple. He used to beg me to come to Alaska and have the fun of catching king salmon and going elk hunting with him. He was the man who introduced both strawberries and potatoes into Alaska, believing that though the season was short, the earth was so rich that anyone could get in one crop before the cold came again. He had eight huge strawberries in one quart mason jar, and some potatoes that were immense. When those families from the Dust Bowl, numbering 700 men and women, were sent to Alaska to take up free claims, they were sent to Uncle Emil Winterberger to settle them in. He said that some of the Swedes and Germans among them only wanted an axe and a few tools and a gun to keep off the curious bears and varmints and they'd have a cabin built and things growing in no time, but that the bums would take the government money and head for the saloon to cry into their beer over their sad lot. He would lecture about Alaska wherever he was invited. I thought he must be like the country, big, vital, laughing, and assured, with a hint of mischief in his eyes and a love of all mankind in his heart. He was bald as an egg and thought it a great joke.

Sometimes in the 1920s Uncle Edwin would visit us, too. He was considered the foremost surgeon in Chicago. He had completed a long and thorough training and was just ready to put up his shingle when World War I was declared in America. He went to France and operated behind the lines 18 hours a day. Surgeons had to take chances or the patient would die anyway, and this constant practice gave him a facility that few doctors enjoyed. He was just the opposite of Uncle Emil, except that he loved the parson, as he called him, best. In Chicago he would drive so fast that he'd get a speed cop after him. He'd lament to the parson that he hoped his parishioners would forgive him if he had to spend some time in the hoosegow. At the last minute he would show the cop his doctor's permit to exceed the speed limit in emergencies.

Uncle Edwin had given all his love to his wife, and when she died giving birth to twin baby girls, he became hard and cynical, marrying a woman who supposedly poisoned him on a train for his money. Before they could get him to a hospital he was dead. I don't blame my mother for liking those two brothers best. They were big, self-reliant men. Uncle Emil didn't constantly moralize. As Emerson said, he put his creed into his deed. I'm sure my mother begged him to convert me, but though he visited us many times, he only mentioned the matter once. We were bass fishing in a strange river, and he said in passing, "Lawrence, in all your searching don't fail to give some time to the study of Jesus Christ."

It did not help my mother's effort to influence me when in May she married the preacher then serving at our church, the Reverend A.C. Loucks. I knew he had been begging her for some time to marry him, and I suppose I was one of the few people who did not think the match ideal. His wife had been dead for a long time, and he badly needed someone to humanize him, for he was a bookish man, a scholar, who gloried in his perfectibility. He would pooh-pooh it, but I could see that he loved to be called the "Saint of Saint Lawrence County," and "God's Good Man." He had a perfect record for godliness. His first wife was from the wealthy Crouse family, the same philanthropists who had given Syracuse University Crouse College, which housed the arts schools. The young lady came to him with a dowry of $80,000, which he persuaded her to give to foreign missions.

He had made Phi Beta Kappa but refused to be initiated because the society had denied admittance to a Jewish student in his class with an equally good record. He begged to be excused from any function that might be considered worldly. His sermons were well-reasoned, lifeless, humorless, scholarly dissertations. He had no tolerance for weakness or what he considered to be evil, and would have been happiest to have lived with the New England Puritans in the days when sinners were put in the stocks. He never said a cross word to me or reproved me. He probably knew that if he did I'd tell him to go to hell. For my mother's sake I tried to put the best face I could upon the marriage. I am sure that it was no love match, that whether she admitted it or not, she wanted help from this man whom she admired for his dedication to the church.

She liked being a preacher's wife, and Glenevieve was religious. Glen liked, and probably pitied, this strange, stiff figure of rectitude who didn't know how to act like a human being. The marriage went off well, for Mother persuaded her beloved brother Emil Winterberger to visit us and perform the marriage ceremony. There could be no silent, reproving look if I made a remark that Dr. Loucks considered "worldly," for Emil would throw a hundred questions at him about what he thought of a certain phase of "the holy land" on his last pilgrimage there, or when was he going to visit Alaska and let the folks on KFQD hear a real sermon from a guest speaker who knew what he was talking about. Dr. Loucks swallowed the compliment, but refused the invitation because of the pressure of work. But in the face of Uncle Emil's enthusiasm, he found it difficult to pick at his plate of food when everyone else was devouring theirs. Later on, when he had settled in, he seldom ate any part of the fine meal that my mother always prepared. His stomach was strong and normal, but he considered tea and coffee stimulating and therefore sinful. He usually had a cup of hot water and often nothing but rice—to mortify the flesh—or because he had read that somewhere in the world people were starving. The implication that the rest of us were all greedy pigs was evident. I couldn't help thinking what a dirty shame it was for the best cook in town to marry a man who looked upon one of her lovely pies as the work of the devil. He wouldn't even let her cook breakfast for him. He usually would poach himself one soft boiled egg and put it on a piece of unbuttered toast and eat it standing up at the kitchen table. In later years he seldom ate with the rest of us at all, but had Mother prepare him a tray, which he could eat in his bedroom, while thumbing through a Biblical concordance. The excuse was that his teeth hurt him. It never occurred to him to have them repaired. That would have cost money. I believe that he had some arrangement with Cazenovia Seminary. Years previously he had given them a large sum of money, and if he needed it he would ask them to send him a certain meager amount. He did this in lieu of life insurance, which of course he thought sinful. I believe my mother insisted that she have a certain fixed allowance for taking care of the house, for she could no longer work in the factory, and I am sure his pride would not let her peddle butter or take in sewing. I don't know their financial arrangements, but I am sure it was enough to see Glenevieve through college. Glen went to Syracuse, helped start a sorority, and graduated four years later, in 1927, Phi Beta Kappa.

9

When I entered Syracuse University in the fall of 1920, all freshmen were required to wear the tiny blue freshman cap, their lid, which made them easy targets for hazing by the sophomores, who were mostly returned soldiers from France. They made our lives miserable, not by the extreme cruelty that often resulted in mutilation or even death, but by little niggling harassments. I remember once approaching a building on my way to class, when a group of sophomores made me stop and push a penny across a ten-foot square of sidewalk cement with my nose.

They also loved to ridicule us ROTC marching squads, as well they might. In our badly wound puttees and sloppy musket handling, we looked like exactly what we were, a great concourse of boys who had elected to take a year of ROTC rather than a year of gym, because it was easier. We had been denied the chance to go to war, and there wasn't another war anywhere in sight. It was the lesser of two boredoms. The only memorable thing about it was the sex lecture. The college decided that we all be herded into one great hall and be told the facts of life by two speakers, one the rarely seen colonel in command of the whole military set-up, the other the secretary of the YMCA. The two speakers were so different in their approach to the unmentionable mystery that the result was hilarious.

The colonel spoke first. He sat uneasily on the edge of the speaker's desk. He was regular Army and had come up through the ranks and though it's impossible to remember his ungrammatical rumblings, punctuated from time to time with an embarrassed, death's-head smile, I'll give you the gist of it. He spent no wasted effort getting to the point:

> Listen, you guys, you know and I know that every so often any normal red-blooded man wants to ... to be with a woman. [Here the smile.] Now in wartime, if and when you're in a foreign country, it ain't likely you'll be sleeping with your wife. Sometimes you have to make do with a piece that ain't much better than a whore. Now, if you do, don't take a chance. Get a shot. You get a shot, you got nothin' to worry about.

> I remember one time the company I commanded was so shot up and bone tired we were given a few days of R&R in this little French town that had been evacuated it was so near the firin' lines. The men was layin' around in the sunshine when this French girl come through town on a bicycle. She was as young and fresh and clean as the finest highborn lady you ever laid your eyes on. She talked English pretty good, too, and not a dirty word come out of her mouth. She said she was so grateful for what our boys was doin' over here for her country that she wondered if there was anything in the world she could do to show her appreciation? Well, sure enough, somebody thought of a way.

Here again the smile, followed by concerted laughter. The colonel continued:

> Before she left she laid the whole damn company, and, man, were those boys clapped up! So for God's sake, fellows, anytime you are with a woman, get a shot!

He nodded and walked out to considerable applause, leaving the field to the YMCA secretary, who was busy at the blackboard, drawing the outline of a limp but wellknown organ, curved slightly. Somebody started to laugh. The secretary frowned and picked up a wooden pointer, indicating his masterpiece. I can give you his words exactly. How could I ever forget them, or his shrill, didactic tones: "The male organ of generation, commonly known as the penis, is, in its quiescent state, from five to seven inches long." This information was greeted with such roars of laughter that he tried, in even shriller tones, to go on. "Aroused, it may attain the formidable—" That's as far as he got. Somebody in the back of the room shouted out, "Cheer up, boys; there ain't no hell!" whereupon the whole roomful rushed toward the exit doors, completely disregarding the shrieks of anger proceeding from the podium.

In 1920, Syracuse University was considered a large university. Compared to the huge enrollments of today, its 8,000 men and women do not make it sound enormous, but so it seemed to me. It was far too large and strung-out for me to feel myself a part of it or to want my children to go there or to care how its athletic teams fared after I had left the place. It might have been different if I had joined a fraternity, though I doubt it. Roy Van Allen was kind enough to write from his fraternity at a different college to the Syracuse chapter, proposing that they look me up, and they invited me to visit them, but I most politely told them I was so poor that all my spare time would be given to paying jobs and that my name would not add any luster to their club. I remember reading somewhere that Stephen Crane, before he wrote *The Red Badge of Courage*, had gone to Syracuse because he loved to play baseball; and because he was good, a fraternity had pledged him and given him a barely habitable room in the attic, but good enough for an athlete. A friend of his told the fraternity that he had despaired of a novel he had written and threw the whole thing down the beams along the side of the building that had a dormer window. Supposedly, years after his death, the fraternity tore out that side of the building down to the first firebreak and found nothing. I would have had them retrieve one cleated baseball shoe with a hole in the bottom.

Anyway, I was a non-entity and a loner and much preferred the company of the one boy who also came from Camden that year, Ludwig Krissler. I was surprised that staid old Camden had questioned the loyalty of the Krissler family during World War I, some of the neighbors even shunning them as German spies. Actually, Lud's father had risked jail to escape to America from the military junta that tried to press him into service. Lud was as poor as I, but we found a clean decent room to rent within walking distance from the college and both were hired as kitchen slaves in the basement of a girl's dormitory. A third boy was a big blond kid named Nicholson. Kitty, the sweet, fat, Irish cook, and her skinny helper Mary, saw to it that we three boys got the best of everything before they sent the loaded plates on the dumbwaiters to the sixty girls above. Our job was to scrape the remaining food off the returned plates into garbage cans, wash the dishes in the two big dishwashers, wipe them if necessary, and stack them for the next meal. That work insured us three hot meals a day and a little pocket money.

Because everyone said a student should have an activity, it occurred to me that I might go out for the rifle team, which wasn't very glorious, so I didn't. In high school I had pitched for the baseball team. I was skinny and couldn't hit, but I had long fingers and an excellent arm, probably because I never went into our pasture without throwing stones at some target. I had a fair in-curve and an excellent out-drop, and could hit the corners pretty well. I was as good as the pitchers on the teams we played against. Two things stand out from those days. Once I very much wanted to catch a pop fly to put out a troublesome batter, but had to wade through the kids seated on the side lines between third and home plate. The ball was coming down on the head of a scrunched-down girl who had linked both hands over her head to protect it. I reached out and speared the ball with my glove. I looked down; the girl looked up. "Did you catch it, Wat?" she said. It was my sister Glenevieve.

I wished the other kids had called me Wat, but someone gave me the nickname of "Butter" and it stuck. Old friends still call me Butter Watkin. I particularly resented it because it was in error. My cousin Earl delivered butter that his mother made on their farm. Someone mistook me for him, and I never pitched a game that the opposing gallery wasn't yelling "Butterfingers" at me. I wished that I could have used it on the ball. Another thing that stands out: Our team to a man used only one word as a curse if we made a bad play. We were at Utica, playing the Utica Free Academy. There was a big crowd of boys, but only five girls had come to watch their big-city heroes wallop the country yokels. The girls sat in a row in the second tier of seats behind the wire backstop. I threw an out-drop that the UFA batter swung on and missed entirely. The ball hit the ground and went right between our catcher's feet. Johnny Eastham, our catcher, yelled out our watchword at the top of his voice: "Shit!"

The five girls arose as one and stalked out of the park.

I knew I wasn't good enough to make the university squad and didn't try. I had met a girl, an art student, a quiet, pretty girl with whom I fell in love. I wanted to take her to Keiths and buy her a sundae at the Cosmo after the show, which meant extra money. All the employment office had was for a strong boy to dig a deep hole for a septic tank out in the sticks at the end of the car line. I took it. I worked at it in my spare time afternoons day after day. When I had dug a wide cavern so deep that I could no longer throw out the dirt easily, the owner wanted it still deeper; so we rigged a scaffold and as I continued to dig I threw the dirt on the scaffold and then out. I was approaching China when the owner said that was deep enough. His wife was so certain of my reliability that she offered me the job of baby sitter. I preferred digging cesspools until I tried singing to the squalling brat, whose savage breast was instantly charmed. In the course of a long life I have found that to be the most often mis-quoted passage in the English language. It is usually given as: "Music hath charms to soothe the savage *beast*," and the source as Pope, but it comes from William Congreve's "Mourning Bride":

> Music hath charms to soothe a savage breast,
> To soften rocks, or bend a knotted oak.

Finding that song put the child to sleep, or at least induced a blessed quietness, I brought out my full repertoire. The lady rec-ommended me to her friends. Soon I had all the baby-charming jobs

I could handle. If the kid was very small, I walked the floor with him, singing *"Sleep, Kentucky Babe."* If the child was older, I sang it all the nonsense songs Uncle Dan had taught me, and a minstrel song my father sang which started:

> Oh, darkeys, have you seen de massa
> Wiv da mustache on his face
> Come 'long the road some time this mawnin'
> Like he's gonna leave de place?
> He saw de smoke way up de ribber
> Where de Lincum gumboats lay
> He tuk his hat and he lef' mighty sudden;
> I specks he's runned away.
> De massa run, ha, ha;
> De darkey stay, ho, ho.
> Mus' be now de kingdom's comin'
> In de year o' jubilo.

There's a lot more of it, and the dialect doesn't improve, but minstrel songs were not written to appeal to the intellect. "Dixie" was written by Dan Emmett, a Yankee minstrel songwriter, and its second verse deserves to be forgotten. The word "Dixie" was originally the name for New Orleans, which printed a ten-dollar bill with *dix*, French for ten, thereon. Soldiers, like children, like songs zany. Witness "Yankee Doodle" or "Mademoiselle from Armentieres." Incidentally, in the song about the plantation master who was running away is the verse:

> There's wine and cider in de cellar
> And the darkeys they'll have some;
> I specks we'll all be confiscated
> When the Lincum soldiers come.

Not understanding the word *confiscated*, I chose to think my father said *corn-fish crated*, which made no sense either. Children often give their own meaning to unfamiliar words. My wife told me that her father always ended his grace before eating with: "For Christ's sake we would ask it." She thought he said, "For Christ's sake weave a basket," and never quite understood why he should burden the Lord with this strange request.

The girl for whom I did all this extra work did not care about money spent upon her. She much preferred to hike to some high spot where we could look down upon the city, which exalted our kissing. She was altogether a very nice girl. All the following summer I wrote her love letters, but when I met her in the fall I noticed something that I had never seen before: she had very large pores in her nose. It wasn't a serious flaw, but to one who had seen only perfection it was a calamity. I don't know how I got through the rest of that evening, and when I got back to my room it was worse. I finally told Lud about it. What could I do? I never wanted to see her again, and I couldn't tell her about it, but it would be cruel just to stay away. But I had to. I begged Lud to answer the phone and if she called tell her I had gone out. He thought the whole thing was ridiculous. What were a few big pores? Maybe the sun did it. They might go away. Yes, but what if they came back, or even got worse? To me she was disfigured for life. I felt like a criminal. What was going through her mind? What had she possibly said that could make me change from hot to cold in a second? I hoped with all my heart that she would meet a man who made me look like the bag of worms I really was.

For months if I saw her at convocation or anywhere else, I rushed away in the opposite direction. Eventually, I got over it, but it took a long time for me to cast off the feeling of guilt. I decided that I was too unstable ever to get married. I stayed away from girls entirely and devoted myself to my schoolwork, which was just as well.

I had no trouble getting good grades in any subject except two: Latin and mathematics. If a Latin word was one from which an English word derived, I took note of it, but I had no interest in it as literature and flunked the final exam by one point, but got a D for the course. As for math, I was utterly hopeless. I had scored a 99 in high-school algebra, but did badly in geometry, and never understood anything whatsoever about the trigonometry I was now taking in college, though a pass was required. I went directly from freshman English class, where the instructor had usually read my theme as outstanding, to trig, where I was a dunce. The professor was a character, whom I immediately liked. His name was Professor Buller, and I believe he was a bachelor. He invariably started the hour with a lecture upon the lack of morals and shocking manners of the younger generation. He told little stories of what he had seen on and off the campus. He damned us not on religious grounds but for openly flaunting sex. One day he came to class with a good six inches of white shirt sticking out of his fly, and as he related the behavior of a young couple who sat in front of him on the street car, we howled with laughter. He simply couldn't understand it. Usually we listened to his diatribes with respect, but today we were worse than the kids on the streetcar. When he quizzed us on the day's assignment, he was unmerciful.

"Mr. Watkin," he said, "can you answer the question I put to Mr. Campbell?"

"No, sir."

"Can you answer half of the question?"

"No, sir."

He went back to Campbell. "Mr. Campbell, I forgot to ask you. Can you answer half the question?"

"No, sir."

Dr. Buller sighed deeply and looked at the ceiling. "Pity," he said in the clipped tones in which every syllable stood out: "I thought that together you might make one man mathematically!"

He waited. No comment. A girl glancing at the piece of shirt-tail uttered a brief, hysterical laugh. He did not look at her, but riveted his eyes on the two of us : "Are you quite sure," he inquired, "that you are on the right hill?"

We both smiled as a tribute to his witticism. The other hill he referred to had the insane asylum.

In 1920 the administration was very forgiving. During the summer you were encouraged to study the subject you had flunked in the spring and take a make-up exam in the fall. When I was 19 I could memorize anything. If I liked it, one reading might be enough. If I loathed it, I could still learn it letter perfect. Now Dr. Buller based all his teaching and every examination, long or short, on the trigo-nometry text he had written. I worked like a Trojan and memorized the whole one hundred pages, including the logarithm tables.

Dr. Buller gave me the make-up exam in his own house, which was nicely furnished. He greeted me politely and offered me a comforta-ble chair, which I carefully drew up to the table. An empty quiz book had been served up and the examination paper lay face down over it. He drew up a similar chair across from me and sat in utter silence while I wrote out a perfect examination and handed it to him. He read it with growing amazement. When he had finished it, he spoke.

"Mr. Watkin," he said, "I know that you cheated, but will you tell me how you managed it?"

"Dr. Buller, I did not cheat in any way, shape, or manner."

"You had to."

"I did not."

He shook his head. He seemed ready to cry. "You won't tell me," he begged, "not even if I don't let it invalidate this examination?"

For a moment I was tempted to tell him, then I thought of all the nasty digs he had given me throughout the previous year. "Dr. Buller," I said, "the only way I can explain it is that you are such a remarkable teacher your instruction must have stuck with me without my knowing it."

I did not speak a word sarcastically; I tried my best to make it sound sincere, but he knew what I really thought of him.

That was the last bout I had with mathematics. My wife balanced the checkbook.

Cheating at Syracuse was widespread. Students did not consider it shameful, unless they were caught. If somebody figured out a new way to cheat beyond the usual cribs secreted in pockets, in watches, in turned-up trouser cuffs, or jottings to jog the memory written in ink inside the left hand, or on the inside of the forearm, he was considered a clever dog, not a dirty one.

Almost everyone was singing the praises of a student so brilliant in psychology that he got all the brothers taking that course through with flying colors. The teacher always gave true and false exams because they were easy to grade. She was so lazy she didn't patrol the exam, but sat at the desk in the center of the room and read a book. The genius sat a little to the right of center and had the brothers staggered still farther to the right. When he decided whether the answer to the first question was a yes or a no, he tapped his desk, once for true, twice for false. Because regularity in tapping might be noticed, any tap beyond one meant false. If the teacher looked his way, she would see a student with a scowl of concentration tapping nervously. If she told him to stop, he would go to finger signals, holding either one or two fingers against his pursed lips. Or he might scratch his head. Or hold them down at his side. Then it was up to the nearest fraternity brother to relay the signal to others farther away. If a brother lost count, he must clear his throat until another came to his aid by writing the number of the question coming up on a piece of scratch paper and showing it to the befuddled man. The genius had even realized that all the brothers involved would finish their exams at the same time. It was up to each man to delay a decent length of time before turning in his paper.

A friend of Lud's, not wanting to prepare his crib at home, came to our room the day before an exam with a snug roll of streamer paper about an inch and a half wide, each end fastened to rollers, so that when it was finished he could roll it backward or forward at will. He fastened one end across the room and ran the tape across a desk near his pen hand. He had the text used in the course and preceded to outline the whole book under chapter headings. He had a pen with a fine point. It took him all day. When he had finished I bet him that he would never have to use it, his review had been so comprehensive. I was right. He knew it so well that he had to ask the teacher for extra time to finish all he had to say. About twenty years later I ran into this fellow again, literally. We were passing in a parlor car headed for New York City. He remembered my face and embraced me. We had only a moment to converse, but he told me with some pride that he was the principal of a high school in one of the towns along the Hudson through which we had just passed. He was the beaming spirit of Rotary, and as we parted he called after me: "By the way, I just introduced the honor system. It's working great!"

10

My sophomore year and the junior and senior years that followed were most pleasant. I liked almost every course I took except that I wished those in French, German, and Spanish had stressed conversation, not grammar.

I got good grades in everything. I had worked like a dog all summer to bring up that math grade in order to stay in college and from this point forward, I did my studying punctually and did it well. Without putting it into words at the time, I realize now that I had been scared into studying, that though I took the matter of flunking lightly before it happened, I would have let my family down and felt disgraced if I hadn't been allowed to return. I experienced no blinding light of conversion, but it happened nevertheless. I had heard students say in countless different ways that they came to college to "find" themselves. That never occurred to me. Nor, unlike my roommate, Ludwig Krissler, who had come to college for one purpose only—to make a financial success—did I stop to consider how the liberal arts courses were preparing me, or not preparing me, for a profession. My father and mother had arrived at middle-class status or better; their friends' children went to college; so should I. My older sister, whom I saw infrequently because of our age difference, was already there, and would graduate and start teaching soon. I simply accepted the fact that college was opening up the world for me, that I loved books, even our despised textbooks, and that I welcomed the chance to write.

It's a commonplace for students to tell you today that they expect to become professional writers. I never, even as a graduate student, thought I was good enough. A writer friend of mine, some forty years later, remarked, "God, Watkin, we're conceited bastards, aren't we?"

"Well, no," I said, "I don't think I'm conceited."

"The hell you don't! Do you think that the average man has the gall to believe that the general public would be interested in what he had to say, or the way he says it?"

"It never occurred to me."

"Well, it should. Next to me you're the most conceited man I ever met. "

There was one great difference between college courses then and now. There was more meat in a course then, fewer crip courses and electives for athletes. The course I had in ancient history was well attended and thought one of the most valuable. It would be a rarity today. Our text, Breasted's *Ancient Times*, devotes 200 pages to the civilizations that flourished before those of Greece and Rome. Most kids currently think of ancient history as starting with Greece, if indeed they would go back that far.

Greek was already in disfavor by the time I went to college, but the Greek professor, a marvelous little man, gave a course supposed to be a crip, but one which exposed us to the mythology of a great many civilizations by reading their national epics, not only *The Iliad* and *The Odyssey*, but *The Aeneid, The Song of Roland, The Cid, The Kalevala*, and *The Nibelungenlied*. I was as familiar with Siegfried as I was with Achilles, all seen through the civilized vision of Professor Davy. It marked the beginning of my interest in all mythology, a private passion. That professor accepted the decline of true erudition with good humor, and if the hoopla on the old oval the day before homecoming sometimes became so noisy it was hard for him to be heard, he would look out the window and remark with a wry wistfulness, "I used to think it unfair that the football coach was paid ten times as much as the Greek professor, but I must admit I never heard 30,000 people cheering a Greek recitation."

I wish I had taken Greek. I would have learned it just to please him. The Latin teacher I had in my freshman year was a stolid, self-satisfied bore, but that little Greek professor, like several other excellent teachers I studied under, had only to hint that a book was worth reading to send me to the library. These unassigned rivulets of reading spilled over into the daily theme course I relished, where we were constrained by no assigned subjects but told to follow our enthusiasms.

I was still a loner, but became one of a small coterie of students who met in the same classes day after day. We wanted to pursue a subject under discussion after the class was over, and drifted out on the steps of the building or down the street to the Cosmo to talk it out over a soda or Coke. I kept meeting them on friendly if not on familiar terms. This was the same group that eventually ran the *Phoenix*, the literary magazine. I wrote the book reviews for it, and yearned for a time to date one of the girls whom I thought exceptionally beautiful, but I never quite dared. I think that she came from an enormously wealthy and socially prominent New York family, and the good breeding that made her so genuinely superior could never have been mimed by an actress. I longed just to touch her. I knew that she would be soft as a seal. I didn't lust for her. That requires a special chemistry. You can walk through a roomful of beauties and only one may stir you. My freshman sweetheart, whom I had treated so shabbily, made me wary of any similar entanglement.

There was another girl who fascinated me. She too was in many of my classes, though she kept herself aloof. She used the library a lot, and I gazed at her and conjectured about her background. She was a Jew; very quiet with a lovely serene face and hair that shone it was so black against the whiteness of her skin. She was highly intelligent. I had heard that some Jews are so brilliant because as the children of a rabbi they are too smart to be impressed until they meet the child o·f another·rabbi, and that this sort of inter-marriage repeated leads to genius. I pictured in my mind the boy she was in love with back home. One day she caught me staring at her, and before I could look away she nodded toward the book she was reading as if to say it was tough going. I nodded toward my own book ruefully. We both smiled and went back to reading. She had a beautiful smile, which I had never seen before, and I only pretended to read after that, thinking that she might come by and make some comment about the course, but she didn't. She had countered my stare politely and decided that was as friendly as she wanted to be. She slipped out quietly without a glance in my direction. Thereafter she did not look at me or at any other male student, but remained true to that rabbi' s son who so much resembled one of those fine pictures of Jesus as a very young, bright-eyed man.

Because my freshman sweetheart had not returned after the midyear exams I no longer had to stay away from Crouse College where I might have run into her. Most of the interesting lectures were given in the Crouse College auditorium, and all the debates.

If the lecturer had a reputation for packing them in, as did that wonderfully witty and delightful speaker Stephen Leacock, a larger auditorium was used, as it was for Vachel Lindsay, who could charm an audience by half chanting, half singing his poetry, but for a more purely literary speaker such as Gilbert Chesterton, the more inti-mate, better designed, and far mare comfortable Crouse College was used. Debates were often mere wrangles, but there was one that brought out the whole sophomore class and a great many others besides. Our classmate, Dan Flood, who was already known as a character because he walked around the campus with a disdainful and supercilious expression on his face, wearing a coat with tails so short that they barely covered his rump, was so chauvinistic that the word, not yet in use, might well have been coined just for him. He was considered, possibly because he considered himself, the number-one debater in the university. To oppose him, the committee had imported from across the sea a real, live English lord. We expected to see the fur fly and were not disappointed. Daniel, regarding his foe with the built-in sneer that suggested he smelled Old World decay, twisted the British lion's tail for round after round. His lordship, a gentleman born and bred, parried Dan's crudities until he could stand it no longer. He suddenly cut loose and demolished this provincial bully, burying Dan under a mountain of facts and figures, with a fine scorn for Dan's illogic. There was a murmur of general approbation from the audience that amounted to applause.

Almost the same thing happened some fifty years later. After spilling his venom on any American who was willing to give away the Panama Canal, Dan was convicted of stealing out of the till, and though many of the charges were dropped in deference to his *service* in the US Congress, his arrest for thievery made television. I hadn't laid eyes on him for fifty years, but as he was led away, the spiky, waxed ends of his mustachios, quivering with indignation, proclaimed him to be the same old Dapper Dan, all-American buffoon, class of '24.

11

I spent one of my college swimmer vacations selling *Pictorial Review* subscriptions with several other students. In return the magazine paid my tuition of $150, or its equivalent, and some expense money. I think this happened in 1921, but I cannot remember exactly. It may have been later. The modern practice of writers to write their biographies before they are half-way through their lives saves them such doubts. Remember Barrie's *The Admirable Crichton* in which one of Lord Loam's daughters says she's not young enough to know everything, and the others thought the intentional epigram a slip of the tongue? Barrie was satirizing Oscar Wilde. Today young writers don't think they know everything, just everything worth knowing. So even if it happened two years later, I'm going to write about it now.

The tour guide of our five-man group was C. Rollin Zane, a tall, competent student who mapped our itinerary and got some store to sponsor us in the next small town. The local paper ran the group picture we had taken earlier. We carried a copy of the paper in our hip pockets and when the lady of the house answered the doorbell, we'd whip it out and inquire, "Did you see our picture in the paper?" That picture meant everything. It had already made us believable as university students; we certainly didn't look like city slickers.

I didn't sell a subscription for two days. Late on the second day, when I was ready to pack it in, a lady said she didn't really need the magazine, but she felt sorry for me and would take it. "Oh no you won't," I said. "If that's your only reason for taking it, I wouldn't think of selling it to you," and stalked away, my pride intact. I told Zane I was quitting and why. He gave me a small lecture about salesmanship. We need not be ashamed of what we were selling; the buyer was getting value for her money; so if I could sell subscriptions by looking pathetic, for the Lord's sake I should cultivate that trait, make it my trademark. He said a lot more, all of it helpful, and sent me out again the next morning with a new feeling of confidence. I found I didn't have to look pathetic. The world was beautiful, I was young and full of beans, and people were nice. They really wanted me to go to college. I sold the first lady I talked to, and I sold the second, or rather her little daughter, who was pawing through my magazine and found the funnies or some cut-outs for doll's dresses, and kept pulling her mother's skirts and telling her to buy. If a woman were doing her washing, I'd help her hang out sheets on the line, for I was no stranger to a clothespin, and we'd start talking about my mother and Camden, and I was in. It was an excellent experience for me; I learned a lot about people, and I came to admire these hard-working women.

We worked the beautiful little towns along the southern shore of Lake Ontario. It was in North Tonawanda that I first noticed something, which I had previously heard mentioned in a poem by H.C. Bunner, entitled "Shake, Mulleary, and Go-ethe" (Shakespeare, Moliere, and Goethe). Bunner was satirizing Joaquin Miller for riming Goethe with teeth. The first verse goes like this:

> I have a bookcase,
> which is what many much better men have not.
> There are no books inside, for books,
> I am afraid, might spoil its looks.
> But I've three busts, all second hand,
> upon the top. You understand
> I could not put them underneath—
> Shake, Mulleary, and Go-ethe.

Well, *in* North Tonawanda I saw living room after living room with two- and three-shelf bookcases, filled with complete sets of the works of Dickens, Shakespeare, Thackeray, Mark Twain, and the like, all in cardboard inserts. Across the room they looked like the real thing. And to prove that America is still provincial and that nothing much has changed, Charles Kuralt, when he was the roving reporter for CBS, discovered a Goethe Street, which the inhabitants pronounced Go-eeth-ee.

A more remarkable article of furniture in the neat little houses along the lake where the German immigrants had settled were the music boxes, some as tall as a man. These held steel records the size of big electric circular saws. Their music was distinct, something like that of a steel guitar. They came in all shapes and sizes and could play a tune as lengthy as that of a Victrola record.Collectors must have had a field day, provided the proud owners would sell. My genuine admiration for these machines from the old country sold a lot of subscriptions for me.

Somewhere along the way Zane bought an old Ford for twenty-five dollars. Since it provided transportation for us all, we were supposed to chunk in a few dollars apiece to reimburse him, but I don't think we did. I'm not sure that Rollin drove it or got it going again when it stopped, but somebody did. I know that when the radiator leaked the same genius bought a package of oatmeal to put in the radiator, and it worked. I recall too that as we were descending a hill, a back wheel came off. The car plowed to a stop but the wheel maintained its balance and went scooting down a stubbly field until it rolled out of sight. It was hunted down and remounted.

This shaky conveyance carried us safely to Montreal and back over a weekend. Prohibition had been voted in, in 1920, out in 1933. None of us got swacked in Montreal, though drinking by the youth of America was obligatory to defy this stupid law. Furthermore, any self-respecting American was supposed to sneak in whatever amount of alcohol he could manage past the hated US Customs officers. The old car did that for us. The springs in the back seat were barely held in place by the upholstery that covered them. We poked in five bottles of cordial that made it even less comfortable for my skinny rump, but I was so tired that when we reached the border at midnight I was sound asleep and barely knew what was going on when the customs man waked me and told me to get out of the car so that he could search the back seat. He shoved the seat from its frame, but the bottles did not clank and he sullenly passed us through as clean. It was a great victory.

Several years later my brother-in-law and I took a similar trip to Montreal. Though we drank very little in Montreal, we had barely entered Canada before we stopped at a roadside tavern for a beer and a sandwich. Because I admired the tray the waiter used, which was a highly colored scene of country dancers advertising old Log Cabin Canadian whiskey, the French-Canadian owner gave it to me as a souvenir. On this trip we had nothing to hide going home, but the sour-faced customs man, his eyes black with hate, spied the tray, snatched it away from me, and because it advertised whiskey, stomped on it with his heavy shoes so that it was bent out of shape before he threw it into the trash.

He kept pawing through our possessions until he ran across the souvenir guidebook I had bought, with maps showing the location of hotels and parks and public buildings in Montreal. Slowly, he perused it, and his face took on the gloat of the fanatic. Page by page he went through it, tearing out any that carried an ad for beer, wine, or whiskey. I thought of Shylock, allowed to take his pound of flesh but not an ounce more. I tried being Portia, saying that I was sure the law might allow him to remove the liquor ads, but did it also permit him to destroy the photographs and information about McGill University on the reverse side of the page, which I, as a college teacher and a great admirer of Stephen Leacock, wished to keep? He merely laughed at me, but I made a great point of taking his name and number. I also looked at my watch, asking Roger, my brother-in-law, to verify the time we had entered customs and how long it had taken him to perform this lint-picking nonsense to process a pair of law-abiding American citizens through customs. That brought a look of pure hate from this crackpot and a tirade. I made a pretense of writing down what he was saying, and kept my pen poised over my notebook. No telling what gnawing fears might lurk in the heart of such a man. It was only a bluff, but if it gave him a bad moment or two it was worthwhile. At least it speeded him up. When he handed the damaged tour book back to me, I said, "Hope you didn't miss any." The implication that he might not have done his full duty, rather than that he had overdone it, almost started him on another search, but I managed to reassure him that I was just kidding.

As I look back on my Syracuse days, I am amazed that I did practically no drinking at all. Religion didn't stop me, nor did my strict upbringing, though I am sure the debt that I owed my mother had its effect. Never in all my life did I purposely do anything to hurt her feelings. If I indulged in any of the vices great or small, I made sure that she should not know. When I visited her, I neither drank nor smoked, nor did I flaunt my unbelief. She would bring that up anyway. I answered her honestly when she wanted to know if I attended church. I told her I did not, except at Harvard. That was later, of course, and I informed her that I had gone to the Unitarian Church a time or two because the preacher had written delightful essays, and that his sermons were similar. She had no use for Unitarians, who left Christ out of their services.

"Not his ideas, just his credentials," I answered.

She thought I might as well be a Catholic. I shook my head and clammed up.

No doubt the real reason that I never drank at all as an undergraduate was lack of money. If I had belonged to a fraternity, I most surely would have indulged. Nor did my roommate. Ludwig and I had a different room every one of the four years, and though some were not improvements over the one we had before, at least they were different. Ludwig studied like a gopher, had even less money than I did, and was obsessed by one ambition: he wanted some day to own and operate his own business school, and one day he did. He was a quick-moving, wisecracking little fellow. Good nature welled up in him. In many respects he resembled Schnozzle Durante, whose humor was based not so much upon wit as upon an excess of animal spirits. Durante didn't play the piano; he pounded it. He didn't sing songs; they exploded from inside him. Before you had a chance to say, "That crack wasn't very funny," you were being assailed with another. He was a walking volcano of good humor, and so was Lud.

Lud was a devout Catholic. I once tried to explain my doubts, but he couldn't understand questioning the established order. Every day on our way to the dormitory kitchen, we would pass Chancellor Day, walking in the flower garden beside his mansion. Ludwig could hardly restrain himself when the Great Man rumbled a "good morning" at us. Ludwig thought he had just been knighted. He couldn't get over the fact that the chancellor—the chancellor himself in the flesh—had demeaned himself by addressing us.

I made some remark about the old crook, whose salary never would have built that palace by itself. Somebody asked him why he needed a house that large and the chancellor replied, "Because, sir, I *coveted* it." Ludwig expected lightning to come down from heaven and strike me dead. But he was an amusing companion, and he thought it a terrible waste of money to drink. Besides, it was against the law.

12

As long as my mother lived in Camden, I went there for all holidays, but in 1922, Dr. Loucks, her new husband, went to Conifer, New York, a little logging town in the Adirondacks, as a substitute preacher for a minister taken sick. We all liked Conifer. The houses were small but comfortable and completely surrounded by the beautiful forest. The sidewalks were uniformly cut and spaced wood planks on runners. A high wooden bridge spanned a ravine to connect the town to the church and schoolhouse. Downtown consisted of a hotel and the company store that housed the post office cage. As in little towns in Ireland, the postmistress read all postcards and would tell my mother as she handed her the mail, "Lawrence will be coming home on the morning train Sunday." Nobody could resent the nosiness; it was given with a spirit of friendliness to be the first with good news.

The tract owned by the Emporium Forestry Company extended from the railroad tracks of the New York Central, a mile and a half to the northwest, to Cranberry Lake, fifteen miles east. There were mills at both places, but the greatest number of logs of big birch and maple trees were cut at Conifer. A logging railroad connected the two towns, and a gasoline-propelled toonerville trolley, a fairly capacious passenger car, kept to a regular schedule.

The owners were the Sykes family, all of whom lived in Conifer, but had beach houses at Cranberry Lake. W.L. Sykes the elder, who started the whole thing, may have taken an active part, but his time seemed mostly spent in tours of inspection, in the mill, the lumber yard, or wherever the spirit moved him. I was working in the lumber yard where boards of the same size had been piled on the little hand cars and rolled out on the track that ran along the top of the 15-foot high docks to be piled in 30-foot high squares until wind and sun had given them a partial drying. Before a workman learned the knack of using the thick, heavy leather apron he wore to slide the board along, and his knee or hip as a fulcrum to lift the end of the board and slide it down to the loader on the dock, or to lift it upward to the dock timber if he were down in a pit, he would try to lift the whole board, and soon tire himself out. The same applied to the loader. He would grab the end presented him and let it slide along some other board until it reached the halfway point. Then he would direct it to its proper place, but he never lifted it. Using whatever fulcrum was handy and sliding the boards along their glossy aprons, two men pushing and pulling in concert could load a handcar with amazing speed and push it into the dry-kiln shed.

I was at the very bottom of the pile, looking up. My muscles still ached from the work I had done the day before, for I was the greenest of greenhorns. I had grabbed a board in the middle with my leather gloves, sat it on end, and let it lean toward the dock. Then I pushed it upward until the loader could grasp its end. I was nauseated.

Dust and cinders on top of the board sifted down it and ran into the top of my wet shirt open at the neck. An old man appeared, squatting down at the forward end of the load, and stared down at me. He began a harangue about how easy the workingman of today has it, compared with when he was getting his start. When he was my age he worked a twelve-hour day, worked like a dog for half the money workers got today. Save our money, we could live like kings. He had no idea who I was, nor did I know him. I was about to tell him to get the hell out of the way and let us earn that big money, when the loader coughed and shook his head. So I nodded politely and tried to smile, and finally he went away. The loader breathed again. He told me that was the king of kings, Ozymandius himself—W.L. Sykes. I went to the edge of the pile and threw up. The loader, a nice guy, climbed down and showed me why I had been straining my stomach. He went over and over it, handling a board with the greatest dexterity from all possible angles, and making me copy his movements. I learned the tricks, added some of my own, and enjoyed the difference. When he got the next pile down to the level of the dock, he swapped places, showing me how to load. Manipulating a board into place was more difficult, calling for a quick decision on the best place to put it, but after I had finished that load and had done another all by myself, I was proud and he was complimentary. "Soon you will be one of us," he flattered me. "Strong back, weak intellect. But before you can be a man you have to chew Old Copenhagen." Spitting out the lump under his upper lip, he took a new pinch from his tin and offered the snuff to me to do likewise. I tried it, had it nicely settled into a round ball, and had already spat forth a stream or two of brown liquid, when the world began to spin around me. I grabbed the empty car and held on tight while he gave me a free ride back to our lumber pile. No alcohol ever made me that tipsy. I threw up again. Before I came out of it the whistle blew. I washed my mouth out thoroughly before going home, and though I was never man enough to chew Copenhagen, I rather liked the job. When it came my turn I served my two weeks on the night shift, tailing the bandsaw. Four o'clock in the morning was the worst. That was the time when the compulsion to sleep became so overpowering that men would fall forward on their spinning saws and lose an arm, hand, or finger. I stayed awake by reciting reams of poetry aloud. Nobody heard it over the screaming saws.

In due course I met the two sons of W.L. Sykes, who actually ran the business. George Sykes was curt and in a hurry, but pleasant enough when you came to know him. He was so violently Republican that he put notes in the pay envelopes of employees, saying that they could vote for Roosevelt if they wished, but if that man became president again, he would close the plant. Ironically, before George could shut down the mills, he received a huge war order from *that man*, which made the company rich. He closed the plant for two weeks not only to keep his word but to prepare for the boom that would tax the company to the limit. George was married to a queenly lady, whom everybody liked. Her people owned Woolrich Wool.

Clyde Sykes was his brother's opposite, slow-speaking, humorous, friendly with everybody. He too married a lady born to the purple, Marian Chappell. Her parents owned the big Chappell Department Store in Syracuse, and she and her brother inherited it, I believe.

Such ladies did a great deal for their husbands and for the community. Without in any way giving the impression that they were lowering themselves, they were universally liked. My sister Glenevieve, recuperating from an illness in Conifer, named both Sykes ladies among the neighbors who called on her so frequently that they made her recuperation a pleasant holiday.

While in Conifer I would often try my level best to like my step-father but rarely succeeded. He did one thing that I greatly admired. At the close of church one Sunday, he dropped out of character and took the congregation into his confidence. It was hard to keep his concentration on his sermon when some straggler would come in twenty minutes late, then another and another.

He had purposely delayed the service to accommodate such latecomers, but it hadn't helped. If they preferred, he would be glad to begin the service at 10:30 or even eleven o'clock, but he wanted them to set the time. He took an informal vote, and the old hour of ten won unanimously; so he let it be understood that he would start at ten precisely. By the following week everybody had forgotten. At ten he started the service, preaching only to my mother and me. People sneaked in sheepishly, and thereafter everybody came to church at ten o'clock exactly. I wondered if he had heard the story about Jonathan Swift, who had the same trouble with his congregation when he was Dean of Saint Patrick's cathedral in Dublin. One Sunday, as the hour for service arrived, Swift ascended his pulpit and began reading the service. The name of the janitor was Roger, which Swift substituted throughout for brethren, beginning, "Dearly beloved Roger, the service moveth thee and me..."

Anyway, I liked him for that, but on the Fourth of July, when he was mowing the lawn, he did a thing I thought unforgivable. A four-year-old neighbor boy by the name of Rutson was shooting off his brand-new cap pistol in the adjoining yard. The kid was mastering the quick draw, killing an occasional Indian lurking behind a bush, looking skyward to knock down an enemy dive bomber, but mostly just standing crouched to shoot it out with gunmen. (I once asked a small boy how he could tell the villain in a movie and he said, "The hero rides a white horse; the bad man wears a vest.") So Rutson was spotting men wearing vests, and having a grand time with his six-gun when Dr. Loucks entered the scene.

"Why do you have that ridiculous cap pistol?" he inquired.

Rutson didn't answer; a man wearing a cowboy hat doesn't disclose his fantasies to everybody.

Dr. Loucks persisted. "See," he said, "I can make just as much noise as that by clapping my hands together." He did so, smartly.

Rutson looked at Dr. Loucks. Dr. Loucks looked scornful. Sadly, Rutson looked at his six-gun. He pulled the trigger. Dr. Loucks clapped his hands together. If anything, the clapped hands made the bigger noise. Without another word or look Rutson went back inside his house to put away his gun forever. At least I never saw him shoot it again. Truth had triumphed.

I didn't tell my mother, but I wanted to kick the ass of God's Good Man all the way around the block.

In the summer of my junior year I planned to work in the lumber-yards again, but had barely started when I noticed a bulletin asking help from any man who could milk a cow. A very few miles east, the first stop on the railroad to Cranberry Lake, was situated a private club of long standing, organized before the Emporium Forestry Company bought the timber, and quite separate from it. The club, owned by wealthy families from several New England states, built a cluster of cottages, a caretaker's house with an ice house nearby, and a cow barn to house a small dairy of ten to twelve cows that grazed on a pasture of maybe twenty acres in a natural clearing. Through the center of the pasture ran a picturesque trout stream wide enough for rowboat or canoe. Fringed with alders, it meandered through the clearing zigzagging from one deep hole to another. If you let a canoe drift quietly around each bend, you were almost certain to rouse a deer who had come there to drink or to stand knee-deep in a shallows to escape the flies. Upon one such excursion I surprised a lordly albino buck, a twelve pointer at least, with a little brown doe, standing in midstream, drinking. As they raised their heads, the water dripping from their muzzles, I'd have had plenty of time for a picture. I would have given anything for a camera, for nobody else had seen an albino deer, and not everybody believed me until two years later a hunter brought in the prize.

Adirondack soil must have been spread over rock, for as they ran for the woods, their hoof beats echoed loudly long after they disappeared from view.

It had been a cinch for me to get this enviable job. Nobody else knew how to milk a cow. There was only one cow in Conifer. Her owner staked her out wherever the grass was high. Schoolchildren would gather around her, not getting too close, for they feared this strange beast. She was their zoo. A deer caused little sensation, but a cow was a seven years' wonder.

The caretaker and his wife, Dan and Addie Hull, were old people. To milk ten cows morning and night was too much for Dan to do by himself. All I was supposed to do was to milk half of them. If I wished to do more, that would be nice, but it was not required of me. After the cows had been turned out to pasture in the morning, I could fish for trout all day if I pleased until milking time came around by late afternoon. I grew very fond of Dan and Addie. I busied myself with whatever job Dan decided to do—carpentry repair, gardening, splitting stove wood, cleaning the stables—and still had time to fish for trout to my heart's content. Dan had been a handsome man and a lady-killer. He had served as a bartender for twenty years: "twelve years drunk, and eight years sober." He was a marvelous storyteller. He didn't care much about fishing, so it became my pleasurable duty to keep the larder full. Only one or two couples appeared to enjoy their resort all summer, and they were too decrepit to do much fishing. So I supplied them, too. That river was teeming with trout, big fellows a foot long or more. I used a worm to catch the first one; then I cut off the ventral fin of that fish and twisted it on the hook so that it would spin when drawn through the water. I'd sit in the bow of a canoe, letting the current drift it down stream, tossing my bait ahead and reeling it toward me. Sometimes I'd catch ten spotted brook trout in an hour's time. It spoiled me for fishing ever after. Addie was an excellent cook, little and quick like my mother. She was skinny as a rail and ate very little herself, but loved to watch Dan and me wolf it down.

Occasionally, the game inspector would drop by for dinner, and when he did Dan would shovel the sawdust aside and bring out a leg of venison from the ice house. Throughout the meal, jokes about the "veal" we were eating flew back and forth.

As an old guide, it never occurred to Dan to get a hunting license or to wait for hunting season to shoot deer. Nor could he bother to tramp around the woods. He left nothing to chance. The deer were part of his herd. If the larder got low, he would salt the stump outside their bedroom and if a deer woke him in the middle of the night, he would crawl to the window and have a look. He hoped it was a dry doe, as was usually the case. So many bucks were killed during hunting season, the only legal game, that many of the does lacked an impregnating partner.

They should have protected the bucks one season, "but them fellers in Albany didn't know a deer from Adam's ox." Twice that summer Dan's twelve-gauge loaded with slugs awoke me in my attic room. I would hastily pull on my oldest clothes and by lantern light help him skin the deer, cut it up into chunks to put down in the ice house, then dig a hole and bury the entrails.

Dan 's right to a deer or two was more than justified. During the winter he would brave the deepest snows to cut the tops of birch trees to keep the deer from starving, or carry provender from the barn to a feeding station. The game wardens knew this when they ate Addie's "veal."

She had her own way of cooking it. While a haunch was still half frozen, she would cut thin strips from it with a straight edge razor and fry the chips in a skillet lined with butter. Venison can be tough, but hers would melt in your mouth.

I have always had an affinity for old people, and those two rank high in my affections. I hated to say goodbye to them when college resumed.

13

My junior year at Syracuse was uneventful. Academically, I cannot remember which courses I had as a junior or a senior, but I took almost everything that the English department had to offer. Particularly enjoyable was Dr. Eaton's course in Chaucer. Eaton, the department head, was informed, witty, and fluent. I owe him a debt of gratitude, for when we were studying the "Pardoner's Tale" of the three revelers in search of Death, he told us an old folktale about a poor woman who, in return for a good deed, was allowed to detain Death in her apple tree until the townspeople, needing his services, made her release him. I couldn't get the story out of my head; it became, a dozen years later, the basis for my novel *On Borrowed Time*, which changed the course of my life. Another fine teacher was Dr. Harrington, a character. To make sure that we would read the medieval or early Renaissance play assigned, he would lower his voice to an apologetic whisper, somewhat questioning its fitness for young ladies in the class to read, saying: "It smacks of the soil." We were prepared for something dirtier, but plowed through to the end, hopefully. And then there was Professor Yerington, who taught poetry like a religion, and wrote it, too. He loved Emerson and so did we.

I don't think it was any of these gentlemen, but some professor in the English department put my mind at rest about the fact that I spelled my name Watkin, not Watkins, in deference to my crotchety old grandfather.

"He knew what he was talking about," the professor said. "It was *kyn* originally. Watkyn meant the sons of Watt. We still say next-of-kin. If you read Piers Plowman, you may come across: "Watkyn the Waster will make fun for us all." Good motto for a game room.

I thanked him and was sorry that my sister Elsie had already graduated. I could explain it to her in a letter, but I probably would never get around to it. Now that Elsie was gone—to Endicott to teach English—I wished I had seen more of her, though our interests were so different. I did take her down to the chop suey restaurant. At my last rooming house I had made friends with a student sent to Syracuse by the Chinese government to study our farm programs. He explained that there were four classes in China and that he was of the upper crust. I was a trifle shocked that he could not enter an American gymnasium without being nauseated by the smell of our sweat. He was so much a man of culture and he knew so much about the world that I did not, it made me revise my attitude about the white man's burden. I even began to have some low doubts about the missionary barrel that held my outgrown garments "to help the starving Armenians." I wondered if some Armenian boy was living high on my cast-offs, or if he passed them along in some missionary barrel his mother sent to the starving Hottentots. At any rate, this Chinese student took me along to the chop suey palace and asked the waiter what they were having in the kitchen. He ordered that. I had my first taste of Chinese food. The cooking was still Cantonese but what a difference! I remember none of the names except that the soup translated meant "needle of the sea."

When I took Elsie to that restaurant and ordered the kitchen fare, she took a small nibble as if she feared she might be eating one of the garden pests she would ordinarily crush under her shoe. One bite led to another until she ate it all. I assured her that all the meat was chicken and pork and that all the vegetables were the ones she ate every day, only prepared differently. That wasn't true, but I'm sure it was an aid to digestion. Some people who gag at the thought of eating calf liver or chicken gizzards eat brains and eggs with gusto. It was important to me that I had impressed her as being a man about town. Many times I have cursed my youthful arrogance. I learned too late that Elsie was someone worth knowing, but I let my conceit stand in the way.

In the fall of 1923, my senior year, my younger sister Glenevieve arrived. Things were reversed. It was impossible to be reserved with Glenevieve. She loved the school, she loved the teachers, she loved the old gray buildings. She was as friendly as a little puppy, whom Southerners say needs two tails, as he can't wiggle hard enough with one. Put her down in a strange street, and inside of a week she'd know everybody in the block. Nobody could resent her enthusiasm because it was real.

I did not pay as much attention to her as I should have at first because my spare time was devoted to reading modern novels to review for the *Phoenix* and a lot more time mooning over a girl in my English History class. I wrote reams of god-awful poetry about her, which I had the sense to destroy as soon as it was written. I had read a great deal of Norse mythology and identified this girl, with her sober demeanor, intense blue eyes, and flaxen hair, with Freya, the goddess from whom we get our Friday. Freya was sometimes called the goddess of love and beauty, but unlike Venus, Freya was not the temptress, but the goddess of hearth and home. Married to Odin, or Woden (Wednesday), she worked at the loom, spinning a mysterious thread of gold. (Incidentally, Thursday is Thor's Day; Tuesday is Tiu's Day.)

By Odin, Freya had a godlike son, Balder, whom everybody loved except Loki, the spirit of evil. As with Achilles, Balder, his mother hoped, might become invulnerable. She took him from Asgard, the Norse Olympus, to Midgard (earth), and made every object swear not to harm him. Since she overlooked the mistletoe as unimportant, Loki, the evil one, made it into a spear for Hoder, Balder's blind brother, to throw at him, joining the game the gods were playing. They hurled spears, swords, axes, and arrows at their friend, only to miss Balder. But Hoder's mistletoe spear pierced him to the heart.

Both William Morris and Matthew Arnold had written poems about it, but I liked Arnold's *Balder Dead* better, and tried to bring the Norse spirit of doom into my puerile verses. The Norsemen thought that at the last day, their gods would be defeated by the giants from whom they had wrested the world in the first place. Death is the reward of every Norse saga, but its sting is taken away because they go down fighting bravely, an end in itself. Sigurd, or Siegfried, and Brynhild is the best known of the sagas, but I never compared this girl to Brynhild. I liked Freya because of her gentler side, and this girl looked that way. Like Freya she was tastefully dressed and wore good jewelry, but not too much. It seemed to me that she must have known instinctively that nothing should be so catching as to detract from the two things that made her outstanding: her wide, lovely blue eyes, and her blonde hair, which she wore in an almost primly straight boyish bob that in no way dispelled her femininity. Her body was strong and erect and it had to be as beautiful as the rest of her. Somehow I was going to have to meet this girl.

There were no assigned seats in the class, so I stationed myself at places where I could see her from different angles without her knowing that I was looking at her. Her nose, not her best feature but sufficient, had no pores, nor her skin any blemish, and her mouth, which was perfect, was also firm enough to indicate character. The class was too big for recitation, so I never heard her speak. I had to presume that her voice was normal. I had only one thing to worry about. She might be dull. I would have to chance that. If I hadn't made such an ass of myself with that art student, I would have asked her for a date before this, but I couldn't bear to repeat that. When it came to girls, it was rather a pity that I didn't belong to a fraternity, where I could have met a lot of girls on a purely social level. If you live for a while in a community you know all about the girls you may want to date, and they know all about you. You can double date at first, which doesn't imply any need to go steady unless you both want to. I had made up my mind that I was going to ask her for a date after the next class. I could kid my way through it and not get serious until I found out more about her. A date didn't have to be a proposal of marriage. We could talk about English history for the first five minutes, though I remembered what a student in that Epics class had told me. He was majoring in Greek and at the age of 21 was a full-fledged classical scholar with a genius IQ. He asked me what I said to girls when I dated them. I said just to kid around at first. He looked so hopeless when I said "kid" that I suggested he might talk about the thing that interested him most and let the girl respond. So he had his date and told me it hadn't worked. Since he was a nice-looking boy, I asked why not. He said that I had told him to talk about the thing he liked most; he inquired of the girl, "What do you think of Socrates?"

She said, "I never heard of him."

So he said, "Well, what do you think of Aristotle?"

And she said, "I never heard of him either."

The next day she saw him coming down the street and she crossed over so she wouldn't have to meet him.

When I returned to the room, Lud had left a message for me to call my sister. I did so and Glenevieve said she had a date for me. The girl she liked best in her sorority had agreed to meet me. She was very shy and didn't date much, but Glen had talked so much about me, she was curious. She warned me that I couldn't trifle with her affections, the way I did with other girls, get them interested, then drop them.

"Name one."

She named a girl in Conifer that I had dated a few times. I told her she didn't know what she was talking about. That girl and I had an understanding from the first that we mustn't get serious. She had already picked out the boy she planned to marry. The most we could ever be was good friends. I'd be going back to college and she never would and that would be that. I had kissed her only once, to say goodbye. She did it to stop my heckling her about it, but she kissed me so tumultuously that I said we hadn't better do that again, or I'd never get back to college. She had grinned, pleased at the compliment.

So that was the extent of the wild life I had led in Conifer.

I then had a few questions. Was this girl fat?

"No!!"

A little on the dull side, maybe? Glen laughed uproariously. She was reputed to have the highest IQ of any student at Syracuse University. I told her all right, but I had my eye on another girl now. Glen asked me just to come over and meet her. We could sit around and talk, then I could take them both to the Cosmos for a soda and I needn't date her alone if I didn't want to.

I walked into the Delta Zeta sorority house at about 7:30 that night, wearing my good suit and a white shirt and tie so that my sister wouldn't be ashamed of me. She introduced me to Dorothy Parke. I was so astonished I don't know what I said, but I think I shook hands. I didn't tell her that I thought her name was Freya and that we had two grown sons named Balder and Hoder. I also think I said that I had seen her in my English History class. Her hair was unforgettable. She seemed apologetic until I added that it was beautiful. In our three-way conversation I learned that there was no Scandinavian strain in her background, only English and Scotch-Irish, that she lived in Mount Vernon, New York, that she had a brother at Colgate, and that her father worked in granite.

I managed to ask her for a date Friday night when Glen wasn't looking and she accepted. After Keith's vaudeville, which was wretched stuff, but all that Syracuse had to offer except an occasional road stock company of a New York play, we walked all the way back from downtown.

She liked to walk, and in the semi-darkness of the streets, safe then for any pedestrian, she told me all sorts of things about herself. She had won a scholarship to Vassar, where her father wanted her to go, but he hadn't objected when a high-school friend talked her into coming to Syracuse. She wanted to be an architect, but the engineering school said she would be the only girl there and discouraged her, so she majored in math, the next best thing. Glen had told her how I passed trigonometry, which she thought a remarkable feat, but trig was so easy she was sure it was bad instruction that made me fail and that she could teach me trig in a minute. I said thanks but no thanks. All math simply confused me, and though Edna St. Vincent Millay had just written a poem "Euclid Alone Has Looked on Beauty Bare," that kind of loveliness was not for me. She said she would swap her mathematical ability for my ability to write. She had learned the rules of grammar and could set forth facts in logical order on paper, but she couldn't *really* write and envied anyone who enjoyed doing it. It was hard work for her. She loved music, especially opera.

But she couldn't carry a tune. She had a theory that if a child took violin lessons when it was very young, hearing the true notes close to its ear would cure that. She had enjoyed singing in a high-school chorus. The supportive voices all around her made her sing on key. Her grandfather had been a great singer, but though he loved her, he had tried to ridicule her into carrying a tune, which was the wrong way to go about it. Grandpa was her mother's father. He was an old Civil War veteran. She thought I'd like him, he was such a character.

When she was with a group, she seldom opened her mouth, but when she was alone with me she chattered like a little squirrel. She loved Glenevieve with whom she felt a closeness she might have had with a real sister.

I learned later why she took so little part when a group gathered together. She was slightly deaf, as the result of a hideous cold she had suffered. All sorts of doctors had examined her eardrums, but none thought that surgery was the answer. It was only a slight impairment, but if people whispered or dropped their voices at the end, or talked in a confused babel, she wasn't always sure of what they said, and she was too sensitive about it to ask them to speak up. So she sometimes had to guess at what they were talking about, and if the subject had been changed and she didn't know it, she might make a remark so belatedly that people thought she was slow-witted.

I was rather pleased that she had some flaw. It made me feel very defensive toward her. That could never have happened to Glen or to me. We would have said, "Speak up; I can't hear you. I'm deaf as a post; didn't you know?" and it wouldn't have worried us in the least. Dot was more like Elsie, and sure enough those two understood each other.

I can't remember when or where I told Dot I wanted to marry her. We were both in love with each other long before we put it into words. I'm not at all sure that I didn't even propose to her by implication while asking her a question, the answer to which would infer that of course we were going to be married. As a matter of fact, a proposal of marriage seldom comes as a surprise. For example, if a couple had been going together for some time and one asked the other if she thought married couples should have children and if so how many, the one so quizzed would not think that the other was merely conducting a sociological poll.

She must have noticed that I had been unusually quiet that evening, turning something over in my mind. We were walking after dark across the old bridge on the road that led to the education school, and I stopped her to say words to this effect: "I believe you told me that your father is a fundamentalist in religion like my mother. Are you? Do you believe literally in a heaven and a hell and eternal damnation unless you accept Christ?"

"Of course not," she said. "I haven't believed any of that since I was a little girl."

"Does your father know of your disbelief?"

"Of course, but he wouldn't try to interfere. He wouldn't think of trying to invade my privacy any more than I would try to invade his."

I thought to myself what a wonderful man he must be. Some of those old New Englanders had codes of conduct that were rare today. I also gave a sigh of relief and apologized for having to know. It had been such a matter of conflict between my mother and me that I just couldn't bear to marry a girl unless we both thought alike on such a fundamental issue. We'd always be on the verge of hurting each other's feelings. I kissed her then and kissed her thereafter whenever possible. I had no fraternity pin to give her and no ring, and to tell the truth it never entered my head that I should furnish something symbolic. It would be a long engagement before I had the money to marry her, but it was no less an engagement. About religion, we both agreed that we were not evangels for atheism. We liked Thomas Henry Huxley's coinage of agnostic, meaning "I don't know." Atheism was, as Shelley said, "A painted devil to frighten the ignorant." We had no wish to make converts, but to follow her father's civilized example.

14

Dot was very good about accepting my poverty. Her father, who was well on his way to making his first million from the granite quarry he owned in Maine, was ruined by World War I. Granite for public buildings and for private ones along Fifth Avenue. had been replaced by cement. The demand for granite did not cease entirely, but a very few of the big companies who had been able to exist in spite of the war were sufficient to supply future needs. Granite was a luxury.

At the beginning of the war after he had sold the percherons who hauled the blocks from the quarry to the ship that took his first and last load to New York, Jesse Battershall Parke was forced to let his quarry machinery rust and to look for a job. The only thing he could find was as a draughtsman for a firm on Long Island that made templates for the Liberty ships. But he had to get up at 1 am to make it to work on time, and he reached home so late at night, he never saw his family. So one day he walked into a broker's office and played the market and made money. He worked at it. If he liked the looks of a stock, he would visit the company in New Jersey and watch their operation before he risked his money. He was most successful. He had always wanted to be a banker and play with figures. So he made graphs and calculations in this fascinating game; but the day the war ended he stopped playing the market. His New England conscience allowed him to do so to feed his family, but now that the few granite firms that were operating were going full tilt, he got a high-paying supervisory job in one of them and could give his daughter anything she wanted. Dot often sent back half of his too generous allowance. One more thing about this man even before we meet him: He played the market for fun until he died, entering his would-be losses and gains every night after supper. His notebooks showed his net worth on paper to be worth several million dollars when Dorothy and her brother cleaned out his roll-top desk after he died.

My own search for part-time work was rewarded by a job that paid well and one which I liked. I was hired by the university to wash the windows on the four-story science building, which was new enough to have properly embedded bolts on which to hook my outside belting. It was a lonesome job. Nobody ever looked up at me and I had to work when the classroom I faced was empty, but one day there was excitement. Though I didn't see it, I heard the jolting report of a pistol in a professor's office. I opened the window, crawled inside the classroom, and was the first person after the custodian to enter the office of the Dean of Science. He lay sprawled on the floor, a bloody dead ragbag after taking four slugs into his body. The professor who had killed him was equally dead from the single bullet he had fired into his own forehead. The custodian shooed me out and shut the door, which he guarded from the curious throng that soon filled the corridor until the police took over.

Chancellor Day had enough influence with the city dailies to keep the story from headline treatment with photographs. He too had played a part in the tragedy, for the professor committing the murder and suicide believed that the deanship should have gone to him. Something like this might be expected of two gangsters, but professors—I had never really thought professors capable of such powerful emotions, or the will to act upon them. They had never seemed quite human before. I think the incident helped me to decide on a teaching career. I could no longer think of them as freaks. I wanted to get married. I could at least do what my older sister was doing. Teaching meant mighty poor pay, but it had supported many wives and children. Just before I received my A.B. degree my professors called me in. Dr. Eaton, Dr. Harrington, and I think Dr. Yerington had all been to Harvard. They considered me a hard worker with enough talent to earn a master's degree in English in a single year. With that I could start teaching right here at Syracuse in the fall of 1925. Though it wouldn't mean much more money at the start, I would be in a whole different league with greater distinction, more interesting students, better research facilities, and eventually be making a good living. I said yes. When I had discussed it with Dot, she was quite willing to wait that extra year.

I worked hard that summer, saved every penny. My sister Elsie had $200 she insisted on lending me. My mother, who had sold our house in Camden to Dr. Loucks, would help if I would let her.

On the train to Harvard a pretty girl came over to sit beside me, indicating that she was bound for one of the girl's schools near Harvard and would be available. I found it difficult to say no. Rollin Zane, the *Pictorial Review* team captain now minded to study law, had found good but not expensive quarters where we might room at 27 Gorham St. The whole second floor housed students. Our melting pot contained Aldo Greco, a huge, friendly student taking business administration; Adrian Richard and his brother, French Canadians and very religious; and in a back room adjoining ours two Jewish boys, one named Sammy as handsome as his roommate was ugly. Sammy couldn't resist women, nor they him. His roommate was forever having to head for the library while Sammy "entertained" a pickup. I don't think it had been a month before he was introducing his latest conquest to all hands so they wouldn't blunder into his room. As I bowed to the girl on the train, who greeted me amiably, I was a little jealous of Sammy. If a girl had a roving eye, Sammy would find her.

I would have too much studying to take on as many side jobs as I had at Syracuse, but to be sure of one good meal a day I became a waiter and kitchen helper at a nearby hash house for breakfast only. I prepared grapefruit halves by separating the nuggets from their pulpy filaments, cutting once around the inside skin, decorating the center with a maraschino cherry. I also prepared shirred eggs for several students and carried in the trays.

At the college I took two courses that I liked, and two that were highly forgettable: Anglo Saxon from an ungifted teacher, and American Literature. The American Lit professor was capable, but the textbook called *Early American Writers* was the dullest collection of the work of pious sermonizers ever taught at any college. It covered the period from 1607 to 1800 and dealt almost exclusively with Puritan divines who had attended Harvard. Here are a few of the humorless literary men we tackled: Bradford, Winthrop, Morton, the writers of the Bay Psalm Book, Cotton, Roger Williams, Peter Folger, Increase and Cotton Mather, Nathanial Ward, Samuel Sewall, Ebenezer Cook...do you want to hear any more?

I had a brief respite with the Virginian William Byrd and his delightful *History of the Dividing Line*. (I don't know how he managed to be slipped in there.) Then came John Seccomb, Jonathan Edwards, and Thomas Godfrey, and finally among the Revolutionary writers: Benjamin Franklin, Patrick Henry, Tom Paine, Jefferson and Hamilton, a good deal of Freneau, Brackenridge, and Thomas Brockden Brown. This was American Literature! I swallowed my distaste, smiled, studied, and passed. The only thing I remember from the whole dolorous mess was the phrase "Silence is that which sleeping rocks do dream of," which I am reasonably sure was written by Jonathan Edwards, though it came from outside reading, not from the text. He could write so powerfully about damnation that his tract on future punishment in hell, and his more famous "Sinners in the Hands of an Angry God," are literary and artistic achievements of a high order, but though he is unmatched in describing eternal death and hellish torture, I found myself unmoved when he described how right God was to redeem some and damn others simply because HE could not be questioned. In two-and-a-half pages he uses the word *sweet* when applied to God 18 times, but never lacks for diversity of phrase in discussing damnation. In a tract called "Early Religious Experience" he has this to say:

> From my childhood my mind had been full of objections against the doctrine of God's sovereignty in choosing whom he would to eternal life, and rejecting whom he pleased, leaving them eternally to perish and be everlastingly tormented in hell. It used to appear like a horrible doctrine to me. But I remember the time very well when I seemed to be convinced and fully satisfied as to this sovereignty of God and the justice of his thus eternally disposing of men according to his sovereign pleasure, but never could give an account how or by what means I was thus convinced.

That struck me as exactly my objection when I argued religion with my mother, but I never had experienced Edwards' sudden alteration when injustice struck him as *sweet* and pleasant.

Very recently I read somewhere this little verse, obviously a jibe at predestination, which once was part of Presbyterianism. Bartlett's has failed me, and so far two librarians, who never are stumped, can't find who said it:

> We are the sweet, elected few;
> May all the rest be damned.
> There's plenty of room in hell for you;
> We don't want heaven crammed.

This sort of thing has bothered me all my life. I have a remarkable memory for anything I like. Everybody has. But if I don't have a pencil handy to jot down the name of the author, I'll remember the selection but not who wrote it. For example, 20 or 30 years ago I came upon this passage:

> Among those pleasures that are pursued by men in the course of their lives all the rest are baubles beside old wood to burn, old wine to drink, old friends to converse with, and old books to read.

Bartlett will give you half a dozen quotations that say somewhat the same thing, but not one with the same style or cadence or felicity of phrasing. Bacon ascribes almost the same thing to Alonzo of Aragon. But he has it "old friends to trust," which is a generalization, not something to do. I wondered if I had changed it to make it more euphonious, but there is that "baubles." I never made up that word.

Back to that American Literature textbook. The author wrote little biographical introductions to explain each writer. When he at last came to a great man and great writer, he treated him as half Rotarian, half children's author. I daresay that in 1925 most Americans regarded Franklin like that, but I have always thought him to be the greatest intellect this country has ever produced. Franklin and George Washington gave us this country. At least I was allowed to write a master's thesis about Franklin. More of that later.

The two courses that made the year at Harvard memorable were a course given by Professor Irving Babbitt in classicism, and the course in writing given by Dean Briggs. I don't remember if we even had a textbook in Professor Babbitt's course. That man was such a fountain of knowledge that after one of his lectures, we all trapped over to the Widener Library to find out what he had been talking about. He never lambasted the romanticists, upon whom we had all been suckled from grammar school up to the present, but made out so powerful a case for sanity, restraint, and artistic unity, truth, and good taste that on the final day of class we rose as one and applauded him. He talked a great deal about the French critic Sainte-Beuve, who started out to be a howling romanticist, like all of us, but in successive periods became, as we did under Dr. Babbitt, a would-be classicist.

Last year a newspaper columnist I had greatly admired reviewed a book I already owned which left a lot of witless sayings we all repeated bleeding on the floor. Among them was the expression: "The exception proves the rule." It was ranked among the more idiotic. I wrote to the columnist saying that I remembered a Harvard professor (Dr. Babbitt) mentioning one day that almost everybody takes the saying to mean, "The exception proves that the rule is true." So read, it's silly. The professor said it merely means that the exception proves there is a rule because without a rule there could be no exception. Read that way, all the "silly" examples immediately made sense. The columnist wrote back that I might have a point, which is further than most columnists will go.

In Dean Briggs' course, he kept us writing papers of various sorts, some of which he read to the class for discussion, but usually saved them for the private conferences he had with each writer. He was the man whose kindness made Charles William Eliot's regimen of improving Harvard workable. You couldn't sit near Dean Briggs for five minutes before you knew you had a friend with a wonderful sense of humor. When he pursed his mouth to smile his eyes smiled, too. He was a magnificent human being. A great many writers ten times more talented than I passed through his class and were the better for it.

Just before our Christmas holiday we turned in half of a long short story he assigned. He would call for the other half later, but needed the vacation time to be sure he could read the total number of pages submitted by each man. Of the several stories he read to the class he chose mine. I haven't the foggiest idea what it was about, but it was an honor to be singled out in that manner. When he came to the second half of my story, turned in after the vacation, he began to chuckle. He said: "Over the vacation Mr. Watkin, who did not keep a copy, forgot the name of his hero. So instead of the given name Charles, we now have John." After the laughter from the class, Dean Briggs continued, "The same thing happened once before several years ago when John Dos Passos took the course. He suffered the same mental lapse that afflicted Mr. Watkin changing the name of his hero in mid-stream, as it were. So for Charles read John."

I cursed my youth. If I had been born six years earlier I might have made a fourth in that Harvard ambulance unit which included E.E. Cummings and Ernest Hemingway, though Hemingway wrote without benefit of Harvard.

After I had graduated in June, I wrote Dean Briggs a brief letter of appreciation for the lessons I had learned in his composition course. I had yet to teach my first class in that subject, but hoped to emulate his attitude of helpfulness and his conscientiousness in reading carefully every theme he assigned. I asked him if there was any one basic bit of advice he could give to make me a good teacher.

This was the letter I got back from 10 University Hall on June 25, 1925:

> Dear Mr. Watkin:
>
> I am ever so much obliged for your letter.
>
> It was good of you to write. Let me say, also, that I enjoyed having you in the course.
>
> I always feel puzzled about teaching English Composition. There seems to be so little that anyone can do. One can sometimes help students in getting rid of hindrances to the expression of what is in them. This is a remark which you have doubtless heard before; but it is as true as ever.
>
> With best wishes for your new work, and with the hope that we shall meet again some time, I am,
>
> Yours sincerely,
>
> L.B.R. Briggs
>
> Mr. Laurence E. Watkin

Notice that his secretary spelled my given name with a "u" not a "w." Dean Briggs would not have done so. He was too meticulous. I took his advice and tried never to ride a kid so hard that he wouldn't open up. A little good-natured raillery is sometimes stimulative, but scorn has no place in teaching.

For a master's thesis I wrote two long papers, one on Poe, which was no great shakes, the other on Benjamin Franklin, which in 1925 was a departure from the usual. I realized later that I might have expanded it and tried to have it published. My thesis over-emphasized the deist, the radical philosopher, the sometimes vulgar human being because the generality thought him a pious, gentle dogooder. It was not until 1938, remember, that Carl Van Doren, in one of the greatest books ever written, gave America and the world a true picture of the brilliant philosopher, the steadfast patriot, the clever, canny politician, and honest, hopeful lover of all that is best in mankind in his 782-page biography of Franklin. All of the occasional despair, the ridicule of shoddiness that appeared in my paper were a part of Van Doren's great work, but were relegated to their proper position.

Before I started my research, I had read enough to know that Franklin's *Autobiography*, by which he is judged, was purposely one-sided to show young Americans that a man may start small and gain stature by thrift and hard work, and that no self-respecting American need any longer kow-tow to older European civilizations.

Every graduate student at Harvard is assigned a small but sufficient desk before a window in the Widener Library stacks. He need not even waste time by searching out and signing for material he wants. If he wants the most private letters of Benjamin Franklin, he has only to explain his desires to one of the handmaidens who are trained to search out and deliver to him quickly the documents. She will also return them to their vault when he is through with them. I found some of Franklin's letters to the British scientist Joseph Priestly morbid and uncharacteristic as though he had struck bottom, as when he so despairs of mankind that he conjectures if scientists, instead of murdering harmless mice in mephitic air, should not use children in their experiments. Whatever his mood, he knew that he could unburden himself to Priestly and it would go no further. Franklin did not let the war interfere with his friendships. He did not hesitate to aid Tory ladies when they were in danger from a patriotic mob, whose intelligence is always that of the lowest mind among them, nor to help his illegitimate son, William, the royal governor of New Jersey and as stubbornly loyalist as Franklin was revolutionary.

Another letter to Priestly was cynical but not morbid. I can quote the substance from memory:

> Mankind is a sort of being very badly constructed. He meets in battle in broad daylight, kills as many as he can, then exaggerates the number slain; but when he would create life he crawls into a dark corner as though ashamed of virtuous action.

He also let Priestly see the ribald satire he had written on the Brussels Royal Academy of Science. Later he told a friend he might print all his little scribblings, but not this one, which was too vulgar for distribution. It is written in the form of a parody as if a member of the Brussels scientific society were proposing an experiment in diet to let a man with a whirlwind in his bowels "express his scentiments, so that instead of offering he would give vent to the pleasing odor of roses or violets." Franklin concludes with another outrageous pun, "that their lucubrations are not worth a FARThing."

Among his frolicsome letters was his famous "Advice To a Young Man on the Choice of a Mistress," in which he tells him to choose an older woman. Debauching a virgin might make him unhappy for life, but an older woman will have more agreeable conversation, more prudence in conducting an intrigue, be a better and more experienced lover, and be more grateful. He ends as he begins by saying that marriage is better than any illicit commerce with women.

Another barb: "I greatly fear that all the warring sects who gather together on the Last Day to see each other damned may have to rest content with their own salvation."

It was as ambassador to France in his gouty old age and his later task as negotiator for America in the treaty of peace that shows Franklin's almost diabolical cleverness. Arriving in Paris wearing a fur hat because he was cold, he was immediately hailed as Jean Jacques Rousseau's *natural man*, right out of the American wilderness and hence a person inherently good because not corrupted by the sophistication of cities. The old fox played the role for all it was worth. He wore homespun made by the best French tailors. He became all the rage, so that young noblemen like Lafayette were as greatly charmed with him as were the wealthy old women who wanted him to add luster to their salons. If they wished to play at shepherds and nymphs in Arcadia, Franklin was their man. Half sick and aching from the gout, he wrote them the kinds of extravagantly graceful love letters they could show to their friends. Franklin did not bed them, but he wooed them and their wealthy husbands and diplomats for America. At first the men of power close to the king sent money and supplies secretly to the brave little country until they were at open war with their old enemy England. Franklin brought them in, and without the French there could have been no victory at Yorktown. He met Voltaire and it was almost a national holiday. The Prussians sent him a drill-master named Von Steuben. Franklin knew he was no general, but he sent him to the colonials as one, with a medal as big as a saucer. With a Prussian general to whip them into shape, Washington's ragged militia responded. After the war, Franklin almost got Canada for us for free. He told the gullible British commissioner that with its French-Catholic citizens England would find Canada only a headache. The British ministry recalled their agent just in time.

My paper showed Franklin to be something more than a printer with a kite, and I wasn't sure how it would be received. But the professor found it acceptable. He may have been as fed up as I with clergymen who had attended Harvard.

One course I did not care to take was Professor Kittredge's course in Shakespeare. Professor Kittredge was king, so he thought. I saw him striding across the square one day. Two students were so deep in conversation they did not know they were blocking the great one's path. He simply whipped his cane back and forth against their ankles until they jumped out of his way.

Now and then I dropped into his class to sit in the back and listen and was lucky enough to be attending the day he barked at a student for rubbing him the wrong way. He told the young man he was no gentleman. The professor made the mistake of addressing an aristocratic Southerner, as imposing as his detractor. The insulted man jumped to his feet and told this Yankee pedagogue a few choice things about gentility that Kittredge had never read in Shakespeare. Then he rushed from the room, barely resisting the temptation to knock the despot down.

Kittredge pretended it hadn't happened, but it had.

I should mention one other thing that greatly influenced my thinking. As you entered the Widener Library, on the right was a reading room with papers, magazines, and a few choice volumes lining the bookcases against the far wall. The deep leather chairs were of that comfortable sort you glimpse through the windows of rich men's clubs. I picked up volume one of Frazer's *Golden Bough*, and before spring had read all twelve volumes of that exhaustive work on folklore. Everybody has one of the single volume distilla-tions, but these were the twelve separate books, a feast for anyone slanted toward folklore.

To read the history of the 20s, and see the pictures of the Jazz Age, the pocket flasks, the rah-rah boys in coonskin coats at football games or in the rumble seats of Fords, the petting parties, and the wild dances was to make me realize that I had not been a part of it. I did see the Charleston danced by Miss Ernalina 11 at the Old Howard in Boston, and I learned to drink but with no great abandon in the company of fellow students who were later to become decorous professors of literature at such places as Duke and Southern Methodist. We met in various rooming houses to read our Anglo-Saxon aloud, imbibing whatever mead the host could lay his hands on to make Beowulf more palatable. I double-dated with Rollin Zane, whose girl brought her roommate along for me. It led to some superficial kissing. The girl was from Mount Vernon, too, and when I brought up the matter of Dorothy Parke this girl spoke slightingly of her. My reaction was to sell the pasture my father had left me, long distance, for a few hundred dollars less than it was worth but sufficient to buy a diamond ring from a fine Boston establishment. The clerk took me to an upstairs room where I might view it in a north light. The store guaranteed it to be free of carbon, a perfect stone for my sweetheart. Until I could give it to her in person I would take it out secretly to gloat over. In my eyes it was a diamond as big as the Ritz.

15

In the fall of 1925 there were 22 instructors teaching Freshman English at Syracuse, each teacher having four classes. We used a combined composition and grammar text, and I think that it had a grid back and front, marked off in squares like my cornfield. Each square was numbered, a labor-saving device for the instructor. Let's say that square 3 said "mixed metaphor." Instead of explaining the mistake, the teacher simply wrote 3 in the left margin opposite the underlined mixed metaphor. The student was supposed to read about mixed metaphors in the text and to sin no more. I never used the numbers, but if there were a lot of mixed metaphors in the twenty-five or thirty themes, I might read aloud a few horrible examples. I never found any as great as the one Sir Arthur Quiller-Couch reported. A student sent his brother a telegram announcing their mother's death: "Regret to inform you—the hand that rocked the cradle has kicked the bucket."

I remember how timid I was at first. I was terrified to notice that two students had the same name. I glanced up to behold a very stylishly dressed lady who was accompanying her daughter through college. I imagined that here was a Madam Helvetius at least and knew that I was no Benjamin Franklin, only to find that the poor thing really should have been in grammar school. One of my most interesting students was a coal-black man who sat between the granddaughter of the Methodist bishop who had great influence in the university and the heiress to the Johnson & Johnson millions. He constantly rocked back and forth in his seat out of pure embarrassment, but he came from one of the colonial possessions controlled by England, spoke beautiful English-English, and wrote like an angel. I tried to make him feel at home; I read one of his themes called "Music in the Jungle" to the class and let his fellow students know who had written it by asking him a few simple questions, but all he would say was, "Beg your pahdon, suh, I wasn't paying attention." It was no better in conferences. Somebody had scared the hell out of him, and he simply wouldn't talk. He evidently thought any kind words or well-meant advice about submitting his stuff to magazines was meant to entrap him. So I had to be content to give him As and a friendly smile whenever possible.

Another student was Lucy Ling, a quiet little Chinese girl who sat next to a Japanese student with the grandiloquent name of Hatsotauro Nakabiashi. Because there were so many teachers, Dr. Eaton made all English instructors teach a different section at mid-years, thinking that the best and worst instructors would be more evenly balanced that way. But Lucy would not leave my class. I let her explain why to a higher authority because she wouldn't tell me. He cross-examined her in the kindest sort of way:

"Is it personal? Have you become fond of Mr. Watkin?"

Lucy shrugged. It wasn't that.

"Is he such a good teacher?"

"He is good..."

But obviously that wasn't all.

"Does he give you better grades than you expected?"

"No...but he gives fair grades."

Both the professor and I were stuck until Lucy burst out: "Oh, Mr. Watkin, I get so *used* to him!"

That did it, I knew the answer. "You mean you have learned my vocabulary and don't want to have a whole new job of translating."

Lucy's face showed that I was right, and the professor ruled that she might stay.

Foreign students can ask embarrassing questions.

Another inquired, "Why do you say, 'In the morning, but at noon?' Why don't you say, 'in the noon'?"

"We call that the vernacular usuage. No rime nor reason. A way back somebody started using a word in a certain way and others followed until it came to be the standard way to say it. You're going to teach English to your countrymen, you told me?"

"Yes, sir."

"Well, if you don't know, either say it's the vernacular usuage or a colloquialism, the genius of the language. Or you can say what Dr. Johnson said. He wrote the first English dictionary and defined pastern as the knee of a horse. A lady asked him why, since the pastern is lower down by the fetlock. He said, "Ignorance, Madam, pure ignorance.""

The year 1926 was a very good one. Dorothy had graduated in 1925, Phi Beta Kappa, and with every other sort of honor the subjects afforded, but to be near me she told her parents she was taking a master's degree in her minor, history, and would do a thesis on the history of arbitration. So that we would not be confined to her sorority, I rented an apartment with another teacher of Freshman English, Matthew Rosa, a big man of Dutch descent with a big mouth, a big smile, a big voice, a lover of poetry and food and beer and H.L. Mencken. We immediately had Dot over to a meal we had cooked jointly. I think it was steak and baked potatoes and a vegetable that not even our cookery could ruin, with wine. Matt thought that Dot was one in a thousand. He told me the next day, "That girl can eat; she'll come through all right." She could drink, too, though she never had. She drank us under the table and wondered why we acted so silly. We never plied her with booze again; it was a waste of good money.

Matt and I agreed about most things: we could barely wait for the new issue of Mencken and Nathan's *The Smart Set*, which became *The American Mercury*. We wanted to see which politician would get the lemon pie award for the month's most outstanding stupidity. We loved to quote him:

"Nero fiddled while Rome burned; Coolidge only snored."

"Never under-estimate the stupidity of the American people."

"The only result of explaining sex in terms of the birds and bees is to make botany obscene."

"A psychologist is a man who sticks pins in a baby to chart the rise and falls of its yells."

Mencken became a fierce outspoken critic of shoddiness in every phase of American life after World War I. He mercilessly ridiculed the shameless way in which fourth-rate frauds led the mob by the nose. He lambasted the spurious in religion, politics, art, education, economics, science, medicine—there was not a thing that escaped him. And he attacked the mob, too, for its whining, its gullibility, its petty selfishness, its readiness to sell out. He made a great many friends among the young and among true patriots who hated to see their country going down the drain. He stiffened the spines of the good people afraid to speak out. He made millions of enemies who wanted to lynch him and run him out of the country; he collected their hate letters and published them in books. He was offered fortunes to come to New York by the big newspapers, but he perversely loved Baltimore and wouldn't leave it. Self-educated, he was such an omnivorous reader that it was hard to put him down. He was constantly besieged by other expatriates who loved music as he did and who enjoyed the freedom in England, France, or Italy from being hounded for having ideas. In refusing to join them, he invariably gave this for his reason: America was the best show on earth. He loved the ribald combats of demagogues, the exquisitely ingenious operations of master rogues, the pursuit of witches and heretics, the desperate struggles of inferior men to claw their way into heaven.

Mencken left one masterwork of sound scholarship behind him in a field almost untouched by the scholars of America, philology. Turn to any page of *The American Language* and you will be entertained and enlightened.

He collected his best work and published it in a series of books called *Prejudices*, stopping at *Prejudices: Sixth Series*. I believe his *Prejudices: Third Series* is the most rewarding. *H.L. Mencken: The American Scene*, collected and annotated by Huntington Cairns in 1965, is excellent.

Never was Mencken so much needed as today, when our politicians are even more debased than during the earlier days, when gurus are rampant, when the mob is transcendent, when education is a joke. We have Archie Bunker, but how Mencken would have roared with laughter to learn that a big part of the television audience applaud Archie's bigotry and take him for their hero.

Mencken would have enjoyed seeing Archie playing Chanticleer to Edith, his Pertelote, but he would not have cared for the occasional show in which the simple goodness of Edith penetrates Archie's thick skull for a moment of tenderness. Mencken wrote caustically about women and marriage, but when he was fifty married a younger woman, a writer named Shara Haardt, and had an idyllic five years with her until she died of meningitis.

He wrote the only intelligent essay ever done on education, laying the blame for its failure in America on two things: the incapacity of some students to receive education and the fallacy that any bright person can learn how to become a good teacher. He rightly observed that no real teacher needs any technical training—only a profound knowledge of the thing taught and an enthusiasm to teach it that never lags.

It is hard to stop writing about Mencken; he was all the dozens of liberal thinkers we have today rolled into one with a good bit of William Buckley thrown in. When I once made my wife accompany me to Luchows, she knew that we were not just patronizing a good German restaurant, but that I was entering a shrine where the great H.L. Mencken enjoyed drinking beer.

Dot was not the only visitor to our apartment. Matt, in no way an alcoholic, was nevertheless a confirmed beer drinker. He was a constant patron of a German restaurant across town and because taxis were expensive he bought a new Ford, which he let me drive. The restaurateur always supplied us with a few bottles to carry home in it. I never gave a damn about beer. I never actually liked the taste of any alcoholic beverage save for a very few fine wines and liqueurs.

Though I had a period in my youth of making cocktails for my friends, I didn't much like them and don't today. But the liquor we stocked attracted several queer ducks. Besides the scholarly George De Mille, one of Matt's acquaintances came for a good reason: he wanted an audience. He had mastered one poem only, Masefield's "Sea Fever," and read only one prose selection, *Walden*. I preferred his rendition of *"Sea Fever,"* because he emphasized words only a drunk would think of. He read it:

> I MUST go down to the sea again
> To the lonely sea and the sky.
> And *all I ask* is a tall ship
> And a star to steer her by.

He read the phrase *all I ask* with an expression that meant what he was asking was a very simple, reasonable request, which only a churl could refuse him. He often spread his hands to enforce the logic of what he was willing to settle for.

I grew weary of his worship of *Walden*. I loved it, too, but his drunken tribute to Thoreau was so repetitious that I put Thoreau down to shut him up or to goad him into finding new words of commendation. I said Thoreau could be very heroic about going to jail for not paying his taxes, knowing that as soon as Emerson heard about it, he'd be over to pay them for him and bail him out. That led to sputtering rage; so I stopped it. But I never tired of *"Sea Fever."* He brought new beauties out of it that wouldn't occur to a sober man.

Matt himself loved poetry and would suddenly break the silence when we were reading to roar out:

> Nor God nor man nor place to stand
> Would be to me essential
> If thou and thy white arms were there
> And the fall to doom a long way.

I might ask him who had written that, but he was so lost in reliving it he would seldom answer me. He was a delightful companion with only one flaw. When it was his week to wash the dirty dishes he would pile them mountain high in the sink until I had to go to the bathroom to find a spigot to get a drink of water.

One last small but significant experience concluded my early education as a teacher. Classes were over for the day. On my way out I noticed a slender coed with her head in her arms crying against a newel post. I waited for another girl to offer consolation. Nobody did; so I put an arm around her and asked what was the trouble? She raised a soppy face and blubbered, "My English teacher said

Christ was not the son of God." For a moment or two, I thought to myself that maybe the Good Samaritan should have passed by, too, but after treading water for a time I struck out in favor of revealed religion. I began asking questions.

"Is this teacher very mature; does he have a doctor's degree in religion and philosophy?"

She blew vigorously and answered in a quavering voice, "I don't think so."

"Well, now, you know that Chancellor Day and Bishop Leonard and practically all the trustees and a great many of our older, wiser professors believe in the divinity of Jesus; so why does it trouble you that this younger, much less mature and learned man should not?"

"I guess because I liked him."

"Well, then, you could do him a great big favor."

She perked up considerably. I went on: "Do you have conferences with him?"

"Yes, at least two more."

"All right; then you tell him this. You tell him that what he said hurt your feelings a great deal, and you thought maybe you should report it to the dean's office, which would probably get him fired, but you were a Christian, and he'd better hope you were. You thought what Jesus said in the Sermon on the Mount was divinely inspired. Do you know what that was?"

"Oh, yes! It said love your enemies and do good to those who have despitefully used you."

"OK. Can you take it from there?"

"I think so."

"If he's nice and says he's sorry he hurt your feelings, then you be nice. But if he's nasty, don't be afraid to tell him that he was guilty of bad manners. If you believe in Mahomet or in Buddha, that's none of his business. The first article in our Bill of Rights guarantees your right to worship as you please. That's the law. You don't have to debate it. So don't you ever cry about it again."

"Thank you," she said. She was smiling.

As I walked away my first thought was that I was a damn hypocrite, but reason convinced me that I was not. If belief meant so much to those youngsters, I decided that I would never try to disillusion them. Argument never convinced anyone who thought with her heart, not her head. Wise old Dean Swift said that happiness was based upon the ability to be perpetually well deceived.

16

Even before Dorothy graduated a second time, this time earning an M.A. in history, we had set the date of our marriage as September 1. We also wrote to a number of places where I could get a teaching job at a smaller college. I had already written a number of schools including one in Puerto Rico, but Dorothy had a sorority manual that listed all the colleges and universities with remarks about each. I wrote to a whole new batch and back came an acceptance from Washington and Lee University at Lexington, Virginia. A professor Moffatt, in charge of Freshman English, appreciated the fact that this was my second letter to them, which indicated a strong interest on my part. All it indicated was that I had kept no record of whom I had written to before. Anyway, it sounded good, and if my abilities matched my letters of recommendation, I should qualify for an assistant professorship after a year as an instructor. So I had a job.

Dorothy's family were as eager to see me as I to see them; so I accepted her mother's invitation to accompany Dorothy back from school, for what the Parke family hoped would be an extended visit. I accepted for a week's stay. Dot's brother Roger appeared from Colgate driving what had been a magnificent Packard open car in 1916. Now, ten years later, it was a museum piece, dwarfing all the low, modern cars. Its front wheels were as tall as my belt; its eight cylinders drank gas like an elephant at a water trough; when its top was up in rainy weather city kids yelled "Fish!" when they saw it coming, but both Roger and his father, who understood machinery, loved to tinker with its engine. They had practically rebuilt it with parts from a factory in New Jersey. When Mr. Parke was along, Roger would drive up to a gas station, his father would say, "Fill her up," and when her monster tank was full some time later, the service man would mention five dollars and twenty cents in a low, apologetic voice, and Papa would pay it without blinking. Having filled the tank of Matt's Ford, I could hardly credit my ears, for gasoline was dirt cheap then. That car would hold as much as a truck. Roger had filled the trunk with his possessions, so we loaded into the back seat my two suitcases, four of Dot's, her five-by-three foot walnut bookcase and the books to fill it, two of her winter coats, and there was room left for Dot and me. Today in

California kids who are surfers often buy old hearses to carry their impediments. Roger's Packard was the equivalent. We rolled along and encountered no problem until we drove through the downtown main street of Albany, New York. The road was paved with cobblestones, which were like glass from a very light mist that was falling. A traffic cop signaled us to stop as he let the noon-hour rush of people cross in front of us, but we couldn't. We were sliding downhill on the cobblestones. The small traffic cop saw the car's locked wheels and heard Roger's shouted explanation. He cleared a path for us so that we slowly slid through the mass of people and stopped against the curb below. He didn't even give us a ticket. Maybe he envied Roger's gigantic bobsled or was Irish enough to think it funny.

We crossed the Hudson and took the road south that paralleled the New York Central Railroad tracks. Along came the flyer, which Roger promptly raced until both passengers and the engineer waved to us. We were doing a hundred miles an hour before the train pulled away. I became fond of Roger. For years, when it was our turn to visit Dot's family on our summer vacation, if Dot didn't want to go out of an evening Roger and I roamed all over the county, stopping at favorite pool halls or bowling alleys. If I won it was as much fun pocketing a dollar as it had been taking seventy-five cents from Matt Rosa at penny-ante poker. I can still see the beautiful grin that covered Matt's face when he drew four aces and how he cursed the rest of us for folding.

Roger had a good mind but no interest in books. He loved to repair things for all the kids in the neighborhood. A giant like his father, he told the young toughs it was sissy to smoke. A real man ate cigarettes. He borrowed one, chewed it up, and swallowed it with apparent relish. When he later taught woodworking and mechanics in a big-city high school, it just suited him. He cared little about money. He left the ordering of his life to his efficient spouse with her Ph.D. He had one great sorrow. She could bear no children. Denied fatherhood, he told life not to bully him, and it never did.

The Parke house was like its owner, big, generous, and substantial. In style Dutch Colonial, it sat up off the street with a spare planted lot on the south side retained by a heavy wall capped with slabs of granite. Its front door was massive. It had been built when golden oak was the mode. Everything inside and out was sound, not crowded, organized, and built to last. The front porch was shaded by awnings, easy to raise and lower. Things worked. Nothing squeaked. The sidewalk that led around the house to a big back yard had no cracks in it. The back porch was as neat as the front. Steps led down to a nice stretch of lawn with a vegetable garden fringed with fruit trees at the rear. Inside was a New England parlor with sliding paneled doors to seal off the piano, the couch, and some fine pieces of furniture. The doors were open now as a sign of hospitality and to stamp my visit as a great occasion. The downstairs also had a big living room with couch and chairs for all the family and for guests. Beyond the stairs was a small cubbyhole for Papa's big roll-top desk. Across from that a guest toilet room had modern fixtures except for one relic of the past that worked smoothly—the tank holding water to flush the throne was high above it with a pull chain hanging down. The lower half of the window was stained glass; the washbowl was modern.

The other half of the downstairs, the dining room with its golden oak sideboard, which matched the table and twelve chairs, and the kitchen, were together about as large as the parlor and living room. The kitchen had a modern stove and a pantry, plentiful cupboards and counter tops, and a tiny separate room to hold the refrigerator with a window behind it. A curtain might have hid that little room, but it had its big, thick, well-hinged door, too, matching the back door, the one leading into the dining room, another to the hallway, and the entrance door to the cellar stairs. There were several rooms in the basement, one a laundry room with a toilet for the maid, a workroom where Roger had re-invented gunpowder, and the heating room.

The stairway leading to the second story was wide with low treads. A big landing half-way up seemed always to catch the sunlight that filtered through a stained-glass window. Here the stairway reversed its direction to reach a wide hallway. On the right side was a suite of rooms with a bathroom between them, one room for Grandma, the other for Grandpa McKelvey. The other suite provided a room for Dot and another for her parents with a similar modern bathroom between. Upstairs on the third floor was a big bedroom for Roger where both of us could bunk. There was a separate storeroom, neat and well lighted unlike the usual littered attic.

It was the kind of house I wouldn't want to leave, nor did any of the Parkes, though the other side of the street was deteriorating into rooming houses. Mrs. Parke had been in dubious health and was not too tall, so her husband had scaled everything in the kitchen to her size. And if anything was said about moving to the swankier part of town where people had garages, Grandma and Grandpa were up in arms. Both were fast approaching their eighties.

Grandma was a tiny wisp of an old lady, deaf, vain, always dressed as if she were going to a party in the 1890s. She was loaded down with jewelry, fingers stiff with rings. On a gold chain around her neck hung a lady's watch, delicately engraved, holding Dorothy or Roger's baby hair inside. She tottered a lot but never fell. All her jewelry came from Tiffany's, where Grandpa had worked for years as an engraver. Now that men no longer wanted big watches with stags engraved on them, his new job was conducting murderers by train to Sing Sing Prison, one of their wrists shackled to his. Though he was even then too old for such perilous work, his brother Frank, superintendent of Brooklyn police, wanted someone he could depend on. To the day he died, Grandpa slept with a gun under his pillow to protect the Parke residence. He figured that sometime a burglar would climb the back porch and enter through the window he kept open for ventilation. When that happened Grandpa aimed to be ready for him. At 80 he went to work every day at the Mount Vernon City Hall, where somebody had figured out a sinecure for an old Civil War veteran who didn't believe in pensions for military service. At first he wouldn't talk about the Civil War, but before he died he told me some of his more grisly experiences. Dot had already filled me in on his early history.

David McKelvey had been born on Staten Island. When he was 16, he invited the teacher out behind the one-room country schoolhouse, told him he was a bully and a lousy teacher, and beat him up. He then ran away and joined the Union Army, giving his age as 18. He was used as a spy. Dressed as a farmer's boy, he carried between the lines messages wrapped in waxed paper in his mouth. If apprehended, he swallowed the pellet. He fought as an infantryman at Gettysburg. A cannon ball took off his buddy's head. He didn't approve of cannon. He would have preferred to fight the whole war with his fists. When he was a civilian again, he tied on a bow of orange ribbon and walked through the Bronx on St. Patrick's Day to come home happily battered until Grandma made him stop it. Her people were peaceful, wealthy citizens, who at one time owned most of Westchester County. She was the only one who hadn't married a man of means. She was heir to some fine old New England furniture including antique spinning wheels, which Grandpa refused to have in the house. He joined the Jungemannichor, a German singing society that traveled all around the country, leaving nagging wives at home, until his wild streak subsided and he settled down to engraving. Even then he was reckless. If the larder was low it didn't stop him from buying Grandma a bangle from Tiffany's where he could get a discount. Grandma scolded him but not too severely. She'd rather be hungry than unadorned.

I thought the Parke family very quiet. J.B. sat and looked over the evening paper and smiled at people but would rather listen to conversation than make it. Grandpa would sometimes make forays to capture someone who would visit him in his room. He didn't join the group for long. Since nobody else used tobacco, he'd not inflict it on others outside of his den, but he hated to be away from his pipe and cigars. Grandma made up for it. She seldom sat down, but would visit each one in turn, smiling down on them, as she demanded a résumé of that day's activity. Roger was her favorite, for he kidded her endlessly. She cackled in delight at his fabrications. She was very gracious to me, made me feel welcome, loudly approving Dorothy's selection.

This mood of serenity lasted only until suppertime. When Mrs. Parke announced that dinner was ready, the soup course had barely been served before all hell broke loose. I *think* it started when Papa made the observation that according to the evening paper U.S. troops had been landed in Nicaragua to quell a rebellion. And I *think* Grandpa said that if Teddy were alive he wouldn't have waited all this time. Teddy, I discovered, was his hero. He had been furious, Dot said, when they wouldn't let him charge up San Juan Hill in the Spanish American War with Teddy's Rough Riders. He joined the Bull Moose Party, which Teddy founded in 1912. Papa never forgave him, for it split the Grand Old Party and let that man Wilson, a Democrat and a college professor, into the White House. I *think* Dorothy said it should have been arbitrated, but I *know* that Dorothy's husband-to-be never joined the melee, but Mrs. Parke did, trying to make her father, the Bull Mooser, and her husband, the loyal Republican, lower their voices. What must their guest think? They both looked at her and at me in consternation. They were just having a little friendly argument. I was most welcome to join in.

Later that night when Dorothy and I were kissing on the parlor couch, she said that I had received the completely wrong impression. Nobody was angry. Everybody in the family argued like that, but they never got their feelings hurt. I said that if I argued that heatedly I'd be mad as hell. She simply couldn't understand that. They felt strongly about politics, but they never insulted anybody. Everybody had a right to his opinion.

"I wonder what your dad would say if he knew how I felt about things he holds dear."

"He knows what you think, and what I think. He doesn't hold that against us even if he doesn't approve."

"How does he know?"

"I told him—what we both believe."

"He must secretly dislike me very much."

"Just the opposite. He thinks you're great. He told me so."

"You're kidding."

"No, I'm not. He wishes Roger had some of your ambition. He likes you already. Can't you tell; can't you feel it?"

I couldn't then, but I did before the week was out. He took an afternoon off and took me on a walking tour of New York City, just the two of us. I visited his office, which was no longer in the Flatiron Building but on the corner of 42nd Street and Fifth Avenue, across the avenue from the New York City Public Library. That's where our tour began, inspecting the lions guarding the side entrance. He showed me the two small patches, one on the flank of each lion. They had been damaged in transit and instead of bringing the sculptor in to make the repair, they plugged the holes with German cement. His mustache quivering with indignation, Papa said, "Think of it! A city with no more self-respect than that—putting cement on a lion's behind!"

We headed up Fifth Ave. I had trouble keeping up with his long strides, but I would have run if necessary to hear the views of this granite man. He knew not only when the public buildings were erected, but as we hiked way up to the Plaza Hotel and beyond, he would stop in front of one mansion after another where the company he had worked for, away back in the 1890s, had added grace and dignity to this modern Athens by building an edifice in imperishable granite. He knew about the owners and how they had made their fortunes. Always he explained the name of the granite and from what quarry in what state it had been cut. I remember being surprised that so many states were represented. The only name I recall was pink Milford, which could just as easily be a marble, with which he seemed equally conversant. Stopping in front of a certain house he told me that in its back yard was a circular swimming pool, thirty feet in diameter, that had been hewn from a single granite block, and of the difficulty in bringing it through the city streets at night and setting it up in its final destination. He was almost equally pleased to have me look through an iron grille in a gutter to a facing under the curb that was granite all the way.

Since the turn of the century he had procured and supervised the installment of the granite that went into the Cathedral of Saint John the Divine. He had done the work as a sideline whenever the bishop could dig up some more money for the project. He would work on it evenings. He was proud of his present company, Grenci & Ellis, for having invented a "saw" that actually cut big granite blocks into smaller and more usable shapes. I think their factory was in Peekskill and I believe they were preparing the abutments following Papa's draughted designs for the great new Hudson Bridge. I recall that there was a young German youth there, son of a German manufacturer, who was studying that saw. He was a handsome young man with beautiful manners, wanting to learn English. Some of the young American boys like Roger told him that the nicest thing he could say to his landlady was, "You, madam, are an old gabby-guts." He practiced it with the accompanying smile and bow.

Papa knew so much more about his job than the ordinary draughtsman that when the workmen got stuck, he was sent to the job to straighten them out. Dorothy and I were to meet him at such an address to pick him up for lunch, and got there early. Over the noise of the pneumatic riveters, I yelled at a workman to tell me where Mr. Parke could be found. He pointed upward. Walking across an open girder with nothing to hold to, at least forty feet above us, was Papa. He was as unperturbed as if the narrow steel beam was a sidewalk. When he reached the other side where two men in steel hats were waiting, he unfolded the blueprint he was carrying and spent some little time in explaining before he came down in the makeshift elevator. I had been frightened but not Dorothy. She said that her father had no fear of heights.

That evening he took us to the opera. He was as wild about opera as the real fans that could afford only standing room in the sixth-floor balcony, but Papa took his guests to the dress circle or to a box so close to the stage that sometimes it was actually over a part of it. Tonight, we were about ten rows back in the very middle of the dress circle. The house lights were flattering to Dot's diamond. She nudged my arm until I forgot about the preliminaries of the orchestra warming up and the mounting excitement. I caught a glimpse of Papa's face and he was blessing us both with his glance.

I was so sorry for Mrs. Parke. She loved the opera, too, but couldn't attend any gathering where she would have to sit for any length of time. Dorothy owed the exuberant health she enjoyed to her mother. She was a remarkably advanced woman in her younger years, and a tenacious student of diet. She did not believe what the doctors told her that a dysfunction of her child's liver would condemn her to invalidism, and by her own research and by applying a Spartan diet she nursed the child into such vigorous health that Dot before her teens could outwrestle and outrun all of the boys her age. Dot inherited from her mother her love of all living things. Neither Dot nor her mother would ever kill a spider or a pestiferous cricket in the house, but would lure them on a sheet of paper and convey them out of the house with some such injunction as "Go on, now; lead your little life somewhere else." Mrs. Parke even fed the mice in a cupboard downstairs so that Papa had to secretly trap them upstairs to restore the balance of nature. But he was too kind to disturb her feeding station. A similar thing happened at the Disney studio. One of the biggest jobs for the police who patrolled the studio grounds at night was catching and disposing of the dozens of unwanted cats, rabbits, and other pets that people who couldn't give them away, and were too lazy to take them to the pound, would drop over the wire fence.

They were sure that nice Mr. Disney would simply love to take care of the darling little bits of fluff. If it hadn't been for the heartless watchman, the studio would have had to shut down.

No mouse ever sent Dot screaming to stand on a chair.

When the thunder roared and the lightning flashed, some mothers shut their children indoors and made them sit in chairs or couches that had no metal showing. One even had her kids put on their boots or rubber overshoes as non-conductors. At the beach at Asbury Park, Dot's mother took her children to the seashore so that they could witness the magnificence of the electric storm over the water.

To please Papa, Dorothy and I attended church with him on the Sunday before I left, but we had a rough time. The preacher had a lisp; he was inveighing against intolerance, and had chosen the text from the first psalm: "Him that sitteth in the seat of the scornful…" He kept referring to it throughout the sermon and every time he did, Dorothy and I had to bury our heads in our arms, for the preacher most plainly said: "Him that shitteth in the sheet of the schcornful." I think I chewed out the lining of both cheeks, trying not to laugh, but others did. Every time the oblivious lisper shat in that sheet, a ripple went over the congregation. Not Papa. He never even smiled, but sat and listened respectfully through it all. He smiled as he shook the hand of the preacher, congratulating him on his splendid sermon. We were several blocks away and I was saying, "Lord, Papa, didn't you hear what the man…"

But Papa didn't hear me. He was roaring with laughter. He let it all out, and had to take several deep breaths to stop. I stopped laughing when I looked ahead three months. Dorothy wanted to be married in that church, but I knew that if that preacher said, "Dorothy, do you take thish man," I would start laughing. Then it occurred to me that my mother was married to a preacher that she could undoubtedly persuade to do the job, and nobody's feelings would be hurt. Dr. Loucks began looking better and better to me.

17

September 1, 1927, was the most memorable day of my life, as it was for Dorothy. Until that time we had both been living nervous lives. It had been rough on me because I was never quite sure that I was doing the right thing in taking this girl away from her sheltering family, even though they approved of me. Like so many solid citizens of that era, they thought that children should not take the plunge until the husband had settled into a secure position. I was used to taking chances and living on a shoestring, but I had made it plain that we were not to be supported by either family; that Dorothy would have to gamble on me and share my comparative poverty until I could improve our position. We had both tried to find out if there was any sure method of birth control, but couldn't. The Syracuse *Daily Orange* had published a long and somewhat satirical article of mine, in which I took exception to recent statements by a Mrs. Knapp, who agreed that birth control should remain a secret except to doctors. She was concerned that the 68th Congress was considering the Cummins-Vaile Bill for repealing parts of Anthony Comstock's restrictive legislation of 1873, which declared birth control pamphlets to be "obscene, lewd, and lascivious." I pointed out that with the exception of Japan we were the only civilized country that banned dissemination of information on this matter. I had good reason to argue. Dot and I both wanted children, but not until we were better prepared to cope. I very much doubted if Lexington had a clinic, but I also thought I could find out.

During the year that I was at Harvard, Dorothy and I discussed all these matters by letters. Before I departed for Cambridge in 1924, I thought we should not announce our engagement until I was sure at least of the masters. Dot agreed, but it was much harder on her. Her sorority sisters suspected that she had pledged herself to me or she wouldn't have refused dates with other men.

Two of her sorority friends told her I was a nice guy but a poor risk, and that she should dump me forthwith. To all this she had to produce a tolerant smile, no matter how much she was seething inside. One of her closest friends had convinced herself that I was taking all I could get from Dot and giving nothing in return. Dot wasn't trying to make things harder for me, but she had to have somebody she could confide in or burst. She wanted me to know that she understood the pressures against us and defied them all. She told me repeatedly that the only thing that meant anything to her was· her love for me, and that she could be happy with me no matter how poor we were as long as she could share. She also gave me steady encouragement when I feared I couldn't make it. If I failed, it would not alter her feeling for me one iota, and she reminded me of the arts course I was sure I had flunked but had emerged with a good grade. All she ever expected of me was that I should do my best. When I gave her that diamond ring which was more than I could afford, and she announced our engagement, she could breathe again.

In the two days before the wedding we decided that everything was going to be great and we began to enjoy ourselves. All summer long Dot had practiced cooking until her family admitted she was good at it. In her intelligent way she even experimented how she could make cheaper cuts of meat tastier. She was just so damned intelligent she would never be unprepared.

I was sorry that Rollin Zane and Matt Rosa couldn't make it, but my high-school friend Fred Pierce was on hand to undertake the duties of best man, and Ludwig Krissler turned up, more sure than ever that he would own a business school someday. He had bought a car and to protect it from accident had a statue of the Virgin Mary inside and so many decals of saints on his windshield, I don't know how he could see out of it; but with the great mother church behind him, New York traffic held no terrors for Lud. He had everybody laughing. We went swimming in Long Island Sound, made sure that our two families liked each other, and went through the wedding rehearsal in the church smoothly. The wedding was to be held at 6 pm.

When the first arrived and we were all getting into our tuxedos, Papa was too excited to tie his bow tie. As I did it for him, he murmured, "Lawrence, please take care of my Dorothy."

"I always will," I said, and I nearly bawled. I loved this big, worried man so much.

The wedding itself was the sort you can't forget. The best man, possessed of a smooth, ruddy complexion, had a carbuncle on his cheek that had been newly lanced and needed a large poultice to contain its eruption; the maid of-honor, pretty enough to be a model, wore a conspicuous cold sore, but nobody looked at them anyway when Dorothy emerged, radiant in an exquisite wedding gown. Dr. Loucks fed us our lines and we recited them without a hitch. But when it came time for Freddie to dig the wedding ring out of his vest pocket and for me to slip it on Dorothy's finger, a high, quavering voice broke the silence. Grandma was deaf and thought she was whispering, but she could be heard a full city block away. "I can't see," she complained crossly. "I want to see him put on the ring!"

Keyed up as I was, I let out a snort of laughter but disguised it as clearing my throat. Freddie mumbled out of the good side of his mouth, "Shut up, you damn fool," which almost made me laugh again. Fortunately, it was time to kiss the bride, which was too wonderful to laugh at.

We let the children throw rice at us as we entered the limousine that drove us the few short blocks to Dorothy's house, where a professional photographer took countless pictures and a caterer served a repast to innumerable aunts and cousins and friends who had driven some distances to honor the occasion. I shook hands and was hugged and kissed until I was limp and Dorothy exhausted. We outstayed them all to please our families, who hated to see us leave for the Pennsylvania Station Hotel. There we would spend the night before taking a mid-morning train to Washington, D.C., for a full week's honeymoon. My mother and sisters and Roger and Papa promised to sort out and mail our plunder to Lexington. Ludwig Krissler insisted on driving us to the hotel. It was after dark before we went aboard his movable shrine and I begged him to drive slowly, for he could not stop talking about the wonderful, wonderful wedding. When he talked, he gesticulated with one hand and sometimes two. Then it was that Saint Christopher from his vantage point on the windshield took over. The blessed wraith, patron saint of travelers, caused the taxi drivers to be especially alert when they saw Lud bearing down on them. Finally, we drew up in front of the station, crawled out weak and shaken but alive, and expressed our thanks to that joyous little man. I would not trust our two heavy suitcases to the porters, which was just as well, because we had barely started across the station toward our hotel when we almost collided with Dr. Loucks, calmly waiting for a late train. His duty done, he would not wait with my mother, who had accepted the Parkes' invitation to tarry a day or two. Without doubt, there was some passage in his Biblical concordance he didn't know by heart, and he must have wanted to get the taste of that rich party food out of his mouth and return to his regimen of rice and hot water with the odd poached egg thrown in for kicks. We managed to make some brief, embarrassed small talk that seemed endless, then repeated our sincere thanks, and staggered on to the elevator. Our room was nice, I think, but we were so beat, all we wanted to do was take a quick bath, make just enough love to say we hadn't failed our wedding night, and fall asleep in each other's arms. We slept so late we barely had time to grab a cup of coffee and make our train for Washington. We had both come alive again. Dorothy was exquisite in her going-away travel suit with handbag trimmed with dark, wine-colored leather and shoes to match. I was so proud of her I found it difficult to behave with the dignity she expected of me in public, but when we reached the Powhatan Hotel, she was as anxious to rip off her clothes as I. It was a long time before we realized we were starving.

That was a delirious week and if we saw the sights of Washington it was because they were reflected in each other's eyes. The Powatan was a nice little hotel. Many years later, when I was stationed for a time in the Navy, a select group of us kept a big round table reserved there for lunch, but it was some time before I recognized it as a place I had visited before.

18

Lexington, Virginia, a small town in the Blue Ridge Mountains, that houses both Washington and Lee University and the Virginia Military Institute, is roughly 40 miles north of Roanoke, thirty miles northwest of Lynchburg, forty miles southwest of Charlottesville, in the west central part of the state. Today, because of its easy access by car from the wide, super-fast highway 81, it is a well-known tourist stop, often considered a shrine of the Confederacy. The brilliant Stonewall Jackson taught mathematics at VMI, and General Robert E. Lee became president of Washington College at the close of the Civil War and is buried in the Lee Chapel on the W&L campus. The Jackson Post at VMI was named a national historical landmark by the Department of the Interior in 1974, and Washington and Lee University was so designated in 1973. The Department of the Interior further called the front campus of W&L one of the most dignified and beautiful college campuses in the nation. Its long colonnade of Tuscan columns, white against the old red brick buildings, makes it for me the loveliest campus in the world.

When Dorothy and I went there in 1926 the Scotch-Irish families of Lexington did not want their town opened up.

Even if I had had a car, the roads were narrow and wretched. The railroad did not go through town, but had to back its cars along a ravine to a ridiculous small station. Dr. Moffatt was there to meet us, and had engaged a room at the Dutch Inn, a hotel much like a French pension, having excellent food. With funds running low, our most pressing need was for an apartment. We found one the next day for $50 a month. It was a second-floor walkup in a private house on the edge of town with a living room, dining room, bedroom, and kitchen. Its back porch overlooked the cemetery. The furniture was something that must have been salvaged when Yankee General Hunter burned part of the town during the Civil War, referred to in Lexington as the War Between the States. Dorothy bore up bravely, but gulped when she beheld the kitchen range, a kerosene stove you would be ashamed to take on a camping trip. The bath room was in the owner's bedroom, an old-fashioned tub behind a screen. It sat against a wall, upon which a wide strip of what had once been blue-and-white checkered linoleum was pasted to protect against splashing. Previous dirty soapy splashes had obliterated its color; so one day Dorothy after bathing had cleaned just one of the blue-and-white squares with her wash cloth. It was startling. The whole linoleum was washed the next day, though the landlady would not speak to us for a week.

Lexington had more quaint characters per square mile than any other town in the world, and our landlady Mrs. Myers was the first of hundreds. She was the most pious woman in town, Presbyterian of course. She lived with her sister, a quiet, inoffensive person, also pious. It was Mrs. Myers who did all the bargaining. She never gave a direct answer about money. She always said, "I'll have to take it to the Lord." Asked when she could expect heaven to settle on an exact figure, she might name tomorrow, or even several days later, but when the Lord answered, that was it. You didn't haggle with a deity.

Mrs. Myers carried on a continual recruitment of Japanese or Chinese plebs from VMI, as first-year students were called. Evidently she had heard of rice Christians and she used the same tactics to convert the unwary foreign kids. She didn't feed them rice; she fed them chicken and black-eyed peas. When they were stuffed, she held a prayer meeting in her parlor. On these days she would pin little notes to our front door, such as "Please pray for the spirit's presence in power." She never would have got me on my knees with her cooking, for I hated the smell of black-eyed peas. She put out poison on strips of bacon to kill the rats, but her cat ate a strip and took a smelly retribution, by crawling under the house to die. Long after, I came home of an afternoon, wrinkled my nose, and said to Mrs. Myers, "Well, I guess the old cat is still with us."

"That's not the cat," she answered. "That's black-eyed peas."

In prayer meetings at church she would always pray *against* someone. If a college professor had too drunken a party at his house she would explain it to the Lord in a long, detailed prayer, making it abundantly clear upon exactly which individual she wished the fire and brimstone to be heaped, concluding, "Oh, Lord , thou knowest who I mean. *Thou* knowest!"

As the man on the scene, my associates among the teachers and some interested townspeople expected me to keep them informed of Mrs. Myers' latest, but I never contributed anything as great as the classic story which concerned her dear, departed husband Mr. Myers, reputed to have been a bit of a rake while living. Another lady asked her how she could *stand* such a man. She answered with her usual composure, "Oh...I let him take his wicked pleasure, and I thought about the missionaries."

Could Dorothy and I be happy in such a place? Indeed we could. I took considerable kidding because I would sprint home between classes to see if Dorothy was all right. She always was. She baked a whole chicken in that disgraceful stove. It was so beautifully browned that I insisted she carry it out in its tin and let me take a picture of it. The picture came out very well, showing the proud young bride and her masterpiece, but when I tried to carve it the knife disclosed that it was raw.

As a wit remarked when he sent back an underdone slice of chicken in a local restaurant, "I've seen a bird hurt worse than that entirely recover."

One pleasant discovery we soon made was that, with a very few exceptions, all the young teachers were as poor as we. They even convinced me that college professors were supposed to be poor and had to charge everything in order to live, paying the grocer whatever they could at the beginning of each new month. The grocer expected it; he made an excellent living, gave us wonderful service, slipped in occasional surcharges if we didn't scan the bills carefully, would laugh delightedly if we caught him in such rascality, and was even known to wait until some old customer died to receive full payment, taking it in the end from his estate. This man, Monks McCoy, was a happy man; he provided us with fine meat and fresh vegetables, and he gave me the same prompt and cheerful delivery when I had no money at all as when I had a lot. I wish I could find such a grocer today.

All the tradesmen in town were pleasant to deal with, though some were almost apologetic for buying and selling. The old snobbery from England that such people were second-class citizens persisted in Lexington, but many were better men than those they served. If you had a sick child, the druggist would go to his shop at three in the morning to supply a medicine for the child and do it uncomplainingly.

A pleasant informality prevailed. Since crimes of violence were rare, babysitters were seldom needed unless the children were very small. If a couple went out for an evening, they told the children their destination, then called the operator, explaining where they were going. All their kids had to do was lift the receiver and the operator would relay the message she had written down and get in touch with the parents in a hurry. She was babysitter for half the town.

The men's clothing store was run by an austere gentleman who didn't need the money his store brought in, but had always wanted to own such an establishment. He carried excellent haberdashery, but had an alcove in the rear where he might play poker with his cronies, or discuss football. Unless you knew the famous athlete who had made the winning touchdown for W&L or VMI, or for that matter Yale or Princeton or Army or Navy, you were not welcome there. The alcove was curtained and a buzzer sounded if anyone opened the front door. If the proprietor and his friends were at a critical point, he would whisper, "Keep quiet; maybe they'll go away."

A customer tried on a suit, couldn't make up his mind, and kept on doing so. The following year he complained that the suit had been marked up from $25.00 to $26.00. The customer had tried it on so many times, the owner had to send it out to be dry-cleaned. If he didn't like somebody, who had been gossiping about him, he wouldn't sell them any merchandise. Such a lady entered his store to buy a shirt for her husband. "We have no shirts," the proprietor said.

She pointed to a plentiful supply in their cubbyholes along the wall.

"What are those?" she said.

"All spoken for, madam. I don't have a shirt in the store. Sorry." He smilingly ushered her out.

He was invaluable when we put on a college play of the last generation. He not only unearthed beautiful wide silken neckties of the past, but showed us how to tie them, too. His prices were negligible.

The college president was a sweet, pink-cheeked old gentleman, who paid duty calls on all new teachers, and had each couple to his house to dinner. He was old, forgetful, but kind-hearted; and his wife, who needed all her wits about her, would know when a couple were overstaying their visit, and was always ready to step into the breach when her husband became confused or unintentionally tactless.

From time to time he issued bulletins to the students, fireside chats, sending a copy to each member of the faculty as well. They were wistful, coming from that delightful old man, and I wish I had kept more of them. I have only two, one dated December 10, 1926, Volume 25, #20. This one was:

THE THREE ELEMENTAL HUNGERS
A Frank Talk to Young Men
on
MANLY SELF-CONTROL
by Henry Louis Smith

The second keepsake I possess;, though published on November 1, 1929, it was a re-issue of the first, Volume 28, #16:

OUR THREE HUMAN HUNGERS
A Very Frank Talk to Young Americans Concerning
CERTAIN PERSONAL PROBLEMS

The message, though paraphrased, repeats that an all-wise Creator has endowed man with three elemental hungers: food-hunger, sex-hunger, and property-hunger. President Smith was a phrase-maker. He always patted your child on the head, remarking, "Ah, the angelic anchor of the home." About sex-hunger he wrote: "Although rooted in the rank, red clay of our animal nature, the mating instinct is not in itself degrading or sinful or unworthy or unfortunate..."

He goes on at great length, saying that when rightly controlled it is the source of home-joys, of music and art and romance, of spiritual hope and aspiration, of the complex loyalties and traditions that weld the warring individuals of the human race into a close-knit social whole. When warped or psychologically perverted it makes him a degenerate, more loathsome than any beast, more cruel than any devil of the pit. He concludes that the only safe path to morality, safety, and stainless honor is a rigid and self-controlled chastity.

About food-hunger he wrote that eating and drinking when controlled led to friendship, hospitality, and social intercourse. Uncontrolled, it creates the glutton, the drunkard, the dope fiend, the raving maniac, the wild beast snarling over his prey. Control food-hunger or be devilized.

Property-hunger, or the passion for acquisition, also comes from God, inspiring our industrialists to add to the riches of the race. Uncontrolled, it forces the weak to the wall, grinds the life out of defenseless women and children and the lower classes. Be honorable, keep your word, and you can be a nice rich man.

I have given you these passages not in ridicule but as a sample of the somewhat childish eloquence of the Victorian Southerner. In general, the faculty was fond of Henry Louis Smith, but I fear that the students considered him a hopeless anachronism.

He published one of his frank talks, though I don't know the subject, which was noteworthy because of the unfortunate phrasing on the cover-title. It concluded:

LET NO YOUNG MAN BE MISLED
by
Henry Louis Smith

The students promised each other that none of them would be. In chuckling over it with our best friends Charley and Catherine McDowell, I mentioned that when I was in my teens I had never heard the word "misled" pronounced and thought of it as "mi-z-ld." Catherine admitted to the same misconception and still thought *mizld* the stronger word. If you are *misled*, you have been only slightly deceived, but when you are *mizld*, you have been cruelly swindled.

Before leaving this fascinating subject, I must mention Governor Letcher, as the son of the Civil War-era Virginia governor was called. He lived on Letcher Avenue, which led to VMI, and was intersected by Maiden Lane. For a time, we lived across from the Lee Chapel and enjoyed watching Governor on his way to work. Governor loved golf and spent his spare time on the little cow pasture golf course on the edge of town. It was so constricted that it was hard not to drive into the foursome ahead of you. When Governor did so, he never yelled "Fore!" He always bellowed, "Watch this if you kindly will." Going to his office, he crossed the lower part of the W&L Campus, using it to practice shots with the niblick he carried. Reaching the parking lot below the chapel, he put the golf ball into his pocket and converted the nine iron into a cane until he had gone out through the entrance gate. As he walked the short block up Jefferson Street, he used the niblick to spear a load of newspapers and other trash that had been blown against the fence and carried it to his office on the lower part of Washington Street, where he disposed of the litter. The inside of his law office was interesting. Inasmuch as radiators with central heating had been added to the building, he used the potbellied stove as a safe for his most valuable deeds of trust. The middle part of the room had neat piles of papers on the floor, with a scrambled alphabet which he had memorized to discourage snoopers. Thus he carried on a successful law practice.

In his house on Letcher Avenue he lived with his brother. The two frugal Scotsmen drew half a tubful of water once a week, which both used of a morning. They fired a maid who flushed it down the drain before the week was out. Furthermore, they did not follow Benjamin Franklin's advice to Americans to open their bedroom windows at night for ventilation. They had their own method of ventilation: they kept an umbrella near the window and took turns getting up during the night, opening the window briefly, and pumping air into the room. I can't vouch for these last two stories though everybody repeated them, but I witnessed the rest.

As we approached World War II, I was invited to a meeting of the Fortnightly Club, a formal dress affair. Governor Letcher read the paper. Though we were not yet in the war, it was plain that we would be, that Hitler was already thinking "America next." Governor gave a shrewd guess on the thinking of the German High Command. First their bombers would try to strike a manufacturing establishment in Buena Vista, a neighboring town, then knock out VMI, leaving us not only lacking in hardware to pursue the war effort, but our soldiers practically leaderless.

As with President Smith we did not jeer at Mr. Letcher. We cherished his idiosyncrasies. He was such a lovable man we wished him long life and happiness. I have considered myself blessed to have known such people, straight out of *Alice in Wonderland*, in person.

Another character I cultivated was Watt Smith, the college plumber. I not only liked to listen to his speech; I liked him. At strategic points around the campus were little boxed-in cutoffs for hose attachments. I had noticed that Watt knelt unduly long at some of them. I asked him why. Pledging me to silence, he showed me that at every station he had hidden a mason jar of corn whiskey. He offered me a snort, but though I refused, I showed my concern that some snoop might make trouble for him. "Now don't you worry none," he reassured me. "I ain't gonna get fahred. I put in this yere plumbin' myse'f and a lot more, and I'm the only one knows where to find it."

19

By 1927 we had moved to an inexpensive house which had the usual rooms downstairs, with a stove, two sizable bedrooms upstairs, and a garage for our Chevrolet, which we had bought on time and which performed perfectly for years, needing few repairs, for built-in obsolescence was not yet in vogue. We had fine neighbors. More of them anon. West Side Court was somewhat nearer the college and the whole set-up ideal for our purposes.

Those early years in Lexington meant a lot of hard work for us both. We had fun, but were often rebuffed and left out of parties simply because we had come from the north. If I had let Dorothy's father buy us fine furniture as he wished to do, it would have made a difference, but neither of us wanted to make friends that way. I was never snubbed directly, but at a large gathering a lady who considered herself the social arbiter said loudly for my benefit, "Where do all these Sears-and-Roebuck professors come from?" After I had published she tried to wangle an invitation to our house, but I didn't know her.

Dot very much wanted to take the grand tour of Europe before we had children, and though I had convinced Dr. Shannon, head of the English department, that I was a conscientious teacher respected by my students, my salary would stay small for some time. He had a chance to size me up; I requested to take his Anglo-Saxon course, having explained what a mediocre one I had had at Harvard. I liked that year because Dr. Shannon made it as much a study of etymology as of Anglo-Saxon. That is why, though I have been reproved for doing so, that I spell *rime* correctly. It comes from the Anglo-Saxon *rim*. Because *rime* and *rhythm* are paired, people think they both derive from Latin *rhythmus*. I even studied my old Latin books on the side and made a 99 on the final exam. We both laughed when I asked Dr. Shannon what I had missed. I would not have taken his Chaucer course. His students read all the Canterbury tales aloud in class, but were forbidden to so much as chuckle when they hit a dirty passage. If I had been reading the Miller's Tale aloud, by the time I came to: "'Tehee!'" quod she, and clapte the window to, and hadn't laughed I'd have choked to death."

Dot decided that if we were to take our trip in 1929, she would have to work to finance it. First, in 1927, she worked in the library, the kind of job that called for a sense of order and a love of books. She was good at it, but told me how rude a certain Southern colonel had been. Every little town in the South had these old phonies in full measure. If a man had made money at any of the low trades which wartime offers and had arrived at the battlefield just in time to see Lee surrender, he still retired as a colonel at least. Some of the thousands of colonels were men of the highest gentility, but they were not the sort who would say to Dot, "Another damn Yankee! I knew you were a Yankee the minute you opened your mouth!" Dot might have told him that she was indeed and that one of her Parke ancestors had a letter of thanks from General George Washington for helping pull the blockage chain across the Hudson to keep the British warships from coming up the river when the general was camped at West Point. Ever since I saw the letter, I visualized Washington not throwing a dollar across the Potomac but standing on one side of the Hudson and hurling the chain across to this gigantic Parke soldier who caught it on the other side.

Dorothy, of course, would never fight back. She merely smiled at the colonel, and asked how he liked the novel he was returning. He wanted another just like it. She produced one. Thereafter, he always went to her for a new book. She had him pegged and never failed to select something that fitted his mentality. When she quit at the end of the year to take a teaching job at the Lexington High School in 1928 for more money ($1,000), the colonel complained bitterly.

With her educational background, Dorothy had no trouble getting a teaching certificate from the State Board of Education at Richmond, but signed for one year only. She had never taught a class in her life and was scared to death, but her students didn't know it. To test her, the principal gave her a classroom that had frightened away far more experienced teachers. It was crammed with hillbillies, some of whom came to school half-drunk, and before long, chalk and erasers would be flying and the room a shambles. I believe that the ringleader was a boy named Raymond Flint, a terrific football player and an incorrigible. But while sizing Dot up, these children were amazed to be called Mister and Miss because Dot didn't know any better. She treated them as if they were ladies and gentlemen at college and discovered to her joy that Mr. Flint had a natural aptitude for mathematics. Her enthusiasm in teaching him math that strained his capabilities astounded him. His excitement at meeting a teacher who thought he had brains engendered mutual admiration. It rubbed off on the other kids, who became interested, and she soon had them eating out of her hand. The traditional hillbilly is too often thought of as a moonshiner with a squirrel rifle, who had been shipped over from England as a felon and took to the hills. Some of them were, but we must remember that in Shakespeare's day and a hundred or two years thereafter a spirited teenager might be sentenced to death in England for, say, snatching a handkerchief from the hands of a fop and throwing it in the gutter because he could not bear to see the sissified jackass making a fool of himself. Not every hillbilly is gifted, and intermarriage with inferiors takes its toll. You don't have many plow-horses in a racing stable. But every so often you will see a tall man from the mountains coming into town with such pride of bearing, such natural dignity, that you know something more than the blood of a surly, furtive cut-purse flows in his veins.

Principal Waddell told one of our friends that Dorothy was the best natural teacher he had met in 20 years. He offered her the moon to stay on, but Dorothy regretfully said no. She had our stake and we were ready to depart.

That year, 1929, was the one in which the *New York Times* published as usual the best similes of the year. The winner was: "As cheaply as a college professor can go abroad." Dorothy was following her life plan. After the tour we would have babies, lots of them. I wanted not more than two, but she finally settled for three. She intended to take care of them and stay at home.

From that point on I was to be the bread winner and provide for them properly. She never had the least doubt that I would do so. She thought she knew me better than other people did. The doctors told her after I had open-heart surgery that I could not live more than three months. She answered calmly, "He hasn't the slightest intention of dying." Again, when it was touch and go with me, she predicted that I would live, saying, "He hasn't finished the script he was working on."

The thing that made our whole tour possible was the planning that Dorothy's friends in the library had worked out for us. All the ladies in the W&L library were women of culture who knew another genuine person when they met one. They fell in love with Dot and she with them. They had all been abroad more than once and had discovered wonderful places to stay at very small expense that Cooks had never heard of. As a matter of fact, their friends and hostesses abroad would never have taken in two Americans unless Dot's friends had vouched for us. Of course, Dorothy was a researcher. She knew in advance what we would enjoy most. She and her sponsors worked out an itinerary that left nothing to chance. There was this lovely room over a bakery in Brussels, a darling little hotel in Paris, a pension in Florence with a lady who has her rooms furnished with the loveliest polished antiques. She loved to cook for Americans, to show them how exquisitely Italian food could taste. Her place was only a stone's throw from the Ponte Vecchio and the Uffizi Gallery, and if she likes you, she'll probably take you through it. Speaks perfect English. You will, of course, stay in this hotel in Rome and the one on the far side of the canal near the Rialto Bridge, where you can always get a gondola. Walk across it, you're in St. Mark's Square. You'll love the Hotel Cocumella in Sorrento; you will never want to leave. In Geneva a pension almost as big as a hotel, then hotels all the way through the Alps, stopping at Interlaken, Lucerne, and Zurich before entering Germany. A boat trip on the Rhine, a stay in Heidelberg, then the Netherlands, a channel crossing, London, and home.

Before her plans were completed Dorothy heard from her college roommate that she and her older sister wanted to accompany us; so by some rapid correspondence abroad Dot managed to change reservations for two to reservations for four.

The roommate would be an addition to any party, but her older sister was one of those one-hundred percent Americans who regard the rest of the world outside the good old USA as savages. In Italy, when we were having a ball with the jolly, outgoing Italians, Sister would not walk on the sidewalks at night where some *foreigner* might spring out of a dark alley and stab her, but kept to the open road. I tried to explain to her that the natives were not now the foreigners, we were, but it only insulted her, and I stopped trying. She never learned the currency of any country: shillings, francs, lira, marks were all dollars to her.

The only time she really smiled wholeheartedly was when our ship returned to New York Harbor and she beheld the Statue of Liberty again. I did not dare tell her that it had been built in Paris by an Alsatian sculptor and donated to the United States by the people of France.

Twenty years later Dorothy and I and our children had crossed the Atlantic on the *Mary* or the *Elizabeth* so many times in both directions it had become commonplace to them and a great big bore to me. I much preferred flying. But on that trip in 1929 everything was exciting. The liner we boarded was a third the tonnage of the Queens; it was a made-over troop ship called the *Minnekada*, all one class, tourist, but it was as big as a football field to us. It sat well down in the water, was stable, and it did not pitch or roll, for the sea was as untroubled as the blue, flawless sky. We took part in all sports. I was chagrined to find that somebody could beat me at ping pong because I had a board in my cellar that I had made myself and thought I was the master at that indoor sport. Most of the voyagers were young like us and spent little time in their deck chairs. I remember that Dorothy and I went into the bar to have a first legal drink. Children of prohibition, we didn't know what to order, but when an older gentleman nearby said martini, we had a martini, too. I remember choking mine down and thinking it wasn't much better than the drug-store alcohol someone had presented me with. I mixed a little grenadine syrup in it and called it a pink lady. It was a cut above the raw moonshine stuff the bootlegger brought us, but I never did like martinis and didn't order the customary three for lunch which put my friends asleep over their typewriters on workday afternoons.

Our cabin was a closet-size room so small that only one could dress in it at a time. I occupied the top bunk. The bulkhead reverberated with the noise of the ship's engines, alarmingly close by, but they only lulled us to sleep. George Bernard Shaw said that youth was too precious to be wasted on the young, but I don't believe we frittered away a single moment that summer.

The highlights of that trip for me stand out most vividly fifty years later. Others that should be important have disappeared along with the millions of brain cells I have lost in my old age, making room, I am sure, for a lot of trash I might better unload. But these are as clear as anything that happened yesterday.

A middle-aged lady on the boat, a high-school teacher from the Midwest, said she never expected to have the money to take a trip abroad, but only a few months ago a friend of hers who played the stock market said that if she would trust him with $200, he would return several thousand to her in a few months, and he did. He did it all with margins, whatever that meant. He was a financial genius. I hope he didn't jump out of a window.

Our hotel room in Paris. I have no idea where it was, but it was clean and the waiters were so happy to serve us they made it a happy place. I can still taste the croissants and hot chocolate they brought to our room for breakfast. We loved the Louvre and found it exhilarating to see the originals of the masterpieces we had studied: the *Mona Lisa*, the *Winged Victory*, and the *Venus de Milo*. I could have spent the summer there, but all we could hope to do in the allotted time was to skim the cream. If I saw a picture or a piece of statuary I didn't understand, I would stop behind a conducted group to retie my shoe laces and to stare around as if hunting for somebody while listening to the lecture from the tour guide. Usually Dorothy had a pamphlet or chart or guide book that informed us. We walked and walked and walked, liking the quayside stalls on the left bank of the Seine, where we picked up prints and books. We looked at the Notre Dame cathedral without entering it, but we did go into the Eiffel Tower and climbed to one of the lower stations for the view. As a language man, I was struck by the spelling on a public scale, which read: WEIGH YOURS ELF.

We made use of the sidewalk cafes for resting, rubbernecking, and dining cheaply, but did one extravagant thing: window shopping the salons on the Rue de la Paix we saw a lady's hat, a simple little hat tight fitting like a helmet that I thought would look wonderful on Dot. It consisted entirely of big fall leaves in two shades of blue and one of purple. I insisted that Dot try it on. She refused, but I won the argument. It was something to wear with evening clothes and when she put it on she was transformed to a bacchante. Of course, it was beyond our means, but I bought it. We had no hat box, or rather we had no room for an extra piece of luggage; so I put it in our small overnight bag that held pajamas, underwear, shaving kit, and things we might use for a one-night stand some place where we didn't want to undo the big suitcases. All summer long I packed and unpacked that damn hat, protecting it by stuffing and surrounding it with freshly laundered materials and taking care not to defile it with the dirty underwear I had to cram into corners.

When we got home Dot often looked at it, but since West Side Court was not the Place Vendome, she never wore it. My packing may have reshaped it slightly, but it was a lovely souvenir.

I planned to return to Paris, and we did more than once, but I never sparked to Rome and didn't go back, though Dorothy did so with the children. We tried to take it all in, but it was too overwhelming. The city I loved was Venice. We had a forgettable hotel near the Rialto Bridge, but could listen to the gondoliers, parked under the bridge as if it were a taxi stand, with their chorus of *gunduhla*, *gunduhla*, *gunduhla*. They accented the first syllable, not at all the way we said it in Camden, New York: *gon-dough-la*. They were cheap but expert oarsmen, and we patronized them often. Night was best. We'd hail a gondola and say we wanted to go out to the *musica*, a big flat raft quite a way out in the Grand Canal. On this nautical stage, wondrous Italian singers would act out or sing selections from the favorite operas. Our gondola would slip into a vacated berth and its skipper would grip the adjacent craft until twelve or more would be locked together. One of them probably held an impresario scouting the inspired singers for whom it was a continuous amateur night. They sang only opera. That's where Caruso and a host of others got their starts. It was magnificent. Dot was in seventh heaven.

By day the approach to the square was across the Rialto Bridge, a wonder in itself. Arched high enough in the center to allow an armed galley to pass under, it was, like the Ponte Vecchio in Florence, crowded with twelve silversmith's shops, no junk-stores, either. It was a busy mart but not as fascinating as St. Mark's Square which holds the basilica, the campanile (bell tower), the Doge's Palace in the background with its famous attached Bridge of Sighs over which condemned men passed to the prisons, and the clock tower, noteworthy that for hundreds of years two bronze morrish automations, as famed as Othello, have struck the hour with their hammers. St. Marks and the Doge's Palace are two dazzling ornate Byzantine pink wedding cakes. I have a snapshot of Dot alone in the great square with these structures in the background. She is half kneeling to feed the hundreds of pigeons around her. She's slim, bareheaded, and happy as a child. When we entered St. Marks, a church of riotous beauty, the ladies had to wear handkerchiefs on their heads in lieu of hats. Sister let the guard know what she thought of such papery.

One of Dorothy's friends had insisted that we go all the way down the west coast to Sorrento. The orange and lemon and olive groves and the masses of flowers everywhere, the winding roads over ancient Roman arched bridges, the grottoed cliffs a hundred stone steps down to warm sandy beaches in the bay mark this as the spot where Ulysses (more properly Odysseus) stuffed his sailors' ears but made them lash him to the mast so that he would not jump overboard as he listened to the sirens' song. We heard it too and stole three extra days from our schedule to stay a full week at the Hotel Cocumella on the solid rock above. Its rooms were large and cool, its gardens luxuriant, its food delicious, napery starched and white, and its service friendly and obliging. On the Fourth of July, each of our desserts was decorated with a tiny American flag.

We hadn't realized it, but we had been going at full speed; we were tired and needed a few days' rest. The climb up those steps from the beach was all the exercise we needed. Soon we were ready for the hot trip to Vesuvius in an open car. It was what we had expected, but since the excavated town of Pompeii with its preserved dummies provided an instant look at the actual past, it was absorbing. We were too young to be affected by the heat, but next day Dorothy noticed that the sun had faded most of the color from the cotton dress she was wearing.

Now we traveled north again to Florence, easily the most artistic city in the world. Just its bridges are worth the trip. The pension run by the lady near the Ponte Vecchio was as superb as we had been led to believe, as was the bridge with its goldsmith and silversmith shops. It was difficult to walk anywhere in that city and not behold a church, a palace, a museum, a column, a statue, a bridge, a tower—all of ancient lineage and exquisite workmanship redolent of medieval and Renaissance aristocracy. Even the citizens who inhabited it in the 20th century appeared more proud and sophisticated than their countrymen elsewhere. The buildings housed so many treasures that the city is one big museum with doorways of gold and bronze figures that may have taken a genius half his life to create, paintings and statues that have never since been equaled. There were so many madonnas with cherubic babies that they all became a jumble in my mind. The things that have stayed with me longest are the exterior of the Palazzo Vecchio with its twenty or so arches in the open-air loggia filled with classical sculptures, among them Benvenuto Cellini's bronze masterpiece of Perseus holding high the head of Medusa in his left hand, in his right the bloody sword. The figure decorates the cover of Edith Hamilton's unrivaled book on mythology.

For works inside the museums, though critics have found minor flaws in it, the heroic statue of David by Michelangelo, found in the Gallery of the Academy, is the work I visualize when Florence is mentioned, along with Botticelli's two paintings *Spring* and *The Birth of Venus*. Though I have no Italian I take it that *Primavera*, the name Botticelli gave his *Spring*, is straight from the Latin, meaning the first or earliest springtime. Its delicate colors, its three graces with their fresh beauty, the flowing movement of the gowns rekindle the love of life we associate with that most hopeful season of the year. *The Birth of Venus*, rising from the sea in her white conch shell, has the same effect upon my mind. Here she is not the temptress, but the Goddess of Beauty greeting the world. She might better be known by her Greek name Aphrodite, for I read somewhere that among other things *aphros* meant *foam*.

From Florence we made the short journey west to Pisa. We viewed the famed leaning tower. In 1929 tourists were allowed to climb its circular stairs, and though I won't swear to it I think we did. From its top balcony during the end of the 1500s Galileo experimented with a pendulum to prove that the earth moved on its own axis around the sun, and by dropping objects of different weight to the ground worked out his theories of gravity. His published work, ably backing the theory of Copernicus that the earth was no longer the fixed center of the universe, got him in trouble with the churchmen, who had built the Christian religion on the Ptolemic (2nd century) astronomical system of the universe in which the sun and the other planets move around the fixed, stable earth, created by God circa 4000 B.C. The church hated science, which was always upsetting its comfortable verities, and would have burned Galileo as a heretic had he not publicly recanted. He had only a few more years to live and thought them valuable, but is said while recanting to have murmured "But it does move."

To get back on schedule from Pisa we struck right out for Switzerland, first stop Geneva. We made it just in time to pick up our reservations at the pension or small hotel on the edge of the lake that the Lexington librarians had so strongly recommended. As with all their selections, this one was excellent and had the added bonus that one of the guests was Clarence Darrow. The notoriety he had won defending Eugene Debs and later keeping Loeb and Leopold from the electric chair was all but forgotten in the fame he achieved nationally defending a high-school teacher, J.T. Scopes, accused of teaching Darwinian theory to his class in Dayton, Tennessee. The Scopes or "Monkey" trial was a drama enacted in July 1925. William Jennings Bryan was the prosecuting attorney. Bryan, the free silver man, ran for the presidency many times and almost made it against McKinley by the backing of Western and Southern yokels. He was Wilson's secretary of state but resigned when he saw the country drifting into the first war against Germany. After the war, he became the great preacher for fundamentalism, a Chautauqua orator.

I had listened to him at Harvard earlier in 1925. On Sunday afternoons, a club invited all sorts of celebrities to speak, and Bryan was one of them. Not a man in that audience believed one word of the childish drivel he roared at us, but our club was known for its tolerance in hearing all sorts of conflicting, even stupid, ideas.

Darrow was not so polite. Putting Bryan on the stand as an authority on the Bible, he led him into wild admissions, the grossest being *that man was not a mammal.* H.L. Mencken covered the trial and sent daily dispatches back to the *Baltimore Evening Sun.* Soon everybody in the country wanted a reprint. Mencken added to his own fame by his caustic reports. Bryan died five days after the trial.

Mencken's most famous dispatch "In Memorium: W.J.B." is a classic that may be found in his *Prejudices: Fifth Series,* 1926; it is the brilliant analysis of a charlatan's wasted life, ending in the madman's hatred.

Darrow, while on vacation at least, was a relaxed and friendly man, ready to pass the time of day with the other visitors not of his coterie. I chatted with him briefly on more than one occasion, longing to ask him what he thought of Mencken, but good manners restrained me as I heard no other mention of the famous trial, now four years behind him. If I had known that in that same year, 1929, he was publishing, with Wallace Rice, a book entitled *Infidels and Heretics*, I might have mentioned that I had just left Pisa and was curious about Galileo's recanting. But I didn't and learned nothing from this renowned man except that he wished to be thought democratic. A young lady artist was trying to paint his portrait, uphill work because he wouldn't freeze like a pointer. He did, however, open his jacket and said to me, "They all want to see my suspenders."

We took one excursion across Lake Geneva to Chillon Castle, toured by Byron's "*Prisoner of Chillon*," then moved up through Switzerland, first stop Interlaken. There we took a side trip to the Jungfrau, a peak that would awe anyone. But once you have seen one alp... I was glad that our stops were few and far between, for though my mother's people had come from these parts, I felt that Switzerland should be left to the Swiss. Very wealthy Americans go there upon occasion to visit their money, and it's a great country to be from. Like Scotland. Scotsmen play their bagpipes and put on their kilts, and they even throw the caber in Sacramento, California. When they get drunk they cry into their beer about "guid auld Scootland," but you couldn't hire one of them to live there.

I know that we paused in Lucerne and at Zurich, and I remember the bracing air and the Disney cottages and the clean streets and the sparkling lakes and the stupendous mountains with their noses stuck in the clouds and the funicular railways that carried us upward in search of them. We even climbed a mountain. The guidebook said 3000 feet, a very moderate ascent. We started out behind our hotel and climbed and climbed until the girls got pooped. I offered to let them take turns hanging on to my belt as I plodded upward, a scrawny beast of burden in city shoes. It was more fun coming down, for the fields had been newly mown and the stubble remaining was so slick that I could squat and grip my ankles and slide short distances downhill, the soles of my shoes were so shiny. I slept most of the next day and didn't climb any other mountain anywhere after that. I thought Switzerland most beautiful, but if any American asks me if he should, for example, spend some time in the Lake Country in England, I tell him no. If your time is limited when you go abroad, spend very little of it looking at scenery. We have lakes, but we don't have a Tower of London.

Pushing on into Germany, there was a scenic trip that was pure delight, traveling up the Rhine on an excursion steamer. It provided a grand view of the little towns and the terraced vineyard that came down in big steps all the way to the water. I remember a G.I. telling me in World War II, "Hitler is crazier than you think. What the hell does he want with the rest of the world when he can have Germany? If I owned the place, I'd put a fence around it."

Several times every year, for the last fifty, when looking at a precious curio, I have thought of the little wood carving I saw in a shop window in Heidelberg. We were staying in a small hotel on the main highway into the city, and every morning at five the creaking farm carts would wake me up in passing as they carried fresh vegetables and dairy products to market. I would lie there struggling with the problem of whether to buy that statuette. It was maybe eight inches tall depicting an old professor reading a book. His spectacles were slanted down, his hair tousled, but his face was alight with the joy of learning. He was completely oblivious to anything except the words on that page. He carried two other books, one stuffed loosely in either pocket. His coat was not frayed, but it was wrinkled, his trousers a bit baggy. His shoes were good but unshined. He had been a tall man but was now stooped. His hands were large and bony. He was not dirty or scruffy, yet he would not let his housekeeper fuss over him, for he cared only for things of the spirit. He was Dean Briggs all over again. He cost ten dollars, which was like a hundred now. I didn't show him to Dot, for she would have made me buy him if we had to write home for money. So I said no. It may be that I have appreciated him more not owning him, but I'd like to have been able to hand him down.

I don't recall visiting any other German city, nor anything in the Netherlands. We spent a lot of weekends in the Netherlands in the years to come, which may be why I draw a blank on anything done in 1929. The same with London, where we lived sometimes for extended periods. We were there in 1947, 1949, 1950, 1951, 1952, 1953, and 1959. What stands out clearly was the channel crossing from Ostende to Dover. A sudden fierce rainstorm came up; our small boat was tossed about until everybody was sick and the decks slippery with vomit. I was sorry for a group of boy scouts homeward bound. They were a soaked, bedraggled mess. Their scout leader worked heroically. Not until we were safe in port and in still water did he run to the rail. He turned around and said to us all apologetically: "It was the beer."

Our hotel in London, where we spent a week, was somewhere just off Piccadilly Circus. It was dull and respectable in 1929, but by 1949 when we looked it up out of pure curiosity, it had gone all the way downhill and was riddled with prostitutes.

I have one glimmer. Dorothy loved maps and was never confused by them. We set out, just the two of us this time, in search of Big Ben. She begged me not to ask a bobby for directions as I usually did, but to let her lead us to it. She did, unerringly. As we stood before them, I said, "Well, you did it. There they are: Westminster Abbey, the Parliament buildings, and Big Ben." She didn't even look up, not until she had made some pencil markings on the map. She said triumphantly, "There they are—right there!" She drew a circle on the map, *then* she looked up.

The homeward trip was fine if on the melancholy side.

After the quiet of London, the noise of New York City and the rudeness of the porters who extracted our suitcases from the frenzied mob made us want to head right back for London, but after we had suffered the insolence of the customs men and saw Papa and Roger and the parents of our two companions waiting for us, we felt better. Papa looked older and Dot's mother was not too well, but after we had distributed our small gifts and discovered that the tiny tapestry we had bought in Rome was made in Japan, we talked for hours. Before we started back to Lexington, Dorothy told her parents that before another summer rolled around she hoped to make them grandparents.

20

After the palaces of Europe we had no trouble adjusting to our tiny house in West Side Court. We were on pleasant speaking terms with our neighbors, maybe twenty in all, for the court was a little square with only a handful of houses. We occupied one of the two identical stucco houses in the middle. The builder may have planned more, for he placed these two very close together on the same side of a central tract the size of a football field. This other house was rented by Dr. Henry Shelley, the Greek and Latin professor, and his spunky little wife, Marian. Like us, they were newcomers from the north. We both started our families there and were always close.

Henry was a gentle soul, a soft touch. Marian had to protect him from deadbeats. He was a handsome man, not fat but with a pot belly that he carried with dignity, even on the tennis court, where he seldom got much exercise, disposing of his most active opponents by beautifully placed shots and cuts and serves that sent him into gales of happy laughter as he watched a more springy victim race back and forth in futility.

His front porch was shaded on our side by a trumpet vine as opaque as an awning. Henry liked to sit there, grading papers. One day an encyclopedia salesman approached my door. We sat on the steps. He was younger than I had been when I sold *Pictorial Review*, so I heard him out. When he had finished I told him that I was simply too broke to buy his encyclopedia, and he could consider that final, but if he had no objection I thought I might be of help if I criticized his sales pitch. He was pleased to listen, thanked me, and went next door to tackle Henry. He scored easily; Henry liked that reference book and was rising to get his checkbook when Marian came out of the house, inquiring pleasantly enough, "What are you selling?" He started his sales pitch on her, but she broke in. "Sorry. We can't afford it; so until we can, we'll have to use the library. Goodbye and good luck."

The boy appealed to Henry. "Nooo, I guess not today," Henry said. The salesman departed.

I waited a decent interval before walking over for a little gossip. I mentioned that an encyclopedia salesman had called upon me earlier today. "Did he hit you?"

"Yeah," said Henry; "he was here, but I sent him packing."

When Dot was away, Marian invited me over for a fine dinner, then they took me to a movie. I wanted to buy the tickets, but Henry wouldn't hear of it. "Marian," he commanded. He yielded his place in line to her as she brought out a change purse and counted out the exact amount. I sat between them during the movie. I thought I heard sniffling and turned to Marian. Tough little Marian was crying unashamed. I heard sobbing and turned the other way. "Henry," I whispered, "are you crying?"

"Oh, yes," he said. "Aren't you?"

The Shelleys had a Buick, a grand little car that should have lasted forever the way Henry drove it, for though a lion on the tennis court he was a mouse in traffic. He never swore except when driving and then mostly under his breath. The car had a single side seat behind the driver and a shelf alongside it that was just right for their first-born son to perch on. Henry was constantly muttering for other drivers to stop crowding him. He didn't realize that his boy could hear him, until one day the kid stuck his head out the window and shouted at a passing car: "Why don't you stay over on your own side, you goddamn bastard?"

Henry never swore again.

To go back a year or two in time, it was in 1927 when we made contact with two other neighbors in the court, both from VMI. Both were majors at the time, I believe, and they shall go nameless for a very good reason: I have forgotten their names. I can see them both as clearly as I see my current neighbors, but nowhere are their names written down. Rather than continue to apologize for this fault, let me quote from a columnist, Charles McCabe, who writes for the *San Francisco Chronicle*. In an article on "*Remembering*," he quotes some guesses from the better scientific sources, to wit:

> 10,000 thoughts pass in and out of your mind every day.
>
> The brain supposedly is composed of ten billion billion working parts and has enough storage capacity to accept ten new facts every second.
>
> After age 35, 100,000 brain cells perish daily.
>
> In time the brain is overloaded and much has to be pushed out to make room for new. Much good stuff is lost with the rubbish.

So I don't know their names. So what?

I remember Major Blank and his wife chiefly as members of a Shakespeare club, a weekly affair started by the professor of

Journalism, whose name I do remember. He was a very nice man. He invited the members; the club met at his house, and he assigned the parts, keeping the best parts for himself. He read very well, rarely being betrayed by his infrequent bouts of stuttering. But when he read Hamlet's great soliloquy, it came out: "To be or not to be. That is the kuh-kuh-kuh-kuhquestion."

We managed to survive that, but were tortured when Mrs. Major Blank was called to the telephone, which was in the meeting room, and tried to describe to Major Blank, who stayed at home that night, babysitting a sick young daughter, how to give the child an enema. "No, no," she kept saying, "not there, the other end!" And that's when the groundlings roared. The club broke up when the professor departed for Columbia University. I survived the loss of culture, but not the entertainment.

I was much closer to the other major and his very attractive wife. He was a cavalry officer at VMI and invited me to watch his instruction. A group of mounted cadets armed with loaded army pistols road pell mell down a hill behind the institute, and as they started up another rise fired their pistols at a man-size target against a bank. He had taught them well. Those kids were terrific. After they were dismissed, he let me fire at the target, not mounted of course. I had never used a pistol with that much recoil, and the first shot went high, but I soon got the hang of it and made a good grade.

He took me to a meet at VMI where he and others jumped horses over high hurdles. A barnstorming aviator, who had previously skimmed his plane close to the stables, flying it upside down, shook his head unbelievingly as he watched the riders taking those high jumps. The major's temper flared; he thought he was being ridiculed until I helped the flyer convince him that he was serious. You knew what a plane could do, but a horse—god-a-mighty!

The major wasn't much of a drinker, but he joined me in an attempt to brew beer in my cellar. When the bottles started to blow up, I called him. He came over. If you tapped one, it would blow off the cork like a handheld Roman candle. We took the whole batch into our coal bin, then empty, and had fun washing down the sides of that bin. Those were the days!

While we still lived in West Side Court we rented the spare bedroom to a student—two, in fact. The first one was remarkable only for his ability to sleep over a three-day weekend, drinking but a part of the milk I would bring him before he would cork off again. The second was my first cousin Emil Stevens, the kid who punched a hole in our cat's ear. He now weighed 195 pounds and played football in the line, then basketball, and once when the heavyweight on our boxing team was sick, Emil went in for him and walked out alive at the end of the bout. In the spring, he was used on the track team. He threw the shot a respectable distance, but what was more remarkable, he usually won the broad jump. Lord, did he ever pay for his athletic scholarship! He was only a kid and when he had his dinner he would come in and try to hit the books, but almost always fell asleep over them. In spite of that he got a degree in business administration after four years, and came back a fifth year at his own expense and got all As and Bs. He said to me, "You thought me stupid, didn't you?" I said, "In only one way, to let those heartless bastards wear you out." He had a successful business career, is retired, and still going strong, with that infectious laugh as hearty as ever. I'll never forget the night when he heard a crash in our bedroom and found us both on the floor after the slats in our antique bed had given way. He felt there could be only one explanation for such an accident, and I thought he'd never stop laughing as I nailed a couple of the slats in place and he helped lift the springs and mattress back where they belonged.

Nor was he surprised when, on June 2, 1930, I was able to call both our families announcing the birth of a son. Emil had joined a fraternity and his bedroom became a nursery. It had been a long slow birth, eighteen hours all told, for Dorothy had insisted the day before that I take her for a jolting ride in the car over rough roads to start matters along. It did the trick, but it also turned the baby around. Old Doctor White, whose type is little known today but lovingly remembered by a few old people like me, took his time to make sure that in a breech birth the baby might very well die unless his arms were crossed before he emerged. He said that Dorothy was the best patient he had ever had, but he almost lost me. I sat outside that delivery room, sick with apprehension, almost continuously. The man occasionally ould emerge and assure me that everything was going to be just fine. At last I heard his rich bass voice saying, "You've got a mighty fine boy there, ma'am."

He told me, "He's going to be a big man, for they always grow to their feet." Dr. White knew all about feet. In World War I, his job was to see that soldiers were properly shod. "Men are more vain than women. If a man gave me his shoe size, I made him get army shoes a size and a half larger. Their civilian shoes were always too small, and when they marched their feet were going to spread." His office was on an incline. He took me to a window. He pointed to a woman in high heels walking uphill. "No problem. Now wait till you see one coming down." One came along and those shoes hurt her feet cruelly and almost toppled her. Believing the practice of medicine to be simple common sense, he never gave high-powered drugs, but mostly bottles of placebos, accompanied by the strictest instructions when to take them, how many, and with what sort of liquid. People always felt better. If they had fever, he got them into bed and got their bowels open, and if that didn't cure them, it was time to consult the medical books. He seldom charged more than two dollars, .and if a woman cried on him that was fifty cents extra. He knew what was in those big books if an emergency occurred. He was a hard act to follow. When his son Reid White set up to be a doctor in Lexington, people would tell him, "Go away, son. We want your daddy."

I brought about half the town in to see my beautiful son. It wasn't until two years later that his baby pictures showed him looking like a little bulldog. It took me that long to forgive my best friend, Charley McDowell, who said, "Watkin, ain't they a hell of a lookin' thing when they're first born."

I realized, of course, that it was pure jealousy, for when Charley's second son John had been born only a month and a few days before my son, I had strained the truth to be complimentary, and his first boy, Charley Boy, had a head too large for his body. But as our children grew I loved them both, and my affection for Charley Boy has increased. I am as proud of his literary accomplishments as any father and wish that Charley Mac could have lived to see those honors piling up and the casual manner in which Charley Boy takes them. He was speaker for the Washington and Lee 1979 spring anniversary class reunion. This is the way the May 1979 alumni magazine encapsulates him:

> Charles R. McDowell Jr. is a 1948 W&L graduate, who is now the Washington D.C. correspondent for the Richmond *Times-Dispatch*. He is son of the late Charles R. McDowell, who taught law at W&L for more than forty years before his death in 1968, and Mrs. C.R. McDowell, "the indispensable Mrs. Mac," secretary to five law deans at the university. (Charley recalls that because of his parent's connection with the law school, when he was growing up he was called "Footnote.")

> He is a columnist in the Russell Baker/James Reston genre, a sometimes television commentator (*Washington Week in Review* on PBS), Gridiron Club panjandrum (largely responsible for the musical spoofs presented at the august organization's annual black tie banquet for the president and other high government targets), National Headline Award Winner, and, hardly least, superlative raconteur.

I am convinced that some day he will write a great book about his father, who was my buddy at W&L from 1927 to the time that I left in 1943. Charley was a many-sided man. He was very much interested in his teaching, in the law school, in his students, and in the whole college, especially in its physical beauty. Before the thirties the law school was called Tucker Hall, a stone Romanesque building at the north end of the colonnade, which completely destroyed its classic harmony. There was a game show once on television called *Joker's Wild*. Part of it consists of pulling a lever to actuate amounts of money appearing in three boxes above. If the devil, a dark, malignant creature, doesn't show up, the contestant may win a thousand dollars. Often he will almost have reached the prize. Two bright white boxes shine with money. Then the devil lets everyone down with a thud. That was old Tucker Hall. Your eye traveled from left to right over harmonious beauty, then ugh, there was that old black devil Tucker Hall. It burned in 1934, and all the professors on campus brought their families to the window to see the sight. When the new beautiful Tucker Hall was rebuilt the following year, Charley labored mightily to have its fittings appropriate. He spent a great deal of time and is responsible for the handsome, sturdy study chairs that were used. He had an office on the second floor. When I asked him if he didn't rate one of those downstairs near the entrance, he grinned. "I'm too smart for that. I insisted that all the other professors pick theirs first, knowing the ones they'd take. So every student and tourist knocks on their doors with questions, and I've got a nice big secluded room where I can get some work done."

I could see the point of that, for Charley loved to talk and tell stories. He would make the rounds of an evening, stopping at the Corner Store, the hub of the college, proceed to the barber shop nearer the center of town, and run by the ancient black barber who advertised his establishment: "If it was good enough for General Lee, it's good enough for you." He and Charley would have great arguments. Once the barber told him, "Don' tell me about the Scotch-Irish, Mister Mac. I reckon I'se got as much Scotch-Irish in me as you'se got in you."

Next was the Greek restaurant, where Charlie'd cash a check for one dollar for cigarettes, then if the haberdashery was open with the curtain alcove in back where athletics were bandied about, Charley was welcome for he had been an all-state football and basketball star from Centre College at Danville, Kentucky, in 1915 and later coached those sports there. He recruited many a fine athlete for W&L. He might end up at McCrums Drug Store. Charley had a great ear for stories he had heard in his native Danville, and he was a great storehouse of material for me. I never tired of these tales from his native heath, no matter how many times he repeated them. He might say, "Larry, did I ever tell you about Stampy Stern the standpipe painter?" I'd always say, "No, I don't think I've ever heard that one," for he would dredge up new beauties in the retelling. Finally, in 1954 he wrote a book about his youth in Danville, called *The Iron Baby Angel*. He thanked me for my help on it, which was absolutely nil, except that I begged him not to listen to the dope at Henry Holt who wanted to retitle it *A Kentucky Odyssey*. The Iron Baby Angel was the Puck or presiding spirit attached to the horse-drinking fountain in front of the court house. The dialect is perfection. No other American writer has ever surpassed it. There isn't a respectable character in the book except the nine-year-old boy from Chicago visiting Danville during the summer. But the eloquence and capabilities of these rag-tag street people and the precious friendships that develop between the boy and these ne'er-do-wells make this book one of the most remarkable, appealing, genuine works of Americana in existence. I did my damndest to persuade Walt Disney to let me give him a screenplay from it, but when Walt had other plans nobody could budge him.

Writing about Charley's book reminds me of two Lexington street characters I should have mentioned in an earlier chapter, Herb the Dog Man and Dixie Nunn. They had nothing in common but both were institutions. Herb the Dog Man took his stand at the sidewalk entrance to the campus, and nobody could pass him without having a look at one of the winsome, tiny puppies peering out from the top of his coat. If you showed any interest you got the full sales spiel about his genuine blooded animals. He sold them for whatever the traffic would bear and relieved the town of the need for a dog pound.

No less appealing was the gigantic black named Dixie Nunn, an ageless grizzled window-washer, reputedly a former slave. He always stepped off the sidewalk into the gutter in way of deferential greeting. The story persisted that in his prime he was so powerful that he had felled a stubborn mule with a single blow of his fist. His feet were so large that no shoes would fit him, so he had improvised footwear of flat board and bran sacking. He walked all the way to Washington D.C., where the authorities took him in and found over five hundred dollars, all in small silver coins, in those shoes. When at his request the police called Lexington, they were assured that Dixie Nunn had earned every one of those coins, wouldn't steal a penny, and was a sound citizen, whereupon he was set free to enjoy his sight-seeing.

We made many close and lasting friends while we were at Washington and Lee University. Though they have been dropping off like flies, more than half of my Christmas card list, still extensive for one of my years, contains the names of those we first met in Lexington, Virginia. Probably the man with whom I spent as much time as I did with Charley Mac was also a law school professor, Ramon T. Johnson. He was my pool partner and though I was much younger, I became his father confessor. Also a Kentuckian, he was a constant wise-cracker. Everybody loved Johnson, who would get off ten jokes to everybody else's one. He had no middle name, but took the initial T, which he stoutly maintained stood for Turkeyfoot. He told me that when he was nine years old, his parents returning from town with another stop to make, sent Ramon with a jug of wine home on a shortcut through a cornfield. When he emerged on the other side of that field he was a drunkard, and never if he could help it, wanted to draw a sober breath thereafter. He fought for sobriety all his life and often achieved it. His drinking did not interfere with his teaching until just before he died. He married a very sweet Kentucky girl named Mary Lee and for her sake remained relatively sober, but if Ramon was drunk, whoever observed it came to the rescue. He was universally loved. If the police saw that his car was wavering when he returned from a party without Mary Lee, they followed him home to make sure that he was safely inside. He was such a magnificent teacher that near the end of his life when he was all alone in a small apartment on campus, the senior law students would go down and get him out of bed and dress him and get some coffee down him and convey him up the hill to class, saying they'd rather listen to Professor Johnson drunk than anyone else sober. He was a little man with tiny hands and a sizable nose and ready smile. He had a voice of deep conviction and a great sense of humor. When the law school burned he thought it would be fun to imply that he had been researching and writing a book, and that years of his life went up in flames. He had no other copy. Of course he had no copy of any sort, but he found infinite amusement in the sympathy bestowed on him for his great loss.

When World War II practically closed down the law school, Ramon secured a job with RCA. He proceeded in his direct fashion to find out where he stood. He visited the chairman of the board and asked him: "How do you want your contract drawn—honest or dishonest?"

"Why...uh..." the man stammered.

"It makes no difference to me." said Ramon. "I just want to know."

"Why, uh...honest, of course."

"You're sure?"

"Yes."

"Good. Honest it is."

He told me that he had stayed sober all that time, and that he had made that company so honest they hated him and were glad to see him go. He asked for a bottle and got one. I didn't sleep much that night, but managed to redirect Ramon to the bathroom when he was under the misapprehension that our bureau was a pissoir. But it was worth it to see that little man again. We had many a pleasant hour playing pill pool in the room above the Corner Store. Jimmy Hamilton, the proprietor, paid me a high compliment while we were shooting pool. "Larry," he said, "is it true that you go up on that hill and talk to students about litachure and writing and such like?"

"Yes, Jimmy, I really do."

"Well, I'll be goddamned. "

When things were going well for us all, Ramon had married the girl he loved best of anything in this world, and built a very nice house for her in a fine new section of town and set out to repay the many social obligations he had incurred as a bachelor. He was a fine host who stayed on his feet at dinner parties. Then they had a son, and Ramon's cup was full. He said that on the way to the hospital, for the first time in his life he took the first curve in the road with extreme caution. He was a father now. Mary Lee was accepted into the bridge club that met on so many afternoons when Catherine McDowel and Dot and Jane Riegel and Evelyn Mapel and Polly Penick and Hazel Helderman and Frances Veech and many others would get together to gossip and swap baby-lore and hold post mortems on the latest party.

We had wild faculty parties, where nothing was obtainable but the raw white-corn whiskey that had never seen the inside of a charred keg, but came to us from our bootlegger in a Mason jar right from the still. We would line up these lethal libations in shot glasses on the mantel piece and with only a cigarette or a glass of water in the other hand knock them off. That always led to singing, which was sometimes harmonious. We would sing "Fireman's Band," "When I Wore My Aprons Low," "Nancy Brown," "Down by the Old Mill Stream," "In the Evening by the Moonlight," "Carry Me Back to Old Virginny," "Let Me Call You Sweetheart," and other songs with which we could harmonize like barber quartets. The noise must have been frightful, for almost everybody had a piano, and a chemistry professor, Monk Farinholt, had a heavy hand and was much given to playing "Anchors A-Weigh." So many of the faculty came to these parties that little was said about them. I admit to being one of the worst offenders and was reprimanded by the administration for being unwise in the use of alcohol. I never passed out and loved the craziness, but I deserved the rebuke and tried to do better. My second novel, *Geese in the Forum*, describes in some detail the sort of thing that went on. Chapter 26, aside from plot changes, deals with one of the parties at our house in West Side Court. I believe upon that occasion Ramon did not attend.

Things went well for Ramon and Mary Lee until late in the 1930s. I do not know the exact date, but it had to be very near the end of that decade, for I had built a house outside of town with a huge game cellar. At one end was a pool table, and I remember the afternoons when just the two of us would have a quiet game. Tragedy struck Ramon. He and his wife were out on the main highway late in the afternoon taking a pleasant ride. Mary Lee was driving. At one of the widest, straightest parts of the road a second-hand car driven by a drunken workman came barreling over a knoll toward them. Mary Lee pulled way over to the right, giving the oncoming driver a good twenty feet of road to pass on the left. But he came straight at them and plowed into their car. Mary Lee died by the side of the road.

I spent that night with Ramon in the hospital. He hadn't been drinking, but he was almost unconscious with grief. He repeated continuously, "That poor girl; she never had a chance." There was not much incentive for him to stay sober after Mary Lee died, but he had stretches of sobriety when he did great teaching. In the end, he lived alone in a small apartment below the law school, and one night a lighted cigarette which he had dropped into the overstuffed chair he occupied caught fire and he was dead from smoke inhalation before the firemen could extinguish the blaze.

Most people make some enemy sometime, but I don't know of any that Ramon had. He was a delightful companion. I believe that it was in the summer of 1939 when we proposed going by car to Washington, New York, New England, Montreal, and home. I did the driving and Ramon sat in the back and kept us laughing all day. He got drunk only once, in New York City, and had his own way of crossing Broadway. He was weaving only slightly. We were in Times Square and looking in a window. I thought he was looking, too, but he had seen something across the street he wanted to investigate, so he simply took off. I heard the screech of brakes and looked around to see Ramon, simply holding his left hand up to stop the speeding cars, his eyes focused ahead on whatever he had seen on the other side of Broadway. He never stopped or gave traffic a thought, but those taxi drivers were used to stopping on a dime and they curled back in a wave, allowing this small man from Kentucky a path as through the Red Sea. All we could do was hold our breath until he had safely reached the other side. He had seen a popcorn wagon and when he had purchased a bag or two he looked around for the rest of us. I motioned for him to wait. We would join him after we had crossed with the light. Either the popcorn or the tearful rebuke of Mary Lee sobered him, and he didn't even have a beer all the rest of that trip.

It was on the coast of Massachusetts that he first saw the ocean, and I feared he would never stop looking. "I don't believe it," he said. "I just don't believe it."

"I thought you were in the Navy in World War I," I said.

"I was. In Chicago. I had one of those little middy blouse suits enlisted men wore, and I was on a ferry boat as a regular passenger, and it was a bit rough. A little girl told her mother in a loud voice, 'Oh, Mama, there's a sailor. We're going to be all right.' And I was the only one who went to the rail to upchuck."

My first novel, *On Borrowed Time*, had been a Broadway play and was made into a movie by MGM with Lionel Barrymore. I had been invited to its opening in Washington, but was so busy I declined. Now, it was paired with a western, and every place we went we just missed it. Finally, we caught up with it in Montreal. We had good seats in a big city theater, and I was feeling rather proud of myself. When the lights came on after the show, a man sitting directly below us got up, stretched and yawned, and said to his wife, "Well, I daresay one has to sit through something like that every once in a while. "

Ramon choked back his laughter, but he never let me hear the end of it either. He could kid you unmercifully, but without malice.

Other delightful friends were Bill and Evelyn Mapel. Bill took over the school of journalism. He did things nobody else would think of doing, or if they had the impulse wouldn't act on them. For example, we once went on a picnic, just the four of us to roast hot dogs, and Bill pulled out a printed sheet he had struck in my honor to celebrate the picnic, the whole thing done in the monumental style. You never knew if he was kidding. He said that journalism had no background of high-sounding terms such as Renaissance or humanism and he was going to give it some. Hereafter, he aimed to call the boss of the print shop the superintendent of the typographical laboratory. When the president of the university hoped to appoint me as a sort of house father to a fraternity, I didn't know how to get out of it. Bill did. Both he and the president belonged to the Phi Gamma Delta fraternity; so Bill immediately pledged me to that one. Thereafter he always greeted me by saying "Perge!" Not long ago, he sent me a book he had researched for some time about both his and his wife's origins. They had traveled far and consulted countless documents to make it authentic. He discovered that the first ancestor of Evelyn in this country was Sir Robert Parke, secretary to Governor Winthrop of Massachusetts in 1630. Dorothy was still alive then and pleased to know that she and Evelyn were related. The Mapels lived near the Johnsons and gave their support when needed.

So did Allen and Polly Penick. Polly was beautiful, Allen was droll. He was the local judge and the cases he would relate about the ruction two hillbillies had over the ownership of a pig would convulse the listener. He was the keenest hunter in the county, a born woodsman. He should have lived in the days of Daniel Boone to be completely happy. When he could stand it no longer, he would leave Polly a note saying he had gone to visit his grandmother, which meant that he had gone to the wildest woods in the vicinity with his hunting dogs to live like an Indian for a few days. He shot just enough game to excuse his trip. To kill more wouldn't have been fair to the wild turkey and deer and the quail he stalked.

Still another character who told me stories was Jimmy Barnes. Deriving from tough old sea captains, Jimmy was highly civilized. He married a girl from the Eastern Shore whom he always called Queeny. She understood machinery and drove the car. Jimmy sat in the back seat, bowing to his friends left and right like the Queen Mother on a royal pilgrimage to greet her loyal subjects. He loved to tell stories about old men and to imitate their shaky voices until he grew to speak that way. Sometimes he came out of character in the classroom, where he taught political science. If the room was hot, he would ask a student to open the window a crack. If the student overdid it, Jimmy would remark, "Son, if you think that's a crack, you're going to be a terribly disappointed boy on your wedding night. " Jimmy loved flowers and could grow anything. He built a house on a side hill. During a spring freshet, rain washed out both beds down the hill. He watched it from the window, remarking, "That's right, God, take it all!" His mother, visiting, fetched him a clout that left him dizzy. "I'll teach you to insult your maker," she said.

Two very good, somewhat older friends were Dr. and Mrs. Desha. Mrs. Desha was witty, like Colonel Forrester, her delightful old father, who had been a Kentucky journalist in the days when the editor of a newspaper in order to print what he pleased had to invite anyone of a contrary opinion out behind the print shop to decide freedom of the press with his fists. Mary Desha could entertain you with tales of an amusing Kentucky childhood, or make the game of bridge, which I hated, bearable for me with her adroit purveying of the latest gossip. Her next-door neighbor, Catherine McDowell, was equally good at it. It was impossible to spend an evening with those two in the room and not laugh. Upon occasion Mrs. Desha's father, who appeared to be asleep in a chair, would speak up. Cats in an alley were making the night hideous. Somebody remarked about it. Colonel Forrester answered, "All you get out of a catfight is more cats."

Dr. Desha had taken over the chemistry department. He recruited able men and was himself a researcher of note. He had one peculiarity that some might consider a fault. Like the friendly Italians he liked to pinch the bottoms of the better-looking faculty wives. Both Dorothy and Catherine complained to Charley and me about it. We gave them small sympathy. I said, "Look, you girls either singly or in concert could easily lick Dr. Desha; so if you don't like it, why don't you pin him to the floor?" They thought that would be disrespectful. I thought they might feel worse if he didn't think them worth pinching. In spite of this irritating habit, he was very much of a gentlemen and would not stoop to an obscenity, but he did play around with suggestive language, some of it not suggestive enough. We were all at a formal dinner party preceding the W&L graduation dance, a splendid affair to which our neighbors on campus, VMI people, had been invited. In turn they had invited a Washington and Lee student of whom they were most fond, and he had brought his date from a nearby college, a truly beautiful girl exquisitely gowned. The boy was embarrassed for his date was not just tight but drunk. She spoke not a word to anybody and at the table kept her head lowered. The host asked Dr. Desha to carve the chicken and serve. He was in fine form. Asking a diner her choice, he responded to her answer of leg with a further question: "Chorus or ballet?"

This was too much for the drunken beauty, who evidently had been listening, for she lifted her head and fixed Dr. Desha with a malevolent eye, making this pronouncement loud and clear: "When I mean shit, I say shit, and when I mean fuck, I *say* fuck." She dropped her head all the way down again and remained silent until all the rest had completed dining, then allowed her hostess to lead her into a bedroom to sleep it off. Dr. Desha, as De Quincey said, smiled horribly, a ghastly smile, but managed to reply, "Yes, don't we all."

I didn't think I was capable of blushing, but I could feel the blood suffusing my neck and traveling upward to the top of my head.

A last word about Dr. Desha. He could take ridicule with a good grace, and when a reader in Lexington who followed the New York columnists tagged this bit, Dr. Desha himself repeated it:

While thumbing idly through *Who's Who*, I ran across the name
Lucius Junius Desha, and my mouth drooled for ripe peaches.

Another couple we were especially fond of was Leonard and Hazel
Helderman. Leonard, a brilliant teacher in the history department,
had a subtle sense of humor and a face so straight that people often
missed his jokes, but I had an ear cocked for them.

The final ones that I shall mention here, because I am speaking
of my oldest friends, are George and Sally Jackson. George was
a Boston Brahmin. We occupied an office together in the earliest days
when space was at a premium. One day the question of dirty speech
came up in connection with an author that we thought had rather
overstepped the bounds of good taste. George and I set out to write
a dirty passage that would not, to quote Sir Walter Scott, "Bring the
blush of shame to the virgin's cheek." Our passage went as follows:

> Why are you embarrassed baskers fluctuating on the sands of
> a beach? Are you waiting to take a ship? No, frigate.

His wife Sally, who worked in the library, had been a librarian in
Atlanta when Margaret Mitchell was working on *Gone with the Wind*.
One day Sally found her slumped on the library steps staring gloom-
ily into space. "What's the matter, Margaret? Book not going well?"

Margaret Mitchell shook her head. "I've got to rewrite seventy-five pages. I have my lady pregnant for 19 months."

Sally suggested: "Why don't you cover it with a footnote, saying it
was the natural conservatism of Southern womanhood?"

This should make it obvious why I dedicated my second novel,
Geese in the Forum, to:

> For Dorothy and Charley and Catherine and Jimmy and Mary
> and Leonard and Sally and Johnny—who tell me stories.

I made many just as brilliant friends later, and would have liked
to know others with whom I had only a speaking acquaintance,
such as the French professor John Graham. I don't believe his
rewritten Mother Goose rimes have ever been published. I remember hearing one:

> Swimming in a septic tank
> For the third time Willie sank,
> Saying, "Really, how absurd,
> Drowning after I'm interred."

21

As I look back upon our early days at W&L, the thing that surprises me is how much fun we had out of life on a starvation salary. I don't remember worrying about money at all; I was sure that something would turn up and something invariably did. We barely had eating money, then along came a father worried about his son's lack of grammar and hired me for several months to tutor the kid three days a week for two hours at a time at the rate of three dollars an hour. He suggested three dollars; I'd have settled for a buck. We couldn't understand why those stock brokers in the fall of 1929 were committing suicide. After all, it was only money. Almost everybody on the faculty was poor. During the Depression, everybody took a ten percent cut, but ten percent of almost nothing was negligible. A new teacher and his wife arrived penniless. They thought they would be paid on the first, rather than the last of the month, and were so proud that they lived on things like mustard and dandelion greens and windfall apples, and not very filling faculty teas for thirty days. We ourselves went out to dinner one night on five dollars that Dot saved. We were giving some good discarded dresses of Dot's and a pair of threadbare golf knickers of mine to the Salvation Army when Dot said, "Wait a minute, please." She reached into the watch pocket of those old knickers and extracted a five-dollar bill that she had put there in case I bet on a game and lost. In those days, all men's trousers had those tiny pockets for your watch just to the right of your belt buckle. Wristwatches made them pointless.

The three-month vacations, of course, were a godsend.

We closed our rented houses up tight, cut off utilities, and headed for Mount Vernon, New York, or Conifer, and, after 1932, Camden. We were in no way imposing on our respective families. Both of them had room for us, and if they could have had their way they would have liked to see us stay twice as long. All grandparents and aunts and uncles couldn't wait to see our son and listen to his prattle. Dot was glad to help in any way she could, and though my mother and sisters expected nothing of me, they found it pleasant to have a handy man around the house.

I felt always indebted to the Parkes, but though they protested against it, I spent a big part of one summer vacation painting the whole exterior of their huge three story house. I was a good painter and though I managed to slop paint in my ears, I never made or left a mess on awnings or porches or sidewalks below.

In 1932, the year that my mother and Dr. Loucks moved back to our house in Camden, Glenevieve and Elsie, both successful teachers, loved the Adirondacks so much that they wanted a place of their own. So they jointly financed a summer camp on Big Simonds pond, an extension of Tupper Lake. The lot cost practically nothing, because at first there was no road through and all building materials had to be hauled by water. Mr. Fuller, our nearest neighbor in Conifer, a superintendent at the Sykes' lumber mill, built a somewhat swankier camp on the adjoining lot. The girls suspected that he gave them a lot of the lumber, and the Sykes family made sure that the prices were minimal. Old W.L. Sykes donated the fireplace andirons, made out of two pieces of railroad track. The living room / dining room had a beautiful hardwood floor. They had a small kitchen with a wood stove and a sink with cold water piped in. My mother's nephew Charlie Kilbourne, whom she had practically raised, understood masonry and constructed the beautiful fireplace out of native stone. Later he returned and with me as his helper built a stone front under the porch. Mr. Zenger, the Conifer mill's best carpenter, did most of the framing and clapboarding alone, but I arrived in time to work with him on shingling the roof. I learned how to lay a chalk line and put on a course well enough that I shingled the whole rear end of the building alone. I had learned to be a good carpenter from teaching the college dramatic group how to build scenery, but nobody could keep up with Mr. Zenger. He was lightning fast and accurate. I did a lot of the finishing work after he had built the basic structure. He built a privy out back, but I added the seats, sawing and contouring them, a completely round one for the ladies, and a round one with an added v in front for the gentlemen. Outhouse humor was going around then because of a book written by a humorist-in-the-rough named Chic Sale. It was crude Midwestern stuff before the Midwest was ridiculed into becoming sophisticated. All those yokels moved to Orange County, California, the latest place for the light of learning to descend. All I recall of Sale's classic was the phrase, "A mighty, mighty pretty privy."

I remembered that phrase again in Paris in 1929, where I saw a gentleman standing at a street pissoir and tipping his hat to a lady of his acquaintance without turning off the spigot. It impelled me to write this limerick:

Montmartre, the Parisian's pride,
Like Broadway is famed far and wide.
That street couldn't fail
To enrapture Chic Sale,
For the plumbing's all on the outside.

About the Left Bank:

Miss Parsons would rather be in at tea
Than doing this doubtful vicinity.
It just makes her shiver
That this side the river
Sees so little point to virginity.

I wrote a lot more, which I have forgotten, but I did one on Professor Moffat's wife, who was still fighting the War Between the States. The Rileys were her very dear friends, but she refused to ride in their car because it was a Lincoln. She held every Northerner personally responsible for causing her grandfather to work himself to death trying single-handed to save the old plantation, somewhere in the misty past of antebellum days. She put the bite on a good many of us crass Yankees in an appealing letter, asking a "loan" of three hundred dollars to help restore this mythical kingdom of beauty and gentility in the deep, deep South. She was a little like what Shelley said about his father-in-law William Godwin, "Preaching and passing the hat." Anyway, the fun I got out of it was well worth the lost $300. It inspired another limerick:

Lila Nance Moffatt sat on her toffet
Under the UDC
While thinkin' how stinkin'
Was Abraham Lincoln
She clean forgot Robert E. Lee.

Pooling our ideas, we came up with a name for the Tucker Lake camp, which sounded Indian: Niktaw Lodge, or Watkin spelled backward. Other contributions I made was to build a cold storage cabinet to act as a refrigerator over the big rock under which the ice-cold spring water bubbled up. Also, I built the stone walkway from the porch down to the boat dock out of flat stepping stones. My sister Elsie supervised the job, and I thought then what a clever psychologist she was. She kept me working hard by saying, "Now don't try to lift that big stone unless you're sure you won't strain yourself," and when I had wrestled it to a walking position and carried it to its resting place, she would exclaim, "Gracious, Lawrence, how strong you are!"

The fishing was great; trolling would get you a walleyed pike, a most savory fish, as long as your arm. To save the job of scaling, I nailed the head to a tree, and with knife and pliers skinned all fish and cleaned them ready for the skillet. The entrails went back in the lake for chumming. There were big bullfrogs across the lake for frogs' legs dinners, and more often than not my mother was there to do the cooking, for she loved this spot. There was a promontory with cranberry bushes, and it was no surprise to see deer coming down to the shore for a drink. After the first summer the county built a road that extended above the two camps, which meant more visitors and more jollification. Our son when he was there always went along in the little red rowboat, trolling with his own small pole and line in the water. He caught a sunfish and asked if that could be considered his very own fish, which he alone could eat. We said yes to all questions. The next time his mother turned around we found him trying to eat that fish right then and there.

Dr. Loucks would visit most infrequently, and no Parke except Roger could get away to come, but those two along with Glenevieve's newly acquired husband, David Currier, a New Englander and a splendid fellow, were all there for Elsie's wedding to Milton Eastham. The road men had finished blasting, but Roger and Dave conspired with them to set off a charge of dynamite right in the middle of the wedding.

Glenevieve wouldn't speak to Dave for two days. I had picked up an antique bellows and swept the floor with it by blowing dirt and dust into the fireplace. The lake was clear and clean, cold underneath but warm on top. I made the two-mile swim over and back, floating twice to rest in between. My wind was good. Neither Dot nor I smoked during these vacations, nor had anything to drink. It was no privation for me. I never have had a drink by myself until recently when I've taken a thimbleful of Irish Mist to follow the Biblical injunction.

When we visited Dot's family we had the room that had been Grandma's, for she had died on April 15, 1928, a year before we went to Europe. Grandpa McKelvey, as is so often the case, died a month later on the May 21 at the age of 84. They were buried in the beautiful Sleepy Hollow Cemetery in Tarrytown. They had lived with Mrs. Parke, their daughter, for thirty years, and it hit her hard to be so suddenly bereft. When our son Lawrence Parke was born, the newly created grandparents were so anxious to see him that Papa left his wife with her old friend, a lady doctor originally trained in Germany. She moved in so that Papa could come down and have a look. To see that huge man carrying the tiny blanketed bundle in his arms, smiling down and talking to Parke, as he came to be called, would melt the most caustic cynic. It disturbed him that the baby appeared to have all the usual things, a playpen, a carriage, a crib. Without our knowledge, he ordered a big white electric refrigerator brought in, one of those earliest boxes that resembled the Civil War Union ironclad the *Monitor*, which had a circular gun turret in the middle of her deck. Referred to as a "cheese box on a raft," she drove off the Confederate ironclad *Merrimac*. Papa explained that this gift, a very expensive one then, was for the baby, not for us. He had no objection to adults keeping their milk in an old-fashioned ice box, but he could not bear to think of that child's formula being kept sweet in anything but the best refrigerator that modern science could devise. Papa hoped that before the summer was over we could put that baby into our Chevy and visit them—driving with proper caution, of course. And so we did. It meant everything to Mrs. Parke, and though we managed to visit Conifer the following summer for a brief time, my mother was generous enough to let us spend the longest time with Dorothy's mother. We would have preferred the mountains, for there is nothing much steamier than New York in the summer time when the humidity stays around 90 all night. That was before the days of air conditioning.

There was another reason for being near New York. I spent several summers at Columbia University taking advanced courses toward the Ph.D. After one in the 18th century, the next two were in drama, both ancient and modern, including a course on staging little theater plays. I had offered to take over the Troubadours, the college dramatic group. It meant a lot of hard extra work without pay, but it had its rewards.

Once I worked in Papa's drafting office. I wrestled with ashlar drawings as hard as Jacob wrestled with the angel, but unlike Jacob I received no blessing.

At one summer's end, we had accumulated $200. Dot asked her father, who was still playing the stock market on paper only, if he had any objection to telling us what to buy. He told her immediately, with the understanding that if he telephoned us to sell, to do so fast. It went up and up. When it had gone from three dollars a share to fourteen he said sell, and we sold. The next day it hit fifteen and I shook my head. The day after that the company went broke and off the board. We had a great winter.

Shortly thereafter we moved to a big house on the campus that had been a money-maker for the previous renter, a department head who had rented the five bedrooms upstairs to students. His family was growing so that the small child's bedroom out behind the kitchen would not accommodate a second child. I solved that by building an absolutely huge double-decker with four-by-four redwood posts and a frame that would support two full-size sets of springs and mattresses with a big, wide ladder an adult could work from. Parke liked to climb up to his aerie, and when in 1935 his baby sister Margaret Jean arrived, he couldn't wait to have her graduate from the cradle in our big bedroom to the bottom bed where he could look after her.

We had had for some time a nurse and all-round helper, and we had extra maids to clean and cook as needed. Black, of course. I knew nothing about blacks, who in those days preferred to be called colored or Negroes, anything but black. When I was growing up in Camden there was only one Negro in the whole town, a friendly old man, who lived by himself and was known as Nigger Bill. He called himself that. When he died at one of those impossible ages blacks sometimes attain, he made the front page of the *New York Times*. When we first moved to West Side Court I hired a white girl, who was a no-good flighty little slob. Charlie MacDowell told me for God's sake to get a "cullud" girl. I learned that in Virginia the Negro was quite content to accept his lot as servitor and was proud of being good at his trade. They lived in good, sometimes beautiful, houses all day, had their own little village on the edge of town, where they spent nights and Sundays. Their children went to a segregated school, but it had the same curriculum as the white school, and if a bright kid wanted to be a chemist, he was not held back. The Ku Klux Klan would not have lasted five minutes in that town. If the maid wished to take slices of the roast home, she didn't have to ask. Nor did she steal. If she got bad sick, our doctor took care of her. If she needed an operation, her employer paid for it by an unwritten law. It was about like slavery under an indulgent master, but if one of them left Lexington for Washington, she came back in a hurry. If a man or woman was witty, he was encouraged and much quoted. I couldn't believe my eyes when I saw a Cadillac pull up in front of the hotel on Main Street and when the black bell-boy came out for the bag, the driver threw an arm around his shoulder and greeted him like an old friend. I thought Negroes would be dirty, but our lovely old nurse Mary said she wouldn't think of coming to work without taking a bath first. When she pushed Parke in that baby carriage, you never saw a more prideful woman. Mary was a philosopher. I heard her telling Parke when he had been naughty, "Boy, the only way to do the right thing is to do the right thing." When Mary was too old, her daughter Janette took over. We'd have given anything to have her live with us in California. The girls corresponded with her. I took one of her letters and read it to a group of friends, asking them to guess at the age, background, and education of the writer. Most of them pegged her as a lady of breeding, probably elderly, a college graduate certainly. Mary and Janette were superior people and became part of our family. I paid them a dollar more a week than the prevailing wage, which made me in a few people's eyes a "nigger lover." When I sold the big house and went with the Navy and rented a place in Alexandria, there was no place for Peggy and her daughter, who had occupied the maid's apartment in our base-ment. I think Janette had married (she most certainly had not been fired); anyway, Peggy was the last. Somebody persuaded her to go to Washington. She had a day off and came to visit us, offering to work for us that day for free. I hired her to come but paid her a good wage. She hated Washington. She said the $25.00 a week didn't begin to let her live as well as did the $8.00 we paid her, with perquisites. And nobody had any fun or peace of mind. The blacks were organized and controlled her every move. She was taught to hate white people, all white people, and she didn't. She especially disliked what she called "irritation night." Her job was to spend an hour or two riding the streetcars or buses, taking a seat beside some white person and crowding him or making herself obnoxious in any way possible.

That big house at 7 University Place put us right in the middle of things. We had some very interesting students who lived upstairs and they are my friends today. Dorothy, who liked big families, enjoyed it more than I did. The two directly above our heads were a remarkable pair, both from families with great wealth. The American boy had his own airplane which he had to keep in a nearby city. His people owned an extensive ranch that produced oranges and fat cattle in that arable valley below Santa Barbara. The other boy came from South America. At Christmas, he would smuggle in machine guns which his mother might need to keep the peons in order. He was a tremendous athlete, boxed light-heavy and wres-tled the same weight and never lost a match, was soft spoken and handsome. He did one thing I used in *Geese in the Forum*. There was a fellow teacher in the English department who could not keep order. The students, usually polite, found that they could bully him and did so. The class waited for him ten minutes, and was storming out only to be met by my South American student at the door, who quietly ordered them back to their seats. They meekly obeyed. He made a small speech, saying that he found it hard to hear what Mr. Blank was trying to say there was always such an uproar. He thought

Professor Blank might have some interesting ideas and he wanted to hear them. Any student who caused the slightest disruption would now answer to him personally. They could go now. Thereafter, Professor Blank blossomed. He never understood it, but he became a teacher, enjoyed the class, and was enjoyed in turn.

In our back room were two brothers, football players from some western state. They were seldom in their rooms, but were nice, affable boys. Often I heard late at night a little *ping* from the direction of their room and never found out what it was. After they had graduated, another student explained. They wanted the window wide open at night, the shade not drawn. That caused a distant streetlight to shine in their eyes. So they took turns before they went to bed shooting it out. The repairmen never could find the faulty circuit, which cured itself. All the students went to Dot for motherly advice. Anything told her in confidence went no further.

A student by the name of Frank, a basketball star, blew his top the day after finals. The coach made him turn in at nine o'clock because of the big game coming up, so he couldn't take the beautiful date he had invited from a nearby woman's college to the dance. A fraternity brother took his place and the next day Frank was livid. I asked him if the fraternity brother had double-crossed him.

"No," Frank blurted out, "it's my goddamn father! Ever since my mother died, he's been stealing my dates. The minute my back is turned he'll cut in and tell them, 'Honey, why don't you come up to New York with me and I'll show you a really good time. Frank's a nice boy, but you're too sophisticated to be playing around with children!' And they take off with that old gray-headed distinguished-looking bastard every time!" Maybe the coach conspired with his father. Frank was so angry he won the game single-handed.

None of the students were really mean, but some of them discovered that Parke at the age of five could be a pest. So, without my knowledge, they teased him unmercifully, holding him over a tubful of water with his clothes on, jackknifing him in a wastebasket and putting him on the mantelpiece, or putting him out on the tin porch roof and locking their windows so he couldn't get back in readily. Students became his enemies. He never complained to me about it; he dealt with it in his own way. A most innocuous, old-maidish, perennial student named Joe Magee, an institution known to one and all, felt his wrath. Parke composed his first jingle about him at age five.

> Joe Magee,
> Where is he? There he is—
> Joe Magee.

More than a decade later I met Joe in New York and invited him to my hotel for lunch. Parke, then a student at Yale, came down to join us. When he excused himself to go to the men's room, Joe turned to me with amazement, saying, "Why, Larry; he's *charming*; he's going to be *all right*!"

"What made you think he wouldn't be?"

"Well, every morning on my way to class, he'd be lying in wait for me behind a bush to stone me. And believe me, that little kid had an arm. And he'd say, 'My father will flunk you, you son-of-a-bitch!'"

Other memorable students were George Foster, who became in a way my protégé; Rawak, a handsome, black-haired student from New York, who loved our children—all children—so much that he took Parke with him on the train to New York when our car was over-crowded with suitcases; Duncan Groner, the son of Judge Groner in Washington, an irascible big hulk, formidable for his biting tongue, but so big-hearted that he secretly put several indigent fraternity brothers through college. His father offered him $500 if he could explain within $500 how he had spent the previous year's allowance. He worked at it all day and failed.

As for students in my classes. I have continued to meet them and follow their often-distinguished careers. Lewis Powell of the Supreme Court, the quiet, perfect student; Tom Sugure, the novelist, who always explained when he wrote too wildly that he had been drunk at the time; Art Buck, the economist and son of an economist, who would drive eighty miles to have lunch with me and give me his views of the world.

There were the Rouse brothers and the McMurran brothers, seven in all. I was visiting at their house in Newport News with the oldest, my friend Lewis. Their father had been a distinguished lawyer, a power at the college before he died. Their remarkable mother was never upset. A younger son walked in. She thought he was at Washington and Lee. "I've just been kicked out of college," he said. "Oh," said Mrs. McMurran. "I think you'll find something to eat in the kitchen," and she went back to her book. Lewis, with one of the finest minds I have ever seen in operation, did everything backward. When he was in the liberal arts school, he studied the law books. When he was in the law school, he usually had a Chaucer book hidden inside the law tome. The two of us discovered that the university owned a deserted factory in the lower part of the main street. We played off one student organization against another for the honor of donating money, gutted the building, brought in seats, designed graceful drapes for the windows, and built a stage with an opening above from which we could fly painted backdrops up and down, using nail kegs filled with sand counterbalanced by pulleys on the sides. We had a catwalk to hold lights, dimmed by a rheostat. To enhance the beauty of the entrance door Lewis suggested that we visit the University of Virginia. We were allowed to search the files until Lewis found a design for a doorway that Jefferson had sketched but not used for Monticello, so he copied that. We thanked the organizations that had given us the money to make the little theater possible, but I don't recall that anybody ever thanked either of us. All it did was get me in more trouble.

Because it was hard to import actresses or to find them in town, I had ventured to write a play or two for the Troubadours with a largely male cast. Some of the townspeople found them dirty, though they were not. So whatever we put on after that the ignorant bluenoses usually credited me with the authorship, and found them all dirty. I got so sick of it I went to the president and said I would do no more plays unless he assigned a faculty committee to declare them decent or indecent. He did so, picking all good men and true. It so happened that after I had published *On Borrowed Time*, the Troubadours were all keen on doing Noel Coward's *Private Lives*. I believe this occurred after McMurran had departed from college, but since it is the final thing I associate with the Troubadour Theater, I'll mention it now. I wrote to Bernice Baumgarten, my New York agent, knowing that they handled Noel Coward, and back came the original script, one that had to be toned down before it could be put on Broadway. I presented it to my committee without comment. Put on their mettle, they voted to a man to present it without changing a word. At that point I didn't give a damn what the small clique of pious objectors thought. We had good actors, and the students loved it. So evidently did the townspeople, but to make sure, I arranged to have my small son Parke sitting in the front row beside Fitz Flournoy, a Rhodes Scholar and a full professor in the English Department, a man whose ancestors were sacrosanct in Lexington. His mother ran the UDC. He was a burly man with a ready laugh that made the welkin ring. Parke laughed at *him*, and the combination of the hearty guffaw and the childish treble was so compelling that the audience roared at every off-color joke. So a play too dirty for Broadway was well received in staid and proper Lexington, Virginia.

A final word or two about Lewis McMurran: people in Lexington sometimes asked me what I ever saw in that screwball. Since I was rude to jerks in those days, I usually answered, "His mind, which is so much better than yours."

His subsequent career has proved me right. He started off by marrying a delightful lady from Prince Edward Island, Canada, formerly Edith Margaret Lea. He decided that he must make money so that he could devote himself to politics, for he loved his native city of Newport News and his state, Virginia. In this, too, he was original: today politicians seek public office to steal out of the till; Lewis, steeped in the historic 18th century tradition that a gentleman served his country, made money by reorganizing a public transit system, founding a couple of banks, and making smart investments, and did it honestly, for, as George Bernard Shaw said, the competition was so stupid that a bright man didn't have time to employ the intricate schemes of dishonesty, and Lewis was in a hurry. An abbreviated list of the chairmanships of important committees in the Virginia House of Delegates at Richmond, where Lewis served for thirty consecutive years representing Newport News, would literally take pages. Someone remarked that if he had held the office for six more years he would have moved the capital to Newport News. He has long been one of the best-informed men in Virginia about her historical greatness. When I knew him as a student, he astounded me by his wide knowledge of both English and early American history.

When he decided in the 1950s to build a house, he knew where the beautiful mantels and woodwork of Tazewell Hall, home of Sir John Randolph of Williamsburg, had been stored when the house was demolished. He bought them and rebuilt the house on the banks of the James River, marrying the splendors of the past with the comforts and conveniences of the present. There he entertained the queen twice (1953 and 1976) and the duke once.

What really interests me about Lewis is his instinctive courtesy and his ability to shut out everything else when concentrating on a problem. In regard to the first, while at Washington and Lee some of his friends thought it would be funny to hire a whore to visit his quarters, while they watched the encounter from an adjacent house. He spoiled their fun without knowing he was doing so. He treated his guest like a lady and served her tea.

I was at W&L from 1926 to 1943 and though I can remember some of my students' handwriting, I can seldom recall whether they arrived early or late. They all seem to have been there as long as I was. Unless I have seen them recently I visualize them as the boys they were then. It seems strange that I have outlived so many. Like the handsome youngster that wrote like an angel and kept me, and all that knew him, enlivened by his wit. He could get away with anything, he appeared so cherubic. In the hospital for some minor complaint, he kept his nurse never knowing what he meant. Using the royalty plural that nurses affect, she inquired , "And how are our bowels today?"

He beamed upon her. "Mine are just fine. How are yours, ma'am?"

He appeared to be truly concerned. There was no hint of ridicule in that winsome face.

"OK, I guess."

"Gooood."

He appeared not to have a care in the world. He made almost perfect grades with ease. There was no more popular kid on campus. Yet one morning, shortly after finals, his distraught parents visited me. Their son had written that I was one of his favorite professors. Did I have any idea why he had committed suicide?

Another boy I regarded with affection died on a beachhead in Italy. More than one succumbed to cancer. I have been fortunate indeed to know so many fine people. I am convinced that the world is full of them. We should not despair.

22

I had been an assistant professor for a long time, knowing that I would neither be made an associate professor nor get an increase in salary until I earned the Ph.D. Though it was taken for granted that I would do so, I was dragging my feet and both Dot and I knew it. She never reproved me.

The real reason was that I secretly despised the Ph.D. I had seen it happen over and over again: once a teacher had achieved the doctorate, his interest, even in his principal subject, waned, and he became satisfied to give the same lecture year after year. Instead of the Ph.D. opening up research, he let it close the door. He had done it; he had achieved tenure, and he ossified. This did not apply to men with inquiring minds, possibly one third of any faculty. In the end, such fellows gravitated to the big centers of learning with their magnificent libraries and the rest went into semi-retirement. Their thesis had been duly printed at their expense and filed away (two copies) never to be heard of again. Now they lived in the past. If a department head were to suggest that every faculty member submit one new original research paper a year to be given to the library, the professors would rise one by one and trot out their favorite speech: *Was this not setting a dangerous precedent?* That old chestnut could always be relied on to preserve the no-sweat status quo.

The president, always a cypher scholastically, would go along. He didn't like men with a lean and hungry look. They thought too much. Such men were dangerous. (Must I tell you who said that?)

So if I scorned the Ph.D. and didn't want to join the musty fraternity, I had to take the greater gamble and become a writer. I had the theme for a novel. Ever since I had heard Dr. Eaton of Syracuse relate in our Chaucer class the tale of Death held captive in a tree, it had churned in my mind. Two things sparked the story for me. The first was the wild imagination of my son Parke. A most unusual five-year-old boy, he easily confused present fact with ancient fantasy, religious or otherwise, and talked aloud to God and Casey Jones in his play, or told me of a mythical king of Massonia he had invented who wore his crown upon his seat. I jotted down all such outpourings. From his earliest days, he read a hundred books to the three or four that satisfied the average child. Dorothy encouraged him; bought books that stretched his mind and explained them. I'll never forget his dear old Sunday School teacher, who called me up fearful that something was wrong with him. She asked for the story of the creation and instead of Adam and Eve Parke related the nebular hypothesis, "all about cloud formations," she told me. I soothed her and promised to give him a better grounding in the Garden of Eden.

The second thing that influenced me was the yearning that Dot's old Grandpa McKelvey had to become a great grandfather. Parke was such a lively little kid it was a pity that Grandpa had died before Parke was born. Old David McKelvey had taken me to the courthouse and introduced me to his cronies as his granddaughter's husband. Hoping to shame me into having children, he would add: "But he's no good; they've been married over a year and nary a chick nor a child." I decided to bring those two together in my story, and the thing began to take shape.

I discovered that writing was damned hard work. I threw away much more than I kept. I had these two characters ready made, but even they had to be changed as the story progressed. Writing bullies you. It takes over your mind. I was too conscientious to slight my classes or let themes pile up, and the Troubadour plays took a lot of time. I went to parties but no longer drank excessively, for I didn't want a hangover on the weekend. I had no study, but we had a wide hallway, and like Papa and his roll-top desk, I put my little desk under the stairs, oblivious to the traffic up and down. If I was going good, Parke could climb up my back and I was barely conscious of it. Working so by fits and starts, I worked on that book for three years at least before I had a few uninterrupted months and a whole empty house to myself.

It was in the summer of 1936 at Camden. The house next door where our old neighbors the Suberts lived would not be rented again until fall. My mother told me I could have the key and she would see that nobody disturbed me. I set my typewriter up on the sturdy old dining room table, and I could strew notes and papers all over the place and leave them there and no one would touch them. That's where I really wrote that book. My sisters were probably at camp, or I might have discussed the book with Elsie, for strangely enough as I thought then, she was the most interested in what I was doing. I have never let anyone, not even Dot, know what I was writing unless it was a screenplay, which is a composite effort. But I must have let Elsie know by letter that I was considering as a character in my novel a neighbor woman who used to amuse our whole family. From that time on Elsie would send me funny bits that she had remembered or quaint phrases, and they were all delightful. She had a great ear, I discovered. One story she mailed me was about this neighbor's irritation with a guest who moved in with her daughter and stayed a month, never lifting a finger to help. The neighbor woman had expostulated to Elsie: "And there she sat, like Mrs. Peacock in the parlor while I washed and scrubbed and cooked. Never even cleaned her own room. I ran a broom under her bed and you should see the dust kittens that came rolling out! And her daughter was just as bad. I said to her, "Claribel, don't you even wash your face? My mother would have put the dingbats to me if I came to the breakfast table with the sleepy seeds still in my eyes."

I don't know if I used that in my book, and I'm certainly not going to reread it to find out, but I know that there was stuff she gave me which I worked in. I think I had the grace to thank her.

As soon as I had finished it, I spent two tormented days trying to find a title. While searching the *Rubaiyat*, "On Borrowed Time" popped into my head, and I started mailing it to publishing companies, twelve in all. Each in turn promptly sent it back with no comments. I didn't think it could be that bad, so I drove over to Boonville to visit Walter Edmonds. A successful novelist—*Rome Haul, Erie Water, Drums Along the Mohawk*—he had played with me on his parent's farm along the Black River when we were both small boys. I recall that he took me into his father's bedroom. His father was a successful New York lawyer, and we counted 22 pairs of what appeared to be shiny new shoes. Neither of us could figure how anybody could use that many shoes. My Uncle Nelson managed their estate. Walter wrote a beautiful story for the Curtis Publishing Company about the two of them finding a newborn calf. Uncle Nelson Charter married my father's only sister, and when she died he lived with us in Camden. He let me shave him with a straight edge before I reached my teens. He would fall asleep and wake up when I nicked him. He taught me to play checkers. If I could get a checker in the king row, I won.

I asked Walter how to get a novel published. He wrote out an address. "Send it to her. She's the best in the business." So I sent it to Bernice Baumgarten of the Brandt & Brandt Agency in New York. There has never been such agent anbefore or since she retired. She took it straight to Alfred Knopf and put it in his hands. Inside of a week, I received a check.

We were never poor again.

23

In 1937 no writer could have asked for a more intelligent publisher than Alfred Knopf, and such a brilliant, honest, hard-working agent as Bernice Baumgarten. She worked miracles for me and never gave me a piece of bad advice. A writer friend of mine who knows which plumbing corporation or oil company today owns the fine old publishing concerns who developed the writers of the 30s and 40s can tell you a tale that would sicken you. I don't mean that every man in a good publishing organization was reliable. Publicity men were as phony then as now. One dreamed up the story that I had written *On Borrowed Time* in a single month. The truth is that I was so tired of thinking about that story I soon got fed up with the hoopla. I reread it only once in 1938 and did not look at it again for forty years. When I was living in Washington, D.C., in 1943, a Navy friend called me from New York. He was reading OBT and after saying it wasn't bad, he said something to this effect: "Now on page 34 that's fine, but on page 128, why did you say so-and-so?"

"I haven't the slightest idea."

"You wrote it."

"Yes, but I'm not a Gila monster."

"What's a Gila monster got to do with it?"

"They regurgitate."

After all my disappointments about the book, the letter I received from Bernice on April 2, 1937, which began "Knopf, to whom I submitted *On Borrowed Time*, found the book charming and would like to take it on the following terms...," was the most exciting one I ever received. Everything thereafter was an anti-climax.

From the hundreds of letters I received, the country as a whole approved of it; the book reviews were more than favorable. A great many people, including my wife, didn't like fantasy, but even some of them found redeeming features.

The most fun was in Lexington. Everybody wanted a copy of the book. My ten free copies were gone the first day, and I spent considerable money buying a new supply and then another and another.

I found it hard to keep my counsel because Lexington people were sure that aside from the grandfather and the boy they saw some friends of theirs drawn to the life, which was absolutely untrue. One of those whom I had supposedly pilloried was a little spitfire I greatly admired. She faced me down, saying, "Mr. Watkin, somebody said that you had put me in your book."

I told her most truthfully, "Mrs. Blank, I wouldn't have dared."

"Huh!" she said. "That's what I told them."

It is almost impossible for a writer to present a well-known character in the flesh. He might do so in a short story, but not in a novel. He could even start out to do it, but the requirements of the plot would soon change him. Half the people in novels are shadowy but distorted images of actual persons, but placed in their new positions with different wives, different children, different jobs, different beliefs to act out different situations, they soon become so imaginary that Thomas Wolfe was not exaggerating when he said that to create a single character a writer might have to turn over half the people in a town.

That first novel saved me from ever again giving a thought to the doctorate. It has proved to be worth two PhDs. It gave me my promotion to the associate professorship I had so long deserved; it acted as the best possible letter of introduction I needed for other forms of writing; and it made me a great deal of money.

Though it was accepted in early spring of 1937, it did not reach the bookstores until late summer. In my ignorance I nearly broke Bernice Baumgarten's heart. I assumed that I would have no further use for her services until I had written another book and wrote her a letter to that effect, not cancelling our contract for that book, but telling her that if and when I wrote anything else, we would start all over again. I was too dumb to realize that she would be selling new rights to this book again and again, and that the secondary rights would make the income from the sale of the novel seem paltry. They resold that book in some form or another for the next 43 years. There was the German, the Italian, and the Swedish version, and the one brought out by Lovat-Dixon in England. When the first two printings by Knopf were exhausted, the Doubleday reprint took over, then the Sundial and Albatross and Pocket books. Over the years Knopf did six reprints in all. As Bernice pointed out, its sales far exceeded that of the usual first novel, but even so the American Booksellers Association thought the book had not been promoted too vigorously. I was invited to a banquet in New York and presented with a bronze paperweight in the form of a book that was inscribed with the 1937 National Book Award for Booksellers Find. It is not only a handsome trinket but also a useful one; it is so heavy considering its small size.

One of the early excitements was an offer from Hollywood to write a screenplay for the projected film *The Wizard of Oz*. I would have been paid fifteen hundred dollars a week for 12 or 15 weeks, and was sorely tempted, but heeded Dot's counsel not to try screenwriting for a while yet. But it was always in the back of my mind. She did not discourage a brief visit to Detroit to make a speech and sign books afterward for a book fair put on by the Hudson Department Store. That turned out to be amusing. Dot and I were lunching at a nearby restaurant before the afternoon shindig. I noticed a heavily built man at a nearby table with a nearly untouched plate of food, nervously knocking off one brandy after another in little snifter glasses. I said to Dot, "I'll bet you that's another victim like me, worrying about what he's going to say at the book fair."

"Don't *you* know?" she asked me.

"In a general way, but I didn't write out anything to memorize. I thought it would sound contrived."

"Oh, you'll be fine," she said with wifely pride. "I don't know how you do it."

"Pride goeth before a fall, and a haughty spirit before a destruction."

Before she could stop me, I went over to his table and said, "You look to me like a man who's going to talk about a book at a book fair."

"How did you guess?"

I pointed to his empty glass, then introduced myself. He did the same and asked if I had brought my wife along for moral support. I said yes and took him over to meet Dot. We had a nice chat, swapped backgrounds, then signed our respective novels and swapped them. He wrote "Cordially, Charles Givens," in a swirling but firm hand, and I was glad to see that the brandy had not got to him.

He lived in and wrote about his hometown of Tirus, Tennessee, which is next door to Dayton. The stories he wrote at the famous monkey trial brought him national recognition as a journalist, but this was his first attempt at fiction. He called it *All Cats Are Gray*. He explained the brandy. He was timid about speech making but more concerned that some of his newspaper buddies on the Detroit paper would attend the speaking and he'd never hear the last of it. Having relieved his mind to Dot and me and been reassured, he had drunk no more brandy, and we walked in together, Dot to take a seat in the audience, Givens and I to take one of the folding wooden funeral chairs at the very back edge of the four-foot-high rostrum that held a speaker's stand up front, facing a large audience for such an occasion. I'll guess that there were 1200 women and right in the middle of them a dozen men, the only ones in evidence. I was too concerned with what I was about to say to know who the other speakers were, though I think there were five of us, one a New York City critic. I was the third speaker and got off to a good start by addressing myself entirely to the tiny, disconsolate group of men whose wives made them embrace culture on this beautiful autumn afternoon instead of going to the football game which was even now being played across town. Everybody started laughing and I began laughing, too. Soon I was enjoying myself, and made a good speech.

Givens was next. I figured that some of his buddies were in that group of men and that I had given him a way to attack them and turn the tables if he explained why they had really attended. But he didn't explain that or anything else. The brandy had taken over and he was out on his feet. Leaning against the speaker's stand, he looked at the audience and murmured not more than 10 completely unintelligible sentences, like "Judge judge blub blub blah blah blee." At first the ladies looked frightened, but as he continued to talk they started laughing. Then they stopped, concerned, for it was plain that he was in deadly earnest and trying to say words. He ended with something that he thought was thank you, walked stiffly back to his chair, turned around so that he knew he would sit in it, and dropped in a sitting position. When he hit the chair with his full weight, the chair broke into a dozen pieces and he fell backward full length upon the floor below. He was out cold. It appeared that he had hit the back of his head against the floor hard enough to knock out any man. That was the end of the meeting. Everybody tried to crowd around and see if he was dead. Store executives got there in a hurry, then a doctor, who found that he was breathing and that his heart was beating. No blood showed at the back of his head. The doctor was puzzled. I told him in a low voice about the brandy, which cleared up the mystery. He said a word or two to the store men, who were somewhat hopeful now that the suit he might bring against the store would not be in the millions. The final speaker or speakers said that they thought further lecturing might be omitted. The master of ceremonies herded all writers to their tables, urging the crowd to take this opportunity to purchase books, which the authors would gladly sign. A few heeded his words, but I don't recall getting writer's cramp that day. Evidently Mr. Givens came to his senses and did not sue, though I feared that I might have to give a deposition.

At the time, it was laughable, but I have often thought since it happened that a public humiliation of that sort might ruin a man. Every so often I take out Mr. Givens' book, so cordially inscribed, intending to read it, then return it to the shelf that holds the books signed by my writer friends. Every year the collection shrinks as other dear friends borrow a copy or two, faithfully promising to return them, but of course they never do.

By far the biggest resale of all was the decision of Jock Whitney, who had backed other plays, to listen to his secretary, a young lady who kept insisting that *On Borrowed Time* should be made into a play for the New York stage. Because of my extensive knowledge of plays, I was given first crack at it late in 1937, but as I said I was already tired of working on it, and approached the project with no enthusiasm. I did a lousy quick synopsis, but I was only going through the motions and was secretly ashamed of presenting such a botched-up job. Bernice tactfully suggested that Mr. Whitney had friends in the theater who were hungrier. The friend was Josh Logan, and *his* friend was Paul Osborn, a dramatist whose first play, *The Vinegar Tree*, had been a success. But that was in 1930. He didn't have another until 1938 when *On Borrowed Time* hit the Longacre Theater on February 3. This is by his own admission, given in an interview with Michiko Kakutani and published in the *New York Times* on April 14, 1980. His follow-up to *On Borrowed Time* was an original, *Mornings at Seven*, in 1939, which got a very poor reception then, but revived in 1980 is a fine success. Asked why his play has succeeded now but failed in 1939, he said: "...in part, in the growing compassion on the part of audiences today for the problems of the aged...production brought out a lot of human qualities that weren't stressed before—before, it was played almost all for laughs."

I did not attend the opening of the play, but I had heard that Paul Osborn was having trouble with writing it. The W&L student I mentioned previously, Joe Magee, was in New York City in 1937–38 working for the William Morris Agency, which was heavily theatrical, and Joe, with his nose for gossip, wrote me letters saying that Osborn's friends told him that if he followed the book so slavishly, he would get small credit as a playwright, and that he tried to change it but couldn't. I was in New York when the grand old actor Bennet was rehearsing the part of Gramp. Bernice took me to the theater where the cast was working. I sat with Osborn alone in the middle of the otherwise empty orchestra circle, watching the poor fellow struggling to remember any of his lines, but he couldn't. Osborn remarked that I was witnessing the end of a distinguished career, and that's all I remember. He was definitely unfriendly, which saddened me, for I was prepared to like him. He made it even more plain after the play was a hit, for when I finally did get around to

see it and read in the program a squib that I had written for it as
requested, I found it innocuous. Not so Mr. Osborn's contribution.
He wrote a tidy little essay comparing the art of the novelist and
that of the dramatist. The dramatist, he wrote, might be compared
to the electrician; the novelist to a plumber. Since he was discussing
On Borrowed Time, I had to infer that he thought of himself as an
electrician, me as a plumber. I was sure of it when I read later that
he had received a master's degree in English from the University of
Michigan and had taught there for two years, felt suffocated, and
entertained the thought of becoming an electrical engineer before
he took up playwriting. A former student of mine at Washington
and Lee wrote me about that statement of Osborn's in the program.
He thought him a horse's ass for insulting me so gratuitously. The
student could not know that I had always admired plumbers as
better men than writers, even more than I admired electricians.

When we were living in a very swanky neighborhood in Newport
Beach, California, I was nailing up a big strip of plywood over
a workbench in my garage as a place to hang my carpenter's tools. The
long nail went through the thin plywood and plaster and punctured
a water pipe. I managed to find the cut-off for the water into the
house and immediately called our plumber. It was late afternoon on
Christmas Eve, and when he understood who was calling, responded
joyfully, "Murry Christmas, Mr. Watkin...Murry Christmas!" I was
still calling drunken plumbers when my daughter and her husband
arrived for the holiday. Fortunately, we had bottled water for drinking, but next morning, Christmas day, my son-inlaw was violently ill
and retching. He attributed it to some clams he had eaten the night
before and to which he later discovered he was allergic. After every
spell of sickness I had to bring in a pail of water from the pool to
flush the toilet. In between times I called plumbers. Most of them
thought it was funny and promised to drink a toast to me, though
one wife snatched the phone from her jovial husband's hand and
asked me who I thought I was. If I worked as hard as that poor man
did, I would know better than to bribe him with triple overtime on
the one day in the year... She choked and slammed down the receiver.

Along came my next-door neighbor, glass in hand. He laughed like
hell, hurried home again, and reappeared with a plumbing kit. Didn't
I know that before he became an inventor he had been a plumber? He
repaired that pipe in a hurry and came in to drink with us.

So Mr. Osborn paid me a high compliment. But over the years
I got a trifle tired of hearing about Paul Osborn's beautiful legend
On Borrowed Time.

I was much more miffed by an interview with Josh Logan, written by Susan Berman, which appeared in the Sunday supplement of the San Francisco *Examiner & Chronicle* on July 18, 1976. It begins:

> Josh Logan is sitting over lunch, remembering his first big hit, *On Borrowed Time*, and the thing you notice about him is his forehead. It's as if the lines to the play are etched there and as he talks in his lyrical way, those intense demarcations over his eyebrows are never still.

She stops to explain that the occasion for the interview is the publication of Mr. Logan's biography. To the musical accompaniment of those lyrical lines in his brow he goes on: Yes, *On Borrowed Time* was his favorite, for it was his first big hit. He gives a quick outline of the script that was stuck under the door of his mother's 114th Street apartment. Then he breaks out: "Oh, I remember agonizing over that play. It was just wonderful. For four months, day and night, we tried to solve the problem of the ending."

Finally, *we* did it. Evidently nobody had told him that there had been a novel written which would have saved him the hundreds of precious man-hours wasted by that gigantic intelligence over any trifling change in the basic story. At least everybody else who compared the two works thought so, including Jock Whitney, who wrote me a nice letter, certain that I would be pleased to find my story intact. Never once does Logan mention Paul Osborn in this interview. It was not Paul Osborn's beautiful legend after all. *On Borrowed Time* was Josh Logan's beautiful legend. And so, it seems, were all the other wonderful, wonderful stories that he had tackled. He had to stop with *Picnic*, for the amount of material he had dictated had been enormous. At the end of the interview he tells Susan Berman that he hopes sometime, somehow to find the energy to dictate volume two of his life and works. The interviewer, limp with hero-worship, is sure that he will. She concludes:

> At sixty-seven Josh Logan is writing and producing. Ideas still spew forth with boundless energy and we all wait with baited breath to see what Josh Logan, Act III, will bring.

I am sure that *baited breath* can only be explained by those touching little advertising stories *spewed* forth on television in which a girl with halitosis hooks a beautiful man after using a mouthwash or a "breath deodorant." If Berman had only read the Bible and noticed that Noah after sending out a dove found that the waters were abated from off the face of the earth, she might have puzzled it out that it didn't mean he was fishing.

24

I am not a methodical person, and find dates difficult. In our many moves I threw away junk I now wish I had kept. Luckily for me, my sister Glenevieve had an attic, a thing unknown in California, and she dug out most of the letters I had written my mother over the years. I seldom added the year, but the envelopes she kept them in supplied postmarks to orient me. Mother never kept one big diary, but she often recorded some special event in a tiny notebook. On August 31, 1926, just before my wedding, Mother visited Cousin Homer Stebbins overnight in Hastings-on-Hudson, New York, before meeting me in Grand Central Station next morning. She writes:

> He took me sightseeing atop a 5th Ave. bus until we reached Riverside Drive and Grant's tomb. The soft purple light coming in at the windows and beating on the bier with the garlands proclaiming him the dead hero was sweet and beautiful. Next, Macy's store proved attractive. We took a ride on the escalator, or moving stairway, which was novel to me. Dinner on the 8th floor balcony would have been lovely, had it not been for the girls smoking around me, and makes me ask what is becoming of our American homes.

She visited us again in May 1937 at Washington and Lee, a month after *On Borrowed Time* had been accepted by Knopf, but since it was not published until fall we had no idea that it would make a big stir. She loved the dogwood and the red bud and the mountain azalea. We had our first nice car, a Buick. I took Mrs. Shannon and Sally Jackson's mother along when we lunched at Forest Tavern. Mother liked *Natural Bridge* but was more enthralled with the Hogarth prints at the tavern. Returning by train, she wrote a verse when the ride became monotonous. She called it an attempt at rhyming:

> Life is good. Would you enjoy it?
> Make the most of every hour;
> Treasure every fleeting moment;
> Keep your mind from going sour.
>
> Life is sweet if you so will it.
> Want to make the hours run?

Face each morn with love and courage
Close each day with work well done.

Life is yours. It is your treasure.
Lift your eyes to greet the sun.
Could the Lord have given you better?
You're alive. And spring has come!

Not bad for a sixty-six-year-old, self-educated woman. My friend, Charley McDowell, said that his elderly aunt belonged to a culture club—like my mother's Philomathic Club—but since she had not been to college and he had, she always expected him to write her papers for her. She made her contribution, however, presenting him with a lengthy list of big words, saying, "Charley, these are my words." She didn't care what he said as long as he worked those words in. My mother never asked for help. She wrote her own.

At least she lived to see her grandchildren. Dorothy's people did not. Her grandfather and grandmother had died before Parke was born and though Dorothy's mother saw Parke, she wanted to have a granddaughter. She died of cancer on January 21, 1935, just before Margaret Jean Watkin, a beautiful little baby, was born on January 26, 1935. Dorothy could not even go to her mother's funeral.

Dorothy had no better luck with her much-adored father. When we visited him later that summer we tried to get him to come visit and eventually live with us after his retirement from the vice-presidency of Grenci and Ellis, which he was considering, now that he was over 65. He was noncommittal, though as loving as ever. During the following summer he and his son Roger worked together like beavers to remake the big Parke house into three apartments, Papa taking the top one for himself and renting the other two. After Roger had to go back to teaching in the fall, Mr. Parke carried on the work of repainting alone. He climbed out on a plank he secured from inside, almost fell, and in catching himself wrenched his back so that he had to wear a brace. Whether Roger knew it or not and had told Dot, I did not know. Papa had remarried a quite unattractive younger woman, Ethel Louise Tuffer, who knew a sex-starved elderly man when she saw one, and had set out to get her hands on his money. In this she had already succeeded for the most part. When we visited Papa we found him in bed, dangerously ill from heart trouble and under a doctor's care. He never even referred to his mistress-wife, but Dorothy and I and Roger confronted her in private, letting her know what we thought of her. Her answer was invariably to fall on her knees beside the chair and pray, which did not interrupt our side of the conversation, though it kept her from answering. Roger had worked

long and hard to make the apartments possible; she had tried from
the first to freeze him out of his home, and succeeded, but her tactics
didn't work on us, who treated her with scorn enough to dispose of
a less-hardened bitch. None of this took place in front of Dorothy's
father, who was pathetically glad to see us. He even cracked little
jokes. The doctor prescribed mild doses of whiskey as a stimulant.
I knew so little about it that the liquor storekeeper sold me Three
Feathers as the best brand. Papa enjoyed this medication so greatly
that he said to me with a chuckle: "It's just as well I never tasted this
stuff before. I like it so much I'm sure I could never have left it alone."

"I'm lucky," I told him. "I don't. I drank that raw moonshine
during Prohibition, but I drink practically nothing now. When I do
I can't work." I told him about my soda and iced tea.

"Good," he said. He put his big warm hand over mine. "Some day
you'll find the boss' daughter all hot and ready."

He used the expression that meant if I kept plugging away, I would
some day be successful, but it sounded so strange coming from him
that he laughed at the startled expression on my face. That's the way
I remember him, for he died February 26, 1937. He left the house
to Roger and Dorothy, which they sold for enough money to cover
the funeral expenses and a headstone. His funeral was at Mount
Vernon, but he was buried beside Dot's mother in the cemetery at
Chatham. I suggested to Dot and Roger that they engrave on his
headstone these words from Swinburne:

> He grew straight in the strength of his spirit. And he lived out
> his life as the light.

Ethel Louise Tuffer did not accompany us to Chatham but
remained in the apartment. Roger let her understand that she was
to leave within a reasonable time and so she did. One morning
when none of us was in the city, a Bekins truck backed up to the
house almost at daybreak and carried out anything of any possible
value. She had rifled his papers and trunks and took anything she
thought she might sell, furniture, bric-a-brac, cutlery, china, linens,
paintings. There wasn't too much, but she left nothing, not even
a forwarding address, and was never heard from again.

Shortly after her mother's death, Papa had given Dot a beautiful
little table that had come from England and all of Grandma's jewelry,
and a tiny note, which she had never shown me. On the outside of it
was written in her father's meticulous hand:

> Found in mother's (grandma's) desk Feb. 12, 1935 and
> opened by Jesse B. Parke in top floor front room, to which

it had been removed after mother's death. Daisy never went through this desk.

It was a pathetic little hand-written will, and among other things it mentions Grandpa's pipe and tobacco, which became a moving sequence in *On Borrowed Time*, but I had never seen the paper until 1980. Though Grandma McKelvey was in no way the Grandma of the play, it is an interesting coincidence.

Mount Vernon Sept. 25, 1913.

At my death

I want Dorothy to have all the furniture in my room but the bureau and bedstead which belong to Daisy. I want Daisy to have my jewelry box and all it contains, also all my clothing and wraps, to do as she pleases with, and I also wish her to have all the money that I have in my possession at the time of my death. This is my wish and I hope it will be carried out.

Harriet Maria McKelvey

Take good care of your father and see that he has his pipe and tobacco.

Mamma.

I don't know whether it was in 1937 or 1938 that Brandt and Brandt sold *On Borrowed Time* to the movies, but I think 1938. I was in the office of Harold Freedman Sr., associated with Brandt and Brandt, when he made the deal in a long-distance call to MGM in California. I have never failed to admire the way agents sell "properties." Plainly the caller on the other end of the line wanted it, but kept interposing objection after objection to get the price down. I could tell from what Freedman said that MGM had no child star for the part of Pud, to which Mr. Freedman answered, "Must I remind you that you have a certain child star named Shirley Temple?" He looked at me and winked, saying, "Mr. Watkin is here in the office and he just said, 'Over my dead body.'" I don't quite know how he made the sale, but he did, and it was hefty enough so that after the commission and Mr. Osborn's 50% had been deducted, there was still a big chunk of money for me.

In 1938, too, Bernice sold the book for a one-shot forty-thousand-word serialization to the *Ladies Home Journal*. They paid well, too, but Knopf got half of that, Osborn nothing since the play was not involved. As a matter of fact, Bernice got me such a remarkably fine contract that an agreement like it is almost unheard of

today. Usually the dramatist gets sixty percent, the novelist forty.
Residuals were almost unknown then, but she covered those and all
other particulars, too.

It all brought in a great deal of money, and though Dorothy and
I tried not to show that it made any difference to us, the public
prints played up the success story. Nothing had changed between
my friends and me, but to the administration I had made the giant
leap from nobody-hood to star status. In the late spring of 1938
I received the long overdue promotion to associate professorship
without asking for it. When Dr. Shannon died suddenly of a heart
attack, I was called upon to take over his Shakespeare class, supposed to be a difficult assignment. Shakespeare held no terrors for
me. I had read every Shakespearean play and sonnet before I even
entered high school and had taken more courses in English drama,
to say nothing of Greek, Roman, and Continental plays, than any
other teacher in the college. It was because of *On Borrowed Time* that
such things about me were suddenly being discovered. I appreciated
the compliment but not the extra 52 exam papers I had to grade
before we could take off for Camden to visit my despairing mother,
who feared that the added encumbrances would keep us away altogether. What's more, I swore I would complete the rough draft of my
second novel and see that work was started on a house we planned
to build atop a six-acre lot I bought from the college. An old stone
hotel, Castle Hill, had once stood there.

Pen Clark, the architect, found that fire had not harmed the stone
blocks from the old hotel and used them for the foundation of the
8-foot-high cellar. He combed through the town for details that
would jibe with the design of the college. Built during deep depression, the contractor worked at a little above cost to keep his crew
together. Starting at the cellarage, we had a gigantic game room with
a big stone fireplace at one end, at the other a pool table; a separate
ping-pong room; a separate furnace room; and a two-room apartment for a maid with laundry tubs across the hallway. The first
floor had a big separate guest room and bath, a formal paneled
study with built-in bookcases, a gracious hallway with stairway
and wide entrance into the living room, formal fireplace at one end,
windows and a glass-paneled doorway to the big slate porch with its
two-story-high columns, a dining room, a butler's pantry where we
often had breakfast, and a fully equipped kitchen with steps down to
a brick walk alongside formal gardens, with a high brick wall on the
other side of the walk that connected the house and the garage. Even
the garage was beautiful with its cupola. The second floor had four

bedrooms, two on each side with baths between. A counterweighted staircase gave access to the attic with a proper floor and cedar walls with louvered windows at either end.

All construction was of oversized brick, a slate roof, and rock wool for insulation. Utilities were brought underground hundreds of yards up the hill, through almost solid rock, by using pneumatic drills. The view through the big columns looked across the east-west highway far below to the rear of the college, probably two miles distant as the crow flies. The several hundred yards of gravel road leading to the main highway and the circling in a loop to a not-too-impressive entrance door was an additional expense but not a great one.

I failed to mention my tiny study, which had a built-in desk; bookshelves along the sound-proofed wall; an opaque glass block on the other side, for I did not want to look at anything but that typewriter; a door into the dining room; and a door with a few steps down to a little patch of turf with a mimosa tree, where all my Kentucky friends went to pee.

No Kentuckian, however well educated, used an indoor toilet if there was any access to the great outdoors. I asked Jesse Stuart if this was generally true, and he told me this story.

During the war a friend asked him, "This man Hitler, causing all this trouble, why don't somebody shoot the son-of-a-bitch?"

"They can't get to him. He lives in a big castle high on a hill, and he's surrounded by guards."

"Hell," said the questioner, "why don't somebody hide in a bush and wait till he comes out to pee?"

I thought that uric acid would kill the mimosa, but it thrived.

I spent all the money I had and paid cash. The whole thing cost just under $30,000, including the cut-glass chandelier over the dining room table. It was the last one the furniture man in Lynchburg could get from Czechoslovakia. He had marked it down to $500.00, but when I started to walk out he offered it to me for fifty bucks. The house must be worth a quarter of a million now. In Beverly Hills today it would easily bring a million and a half, since there's plenty of room for tennis courts, pool, stables, or whatever. When it became obvious some time later that we were heading for California and would probably never again live in Virginia, I sold it to a doctor who had greatly overcharged me for two or three visits to see that our children were OK while Dot and I took a small trip out of town. I'm glad he did. Who but a doctor would have $20,000 to buy it?

Though the previous paragraph was added to round out the history of our house known as Castle Hill, it may have given the false impression that we built it on the spur of an ostentatious moment, never really thinking of it as a permanent residence. That indeed was not the case. We planned to live and die there. Dot had even considered the extra expense of a circular staircase, down which our daughters might walk when they were married and toss out their bouquets. She decided against it, for even at the bargain rates money was getting low. The room at the head of the stairs, the nursery, had its tenant ready, for on April 1, 1939, our second daughter, Anne Caroline, was born. We were all so sure that it would be a boy that we had only the one name ready: George Edward, after my father. But she fooled us, and I'm glad she did, for being nearer the age of Margaret Jean, the two girls would be more company for each other. The four bedrooms upstairs were all equally large with two windows in each for cross-ventilation and with big closets. We couldn't wait to see the beautiful new baby in a setting worthy of her, and both Parke and Margaret Jean deserved luxurious quarters. But though the workmen were doing their level best we had to find brief temporary quarters. Luckily we discovered a big brick house, where only one remarkable incident occurred, which I have seldom mentioned because nobody believes me.

The chairs in the dining room being more comfortable than those in the sitting room, Dot and I spent our evenings reading at the big table. The overhead light from the chandelier accommodated us both. We had not stirred or uttered a sound when I was conscious of Dot staring at me. Without any noticeable turning of her head her eyes rolled toward the direction of the big wooden double doors that separated the dining room from the kitchen. They were closed now and fitted loosely together at the bottom. They ran in no groove, which would have caused a stumbling obstruction. Dot wanted me to see the tiny mouse squeezing between the two doors. In a moment, another mouse, then another and another appeared from under the doors or through the same crevice until at least half a dozen mice occupied the six-by-six-foot space of smooth hardwood floor between us and the double doors. They were not searching for anything such as crumbs, nor did they show any curiosity about us. At no time did they come near our feet. We scarcely breathed. They gave the tiniest squeaks, as they appeared to be holding a confer-ence. Then they began to dance. I mean it; they really danced, not touching each other but passing close as in a ballet and one or two of them scuttled around on their hind legs only, like diminutive birds. That's the hard part to believe, but it's true. Neither of us had had a drink. That's what they did and we saw it, and I never watched anything more graceful. I don't know how long it went on, but suddenly an outside noise scared them and they were gone.

After that I joined Dot and Mrs. Parke. I couldn't kill one. In another house we owned later Maggie came rushing in to her mother and said, "Mama, there's a mouse in my waste basket." So Dot went in and caught him with her bare hands and put him outdoors, warning him gently not to be so foolhardy.

As I grew older, I often kicked myself that I had made a bargain with Dot to have only three children. She would have liked eight. I don't think any other couple ever had three such perfect children: Parke with his quick mind always tipping something over to satisfy his curiosity; Margaret Jean, born good and concerned about others; Anne quietly independent, a natural athlete and beautiful like her sister. I told Dot I didn't object to her having Anne if she promised I'd never have to give her a bottle or change her diaper. She promised, but when we moved into the new house, I was a light sleeper and at six I heard Anne talking to herself. She never cried, but when that beautiful child gave me a big smile, I not only made sure that she was dry, but also might want a bottle or at least a drink of water. Except for Dorothy, who knew instinctively how to bring up a husband, I'd have had that darling little baby in bed with me and spoiled her rotten. Dot let both husband and child think they were getting their way, but she knew when to clamp down on—or rather divert—the transgressor before any real harm could be done.

We all worked hard at Castle Hill. Dot planted the flowerbeds that had been designed by a landscape architect from Richmond; I made a vegetable garden on a plateau part way down the hill. I don't remember what vegetables I grew, but Dorothy, thirty years later, could name every shrub and bulb and how it was placed. No matter where we had lived, she remembered her gardens. They were living things to her. Sometimes before we went to sleep at night she would wonder out loud how a certain plant was doing, and how I could have forgotten it. "So nice and uncomplicated," she would say. "You gave it water and it gave you flowers."

25

My second novel, *Geese in the Forum*, took its title from a letter written by Elizabeth Barrett Browning:

> The curious thing in this world is not the stupidity but the upper-handism of the stupidity. The geese are in the capitol and the Romans in the farmyard, and it seems all quite natural that it should be so, both to geese and Romans.

Knopf brought it out in July of 1940, though I had finished it in late 1939, and it disappointed what audience I had created by *On Borrowed Time*, who expected more sweetness and light, not satire. I never worried about that. I was and still am proud of the way I ridiculed the self-seeking administration of the colleges, in which a president and a board of trustees, who cared not a fig for basic education or freedom of the intellect, tried to whip the faculty into line by withholding salary raises and promotions from everybody but yes-men. It was a critical success, but not a popular one. It received high praise for showing what went on behind the scenes in the colleges and showing that college teachers were human beings. What I did not realize then or indeed until some forty years later when I re-read the book was that the love scene was tenth rate and that the ending of the book was just plain awful. If only someone like Bernice Baumgarten had told me to cut out the whole silly romantic mess and make the plight of the professor even stronger, the book would have been immeasurably improved.

In a letter I wrote my mother in 1940, knowing that she must have highly disapproved of the book, I mentioned the wife of a neighbor who lived across the street from us in Camden, Floyd Fish, then a teacher at Virginia Polytechnic Institute:

> I got a letter the other day from the wife of Floyd Fish at Blacksburg about my last book. She said that a group of women in the VPI Woman's Club had got together and decided they'd write up a book from the faculty point of view, and that when my book came out, they said: 'There is the book we've been trying to write,' and that I stole their thunder and put an end to their project. They want me to come down and address them, and I may after I get this other thing off.

I got a review of *Geese* the other day in the AAUP magazine, an organization of associated professors. We have a chapter here. It tries to get a fair deal for the teacher. The review was by Burgess Johnson, who taught for years at Syracuse. He called it: "A significant contribution to the cause of academic freedom"which didn't make me feel bad at all.

In the same letter, I enclosed a letter I had written the *New York Times*, joyfully hailing the third term of Roosevelt in 1940. I wrote:

I enclose the little essay I sent to the New York paper in September. I got back a hundred letters and telegrams about it, most complimentary, but some so childish and threatening I answered them. Every one of the objectors were bankers or manufacturers or investment brokers, and not one reference did any one of them make to the fact that this was a time of national emergency. They all argued that they wanted to put their money to work and that Roosevelt was pinching them. They have had their feet in the trough so long they think they are the country.

I had a very angry interchange from the vice president of the W&L Alumni Association who used all kinds of personal nastiness in his letter and talked about running me out of town. I really burned him up, asked him to come down and try it; said next time he got mad to go out and bite a WPA worker, but not to try to argue with his intellectual superiors. He said if he had a son he'd yank him right out of college if he were under a man who thought as I did politically. I suggested that he had the intellectual integrity of a rabbit and that he was quite welcome to take his nonexistent son out of college. After we had exchanged three of these letters, I told him he bored me and I'd read no more of his silliness. Thereupon I got a telegram from him, begging me to read his next letter, and I got the nicest letter imaginable, wherein he said that a lot I had said was true, that his letters had been stupid and insulting because he was mad about Roosevelt, that I was a good guy, and he'd send any son of his to college just to be under me if he had one, and wanted to know if he could come down and visit me. Of course I told him the latchstring was always out. I guess it doesn't pay to kowtow to such people.

The fun that I had locally from the publication of *Geese* was well worth the fact that the administration had become my implacable foe. The faculty was delighted with the book almost to a man; so were my former students who in no way thought I had debased the school. For one thing, it was funny. Not many months ago a book review for the alumni magazine picked three books that had come from and been inspired by Washington and Lee. The reviewer quotes dozens of remarks that I had forgotten, observing:

> One can almost hear Watkin's laughter as he good-naturedly aims his bazooka at one sacred cow after another, including even Omicron Delta Kappa: "An honors fraternity, thriving chiefly in the South and Middle West. It stimulates the wily fraternity politician to be slicker, the activities hound to be more active, the good Joe to be more unctuously self-righteous. It fills a great need on the campus, for it keeps the chain of American success unbroken. The Eagle Scout becomes an ODK, the ODK a thirty-third-degree Mason..." Dr. Worthington, who had observed that a man's intelligence is inversely proportional to the number of pins he wears on his belly, said that the order would disappear if they'd require all members to wear their keys in their pockets.

If I had what I thought was a good crack, I invariably put it into the mouth of Dr. Worthington:

> The mob is turning our college into something cheap; we're not changing them. I still believe the function of a college is to prepare the best man to lead the mob in the right direction. We'd better see to it that we run our school for the cream of the Southland—not the clabber of New Jersey.

Again:

> It's unbelievable what mothers expect of a college. College is a place where we turn them into great lawyers and doctors and financiers overnight. That' s my part. All they expect of the administration is to place them with perfect roommates, censor their mail, and teach them not to wet the bed.

The reviewer reminded me of the guessing games that went on. Who was who? He writes:

> There is a little bit of a lot of Lexington people in Watkin's sometimes thinly veiled caricatures, and it has been said that in the 1940s more than a few folks in these parts were scandalized to find themselves portrayed with warts and all.

I have already answered that charge in discussing *On Borrowed Time*, but though there is much more reason to think that in *Geese* I was copying people from life, the very fact that when friends were certain they could read my mind they always guessed wrong should be enough to prove that I was dealing with types rather than with certain personalities. I see no point in not telling truthfully what individuals I really did visualize.

Several friends wrote me that they were certain Dr. Helderman of the history department was the prototype for Dr. Worthington. They could not have been more wrong. When I thought of Worthington, I saw the face of Dean Moreland of the law school, a man I did not even know very well. Dean Moreland and Dorothy and Catherine McDowell often tried to guess the murderer in the latest Agatha Christie magazine serialization. But though I had passed the time of day with him and admired everything I ever heard about him, I sensed that here was a man of steel, who feared nobody. As for Uncle Jack, that was obviously Charley McDowell, though a few years older, but I doubt if either Charley or Catherine knew it. The third person was the president, but not the president of Washington and Lee. Never once did I see his face, but only that of Chancellor Day of Syracuse. I wanted a physically more imposing president, more violent, outspoken, and arrogant. Had I been describing our president I would have taken him to task for personal characteristics, among them Southern-fried oratory, which was no part of my imaginary President Burkholder. I say imaginary, for I haven't the foggiest idea how Chancellor Day conducted a faculty meeting. When I said on the jacket blurb that I was dealing with a national problem, I was telling the simple truth. Had I been teaching at any other Southern college, its president would have sworn that I was ridiculing him, and I would have been, for all except the few old-timers were equally guilty.

By 1940 everyone with bat brains knew that a war with Germany was inevitable, but while we waited we enjoyed our new house. We still threw parties, but they were comparatively mild. Much more pleasurable were the Fourth of July celebrations. I bought all the sky-rockets I could afford and invited a great number of friends, telling them each to bring a pint of booze and a few fireworks. I spent most of the day building chutes along the very edge of the bank that faced the highway far below. I also erected sturdy posts where pinwheels could be nailed and marked out places where the kids could fire off crackers and plant their sparklers, for whole families were invited. Dot and the maid spent the day making lemonade and cookies. As soon as it was dark the first rocket went skyward and for the next hour we put on a display that was worthy of any town organization. It suddenly occurred to me that we might be bombarding the filling station on the highway below, and so I called the owner, who said he didn't care if an occasional burnt-out stick hit the roof. They had the hose ready, and they had never enjoyed a display more, and for God's sake keep them coming. We did that for two years without any fatality. Friends have often written me mournfully that the Fourth of July meant nothing after we left town.

Another kick I got out of that house. The cow-pasture golf course was visible and within walking distance, and I was delighted to see more than one of the town fathers, pillars of the Presbyterian Church and staunch teetotalers, climbing through the fence and making their way to pay me a little social call. I knew what they wanted and always had the finest bottle of bourbon that money could buy ready for their jolly visits. They knew that I would not betray them. They always refused the second highball of bourbon and branch but gave in gracefully when I forced it on them. At Christmas they often brought their wives to our open house, where the ladies encouraged each other to have another small glass of the innocuous punch I had for them. "Nothing but froo-joozes," they said. I discovered that I liked them very much.

When old friends dropped in unannounced of an evening, I stuck to my iced tea and soda so that I could finish up the historical novel I was writing, which I called *Gentleman from England*. Though it passed practically unnoticed in the excitement of the approaching war, it was so innocent that I could dedicate it to my mother, who was pleased. I also wrote a short story for *Colliers* about the college night watchman, who stopped to chat with me when I was making my rounds at the college. It served excellently 20 years later. I did another for *Esquire* about old Doctor White and one for *Story* magazine in 1939 called "American Idyll" about my mother trying to help a poor family who lived like animals in a shack in Conifer. The poor woman couldn't cope with her too-numerous children, and though we ordered an ambulance to rush her to a hospital so she wouldn't have her latest baby unattended, she wouldn't leave until they fished out from under the bed her bedraggled but prized hat which she clutched to her body as they carried her away. My mother was great when anyone needed help. *Scribners* apologized twice to Bernice for not taking it, praising it to the skies while refusing it. I treasure it for two reasons: Bernice's refusal ever to give up when she knew something was good, and the fan letter sent me by a lady in New York, the only fan letter she had ever written and the best I ever received.

26

To gain his third term and break tradition, Roosevelt had been forced to tell the country he would keep America out of war. By the time Japan made her sneak attack on Pearl Harbor on December 7, 1941, America was more than ready to declare war against the Axis, Japan in the Pacific and Germany and Italy in the Atlantic.

Unless you had lived through those days it would be almost impossible to make you understand the wave of patriotism that swept this country and the eagerness to enlist and be a part of it, especially if, like me, you had just missed the First World War. Everybody quoted the stirring phrase Winston Churchill used when he took over the British Parliament in May of 1940: "I have nothing to offer but blood, toil, sweat, and tears." Almost everybody thought he had coined the expression. Actually he had merely added the "toil." John Donne had used blood, sweat, and tears in 1611, and Byron had repeated it in the century before Churchill. But when Churchill said it in his bulldog growl, it stiffened his countrymen's spines and brought a tingle to ours in America.

Two days after Pearl Harbor, on December 9, 1941, I had just turned 40. I had a wife and three dependent children and I wasn't expected to go. But I had perfect health and was stronger than I looked. During a party at our house Tex Tilson, the head football coach; Jack Hennemeier, associate coach; and Cy Young, also a coach and the most famous athlete that ever attended the school, were wandering around the grounds for a breath of air. We had stopped beside a mock orange tree. I picked up one arm and offered to bet each one of them a dollar that I could throw a mock orange farther than any one of them.

They all pulled out a buck to make some of that easy money. I collected dollar after dollar until they gave up in disgust. But the armed forces weren't looking for men who could throw the enemy out at the plate and before the year was up I was a wreck, trying to find some branch of the service that would take me. Dorothy knew that I'd never be happy until I had landed something. She encouraged me to go. It was her suggestion that we rent our house to a fraternity and she and the kids would take a small apartment on the campus and sit out the war if and when I could turn up something. All the young professors felt as I did; only a few of the older men finally remained to teach in the special service school the college was planning to rent out where actors and entertainers could be trained as morale builders in the war effort. Charley McDowell, who had undergone training in Pensacola, Florida, to become a Navy fighter pilot in World War I and was about to see active duty when that war ended, was pulling every possible string to get back into a fighter plane. Whenever our old gang met and partied, that's all we talked about. Catherine and Dot and Polly Penick agreed that if a man felt strongly about it he should go. Other wives disagreed. None of us was 20 any more and they thought we were talking silly

We were being entertained by Wally and Alma Cronin. Wally was an athlete, a big, sweet, handsome man, and an electrical engineer who kept the moving-picture equipment in order for the entire valley. He wanted to go, too, but he didn't have a prayer, for he was a diabetic dependent on daily shots of insulin for his very life. Alma, a big, handsome woman, would have enlisted as a foot soldier if she had been a man, and she would have been a good one. My next-door neighbor, a slightly effeminate man with a belly, was desperately in love with Alma and when he had had a few drinks, he declared it in front of his wife and Wally and Alma herself, who thought it funny. Tonight he had drunk enough to be maudlin. With a shaky voice he told Wally, the husband, what torture it was to be hopelessly in love. Wally put his arms around him and patted his arm, saying, "There, there." A little later he disappeared and we didn't find out until the next day what had happened to him. Determined that the woman he loved would be proud of him, he had driven alone half the night all the way to Richmond. The recruiting office for the Navy was closed, but the Marines were open, so he offered the Marines his body to be used as they saw fit in the service of his country. The recruiting sergeant took one look at that body and put it to bed, and when he had slept it off in the morning, they gave him some coffee, thanked him, and sent him back home.

Eventually, Charley and I both got desk jobs in the Navy, Charley in Pensacola, I in Richmond. The Navy officer promised me sea duty if first I would become the commander's right hand man in a special procurement office. I thought procurement meant supplies, but not this one. Since I knew a lot about other colleges in the vicinity, they wanted me to head two other interviewers to procure and place college professors who qualified both physically and mentally for induction into a U.S. Naval Reserve officers training program. There were nowhere near enough regular officers to man the ships and the training jobs the expanding Navy would need, and though we were not limited to college professors by any means, here was a great source of material. When the supply was more or less exhausted, I could have my sea duty. I would be serving my country at this somewhat inglorious task far better than anything else I could do. Dorothy agreed.

We rented the house to the small fraternity; she took an apartment on the campus almost next door to her best friend Catherine McDowell. For the time I served in procurement it was decided that I rent a tiny single room apartment in Richmond. I kept the car, a newer, luxurious big Buick, and would drive up to Lexington as long as I could get the gas. She didn't like to drive and would have no use for it, being so centrally located. Inasmuch as Mary Desha lived close by, too, I figured that enough bridge would be played to outlast three wars.

The Navy procurement office was a huge room on the second floor of what had been a storage room in a Chevrolet parts building. It was now compartmentalized. Each applicant started with my office where his preliminary file was examined and all sorts of questions asked to be sure that his qualifications could be seen at a glance. A very few were marked by the Secret Service in advance with a symbol that the man was thought to be a bad security risk and should be turned away tactfully before he went any further. If he looked promising to me or to my fellow interviewers, Ensign Tom Sullivan, a jolly Irishman with a delightful sense of humor, or Lieutenant J.G. Randy Turner, a VMI graduate, a born gentleman and good companion, he was sent along to take a physical examination, where he must prove to have near-perfect vision and good general health. One of the greatest stumbling blocks occurred when an applicant's urine was boiled and was shown to have albumen. Usually all it meant was that the man had been toasted the night before too thoroughly by friends who saw him as well on his way to being an officer and a gentleman by act of Congress. That meant he had to stay sober for a week or two and come down again, which usually did the job. He would then be sent for a month to an officer's training school, learn Navy regs, harden his body, and determine where he would fit in best. If young and with a flair for engineering, he most often rated combat ship duty. Quite often a hardened old captain of a destroyer or even a carrier would notice that this civilian in Navy uniform had what it takes. Such a man was my friend Bill Drewry, who worked in the office next to the Corner Store in Lexington. It never occurred to me as I went in to pay him my gas bill that the captain on the destroyer in the Pacific who gave close support to the Marines going ashore would take Bill aside and ask him if he would really like to learn how a man who fought a ship did the job, and when Bill said yes, give him an indoctrination he could never have come close to getting at Annapolis. Not many people knew that Bill had most of his stomach shot out, which surgery has corrected and that of all the local heroes that came out of the war there, this unassuming man has best right to the title.

Our commander officer had got a free education at Annapolis and undoubtedly had learned to sail little boats on the Severn, but had spent his life as a stockbroker. But when the bugles sounded, his old Navy training made him spring to the second deck of the Navy procurement office in Richmond where he ran a taut ship. One reason it was taught was Lt. Leonard Reichle, who had yellow hair that stuck straight up. Reichle's Teutonic heritage made him a stickler for order. He was always rearranging the files and the chairs and desks in the middle of the room to make the maze more comprehensible.

When it came time for Commander Moise to turn in our fitness reports every man there asked for sea duty except Reichle. He was having too much fun moving the chairs around.

One interlude in our daily grind was the visit a group of us paid Admiral Halsey. He had been afflicted by a strange malady, a rash that had broken out on his body. None of the Navy doctors could explain it, and because at that time the reputedly greatest living allergist lived in Richmond, Halsey had come here to be cured of the complaint. He was lonely. He had requested that if any naval officers were in the vicinity, they visit him. We were the nearest who answered to that description, so Moise led a delegation to the admiral's quarters. He didn't seem to be violently ill, but he paced like a caged animal. In the middle of a conversation he abruptly ripped off his shirt and showed us his torso, covered with a rash so fine and so extensive that you could not put your finger down between one tiny pimple and the next. Halsey said:

> Nobody knows what the hell caused it. They even suggested fright, for recently a Jap bomb exploded near me on the deck, but hell, fear is part of our business. I've been afraid any number of times, but I haven't let it prey on my mind.

Eventually, the allergist found the cause. Two of "Bull" Halsey's teeth were extracted, and the rash departed.

Another remarkable man washed ashore to us was John Adams. He was so young that I gave him the name of Schoolboy Adams, which stuck. A tremendous athlete who had rowed on the Washington crew, tall and aristocratic looking, he had graduated under Cushing at Harvard as the young brain surgeon most likely to succeed. But instead of rating a hospital or like my uncle in World War I, who had operated behind the lines every day, some brilliant placement officer had put him in charge of a unit that any hack could have run, and he was most bitter about it. But he was conscientious and it pained him to have to tell a hopeful applicant that he had a hernia. He sent such a man back to me. I told him that he should have an operation to correct it while it was small, and that he should not hurry his convalescence until he was quite well and strong again. The war wouldn't end tomorrow. They often left me white and shaking, but they generally had it done, though they always came back too soon. Usually, Schoolboy Adams gave them a bit of good advice to wait another two weeks before they took on the rigors of the indoctrination school.

About the last procurement stunt that Commander Moise pulled was to send me with Tom Sullivan as a second interviewer, Schoolboy Adams as the doctor, and pharmacist's mate Martire to far-off Charleston, West Virginia, to procure officers on the spot. Instead of having the applicants come to Richmond, we would send the substitute procurement office to them. I knew what Moise was doing; he was getting me out of the way while he broke in another chief interviewer. The scuttlebutt was that I was to take over his job and run the office for the rest of the war. I had other ideas. I had often had correspondence with a character in the Pentagon who seemed to be able to place men intelligently if I gave him a special tip about them. So I called him now and told him the plight I was in. I'd rather handle a gun crew on a Liberty ship in convoy to England then be stuck with this stinking job, which any smart store clerk could handle. He agreed. He knew all about me and he had a spot picked out where my talents would be used for the good of the Navy. "You'll get orders very shortly," he said "and there's nothing that Commander Moise can do to countermand them. Bye."

When I received them, I told Dot to go back to Castle Hill and start packing. We'd sell it if she agreed; otherwise, put a caretaker in charge. After this trip to Charleston I was going to slip up to Washington and find a nice new apartment in Arlington I had heard about where we could live together as a family again.

In Charleston, with the help of two old W&L students, we set up a good hotel and did a land office business. When we milked the place dry, we headed back for Richmond. Tom Sullivan as a young unmarried man in uniform said hello and goodbye to a great many young ladies, but his nose was somewhat put out of joint as the three of us were walking downtown when we beheld a ravishing beauty driving a sports Cadillac past us while our pharmacist's mate sat beside her sending her into gales of laughter. We had never noticed that Martire had coal black hair and a roguish smile and big brown eyes, but the prettiest girl in town had been more observant.

We drove back to Richmond by way of Lexington, and it just happened that Dot had our maid back and was ready to put up the three extra guests at Castle Hill. Jimmy Barnes had been over twice to the procurement office and both times had been found fit for a commission except that he had been given a party the night before and still had albumen in his pee. This time, on a Friday night he was giving the party for us and swore that he hadn't had a drink in a week and would not have one tonight. I told him my stunt of drinking iced tea and soda and he promised to follow my example. But by midnight he was drunk. I called him the next day around noon, told him to take something for his hangover, look alive, and follow my instructions, and I'd get him into the Navy. I had picked him out to be Moise's replacement. He'd adore the job; he looked good on paper, he was smart and knew how to get along with people, and he had friends in Richmond to recommend him.

Schoolboy Adams said another exam was a waste of time; Jimmy was drunk last night and it would show up in his pee. I told him about my talk with Jimmy and how he had been drinking tea and soda, but was a great actor. I had used him in every play we ever put on. He was playing the drunk to act as a good host. Schoolboy said OK, but if that albumen showed up, he was going to record it.

Schoolboy Adams and Martire set up their examining equipment in Parke's room, the front room across from ours. On that side was a bathroom, then the baby's room. I sat on the bed watching the exam, which went off well. Then Jimmy was handed a bottle and told to go into the bathroom and bring back a sizable sample. He went into the bathroom, shut the door modestly behind him, and in due course returned with the sample. Schoolboy handed the bottle to Martire who put it under his spirit lamp. In due course, he held it up to the light. Clear as a bell. And Fletcher James Barnes II became the commander of the procurement office, directing it to everybody's satisfaction. But only Jimmy and I and my son Parke knew that it was Parke's urine that put him there.

I committed one other minor sin. Alan Penick was a lawyer. He would never have any duties connected with the Navy that did not pertain to the law. But he had one eye not quite blind but near enough. Yet he was the best shot in the county and one of the best physical specimens. One-legged men were flying supply planes in Great Britain. The lame, the halt, and the well-nigh blind were doing wonders over there. So I copied the eye chart and sent it to Allen and told him to memorize it upside down and cattycorner, but never to read it with his bad eye nearer than five feet. The Navy would allow lawyers that. So he did and went away to indoctrination school. There he set up physical fitness records which added to his years; I know that he did over a hundred pushups. He too served with great distinction both in the states and on Pacific islands.

If either of these fellows had been young enough or had the slightest chance of being in a combat situation where eyes were important, I would never have resorted to such chicanery. But even then I'd have bet on Penick over most of the fighting men I met.

As for me, I was given the rank of lieutenant commander to preside over a roomful of the craziest writers ever to be assembled in one place. It was pure delight.

27

The Department of the Navy was then in one of the old buildings in Pennsylvania Avenue, not in the Pentagon. Our room, known as the writers unit, was under Admiral McCain, Deputy Chief of Naval Operations for Air. There were a whole string of offices on the fourth floor of units dealing with naval aviation. These occupied the rear of the building. Next to ours was the unit devoted to advertising, next to that photography, and so on. These units housed the working officers, probably as many as 30 to a room. Across the hall was the commanding officer for each unit, ours being at present Admiral "Min" Miller and his aide, Major Donald Keyhoe. Both had been to Annapolis. We had a succession of commanding officers, Admiral Miller climbing over one back after another to get himself set outside the Navy after the war, for in his ascent he had made too many enemies to stay in it. Most of his replacements were fighting men, who came in for a rest. If they had so much as written a term paper at Annapolis, that marked them as "literary" and thus able to deal with a stable of writers. Keyhoe, a not very successful journalist before the war, remained at his post. The smart woman who was tabbed to become his secretary prepared herself by reading all she could find about paranoia in the advanced psychology books. After the war Keyhoe made quite a stir. He was one of those journalists, if not the very first, to witness saucers from outer space. I believe he was on somewhat intimate terms with various non-terrestrial beings. His long-suffering secretary came in one morning looking a bit bedraggled to explain in her gentle Kentucky drawl: "If all the hangovers in the world were laid end to end, mine would stand up in the corner and sneer at them."

In reading over my letters to my mother, I was surprised to discover that I barely mentioned any of the amusing people in that unit. Perhaps I thought it might have shocked her to hear about the unmilitary behavior of our unit. I am sure she would not have been pleased to learn that some of the high-ranking officers who ordered our brave soldiers and sailors into combat were dolts and blackguards. I never let her know that when I was in Washington I was so ashamed to wear the Navy uniform, I wanted to hide, but that when I went to the South Pacific and met the men who were actually waging the war I was so proud of them I never wanted to come back to that verminous department. In Washington I was working with Navy desk thumpers who had been called in where they could do the least harm. I am not talking about men like Admiral McCain, but about the blowhards who had been to Annapolis and had to be kept busy with paperwork, never allowed to order a ship or an airplane squadron for fear of getting them sunk.

So I told my mother about the way I had bedeviled the rental officers who had charge of the whole new town that was being built in Alexandria, and that we were to have the coveted end unit that would have a lovely kitchen and a separate bedroom for all the kids, an apartment where a new school was going up just across the way. It would be right in the middle of Parke's paper route. He was terrifically proud of the money it earned him. He bought most of his new clothes for fall. Dot enjoyed the fine meals she was cooking for us. A doctor and his family lived next door. All the neighbors were congenial and Maggie enjoyed playing with Marcia Rodd, who became a well-known actress. It was only a step to the bus which I took at 6:30 am. By 7:00 it landed me right in front of the naval building, where I had a nice breakfast before I went upstairs to be in my office at eight. At 6:30 pm I took the bus home and arrived at 7:00. We had no use for the big car, which we sold. The excess furniture from Castle Hill was in dead storage in Lexington, and though I didn't know what I would do after the war, I was sure it would not be in Lexington.

That was the thing my mother wanted to hear, about Larry, the family man, proud of his brilliant wife and big, smart, likable son, and his two beautiful little daughters. Never a letter went out to her without an invitation to come down and see the sights in our nation's capital.

As for the unit, they were hard to believe. Few of them had been away to any quickie indoctrination school for officers, but like me had simply been sworn in and started working. They were with a few exceptions the most unmilitary unit in any branch of the service anywhere. There were all sorts of reasons for this.

Almost all writers despised the professional soldier for his low ideals, his pretense of patriotism while stealing all he could, his basic ignorance about anything not dealing with engineering; his social prejudices, his arrogance, his underlying cruelty, his hatred of change, his toadyism of higher-ranking officers, his bullying of those beneath, and his essential laziness.

A few of my superior officers were men I was glad to serve, but it was galling to be ordered about by the phonies. Sometimes we were going great, and in general we had reason to be proud of what we did, then along would come a new boss across the hall and because he didn't understand, he would simply shove everything we sent him into a desk and kill it until he had been indoctrinated. It was then that we cut loose, playing baseball with a wadded-up ball contrived out of wads of directives bound with scotch tape. USN shunned our office, not knowing quite what to do if they put the whole unit on report. An old-timer, J. Clarke Mattimore, one of the few advertising men I respect, said it had always been that way and that once when Admiral Miller dropped in, he pleaded with our best writer Bob Taylor to put away his sling shot because it just wouldn't look right to have an admiral bring court-martial proceedings against a lieutenant for hitting him with paper clips. Miller was a rascal, but he did have a sense of humor.

Our unit did everything. It was in the business of writing training manuals for Navy flyers, some serious, some light-hearted. The serious ones meant that some one of us had to write a manual about a certain new airplane, let's say, or something that a pilot should have learned in his brief indoctrination at flight school, but hadn't. Like everyone else, they were very young and very ignorant about these complicated, lethal machines. They were barely introduced to them before they were out in the Pacific flying them against a better-trained enemy, and a lot of them were getting killed through ignorance. Furthermore, they were hardly ever engineers and they didn't know what the engineers were talking about. Neither did the journalist or novelist sent down from our unit, but our writer had to keep at it until he understood what in the hell the engineer was talking about, then he would translate it into standard English that a young flyer could comprehend. That helped.

Even more so, the admirals who were on the carriers or the land-based Marine captains and generals discovered that sometimes pure carelessness on the part of a flyer was causing fatal accidents. For example, a flyer in the excitement of a first mission might forget to turn on his IFF, which meant that an opposing plane was to identify itself as friend if indeed it was such. IFF meant "Identify—Friend or Foe." Or he might be captured, but he had no idea what under the provisions of the Geneva Conference he was supposed to tell his captors, and what he was not to tell. And suppose he had to land his plane, which was not amphibious, in the ocean; what was the best way to do it and how might he possibly cling to it and signal for help?

To answer these seemingly inconsequential matters, our department put out a series of tiny booklets called the Sense Manuals. I believe that we took the idea from the British. Anyway, it worked. We had a brilliant cartoonist, named Bob Osborne, who caricatured a Navy flyer named Dilbert. He did everything wrong. Dilbert was a goon, stupid, conceited, who made amusingly stupid blunders. He got other people killed. His superior officer, a nice guy, told him what to do, but Dilbert did everything *his* way. He was an interesting character, no meanness in him, just an eager stupidity that always brought him to grief. The flyers took one of these pamphlets along when they went to the head, the way some toilet sitters read comic books, and because they were humorous and the cartoons graphic, they remembered. Often we got letters from the flyers saying, "You saved my life."

So *Prisoner Sense*, *Dunking Sense*, and the like had already been published before I even arrived and were established as desirables with constant requests for more. I hated the paperwork that fell to my lot, but as I was the man with the most stripes, two and a half, I was it. It was up to me to deal with the professional bosses across the hall, plead with them when we wanted something done, cajole them, make out fitness reports. I especially disliked that job and begged my charges to give me something good about themselves unless they were unhappy and wanted to be transferred. Everybody soon understood that I was one of them, that I had no desire to presume upon my position, and they were all my friends. Only that old devil Roark Bradford, who sat on my left in the corner, drank coffee all day long and made it for the rest of us, would not cooperate. He was the spirit of mischief, and if I asked him for a note to help me in a fitness report, I would get back a letter done in complete Navy reg style:

> From: Lt. Roark Bradford To: Lt. Comdr. Lawrence Edward Watkin. Subject: Progress. The communication property: No progress, signed Lt. Roark Bradford USNR.

Brad had been in the First World War, and he owned a plantation in Louisiana, which must have been the worst managed place in the world, for he loved the old-fashioned Negro in all his simplicity. The plantation was his laboratory. He had a fine house in New Orleans, but he preferred to live with Negroes. He wrote such hilarious books as *Old Man Adam and His Chillun*, from which the play *Green Pastures* was made with Marc Connelly. I read the original to a college class in 1965 and it broke them up. They had never heard of Roark Bradford, for his books were strictly forbidden by the new Negro who wanted nothing that smacked of Uncle Tom. Eventually if they ever feel secure they may thank Roark Bradford for preserving their inherent gift of tongues and their vivid imaginations, which is quite as valuable to the history of their race as the distorted picture Haley draws in *Roots* of a nation of brave martyrs with no sense of humor whatsoever. It makes no difference that Haley was a plagiarist; he is god, Bradford a devil. Bradford always attended their church services and occasionally it delighted his elfin sense of mischief to bring one of his wealthy but penny-pinching friends to a Negro service and introduce him to the worshippers, who would applaud him roundly, for any friend of Mister Bradford's was welcome. The visitor would just start liking the attention he was getting as a "biiiig man, a real *biiiig* man," when Brad would mention in passing that his friend insisted he wanted to write them out a check for four hundred dollars, which added to what they had already saved for a real church organ, would put them over the top. The tightwad would then become wildly applauded so that part of the sickly smile would leave his face. It was tax deductible, of course.

When some Navy flyer would give several of us a free ride to New York over a weekend, most of us would go to a play. Not Brad. He'd hop a train for Ossining, New York, and visit Sing Sing, asking to see a Negro preacher he had heard was incarcerated. Brad always sparred with the inmate, saying: "Don't give me that sob story. I know why you're in here. You were with a woman when her husband came home and you cut him up real bad with a razor. Now aren't you ashamed of yourself, you old sinner, you."

The preacher, whom Brad once described as a man with a big dick and a bass voice, and had the phrase published in a national magazine, answered, "Now Mister Bradford, you know with a nice clean woman that ain't no sin," and Brad would consider his train fare well spent.

He was a great source of cheerfulness. When some ass in Navy administration sent us a directive criticizing the time some Navy personnel spent going to the toilet, Brad would immediately follow it up with one of his own, couched in military jargon—SUBJECT: Bloated Bowels and Bulbous Bladders—all for the war effort, and men who were so angry they swore they would never write another word for the chickenshit Navy would soon be laughing and have their typewriters humming. He would often greet us in the morning just before eight o'clock doing a funny little dance, a kind of shuffle all the way across the room to his desk. In pantomime, he would put a piece of meat in a skillet and hold it over an imaginary fire before him, flipping it once to brown it nicely. He said he was dancing the poke chop until he fell into his chair exhausted. Or he might sing a doleful little chant, which went:

> A*way* out in Cal if *for nigh aye*
> There was a *race* hoss with two *white feet*
> An' he had a *white star*
> On his *haid*, his *haid*.
> You better bet on Stewball;
> You might *win, win.*
> You better bet on Stewball;
> You might win!

He would then announce loudly, "I brought religion to the 1930s!"

Whereupon Taylor would announce in reply: "You wicked old phony! You reduced religion to the status of a fish-fry."

"My son," Roark would respond sadly, "you should pray more and write less."

They loved each other. Everybody loved Brad, who was often tormented by the commander of the advertising unit in the next room, a former advertising man named Hewitt, who won his commission by being the nephew of some Navy admiral or other and who tried to exert a strict military discipline over the men under him, all of whom heartily hated him. He bustled when he walked, carrying a rolled-up newspaper in one hand and slapping it smack into the other. He once went into the Navy barber shop and commanded: "Give me a shave. I'm in a hurry. Put two men on it!"

Somehow or other he got hold of something that Brad had written and came bursting into the room, waving the script, whatever it was. Without so much as "by your leave," he stormed up to Brad, saying, "You know, this is good. If you let me handle you, I can put you in the slicks."

Brad took the papers and shoved them into his desk, saying in clear, ringing tones, "Listen, Buster, you stupid little donkey, since the death of Irvin S. Cobb, I am the highest paid writer for the *slicks* as you so ignorantly call them, still living today. Now get your ass out of here or I'll sic the dogs on you."

Since Hewitt could not understand insult, he tried to argue. "I can get you more," he said. Then he noticed that not only Brad, but that practically every man in the room was starting to get out of his chair; so he beat a hasty retreat. Brad sat down and wrote a long eloquent disquisition on advertising men, which I have and cherish.

Hewitt met his nemesis. Near the end of the war, it occurred to that nimble-witted Lieutenant Mattimore that if we brought into our unit a crazy, humorous, worn-out young pilot, who deserved a break, being the only surviving flyer of a Navy squadron stationed in the Aleutians, which he explained by saying, "I flew my way, and everybody else flew the Navy way," we could pick up a lot of useful slang that would make our Sense Manuals more realistic. I seconded the motion and the brass agreed, but the big, good-natured, overgrown kid who showed up had to have his desk in Hewitt's room, since our room was crammed. He turned out to be the curse of Hewitt's existence, because though he worked out every morning on the link trainer to keep his flying sharp, as he was allowed to do, he didn't let Hewitt know why he never reported to his desk until nine or nine-thirty. Hewitt would rap on his desk in a fury and bawl him out in front of the whole room, saying crisply: "Lt. Blank, you are under orders to report to this room at 0800 every morning!" Every time Hewitt would lecture him, his tormentor would put his head in his arms on his desk and sob loudly. At last Hewitt could stand the ridicule no longer and one morning threatened to have him court-martialed for insubordination. This time instead of pretending to sob, the big hulk rose to his full height, saying quietly, "You stupid little bastard, I am following orders by coming late here every morning, and I don't intend to explain what I am doing. I do, however, want you to understand this: I give you my word of honor that the day the war is over, I'm going to come looking for you wherever you may be, and I'm going to beat the absolute living shit out of you and you can count on that!" Whereupon he sat down. Hewitt never spoke to him again.

I don't know if he made good his threat. I doubt it, he was too good-natured, but I do know of a similar case. A quiet, diligent officer had been shamefully bullied by another civilian in uniform with more rank. The guy talked it over with his wife; they lived in Philadelphia and didn't have money to waste. The bully lived in San Francisco. The wife went down and bought her husband a round-trip ticket on a plane. He kissed her, flew to San Francisco, found his tormentor alone in a hotel room, beat him up, left him with two black eyes, and told him that in the future he should not browbeat his betters because of any position of authority he might hold, went back to work with a mind at ease, and lived a nice quiet life, full of well-earned success and satisfaction.

Which brings us to the gentleman who sat upon my right, Lt. Robert Taylor, a former writer for *The New Yorker*, the man who became and has remained one of my most valued friends. Though he couldn't help wanting to make money, unlike many of his comrades he did not continue to send pieces to *The New Yorker* and do an occasional job for the Navy. He probably wrote more good stuff which the Navy printed than any other man who ever hit a typewriter on behalf of his country. Nobody signed any of the Sense Manuals, but I'll venture to say that he wrote all the best ones and set the tone for the whole series. Brad was a humorist; Bob Taylor was a wit and he kept that wit razor sharp.

He couldn't open his mouth without saying something funny. I hadn't been working in the writers unit long before it occurred to me that my unit might provide a special service for Admiral McCain, the top dog in our outfit and a man I sincerely admired. I suggested that his fellow admirals might like to have their morale speeches written for them. He thought that was a great idea. I wrote all this myself and he was most appreciative. He'd call me down and say, "Watkin, one of our men has got to make a speech tonight to the workers in a certain fuel high-octane cracking plant in New Jersey."

"Coming right up," I'd tell him. "Anything special."

"No, just the usual. Tell them that our flyers in the Pacific would all be grounded except for the magnificent work their factory is doing. Five minutes and make it inspirational."

"Yes, sir."

I asked Bob Taylor, "Just for the hell of it, would you like to write one of these speeches for our tongue-tied admirals?"

"I'd be delighted. How long?"

"Not more than five pages double spaced."

Taylor knocked that out in record time. I was too busy to read it but delivered it to Admiral McCain, who was too busy to read it, too, but thanked me and gave it to an Admiral Ramsey, who was too busy to read it in advance, but started to read it with vigor to his audience. He hadn't got far before the men started laughing. He himself chuckled. He read some more, took off his glasses, wiped them, laughed, and said to the audience, "Hey, you know, this stuff is pretty good." He and his audience laughed all the way through until he got to the end, when he found a conclusion that sounded All American and sincere. He was cheered wildly. After that, he became our favorite admiral, for the thing the men appreciated most was the surprised laughter he gave vent to and his honesty in not pretending that the wit was his. We thought that man was one in a thousand.

I wrote the afterword to the 1969 Signet edition of Taylor's *The Travels of Jaimie McPheeters* which had won the Pulitzer Prize ten years earlier and at the end after discussing its place in the history of the picaresque novel, I wrote: "Little has been said about the satire, but it glides through the book, getting in many a swift jab." Taylor had been born with a waggish irreverence. Once during World War II, he had to serve under a naval reserve officer with a higher rank.

(This was in New York, under a former history professor.) This former pedagogue, who stuck rigidly to his new textbook, *Navy Regulations*, reprimanded Taylor for leaving notes about bearing the word radar. Spelled backward or forward, that hush-hush word was still classified. Taylor contritely agreed that he had imperiled his country. Not only did he lock his notes in the confidential file, he pointed out to his superior the same fearsome word on the front page of *the Washington Post*. Determined that such top-secret stuff should not fall into enemy hands, Taylor tore a snippet out of the paper, grimly popped it into his mouth, and patriotically munched and swallowed it.

It particularly delighted Taylor to write letters to large companies, taking them to task for not doing their full part for the war effort. He wrote dozens of them, always sending them to the Office of the President of the particular company, and he invariably received apologetic replies, which would make his day. One such was to the chairman of the board of a jelly bean company, for Bob was an addict. He said that he had noticed that the cheery red jelly beans were growing fewer and fewer in every package, whereas the black, morose, dispiriting beans were increasing. He asked: "Do you think that in these trying times you are doing your part for the war effort?" Back came the reply. The president thought at first the letter might be from a crank, but just to be sure, he had a great number of packages counted and found that Mr. Taylor was absolutely right. It had been their aim to put in 10% of each color, but a tally showed that the red beans had dropped to eight percent and the blacks had gone up to 12%. So they were reversing matters. Hereafter, there would be only 8% blacks and 12% reds for the duration. They were so grateful for Mr. Taylor calling their attention to the matter that they were sending him under separate cover 25 packages of all red jelly beans.

Taylor gave up shooting paper clips, and for a month the scuppers of the Navy department ran red.

I had spent so much time at the procurement office that I did not reach the writer's unit until late 1943 or early 1944. So, I am in no way prepared to write a proper history of the manuals, which were well established before I arrived. Ed Erich was on the point of departure, and though Don Thorburn, an advertising copy writer, was there long enough for me to discover that he was a wit, he didn't stay long. Soon to depart, but one who was around long enough for me to appreciate the good work he did, was Bernard Livingstone (Associated Press); also, a genial hard worker always ready to do anything for the good of the Navy, Russ Thackrey. Having done his stint, he was released to become dean of administration at Kansas

State College. I had no hand or choice in selecting men for the unit, nor do I think that Keyhoe or Miller or later Hollinsworth recruited them either. Sometimes they would send us a man whose talents were so far removed from the sort of man we needed that he might spend a full year with us but not accomplish a single thing that we could use. At least they, whoever *they* were, sent us writers, sometimes famous ones. We heard of true cases that were all but tragic. If a placement officer thought that the applicant was trying too hard to make the decision for him, he would show him a thing or two. A man was to go where the Navy sent him and like it! I met a man in the islands attached to the Seabees who was a poet. He was known as one, had published many fine verses in poetry magazines, but the Navy sent him to the Seabees as a construction man. His brother, an engineer, who would have given anything to be with the Seabees, was assigned to a writing job in the Navy department. I'll never forget Steinberg, the man who did so many of those crazy angular covers for *The New Yorker*. He had heard about our unit and had come to see if Bob Osborne, our cartoonist, could use an assistant. Things were slacking off and Osborne couldn't in all good conscience request the man, but Steinberg told me his story anyway.

He had been an architect and was just doing well with *The New Yorker* when the Navy begged him to accept an officer's commission. This man was such a great linguist that he would be invaluable to the Navy, whose plans included maneuvers off Italy. The trouble was he had lived in the United States long enough to apply for citizenship, but he would be so useful to the Navy as a translator that they had to have him. His citizenship papers and his naval commission came through on practically the same day, he was so greatly needed in Southern Europe. Whereupon he was immediately ordered to China and had been there ever since trying to work out some goofy symbols on the typewriter that could be used by the Naval Secret Service. His mustache drooped; he drooped all over. Did anything in the Navy make any sense?

I didn't think so a few days later when Major Keyhoe U.S.M.C. and Robert Taylor U.S.N.R. came into the room, arguing furiously with white drawn faces and both shaking with anger. I never did find out what the dispute was all about, except that Keyhoe wanted me to send Taylor to Portsmouth for insulting a superior officer. Taylor should be court-martialed and it was up to me to put him on report. I tried to calm Taylor down, for he was a tremendous athlete with almost lethal fists and had it firmly in mind that he should kill Keyhoe. I then told Keyhoe that I had no quarrel with Taylor. He had always done more than his duty. Furthermore, I had been brought here as just another writer and put in charge because of my age, not because of my abilities as a military commander. Hell, I hadn't even been away to indoctrination school. But if I were called upon to testify I would have to report that I considered Major Keyhoe a troublemaker, who tried to throw his not very heavy weight around. If Keyhoe wanted to have Taylor or me or anybody else court-martialed, he would have to start the proceedings himself. Keyhoe rushed out of the room and that's the last we ever heard about it.

Some time before that it was Major Keyhoe who gave me my first writing assignment. I was to write a small manual for Navy flyers who came back to the States on leave, telling them that they were no longer in a combat condition when they landed wherever and however they pleased. They must realize that in order to keep air traffic moving safely, they must first file a flight plan and obey the commands given by the control tower. They must not take off until the control tower told them that a certain runway was cleared for them, and they must join the circle of planes who were responding to the control tower at their destination, and land when it was their turn. It wasn't a matter of good manners; it meant life or death if they did not cooperate.

I was doing a very good job, I thought; I had the facts and the jargon down cold and had the manual almost completed when I ran into an Air Force officer who told me that the Army already had such a booklet in print and there was no reason not to use it. I took the matter back to Keyhoe, who told me this: "Listen, it's time you found out that there's an Army and there's a Navy, and we don't give a damn what they're doing. You go ahead and finish your manual and if it's okay, we'll print it."

And that's exactly what happened, though the duplication seemed pointless and silly to me.

So did it, much, much later, to an Army general in the Pentagon, who called me up one day and said he heard we had a little "brokure" telling a prisoner his rights under the Geneva Convention.

"Yes, sir," I said. "We call it *Prisoner Sense*."

"Bring me over a copy," he ordered.

"Yes, sir."

I walked into his office and he took the manual. "I'll read it and get back to you. The way I see it, we're all fighting the same enemy."

He pounded his desk. "This duplicity of effort must cease!"

"Yes, sir," I said, choking back my laughter. I gave him the number of the big brass across the hall, saying that he would save time to talk to my superior officer.

I never heard any more about that either.

The event that seems best to explain our writers unit was the Propeller Conference. One morning a diminutive woman with Steno book and pencil in hand stuck her head hesitantly inside the door. She didn't quite know whom to address; so I said aloud, "Yes, my dear?"

"Is this where the Propeller Conference is being held?"

"Yes, indeed," I told her. "Come right in."

Everybody was pretty much in the doldrums, so I rapped with a pencil to get their attention, and said, "Gentlemen, the Propeller Conference." Mattimore, whose desk was near the center of the room, gave her his desk and everybody else gathered around.

"Can you take fast dictation?" I asked her.

She said sixty words a minute, so I told her we would try to be slow and distinct, but to stop if she missed anything. She cocked her pencil at the ready.

I did not dare call on Mattimore because I could see that he was having trouble keeping his face straight before we had even begun. I believe I asked Lt. Livingston for his views and he said something like this: "We have been getting a great many complaints about the slant of the cam."

The woman looked up questioningly.

"The cam...c-a-m...for camshaft," he explained. She nodded and waited.

He went on. "I suggest that instead of its present position, we try 2-3-6-7-Z squared."

She had that, too.

Several other officers gave gobbledeguck opinions. "Lieutenant Bradford?"

Brad said softly: "There have been so many failures because at top speeds the synchronization of the guns shooting through the prop blades has been so bad that they shoot off the propellers themselves. I submit we can no longer use the single-prop plane as our fighter. We will have to make two-engine planes to give the guns in the middle maximum effectiveness."

Somebody sniggered. The woman looked suspicious, but she took it down.

"Lieutenant Taylor," I said, "we haven't heard from you."

Taylor came very close to the woman and scowled down at her. "I propose," he growled, raising both arms slowly, "that we dispense with the propeller entirely. Hereafter the airplane will flap its wings!" He demonstrated by waving his arms like a great hawk about to pounce on the poor woman. With a cry of alarm, she slipped out of her seat and ran at full speed out of the room, while the whole unit roared with laughter.

At least every two or three weeks after that, she would look in at the door and giggle at us. She wanted to make sure that our typewriters were humming merrily, that none of us was in irons, and that all was well in Cloud Cuckoo Land.

28

I had another brainstorm, which I chewed over by myself quite awhile before getting up my courage to propose it to Admiral McCain. I told him that if he would send me out to the Pacific to see at first-hand what the Navy flyers were up against, it would help our manuals to be more authentic in every way. I also would like to have Lieutenant Taylor, a fine writer with a background of newspaper work that made him a real gopher when it came to digging up facts, accompany me. The admiral thought it a splendid idea. We should take a complete tour and see it all. After that, he would like me to recommend other men in the unit who were deserving to go singly or in pairs to get a new perspective. He thought something of the sort might apply also to the photographers Steichen had trained. They might get a record of the whole war. He told me to ask around and investigate the thing thoroughly, write up the orders myself, and he'd sign them. I'm sure he didn't read them, but more than once when we were reporting to some new Pacific Station, the chief petty officer would exclaim, "Jee-sus! I never saw orders like these. You can visit, revisit, vary, omit. You can bump a four-striper off a plane!!"

"I just put that in for laughs," I told him. "I'd know better than to do it."

Sometimes if I phoned ahead about quarters, I'd be asked excitedly, "Is this the *real* Robert Taylor who's coming with you?"

"It certainly is. You don't think I'd be traveling with Spangler Arlington Brugghe, do you?"

Bob, who couldn't help teasing anybody, was once at a dance and kidded the movie actor. "My name is Robert Taylor. What's your name?"

I could have told him many years later that he'd have liked Robert Taylor, a very nice man.

Before we departed a strange thing happened, or so it seemed to us at the time. James Forrestal, the new Secretary of the Navy since the preceding spring of 1943, called us into his office in January 1944 and said he had a special mission for us. He wanted us pledged to silence but upon our return to give him a report of exactly what was happening out there in the Pacific. He took us into a nearby empty room before he said anything and looked around quickly to see if it was bugged. We promised to keep our eyes open and to hand him a complete report when we returned, and we did so.

The log I kept of our trip showed that we left Washington in mid-January, but did not reach Los Angeles via the Chief, a passenger train, until January 17 nor San Francisco until January 22, also by train; but though we reported promptly to Navy headquarters as soon as we arrived anywhere, we always had to wait, sometimes days, before transportation was provided to send us on our way. We never were provided with Navy quarters while in the United States, and though we called in sometimes several times a day about transportation, we were told to wait. In Los Angeles, we had no problem finding a hotel, but in San Francisco we were ordered to cool our heels and bunk wherever we could. There were no hotels that could put us up. I would have given up after trying ten or fifteen and have gone to sleep in the railroad station, but not Taylor. His newspaper training told him never to say die. After the better part of an hour, he found one that would take us. I don't remember its name, but it was a nice little hotel on a side street with good food, especially breakfasts, so we set out to see the sights like a couple of tourists.

Finally, the Navy put us on something worth waiting for, a four-engine Pan American clipper ship that got us into Pearl Harbor at noon on January 26. Our seats were so comfortable that we had no trouble sleeping in them the previous night. Here we reported to NATS (Naval Air Transportation Service) and hereafter NATS was the organization that kept us waiting. We had invariably done what needed doing in a day or two, though at Bougainville there was so much going on that we kept busy for a week, but usually it meant that NATS was trying to put us on any old plane going in our direction. At Pearl, strangely enough, we occupied Navy quarters, none other than the Royal Hawaiian Hotel itself, which had been commandeered for the week or so of R&R the submariners received after a long, claustrophobic duty, on the principle that the roughest duty deserved the best place to recreate themselves. I might have been given a room there anyway, for when I walked up to the desk, whom did I find in charge but an old Washington & Lee student, Herbert Dollahite, not a priss, but the fastidious scion of a fine old Southern family. Herbert underwent the tortures of the damned for what the submariners were doing to his hotel. While we were talking, one walked in and climbed the stairs. On the first and lower landing a small palm tree stood in a huge earthen pot. The beautiful, great, priceless porcelain that ordinarily held it had been stored away, but as the seaman approached it and paused, Herbert shut his eyes. He opened them again, looking at me questioningly. I nodded. It seemed that no enlisted man could pass that palm without letting fly a brown stream of tobacco juice. Herbert shuddered slightly. His friends thought he had the cushiest job in the Navy, but I knew that he spent several of those years in hell.

What enlivened Pearl for us was that Bob's friend Hodge did have the best duty in the Coast Guard. The one officer above him turned the small details of the job over to Hodge, while he fought the war on the golf course. I think Hodge had a first name, Clarence, but he was known to one and all as Hodge, and if Taylor was a character, Hodge was doubly so. They had played together from the time they were small boys, went to the same university, and were equally fine athletes, light heavyweights. When they played on the football or baseball or basketball team, they were co-equal stars, but they flipped a coin to see which would go out for the boxing team, which the wrestling team, for if they had to compete against each other one of them might have been killed, they were such stubborn competitors. Hodge got out a football to play three-cornered catch and whichever one threw the ball to me it almost knocked me down. Bob was taller and more graceful, but Hodge was chunkier and just as powerful.

The first evening after supper Taylor said to his buddy, "You're not getting fat, are you, working two hours a day and making a million on the side?" He referred to the fact that Hodge had written a little pamphlet, "*Welcome to Hawaii*," well illustrated, which he sold for a dollar, and almost every enlisted man of whatever service bought the booklet. Hodge's eyes began to sparkle; his wife closed hers and she sighed quietly. "What have you got in mind?" he asked Taylor. Taylor slid out of his chair and did a handstand, sat down, and waited. Hodge was barefooted. "You call that a handstand?" he said scornfully. He duplicated the feat, but when he came back down he hit his bare foot against a chair. He had broken two toes, but slipping on his socks pretended that he had just barely nicked them. He bore the pain for two days until his wife made him see a doctor and have them set, but he never stopped laughing or kidding in all that time.

He knew that Taylor, for all his personal courage, was leery about airplanes and hated them. Never a plane took off for the South Seas but Hodge would stop and call our attention to it. "Look, it's going to crash. It's too heavily loaded. It'll never get over the barrier." When it did, he would shake his head. "I don't know what keeps any of them up," he would say.

Hodge had decided that quite often he could not devote full time to entertaining guests like Taylor and me. He told his commanding officer he had to have help. One enlisted man would do it. The Coast Guard brass immediately had such a man ordered. We were there when he arrived, a big fellow, but not very pretentious-appearing in his white togs. Hodge, sitting at his ease behind his desk, didn't bother looking at his papers, but grabbed up a sheet of foolscap and a pen and began questioning the fellow.

"Name?" Hodge inquired. "Romero."

"I didn't quite catch that," said Hodge "Romero, sir ."

"That's better. You got a first name?"

"Cesar, sir."

"Come off it. Quit kidding."

"I am not, sir. That is my name: Cesar Romero." Hodge waited. "Cesar Romero, sir," the man amended.

"Well, I'll be damned, Ces; that's quite a name. Now, Ces ('Seize'), what did you do as a civilian?"

"I was an actor, sir."

"An actor? Where did you act?"

"In the movies, sir."

Hodge had never been to a movie in his life and had honestly never heard of Cesar Romero, but he played along. "What parts did you play in the movies, Ces?"

"I was usually the hero, sir, the love interest."

Hodge burst into a roar of laughter. He looked at us delighted as much as to say, "Isn't this guy something? And he's still got a straight face."

"Well, that's great Ces. I can see we're going to get along just fine. Now you take the rest of the day off and get settled. Come in tomorrow about 8 or 9 and put everything shipshape and I'll be in about ten."

"Yes, sir. Thank you, sir."

Bob and I never told Hodge that Cesar Romero was for real. We hoped that some day he might see that name on a billboard and wander in to see his man Friday done up in breastplate and helmet in the part of a Roman gladiator. Henry Shelley told me that the Romans had a word for a gladiator meaning *the sigh of the girls*," the love interest. I never heard how it came out, but I'll wager that Ces and Hodge became friends. It would be hard to dislike Taylor's buddy.

The plane we boarded which would take us to Espiritu Santos left Pearl on January 28. It was a lumbering big B-24, a transport plane, and was loaded so heavily with wooden boxes all of the same size that both of us questioned if it could take off. We were the only passengers and there were just the two seats midway up the aisle which ended amidships. At each side and behind, seats had been removed for the cargo. Finally, when it was above the clouds, we asked the one duty officer who did not fly, but who whipped up remarkably tasty meals on his tiny stove, what those boxes contained.

"Condoms for the Marines," he said. We didn't think that the whole Marine Corps stateside could use that many condoms, but it seemed that the Marines, who slogged around in swamps, slipped them over the muzzles of their guns to keep the muck and the water out. They could be yanked off quickly if there was any firing to do. Mud in the muzzle might have blown their weapons up.

The plane stopped for refueling at Palmyra where we spent the night and took off next morning for Canton, passed it and headed for Espiritu, but storms or engine trouble or both made the plane go slightly out of its way and put down for repairs at Fiji. When the pilot told us it would take 3 or 4 days before repair could be made, he suggested that we get a jeep and head for Suva, the capital, but to call them twice a day to find out when we could proceed. Taylor was overjoyed. He had been to Suva several years ago as a *young* man bumming around to see the world. He was now 32, while I was 43, but he was right. I loved Suva. There was a fine old hotel we patronized and the town was great. The policemen are huge fellows, who directed traffic, both cars and pedestrians, with the verve of an orchestra leader. The natives are more brown than black and both the men and the women are big, gracious, and handsome. We watched a thirteen-year-old boy kick an American football off his bare foot a good fifty yards. The University at Sydney taught them to play soccer. They sent a team over and beat the Aussies so badly they never asked them back. When the war started a group of them had heard about commandos and wanted to play the game. The Aussies gave them chalk. They were to make a chalk mark if and wherever they could sneak into the military barracks at night. In spite of the doubled guard, the Australians, keen men themselves, had never heard a sound, but chalk marks were everywhere all over the commandant's desk.

Later, in Bougainville I met a contingent of these Fijians, who were playing commando with a vengeance. The island housed thousands of Japanese just beyond the three-mile strip the military had marked out and defended as an airfield, from which our fighting planes took off to bomb Rabaul. Coast watchers, Aussies or New Zealanders who before the Japs landed had taken in radio equipment and supplies and lived in hiding to radio to our headquarters when one of our planes went down, themselves might need to be rescued. Sometimes one heard from friendly natives that the Japs knew of his hiding place and were coming to kill him. When he radioed for help, a picked company, maybe 30 or so Fijians, were sent in. I interviewed such a group and so did Bob right after they had rescued the coast watcher. Three giants towered over me, standing stiffly at attention all the time we were talking. They didn't want to be at ease. They loved the military posture. I also talked to the one white man who had accompanied them, an army photographer. He said that each man used his own selection of tufts of grass and berry juice to make his almost naked body camouflaged so that it melted him into the jungle. He was given two bat boys both in their teens to watch over him. Though he had heard or seen no sign of an enemy, they suddenly pulled him down, making him lie flat on the jungle floor.

Now the big Fijian explained what happened. "Jap think he see us. He shoot here and here and here. When he stop shooting, we kill Jap." They simply wiped out a superior number of Japanese whenever they met a patrol, and brought out the coast watcher unharmed.

By the way, if a native gave helpful information to a coast watcher, the white man would give him a note, as good as money. All the native had to do was present it to an American or Australian or New Zealander, telling the Yank or whoever to buy the fellow whatever he wanted, and it was done.

We were saddened to learn that the East Indians who had come to work on the plantations at Fiji for ten years refused to go home after their ten years were up and were hiring smart lawyers to take from the good-natured Fijians whatever they could steal. We hated those sneaky little men, Gandhi or no Gandhi.

In general, the farther east you went in the Pacific, the more handsome and civilized the natives, and the farther west, the lower the intelligence. I saw a Fijian bringing a native back out of the jungle, where they stood behind the whites watching the nightly movie, always shown out of doors, rain or shine. The Fijian watched with evident relish; the little native, exactly half his size, watched stolidly for ten minutes, then turned silently and disappeared into the jungle. I was told that if a native lost a spear, he wouldn't take the trouble to look for it. He just made another.

On January 31, our B-24 was ready to fly again. The captain told us in late afternoon that we would arrive in Espiritu at 7:10.

"Or thereabouts," I said.

"No, at 7:10."

Those fellows had been flying Pan American for years and depended on celestial navigation when they needed to. I thought they were so efficient they wouldn't know how to let down and have fun. But they quietly kidded each other. The navigator couldn't spell, so they meticulously drew in three extra stars on his maps, labeling them Venious, Dubious, and Serious, spacing them well apart.

The navigator may not have been able to spell, but we circled the harbor about Espiritu Santos and touched down at exactly 7:10.

Espiritu and Guadalcanal were very similar in 1944. The war had passed them by, but they were huge supply bases and points of departure for planes and ships that were carrying the war farther and farther toward Japan itself.

Guadalcanal had experienced such long and heavy bombardment that most of the small trees had been sawed off eight or ten feet up. Already the vines were taking over. Everywhere they grew so fast that after a year or two they had grown a new roof over the jungle. From above you could fly over installations that were humming with life but from the air nothing could be seen. The Seabees built firm coral roads as durable as asphalt that glowed with a blinding whiteness for a time, but without constant care the great vine leaves would soon cover them. The only trees visible above the soft green roof made by leafy vines have a gentle north Italian look about them. Step off the Seabee-built road underneath that cover, and you find enormous trees, like the banyan, which as an afterthought drips down roots from outer limbs to support its old age until the original trunk is completely hidden in a bundle of fasces, all intertwined with lesser vines in an impenetrable maze.

From an airplane, it looks soft enough to support you should your plane spin in. But a pilot who did just that within a mile of a well-traveled road, and whose disappearance point was well noted, could not be found for four days. One of Steichen's photographers volunteered to ride in the rear seat of an SBD and cover every foot of suspected territory. Not a hint did those films show. The jungle had swallowed the plane. Native patrols had no better luck. Four days later two Marines cut their way in with machetes. All that was left after that plane hit those great trees was matchsticks.

There are no words to describe the jungle, but Bob and I overheard two black Marines on a Honolulu street car come close.

Said the sergeant, "Wait till you see that jungle. She is really rugged, what I mean."

"Ain't no jungle gon trouble me," said the private. "I was born in the Evahglades."

"Listen, Big Boy, a sergeant knows more than a private, and I know what you know, but you don' know what I know. I'm tellin' you right now: when you see that jungle, you is gain' to admit self-defeat!"

Reporting at Espiratu, we were surprised that the tall coconut palm trees of the copra plantation extended for miles along the shore, hiding roads, storehouses, Quonset huts and small individual single dwelling huts, roadfuls of bombs on their carriages, planes, trucks, jeeps—a little of everything. The palm trees were loaded with fruit and so was the ground where you might stumble over a ripening coconut shell. The palms were planted in perfectly regular lines and the winds had blown thousands of coconuts down from the tall trees. As I went about the more important job of learning about a supply base, I also had a small side question I asked everybody: with all those thousands of men and thousands of coconuts, hadn't somebody been beaned? The answer was always no, but I persisted and finally I found my man. His name was Mac Donald and it had given him a concussion. He had spent a considerable time in the hospital. Then he added, "But that was a long while ago—in Miami."

Island pigs, originally domesticated, wander wild through the military camps, poking around the doorsteps of huts as casually as did swine in Washington during earliest days. So many of these pigs were accidentally shot by spam-ridden personnel, who mistook them for wild boars, that hunting licenses had to be issued. Copra owners charge exorbitant prices for barbecued livestock.

The plantation owners, many of them degenerate half breeds, would have lost everything if it hadn't been for the Americans. As it is, they snooze in their native huts, waking periodically to hold meetings of protest that the United States government should do right by them. If their cows, brought in to keep down the under-growth, walk out on the airstrips and wreck the planes that are saving their scurvy hides, they don't even turn in their sleep.

It seemed always to be raining in Espiritu. Talk about sheets of water! It rained there in 7 days as much as the total rainfall for New York City for one year. We were glad to board a sizable ship bound for Guadalcanal. On it we met a very disgruntled actor in charge of a bevy of movie stars who had been up the slot in the Solomons, making the dreams of the enlisted men more lustful than usual. There was one little slut who gave him a great deal of trouble. Asked if she would sneak off to the huts and tents, he explained her psy-chology. That would require a certain generosity on her part. She used her body entirely for publicity purposes. If she could be raped by a venomous-looking Jap under the most powerful spotlights with two opposing armies lined up to watch, she would gladly have given herself up the minute she was sure the cameras were rolling. She fascinated me for a while, too, then I found at the very bow of the ship a more seductive sight, a beautiful porpoise keeping just ahead of the ship. I had no sense of the speed we were making until I watched that porpoise swimming possibly ten to twelve feet down. I had heard that they led ships into harbor, and he was beautiful, golden in the hot rays of the midday sun. Such images never leave your mind. The prow above knifed through the water, curling back a tiny wave in satiny, shimmering décolletage, while below, this harbinger of goodwill, its frolicsome dives forgotten, slipped swiftly through the water like an unerring torpedo with so little motion that it seemed to be propelled by inner dynamos, leading the behemoth behind it into a safe harbor.

Guadalcanal was an ugly place. The speeding trucks stirred up clouds of coral dust from the roads, and this particular coral dust covers everything. It can rain all night and by noon the trucks will be whirling the dust clouds. Step off the road, you're up to your hips in mud. Here the huts are all built on a foundation a step or two off the ground. Whether from mahogany, rough cut by the Seabees' power saws, or a plywood square, they are equally unbeautiful but necessary.

The standard building is the Quonset. Hospitals, storehouses, hotels for transient officers—invariably called Hotel de Gink. An admiral's office will be in a Quonset, and so will his house, though interiors differ. Floor lamps, chairs, flowerpots, even indirect lighting, and an occasional painting, done by a Seabee of course, dignify an officers' club or an admiral's quarters. The enlisted man seldom has such refinements inside his hut, which is often given a name like "Cesspool Villa," but his tiny yard or garden may be brave with exotic flowers or garden vegetables from seed supplied by Pearl. His garden will be fenced by rows of inverted beer bottles. If he knows he's here for the duration, he may have rigged up bedsprings interwoven by strips of live rubber, and to protect his best clothes from mildew he may have an electric light eternally burning in a clothes closet.

I interviewed the admiral in charge of the South Pacific Naval Aviation more than once, and came to like him so well that I wrote an article about him in *Flying* magazine. Admiral Fitch made it plain what he thought of the floods of pamphlets and directives that flowed out from Washington. "Watkin," he said, "see that captain? He's my aide. If any of that stuff you fellows write in Washington gets from his desk to mine, he is automatically fired. We're fighting a war out here, and we know how to fight it, and we don't have the time to read bullshit."

In spite of that introduction, we found him to be a reasonable man, who answered our questions. We discovered that he gave any journalist, of whatever reputation, such a low priority on a plane that if the guy ever managed to reach his office—as we had, thanks to Admiral McCain—he might as well head for home in a rowboat. He had no publicity staff of any sort whatever. He had an officer who wrote up a dignified account of an action without giving away any secrets. This he took in the admiral's barge every morning across the bay to the news conference being held by General MacArthur. No wonder that Secretary Forrestal wondered what the Navy was doing. Before the admiral's dispatch even reached the news conference, yesterday's events had been chronicled. By asking around Bob discovered that MacArthur sometimes had fifty American journalists at a time at his camp. Not only were they given high priority on any plane, but if they were top-notch men, planes were sent to Pearl to fly them out to be royally entertained while they watched MacArthur win the war single-handed.

One dispatch from Fitch reported that Army / Air Force planes had hit Rabaul, causing great havoc. Not only were half a dozen Zekes (Jap fighters) shot down, but extreme damage had been done to Japanese shipping in the harbor and to supply dumps. It added that allied planes also took part in the strike. The allies mentioned included the Navy, the New Zealanders, and the Aussies.

When we reached Bougainville, the farthest the Navy and Marines had proceeded up the slot early in 1944, we found out what really happened. What's more, Navy cameramen recorded the truth. In 1940 the Navy had only 1800 airplanes, old and out of date. In 1944 it was flying some 20,000, the great preponderance from carriers in the Pacific. In such a fight as the dispatch described, several squadrons of the best Navy fighting planes had taken off from their land base at Bougainville, engaged the Japanese fighters, and shot them down. Navy or Marine SBDs which was the Navy's single-engine light bomber, came out of the clouds and attacked the shipping. The SBD flew straight down, its machine guns strafing the enemy ship, not releasing its bomb or pulling out until it had almost crashed into the enemy's deck. Army dive bombers glided down on an angle; the SBDs went straight down, presenting a smaller target. At the same time the Navy's light-heavy twin-engine plane, the TBF, capable of very high speeds, carried a heavy torpedo bomb. It swooped down toward the broad side of the enemy ship, holding its torpedo from the water until it was so close to the ship that again its bomb couldn't miss, before it pulled up to escape, always dangerously close above the enemy ship. It took guts to withhold the bomb for a sure hit, but such a hit was lethal.

The Army planes operated at a height of 22,000 feet. They dropped huge bombs, which the ship could often dodge by taking evasive action. Those big planes were great against Germany, where they could flatten whole cities, but in the Pacific the Navy shot down the planes and sank the ships, and the Army planes killed fish.

MacArthur with his unbelievable arrogance and pomposity was probably the most disliked man in the Pacific. He regarded the whole ocean and all its islands as his domain. He didn't want the United States military to come in there except on his terms. He expected his personal lawyers to draw up papers. While we were there MacArthur reviewed a company of Marines, far and away the best fighting men in the war, and the most devil-may-care. One of them had put up a placard:

> With the help of God
> And a few Marines
> MacArthur retakes
> The Philippines.

He put the whole company on report, and I am sure that Fitch did his best to help, but the culprit was never found. After the war, I saw in the Warner Bros studio library a history in which MacArthur was pictured as a tail gunner in an Army plane. He actually had one hand on a machine gun, the other on a long feeder cartridge belt slung heroically over one shoulder. No doubt some wag had convinced him that such a fighting pose would mean a lot to the folks back home, but his pomposity was built in. I saw him at Washington and Lee long before the war as an honored guest at the W&L final ball, and he was arrogant then. When little Truman went out and fired the great man, countless people wanted to hug the peppery little president.

MacArthur did two fine things: he did great work with Nimitz as a strategist, and a Japanese gentleman told me that the people of Tokyo were so astounded by the perfect behavior of the army of occupation because of MacArthur's strict commands for proper discipline there, that the whole friendship of the two nations was built upon that good conduct. Now that I have given the devil his due, thank God he has faded away.

Bougainville was a beautiful place. The earth was soft loam; homemade sprinklers and scrapers and rollers made the roads pleasant to drive on (speed limit strictly 25 miles an hour). The Seabees had outdone themselves. After the Marines had gone ashore and taken the island, the Seabees put down their waffle-strip takeoff and landing runways, and they constructed all sorts of huts with double-decker beds as well as wooden platforms where a man could stand naked and take a shower from an overhead installation. They sent their tractors through the jungle to build ammo dumps and revetments where the 1,000 lb. bombs were stored ready to be wheeled out to the TBFs. They put up poles and strung telephone wires and at the perimeter they dug emplacements for the Army to put their guns to guard the narrow domain from the thousands of Japs who were isolated in the jungle. They could not be supplied, so they had learned which jungle things were edible and had their own gardens. When a Jap body had to be buried, the flyers buried him just outside their own tiny grassy cemetery with its white crosses, putting up a black cross over his final resting place with the legend PUBLIC ENEMY NUMBER ONE.

I never thought of the Japanese that way, for in the secret file in the Department of the Navy, which because of my rank I had access to, I read from a Japanese flyer's diary a statement that could only be written by a civilized and perceptive man. He had noted that tomorrow they were ordered to bomb the American encampment. It would be on Christmas Day, December 25, which meant nothing to the writer, but it meant a lot to the Americans. It was their holy day when they worshipped their God and exchanged loving gifts and feasted and made merry. They thought they would be safe to enjoy such a day. It seemed a pity to intrude upon their happiness, surprise and probably kill a great many of them. He knew how he would feel if the American flyers did that to him.

It reminded me of the brotherhood of man and of Hardy's little verse about his foe:

> How quaint and curious war is
> You shoot a fellow down
> You'd treat if met where any bar is,
> Or help to half a crown.

The Third Marine Division had put up a sign along one of the roads:

> So when we reach the isle of Japan
> With our caps at a jaunty tilt,
> We'll enter the City of Tokyo
> On the roads the Seabees built.

Bob and I first hit Bougainville on February 16 on temporary additional orders supplied by ComAirSoPac, and retained by them, in other words by orders from Admiral Fitch. I had made friends with him in a way. I let him know that I wanted to do a brief but dignified article for *Flying* magazine on the great job he was doing for Naval Aviation. I talked to him enough to let him know that it was sincere admiration that impelled it, but I knew better than to drown him with flattery, and he began to talk. I mentioned Pappy Boyington, recently shot down by the Japs, but did not tell him all I knew. He responded by saying that he couldn't discipline such people too harshly. If they were not overgrown crazy kids, they wouldn't go up day after day risking their lives the way they did. When we reached Bougainville, I heard the full story. Almost daily Boyington would go up and let the Japs tune in on his frequency, then bait them with a newscast of what really happened to their friends in yesterday's strike, warning them against putting their trust in that hogwash from Tokyo.

A polite foreign voice would ask in precise English, "Won't you come down, Maychor Poyington?"

So the slap-happy Marine flyer would barrel on down, gun their field, roar back up again, and taunt them to pay him a visit. Once they did, in broad daylight. Boyington ran out and tried to shoot down an enemy plane with his service revolver. His bunkmate risked *his* life to run out and get a snapshot of Boyington's savage face. Steichen told me that that was the greatest picture to come out of World War II and that it had been taken on an old Brownie Camera.

In the naval building back in Washington, I had often passed the door of Colonel Joseph Smoak, USMC. He happened to be the officer who gave Boyington his orders on Bougainville, all of which Boyington resented. His squadron loved Boyington. They would do anything for him and vice-versa. He hated the attempts of Colonel Smoak to discipline him. One day Smoak put him on report and gave him strict orders not to leave his tent until the colonel so directed. The minute the coast was clear Boyington ran out, hopped into his plane, and took off for Guadalcanal. He ran straight to Admiral Fitch and told him breathlessly that Smoak was going to take his command away from him.

"Hell, he can't do that, can he?"

"No, I won't let him do that, but look, Pappy; you're going to have to be a better boy. We couldn't run an organization of this size if everybody acted the way you do, just did anything he damned pleased. Now I want you to behave yourself, do you understand?"

"Yessir. Thank you, sir."

He tore back home to tell his men the good news. He was most polite to Colonel Joseph Smoak, witih one exception. Every squadron had its own radio signal, by which a flyer first identified himself before he gave a message or asked for instructions. Boyington's squadron changed its signal. Hereafter any member of that squadron called out: "Fuck Joe Smoak."

When the Japanese held him prisoner they beat him with baseball bats; they did everything to break his spirit, but in this they never succeeded. He survived.

The man who told me those things was a Marine flyer of an SBO. I made friends with him and asked if I could go along the next time he did a run on a particular bridge not far inside the jungle. The Japs wanted that bridge held, though it spanned only a small stream, and the Navy or Marines sent a plane down infrequently to knock out the machine gun nests on either side. "I don't want to be a hero; I'm just a tourist, but I'm curious."

Finally, he said OK and early one morning they strapped me into the seat of the rear-seat gunner. Then they strapped down the guns, so that I could face forward. There was an intercom; otherwise, the two compartments were sealed off from each other. It was exhilarating flying straight down, and I could smell the powder when my pilot began shooting. "Why don't they shoot back?" I inquired.

"They are," he answered pleasantly just as he started to pull out. That part was not exhilarating. He pulled out over the top of the tallest tree and started for Bouganville, but every bit of blood in my body had left it and settled in my toes, I felt sure. It was the most horrible sensation I had ever experienced. I was afraid I was going to die, then afraid I wouldn't, but by the time we landed my circulation was nearly back to normal. The pilot saw that I was pretty sick and said, "Hell, I should have given you a corset to wear."

He explained that on their visits to Auckland or Sydney for their two weeks of rest and rehabilitation—R&R—they bought women's corsets in the department stores and strapped them around their middles to keep the blood from coursing downwards. I believe that was the beginning of the pressure suits that pilots were wearing before the war ended. He told me so many stories about the Yanks on holiday that I wanted to see that, too.

Before we left the plane, he pointed out the six bullet holes the Japs had left, two through the right wing and four through the left. They didn't impress me. I was one of those foolish people who never expected to be killed. It has nothing to do with courage. The courageous man is the one who expects to be killed but does his duty anyway. I was in search of excitement, using the excuse that I'd do better with the manuals. But I did go a long way and learned a lot.

I flew with the night fighters when they were teaming up with Swift Boats below to knock off barges the Japs were running at night to supply the all-but-isolated men on certain Islands. The night fighter was the old PBY amphibious plane painted black, that most reliable of transport planes, the DC6. If it spotted a barge it radioed its position to the Swift Boat below that would zoom out from shore and make the kill. I once had the pleasure of introducing men from a Swift Boat to the flyers they had often talked to at night but never seen when both by accident were at a shore installation overnight with orders that sent them in opposite directions.

Bob Taylor, who had worked like a madman at Bougainville to get the stories of all the fighter squadrons, had finished his job there and suggested that we pull out. He he told me that an uncle (or first cousin) of his was in command of the army contingent that was protecting the island from those thousand of Japs in the jungle, that his relative wasn't very bright, which was why his family got him into the Army, and he was sure that when those Japs found out how dumb Uncle Blank was, they were going to come out of that jungle and cream Uncle Blank. He felt it in his bones. That's exactly what happened, we learned later. My friend, the SBD pilot, loved to take recordings of the ground crew in his command and sent me a record when I was back in the naval building. You could hear the Jap shells hitting the runways with a dull boom, while the pilot interviewed some of the men, calling upon them by name. He asked one where he'd like to be right now. The man answered, "I'd sure as hell like to be back in the good ol' USA." Another man with a lovely accent said, "USA, hell, I'd like to be back in good ol' Texas." I have that record somewhere among my effects.

At Espiritu, I wanted to go on to Auckland and Sydney, Brisbane, Noumea, Espiritu, Palmyra, and Pearl. Taylor wanted to go via the central Pacific. He never mentioned it, but he wanted to edit the 1944 Edition of *Flying* magazine, and he eventually did so. I was so amused by the stories about Auckland and Sydney, and the way they entertained the Navy flyers, that I struck out in that direction. I wrote one article for that 1944 issue of *Flying* about R&R at Auckland, opposite another light piece called *"African Wing Ding"* by Brad, whom I suggested visit the west coast of Africa, where he could be near his beloved blacks.

Flying was rough. The storms were of such velocity that the NATS pilot had to bring his plane down within fifty feet of the water to escape the worst winds. The waves below looked at least that high. I was as near frightened as I'll ever be aboard an airplane. I wrote my mother that we had been through some small cyclonic disturbances, which made the cloud formations even more beautiful.

Seen from above, they are very wonderful, especially at daybreak. Some look like cotton, some like smoke, some like that white-spun candy you get at the beach, some like glaciers—mostly like glaciers.

I told her about the leaves of the taro plant as big as a man, and the thousands of coconut trees, and the green orchid, not a cymbidium, an orchid, in a tree at Guadalcanal; and at Noumea the trees with gnarled woodcut trunks and the yellow flowers, pure saffron, shaped like the single petal of a hollyhock, the flame trees, honeysuckle blossoms poking through mimosa-like leaves. I tried to let her see the wonder and the brilliance and immensity and never mentioned the discomforts. I have an idea that's what the service men remember, for there is no ocean with such a dependable blue, or moonlight more intense, or coral reefs more dazzling, or breezes softer when the weather is fine, or rain that is wetter when it isn't.

I could write unendingly about the unmilitary side of the South Pacific, but I must bring this to a halt. When I reached Auckland, I found that the New Zealanders were so grateful to the Navy flyers who had saved their country from the Japanese invader that they all conspired to make his week's visit a happy one. The officer made the choice; he could visit the peaceful and beautiful estate of Kenneth Meyer called Glen Innes which the owner turned over to the Navy as a rest home, run by the Red Cross, where a man who had starved for milk and butter and ice cream and juicy steaks could stuff himself or just sleep, or meet the beautiful and talented daughters of the aristocracy for dance and romance. After the war more than one of these ladies went back to the States as brides. You would hear the boys talking, amazed that the girl would even look at them: "I never met such a girl before. She spun me in." They thought highly of the New Zealand flyers they met who had practically no equipment; so, when one of our P-40s was shot down, our flyers, who hated that plane, were happy to leave it in the bay. But the New Zealanders dredged it up and soon had it flying again. On its first solo mission the New Zealand pilot radioed down, "Hey, Yanks, come on up. I've got seven Zekes *surrounded*."

In reporting to transportation, I met another former Washington and Lee student. They were everywhere. (Later, in New York City, a car almost ran me down and the two boys in uniform called out, "Hey there, Professor Watkin. Almost got you that time.") This character, a former director of the Fancy Dress Ball, thought it would be unsuitable for a W&L prof to fly NATS. He presented me with a first-class ticket on the Tasman Airways Clipper to Sydney.

Sydney was more cosmopolitan. There I met a Helldiver pilot who told me how he had spent *his* week. He was met by a guide who gave him directions to his hostelry, which happened to be in the beautiful house of a wealthy retired old lady, keen to do her part for the war effort. The guide also presented him with two bottles of very fine whiskey. He noticed that women and girls were doing work ordinarily done by men. It made no difference how rich or well-bred you were; if you were young and strong, you must by law take a job ordinarily performed by a man away at the front. If you passed certain tests, your job might be interesting; otherwise, you worked in a munitions factory. The Yank flyer had noticed a stunning girl driving a streetcar, so he swung aboard and went all the way to the end of the line, which ended in a park. He asked the girl if she had time for a short snort. She took the time and they sat on the grass swapping confidences. She was a banker's daughter, whose father had wrangled this marvelous job for her. She couldn't drink too much now, but would accept his invitation to sample the bottle again as soon as she was off duty. She was even more beautiful when she was dressed for the evening and out of her motorman's uniform. Very late at night they tiptoed into his room, where she went to bed with him. Much too early the next morning their elderly hostess tapped on the door. They pulled the blankets around them and our hero, feeling like the most shameful heel that ever walked the earth, said, "Come in." The old lady had made him a tray of hot tea. When she saw that he had company, she put the tray down, said, "Oh, dear," and departed, soon to return with a second cup. She served them both a bountiful breakfast and welcomed them back for the rest of the week.

"Will you marry her?" I asked.

"A clot like me! Not bloody likely."

"You've picked up the lingo."

"I learned a lot more than that. There's a difference. I may go back to school on the GI Bill."

At Brisbane before I took the NATS plane for Espiritu, I watched a timid little Australian girl trying to get people to put a few coppers into her basket for the Red Cross. Two Aussies wear breezy uniforms like the Scots, and big hats. They are like our American cowboys. They went into a store, borrowed a blanket, came back to the street, winked at the girl, and shook their blanket in the face of every passerby, intoning, "Give, give, give to the Red Cross." Everybody gave; they made damn sure of that. Then they emptied their own pockets into the blanket, poured the considerable contents into the girl's basket, and turned to me. They hadn't asked me to contribute. They were saving me. Gesturing toward a pub, they said, "Come on, Yank, buy us a drink." An Aussie always said, "Come on." Their officers never ordered them to charge. They charged and told their men to follow.

In the course of two days NATS flew me from Brisbane to Noumea to Espiritu to Funafuti to Canton and finally to Palmyra, the last stopover point before Pearl, or so I thought. But when we started out in the morning for Pearl we were not quite half-way when one of the two engines on the PBY conked out; so, we returned. Most of the next day was spent with a young officer educated at one of the universities to the north, on the west coast. He was used because of his ability to write Japanese, which he knew perfectly along with several other foreign tongues. I don't remember his name because I always called him Lavengro. He had a hobby he could now use while we waited, ornithology. I had made friends with some of the house boys that came from an island in the central Pacific, Ellice, but the one I liked best, Joe Papua, came from Nui. The pharmacist's mate who had examined these twenty-odd young men said that he had never seen such Form Ys, which I new about from the procurement office in Richmond. He could find nothing wrong organically and not so much as a single cavity in any of their teeth. They were used in the NATS' Hotel de Gink for waiters, cleaners, cooks, or whatever, and were always cheerful and smiling.

So Joe went along while Lavengro showed me the birds, collecting eggs and taking notes for a Washington state museum. He showed us the different kinds of boobies, so awkward on land, so beautiful in flight. Here they had no natural enemies, so instead of hiding their nests in trees, they scratched together some twigs and leaves and sand and laid their eggs there. You could even poke a stick at them and they wouldn't move, not until the white eggs had hatched. More interesting than the boobies were the fairy terns, pure white, that fluttered daintily in the tops of the palms. No bigger than a swallow they were, Lavengro said, and such powerful flyers that they could travel a hundred miles out to sea and back. They were even more careless about nests than the boobies. In the bare crotch of a tree they laid a big spotted egg out of all proportion to their small size to give the fledgling a better start in life and both they and their mates took turns hatching it. The baby bird turns out to be a knot of brown fuzz that sits like a bump on a log holding on for dear life and maturity. The last bird we saw was a gaunt grey bundle of feathers, ugly as sin. He sat beside a boobie that had caught a fish, never moving.

Maybe he cursed under his breath, but he frightened the boobie so much that before his fish was half devoured, he dropped it into the water. Then the frigate bird swooped down and gobbled it up. As funny as that seemed to us was the attitude of the boobie, who knew what would happen but lighted on the limb beside the albatross with the same resigned air that people take toward lawyers.

Joe Papua was a sweet, benevolent man. He hated the Japs because in the early days the Japs had bombed the Nui church until an American flyer closed with the pilot and shot him down. Joe said that when the Jap plane hit the water, its engine came clear of the plane and skipped across the water like a skipping stone until it rested on the beach. The Jap was dead, but the islanders rescued the American pilot and took him inside the chief's hut, where he was nursed back to health and feasted most royally.

"And I suppose," I said, "he repaid that kindness by making love to the chief's daughter."

"Oh, no," said Joe. "He was a gentleman."

I thought Mr. Papua was being a bit unctuous. "I believe your women are very beautiful. If you had been that pilot, wouldn't you have made love to them?"

"Oh, yes," said Joe, easily and without any smile of evasion, "but I am a cowboy."

We went out the second day and again had to turn back because of engine trouble. Joe kept us from the boredom of gin rummy by inviting us both to a dance the Ellice Islanders put on. At the open end of their hut twelve natives sit in a circle around their drum, made of a mat covering a wooden box. For fancy effects one boy vibrates an empty gasoline tin. All start beating on the drum slowly and rhythmically, and begin a low chant. Then half of them rise and face us like a chorus, while the others continue the background chant and beating of the drum. The chorus begins a dance and a song. Their hands add to the accompaniment by smacking folded arms and the flat of bare thighs.

The chief or head dancer may rise while all others sit. Instead of singing words, he makes a *ste, ste, ste* hissing noise throughout the whole dance. Tucking in his red loincloth, he points to face, hands, breast, and hips, concluding with convolutions and convulsions representing lovemaking, done with infinite humor. The half-squatting stance of the Hawaiian is used throughout, but there is no shimmying. The end is a crescendo. The heavy, wild, resistless rhythm of the drum goes faster and faster, building to a final shattering thunderclap, a wild shout. The dancer flings his arms upward. It is over; there is no diminishing, only immediate cessation, grins, down sitting, brown muscles glistening with a healthy sweat.

Those boys liked the Americans because they were so friendly. Papua said they all wanted to go to the States after the war, especially to New York. Some promoter should have taken them there. They'd have been a sensation in a night club.

Before I left, Joe Papua brought me a gift, a coconut crab, a blue monster crustacean larger than a lobster and more dangerous. His great claws could crack a half-inch board. Joe said he pulled him out of a hollow log by reaching his hand in quickly. Though a daredevil enlisted man barely had the crab in his hands before he dropped him again, Joe handled him with smiling ease, his lightning fingers anticipating the deadly darting claws. He held him from underneath by the curled-up tail.

Joe said they were very good to eat, but I apologized by explaining that such things were forbidden on planes. We shook hands instead. It was my goodbye to the South Pacific. He said to come back. I said I would.

29

Bob and I gave Secretary Forrestal a joint twenty-page report, and he thanked us. I wish I had kept a copy. Some years later when I read that he was in a Bethesda Hospital, quite insane, I remembered his looking for hidden listening devices in the conference room. (He jumped from a high window to commit suicide.) I also heard it whispered that he had not jumped from that window, but was pushed. Such a thing was unthinkable then, but nobody appears to be greatly surprised at assassination these days.

I was proud that Bob Taylor used those carefully taken notes and had the names of officers to write to for more information when he became the editor of the 1944 October issue of *Flying* magazine, which was a sizable book with over 300 pages devoted to the single subject *U.S. Naval Aviation at War, 1944*. The table of contents lists almost 40 articles, but the only writer named was the Hon. Artemus L. Gates, Assistant Secretary of the Navy for Air, who in the introduction pulled no punches in stating that the Navy's new weapon, the Carrier Task Force, made possible the landing of marines and MacArthur's army forces on island after island by knocking out enemy planes before the landings and providing close-range bombing and strafing cover for the invading troops. He might have said what became a bitter pill for the battleship admirals to swallow—that they dared not leave their harbors without carriers to protect them. On the opposite page, signed by *the editors* and plainly the work of Bob Taylor, it was mentioned that almost all the articles were prepared by the Aviation Training Division, submitted by various officers of the Navy, Marine Corps, and Coast Guard. He also mentioned that most of the beautiful photographs were taken by the men from Steichen's unit, though he did not mention Steichen by name. That marvelous man, Edward Steichen, had been the commander of the photographic division of the Air Service in World War I, but when he offered his services again in World War II, the Army thought him too old. The Navy had better sense. He was known as American's most famous photographer after World War II. In 1947 he became the director of photography for the Museum of Modern Art in New York. He was then just getting started. Thank

God the youngest branch of the Navy picked the youngest in spirit for its photography.

Taylor lamented that it was too late to include the unbelievable record of Task Force 58 which in 13 days of June 1944, destroyed 747 Japanese aircraft, 30 ships, and 13 barges with negligible losses. Not bad for the *Allied* airplanes that also took part.

But that issue of *Flying* was more than that. It became a history of the early rough war in the Pacific and a tribute to the units left behind who played their part when the war was toughest and who still maintained what they and others had won, for the war was not over yet, though the end seemed in sight. The most famous war correspondent, who eventually met his death before t war ended, *Ernie Pyle*, called that issue the greatest tribute and morale builder yet to appear in World War II.

I claim little credit for the success of that venture. Taylor and Bradford and I left for Chicago to talk with the editorial staff of *Flying*. Brad stayed on to help Taylor, but since my experience with magazines was nil, I went back to Washington after a few days. The place was never quite the same, and they never returned, for after *Flying*, somebody on the staff of Admiral King, the commander-in-chief of the Navy, wanted them both ordered to New York to work upon a history of the Navy in World War II. They visited us in Washington from time to time, and we never were out of touch thereafter until Brad's death in 1948.

I don't know what became of their project or when they got out of the Navy. In our exchange of visits and letters New York was never mentioned. I think there were too many Hewitts around. Speaking of that gentleman, when things began to slow down, he used nepotism to get out of the Navy ensuring him a head start on other advertising men still serving. Nepotism got him into his good Navy job and asthma kept him from more strenuous duty, but when he wanted out, the asthma was miraculously cured.

There were still some amusing characters that remained. Their talents were genuine, though so different from what we needed that they made no appreciable written contribution. It was a joy to the rest just to have them present. All became my good friends and remained such, for they were lovable and fascinating human beings. Like Jesse Stuart, a Kentucky mountain man, reincarnated straight out of the days of Daniel Boone. He had just written *Taps for Private Tussie*, which was so genuine in its understanding of these modern mountain people that the book deserved to be a best seller. Its charm was that it was a straight relation of a group of people out of the past but living in the hills of Kentucky today. We could not revamp our war to use an anachronism, however personally lovable. When the war finally ended, there was no possible reason why we were not all immediately released. I remember Jesse spoke up, saying, "When the Civil War was over my granddaddy laid down his musket and went on home." He said it aloud so that all the unit heard, and he simply did not understand when one of our taskmasters from across the hall came over and made a little speech, saying, "Training is going to be bigger than ever. We need ninety new men!" Most of us gave him a cynical laugh that rolled across the room, and he soon departed. Jesse looked dumbfounded. So, I explained to him what everybody else knew without having to be told: "What he means is that the rank he holds now is because he is in charge of a sizable command. He wants to keep that extra stripe and have it made permanent before we all slip away. And what about Major Keyhoe? Do you think he wants to go back to being a nobody again?"

I told Jesse privately that unlike his grandpop, he was not going to lay down his typewriter and go home. But since there was no assignment for him it would not be unethical if he sat down at the typewriter and wrote up all those great stories he had been telling us, about the time when the Northern Lights came far enough south to hit that little town in Kentucky where he was living. So that's what he did and was completely happy doing. Those stories, which I remember he told us straight-faced, were marvelous. We were living at Castle Hill then, which was in about the same parallel and it was the first time that a lot of the Virginia children had ever seen the Northern Lights, though they were not miraculous to me, for they were commonplace enough in upstate New York. Lexingtonians enjoyed them for what they were. Jesse's hillbillies thought it was the end of the world and behaved accordingly. The village atheist pounded on the empty church door, saying, "Oh, Lord, if you'll stay yore hand till mornin' I'll jine ye."

His best story was about a hard-working farmer who labored during the day but got drunk every evening after supper on his own corn liquor. He had a tough-minded, devoted wife and three stalwart sons she managed to keep sober. When the end of the world was at hand, the old lady sent her boys out to find Pa and bring him home before Gabriel blew that horn. They hitched up the team to a stone boat, which is a low box with wooden runners that the team pulls over the dry grass with its load of stones. It clears the fields for plowing and makes the material for a stone wall outlining the property.

The boys found Pappy skunk-drunk in a field and when he saw them coming he rolled over to a barbed wire fence and clamped his teeth across the smooth wire between two barbs. One of the boys who always carried a file in his hip pocket, its spiked end stuck into half a corncob, took out the file and pried his father's teeth apart. They carried him home on the stone boat and into the parlor where their Ma ordered him deposited on the floor. There she stripped off her husband's filthy clothes, washed his face and hands, put on his clean shirt and his go-to-meeting suit, and laid him out real nice. Then she relaxed, took off her own shoes which pinched her feet, and began rocking in her favorite chair. "Now, then, Lord," she said, "let 'er come!" I gave Jesse the title for that book, *Foretaste of Glory*, and wrote a florid introduction for it. When it came out in 1946, it was dedicated to Lawrence Edward Watkin, for "encouragement and friendship," and he wrote in the flyleaf:

> Feb. 14th 1946
>
> W-Hollow Riverton, Ky
>
> To Larry Watkin with all best wishes. Here it is and I hope you'll think it's okay. You know already without reading it, about all the characters who took off that eventful night of Sept. 18th 1941 in the little town of Blakesburg. You told me to write this; otherwise it would not have been written. Again, best wishes to you and family in sunny California from Deane Jane and me over here in zero weather among these snow-clad Kentucky Hills.
>
> Jesse Stuart

Fine. I was pleased, but when I read the book not one of the wonderful stories that had kept the unit laughing appeared. It was all about rednecks, and not very funny.

I think that Jesse made other people laugh by depicting the mountain people the way they were. He was no kidder, but I used to kid him. I knew that he was a landsman and had no interest in any ship, so I suggested that any time he wished to talk with me privately about sea duty, I'd be happy to discuss it with him. He asked for a conference. He wanted to know if he might be sent to sea. I told him I had no idea. Such things were out of my hands, but after all we had volunteered for the Navy, which might very well mean sea duty. He knew that, of course? Oh, yes, yes, of course. If he had to go, what kind of ship might they put him on? I couldn't even guess. He might be lucky enough to rate a carrier. A long pause, then, "If I got a carrier what provision would they have for my wife and daughter?"

"Oh, they'd send them your check, if you requested it."

"I don't mean that. I mean what sort of place would they have on the carrier for them?"

"Oh, Jesse, I don't think they'd want your womenfolk aboard a carrier."

"I don't see why not. We've always been pretty close."

Another good friend was John Faulkner, who had written a book about the WPA (Works Progress Administration) called *Men Working*. We prized him for his stories about his famous brother William Faulkner, whose work was just being understood about this time. William received the Nobel Prize five years later, in 1949. John looked like him. They were both slight men with military bearings, individualists, who could drink great quantities of liquor without showing it. John called his brother William "Bill," which he pronounced "Beale." He said that Beale had been writing since he was a kid, and finally John thought that if Beale could make a living at it so could he. The stories he told us were the same that Roark Bradford, a fast friend, had told; and later, when I worked briefly at Warner Bros, were told me by my secretary at Warner's, who had also served William Faulkner; so, they must have been true. I will tell only the one I like best.

Jack Warner wanted (and got) Nunnally Johnson, the successful screenwriter, to be a story editor. Though Johnson was a writer himself he stood in awe of other writers, and if he had to talk with them, he wanted a large bare office with a big desk at the far end of the room so that writers would feel ill at ease. Then he wanted one other chair only beside his desk, a chair so deep that the writer would sink way down in it and thus feel at a further disadvantage. When William Faulkner arrived in town, Nunnally was apprehensive. He had heard that Beale disliked most people unless they were real bastards and wondered if he would qualify. Beale entered blithely, marched up to Nunnally's desk, and stuck out his hand. "Mistah Johnson, name's Faulkner." They shook. Faulkner brushed aside the offer to be seated, saying, "Mist' Johnson, are you a drinkin' man?"

Johnson admitted that he occasionally had a snort. "Good," said Beale. He was carrying what appeared to be an old-fashioned carpet bag; he stuck his hand inside, brought out a full pint, and thrust it into Nunnally's hand, nodding for him to take a swig straight. Mr. Johnson did so, then returned it.

"No," said Beale, "Take half."

Mr. Johnson felt that his honor as a writer was at stake and drank a half pint. Beale then took it and knocked off the rest. Then they went out on the town together for two days.

When Beale had been squared away in a hotel and been shown the back room at Musso-Franks where all the screen writers forgathered every day to drink and/or to eat lunch, Nunnally went back to his office, having told Beale he'd call him in due course. Finally, he did so. Jack Warner was having a story conference, discussing the story with Johnson and writers he knew best. At length he said, "What this film needs is horror." He shuffled through a pile of cards and said, "Faulkner...William Faulkner?"

Beale raised his hand.

"Give me thirty pages of horror," said Jack.

"Yessir."

After the meeting Nunnally took Faulkner into the office assigned him, introduced him to his secretary, who would help him with screenplay form, and translated what Jack Warner wanted. Beale went to work, but wasn't getting anywhere. In a few days, his telephone rang and Johnson asked him how he was faring.

"All right," said Beale, "but I can't work in an office. I'm used to working at home."

"That's OK. You don't need to come in. If you want to kick it around, give me a call any time."

Nunnally, who often passed by Beale's office, finally asked the secretary if she had heard from him. "No," she said, "you said he could work at home."

"Call his hotel room, will you, please?"

"He's not there; he's gone home. Oxford, Mississippi."

John himself came in one morning, giggling, half tight. He assured us that we were going to have a visitor a bit later that morning. His wife, whom he always referred to as *Mama*, was out of town for a few days, so he went out to a joint to get something to eat and there met a very beautiful woman and over a few drinks he told her what a crazy place he worked in and what a bunch of characters we all were—ol' Larry Watkin and ol' Jesse Stuart and ol' Mattimore and ol' Hannibal Coons—and she said she'd give anything to see us; so he invited her up. Reckoned she'd be here around eleven o'clock. "Tee, hee, hee," he giggled at the treat she had in store.

I asked him where he had slept. "At home," he said, "but I'll tell you the truth, Pud—he always called me Pud—I almost didn't. We had quite a lot to drink and I was walkin' along the street with her, slippin' my hand inside her dress, when it stuck me what I was doin'. I said to myse'f, John Faulkner, what would Mama say if she saw you now—three o'clock in the mornin' walkin' along the street feelin' a strange woman's thigh? And right then I tol' her goodnight and I'd see her up here this mornin' and I went home and hit that typewriter until it fell on the floor, and I got down on my belly and kep' on writin' until I couldn't see the keys; so, I wrote THE END. In caps."

All day long John waited for the beautiful lady to show up and view the zoo, but she never came. He was happy when Mama came home.

I should at least mention Hannibal Coons, though there will be more of him later. Coons was a super salesman. He managed to make the procurement officer think he was a prolific writer, putting out reams of stuff for the *Saturday Evening Post* and *Colliers*, and he took a rather high critical tone with each one of us, getting our published works and trying to put us on the defensive about them. We all reacted in different ways. It was Dot who finally unmasked him when we visited them one evening. She said that she read magazines, though the rest of us did not (with the possible exception of *The New Yorker* and occasionally *Esquire*), and she had never seen his name in print. What had he actually written? Coons said it had been mostly for *Colliers*. She said to get out a copy and show her. He could produce only two, one on tattooing and the other of equal moment in collaboration with another writer. She insisted he find the rest. She was tired of hearing about his literary exploits when in reality he had written nothing at all. He said he hadn't kept the others. Because there were no others, were there? If he did not produce the others, she was going to write to *Colliers* and ask for anything else by Hannibal Coons, and she was going to search the *Reader's Guide for Periodical Literature*. He finally admitted the truth.

Coons idolized Brad, but beat on him hardest of all. Since Hannibal was a funny lovable big fat guy with a fine sense of humor, Brad would never answer his attacks. He would just look up toward the sky and say in a variety of different ways: "Coons...Coons, Hannibal Coons," and chuckle a bit. I discovered that his name was really Stanley J. Coons, which was how he had registered with the Navy and that his wife's name had been Lucille. Furthermore, they had been living together not married but had married before he joined up. She was a big handsome athletic woman, a beautiful swimmer, with a violent temper and a basic kindness underneath. Coons had always hated the name Stanley; so, the couple consulted a numerologist, who came up with Hannibal and Helgar, or Helga, and he had been crossing the Alps ever since. If he picked on me I called him Stanley. If he picked on Taylor, Taylor would grab from him whatever he was writing, pepper it with signs and symbols and comments that an editor might make on a sloppy piece of writing, hand it back sternly with a "Here!" Coons would study it, find that many of the lightning-fast corrections were justified, and walked away shaking his head.

Everybody learned to love Coons. He simply could not get up in the morning. Taylor would stop and honk for him in his old Ford. Helgar would come to the window naked, displaying her magnificent breasts like a sleepwalker, murmuring that Hannibal would be down in a minute, and soon the man of Mars would appear at the door dressed in only his pants and undershirt, carrying his shirt, tan jacket, cap, and shoes.

He would puff his way into the back of Taylor's car where he would get dressed and appear shortly after Taylor did. He had claustrophobia and hated to look toward a window. He would say, "Good morning, troops," sigh, take a cup of coffee from Brad, remove his cap and outer jacket, and try to correct his shirt, which was always buttoned wrong. His tie was askew, the silver clip denoting his rank as Lt. J.G. was invariably missing, a ring of sweat showed around each underarm. He would eat a whole box of Luden's cough drops for his breakfast and when he had crunched the last one down would lean against the wall and sleep for an hour or two, wake up and get out his typed sheets, grip the two ping-pong paddles he kept in his desk, and spend hours waving the planes aboard a carrier. He spent all of the time he was in our unit doing that and though the flight deck men brought the planes aboard without Coons' manual, which may have been completed in time for World War III, he didn't finish it to my knowledge for use against Japan. As a matter of fact, he never wrote a word that the Navy could use, nor did Jesse or John Faulkner, but they were there. All the big brass liked Coons because he treated them with reverence. In a meeting, he would stand, hands clasped behind him, bent in a half bow from the waist, his features stiff with deferential gravity.

He loved all children, and they him. My two daughters called him Uncle Hannibal. We will meet him again in California.

While everyone was concerned about the coming of peace and what they would do, I wanted to finish one last Sense Manual for the Navy. I had that small experience in the Pacific and decided to go down to Vero Beach where the Night Fighters were training and fly with them before I wrote the manual. I took Dot along, leaving the kids in good hands. She had had a pretty thin time of it, so at our own expense we put up at a beautiful inn on the beach, where we swam and ate good food, and I wrote the manual after flying with the young trainees at night. It was no longer one PBY and a speedboat below. There were a lot of them flying in formation and learning how to keep from smashing into each other. They were much used now to protect carriers at night. I wrote it as *Night Fighter Sense, or Who Killed the Japanese Sandman*, a satirical parody vs. our enemy Dilbert, in the form of an English whodunit. Osborne did some great illustrations.

In the spring of 1945 the war was closing down. Germany surrendered on May 7, 1945. Japan stubbornly refused. On August 6 Hiroshima took an A-bomb and on August 9 one was dropped on Nagasaki. On August 14 Japan said enough and formally surrendered September 2, 1945, on the battleship *Missouri* in Tokyo Bay. Even before that I too began to give some thought about how I should make my living. The Navy, greatly concerned about losing all those USNR officers it had come to depend upon, offered me a remarkable deal, four stripes or a captaincy if I would remain and eventually become the head of a peacetime writer's unit. It was a temptation, for it meant a big salary, innumerable perquisites, and a big fat pension in not so many years. The problem was that not only would my pen be for hire in the worse way, but I would have to hob-nob with a great many regular military phonies I despised. I said no. I wanted out— all the way out, no part-time duty which would lead to the sort of thing I wanted to avoid. I was tempted with all sorts of small inducements like being able to get supplies and cigarettes cheaper here, and abroad if I should travel. I politely declined. One of the very last things I did for the Navy was to write Admiral Mitscher's speech when he came in from the Pacific. He was to give it in an outdoor setting at the Pratt & Whitney plant, and the then big boss across the hall, a tough character whom I liked because he said he hadn't learned much about engineering at Annapolis, but had learned a lot at Georgia Tech, asked me if I'd like to fly up with him and hear my speech read. I said I would. This officer, who was a smart cookie and already interested in rocketry as the carrier weapon of the future, let me fly the plane, a sizable one. It was like keeping your balance on a teeter-totter and he said I showed an aptitude.

The extensive Pratt & Whitney grounds had been trimmed. A speaker's platform had been erected and draped with bunting, and a big circle of funeral chairs arranged for the officers in front of it. Others sat on the grass. Mitscher spoke first and read my speech very creditably, not stumbling over unfamiliar words. Then came an Air Force general, whose name I have forgotten, and he botched things up all the way through. As he plowed his way through to the end, mispronouncing almost every other word and shaming

the English department at West Point, I noticed a slim Army lieutenant a few rows before me squirming in his seat. When it was
over I slipped down and tapped him on the shoulder. "Nice speech,
General," I told him.

A shadow of fear touched his face, then he grinned. "Oh!" he said,
"you're Mitscher."

I grinned back.

"Your man did all right," he said, "but I think I should have been
warned." He lowered his voice. "I could have kept it to words of
one syllable."

I think that was my last official act for the Navy. I sat idly like
the rest, anxious to be released, but not quite knowing what the
future held.

When I sold my house, I had severed my ties with Washington
and Lee. I did not want to go back there anyway. I had seen enough of
the great world to make me restless. My last novel, written in haste,
had not done well, and I didn't think I had any great talent for short
fiction. I should probably take a teaching job somewhere and was
considering the University of North Carolina when I received a bulky
package from the story department of Samuel Goldwyn Studios in
Hollywood. Max Wilkinson, story editor at *Colliers*, was now story
editor for Sam Goldwyn. He asked if I had ever considered screen
writing. If so, the enclosed screenplay, called *The Bishop's Wife*, had
been bought by Goldwyn for the staggering price of $200,000.
Nobody was just sure what to do about that screenplay to save it. It
had been done by a writer named Leonardo Bercovici from the novel
of that name by Robert Nathan. My respect for Robert Nathan has
never diminished. He is the one writer who has continued to write
wonderful straight fantasy and sell it in an age when science fiction
has all but driven real fantasy out of existence. But after reading
Bercovici's screenplay I had no respect for him at all. Nor have I ever
changed my mind about the fellow. It was a piece of cheese worth
roughly $1.98 for the small amount of Nathan left in it. I read Nathan,
then Bercovici, and finally wrote Max a fifteen-page letter, saying I'd
throw the Bercovici thing in the trash and start from scratch.

The story was as Nathan tells it simply this: An Episcopal bishop's
wife found her plodding husband unbearably dull; so, an angel comes
down from heaven and has an affair with her, an actual physical
romance which straightens her out. It seems neither pornographic
nor unbelievable the way Nathan handles it, but Bercovici, knowing
that it could not be shown on the screen, doesn't even try. It's as dull
as I thought Bercovici himself was when I met him. I told Max that

I didn't know how to deal with the big casino at this point, but thought if I began honestly it would be there when I got to it. Besides, all he asked me was did I think I could write screenplays. Since I didn't know camera angles, I'd have to fake that part, but I'd do quite a few pages to show how I visualized the way to start it off. I think I may have written 15 or 20 pages in all as a generous sample and returned the script and the long letter to him. I had waited a week or so and more or less forgotten about it when I suddenly received a long telegram from Max saying that Mr. Goldwyn had read my letter and had read *On Borrowed Time* and said to get that man Watkin out here as fast as he could be released from the Navy. Max further said he knew I would not leave my family behind, so they were offering me all expenses paid to move my family and belongings to the West Coast with a contract for one year at a guarantee of $25,000. After conferring with Dot, she was all for it; so, I told Max it might take me a month to get out of the Navy and drive out by car with the further stipulation that the studio would have to get me something decent to rent to house a family of five, for I had heard that Los Angeles was jammed with service men returning from the Pacific who didn't want to go any farther east. Max said to come as soon as I could and I'd be welcome.

We collected our furniture we'd stored in Lexington, and at last we had everything ready and our suitcases packed in an ancient Packard owned previously by the W&L dean of men. We drove to Camden that fall to say a brief goodbye to my family. Fortunately, the radiator went out before we had gone very far but were near enough expert mechanics to have it replaced and in general over-hauled. How I cursed myself for selling our big, almost new Buick at the beginning of the war. At least the old Packard held a lot of suitcases. When we hit the desert roads in Texas and Arizona, we often traveled twenty or thirty miles without meeting another conveyance of any sort. It was on one of these lonesome stretches when I smelled gas and stopped the car, threw up the hood, and saw a stream of gasoline flowing out of the bottom of what I learned later was the carburetor. I held my thumb over it and told my fifteen-year-old son where to find my jackknife in the glove compartment and told him to cut me an inch thick splinter off a fencepost. Then he put his finger in the dyke while I whittled a short plug with a notched end. I pounded it in with a stone and it fitted tightly. To be sure of it, I secured a piece of wire from another fence, ran it through the groove in the bottom of the plug, tightened it by twisting the pieces together at the top with a pair of pliers, and we proceeded to the next town, where an excellent mechanic found a screw that repaired it quickly, but said, "Dunno what you need it for. I never seen a better plug." I think the town was Amarillo. We thought we had been lucky and that our troubles were over, for actually we had made good time and the three children were good as gold, the only trouble being that we had just got going nicely each morning when first one, then the other would say, "Daddy, I have to wee-wee," or worse. I said they simply would have to synchronize their bowels and bladders, but they never did. When we hit the wastelands, we carried a roll of toilet paper. Any place along the roadside became a rest stop.

Barely had we reached Tucumcari in New Mexico before we broke down again. This time it was a leak of a spring and we had to wait two days. But that was the last of our problems. We struck out for Santa Fe where Brad and his wife Mary Rose and young son Richard had a small house. I don't know why Brad was there, but he seemed to like it. The house was quaint with a little adobe fireplace across one corner of the living room. It was only a block to the best hotel, the La Fonda in the Plaza. Brad had reserved us a fitting room. He told the manager, "Mr. Watkin is a very famous writer—he's a biiiiig man! You'll have to give him the Presidential Suite!" I can see old Brad chuckling now. It cost me a pretty penny, but it was worth it. The children loved it. It had at least ten rooms, I am sure, and a big second-story porch looking down on a terrace. The kids went around hunting bathrooms and the lord knows how many toilets they pressed into service; they never patronized the same one twice and as we spent an extra day, I believe when we left they were all peed out. The beds were antique Spanish so high off the floor we had little stepping stools to let us climb into them.

Good ol' Brad, with his big brown eyes glinting with mischief. He was a lovely man.

None of the filling-station men who had the keys to the car while we were lunching stole anything until we stopped in San Bernadino, California. There one of the mechanics opened the glove compartment and took out my twenty-two caliber target pistol, the clips, and the ammunition. I could not have told which station it was by the time I discovered the theft, but since the car was not unlocked from that time until we drove it into the garage at the beach house in Malibu, the nearest vacancy of any sort the studio could find for us, the thieves, though known, were not worth pursuing.

Goldwyn was in Europe by the time we reached there, but I reported in to work every day and went ahead on my own, first learning screenplay form from reading samples that Max dug out for me, and from the secretary assigned me, a young and very beautiful girl except that she was skinny. There was something else wrong with her, too, which may have been a virtue.

When I left for Hollywood all my friends said doleful goodbyes. Before anybody knew I was leaving, I wrote a letter to the president of Washington & Lee University, saying that a lot of very fine teachers who had left when the students left and had gone into the various industries where their talents were needed had done so well that they might be loathe to return. Yet many were so devoted to the college that they would return if he would put out a form letter welcoming them back. It was only a trickle now, but when the dam burst and the boys flooded the campus again, such teachers might be sorely needed and not easy to replace. I most certainly was not trying to tell him how to run the university, but I had talked with many such teachers who right now were sizing up their futures, and this letter was impelled only by my high regard for W&L.

He hated me so much he never answered me, but three days later I received a form letter he sent out to all W&L teachers explaining that the college still was committed to the Army Division that had taken it over for special programs during the war years. Of course, he wrote, the board of trustees had instructed him to honor all previous commitments. It was a damn poor welcome. I am sure he thought I was talking about myself, and was begging to have him invite me back. As it happened I was practically the only one who did not return. When Charlie MacDowell bade goodbye to me he said, "Larry, there is only one man in this whole damn village and this whole damn town who doesn't want you to return, and to hell with him."

When I told them about the contract I had signed, I came in for the wildest sort of kidding. They visualized me shacking up with a succession of beautiful starlets, and please to save one for them. So, when I wrote to tell them that I had a secretary beautiful enough to be a starlet herself, but that she was a lesbian, I received hilarious letters in return.

It happened like this. Hedy Lamarr was doing a movie at the studio. The set on that stage was closed. Nobody could get a peek at her. However, she had discovered that right underneath my office window, there was a small patch of grass in an alley between the studio and a high wall. The midday sun beat straight down on that tiny patch of greenery and every noon hour the beautiful star of *Ecstasy* sneaked up there, spread a small blanket, and lay down to get a sun tan. Then she sat up, glanced around, undid her halter, and exposed herself to the sun and to me. For days I denied myself lunch, for as Walt Disney said to me in the only indelicate speech

I ever heard him utter, when the two of us were discussing that fine actress Maureen O'Hara, "She's got 'em, you know." I may say that Miss Lamarr had them, too, and in the name of art I compared them to those of the *Venus de Milo*, the *Reclining Venus* by Titian, *Diana at the Bath*, and other famous thems. Actually, that was true, for near perfection is more likely to excite admiration than lust. That did not apply to my secretary, who had tiptoed in and was looking down over my shoulder. "Ohhhh," she groaned, "I'll bet she's gay."

"Are you?"

"Oh, yes."

"And what is your persuasion, femme or butch?"

"Butch," she said.

"Then get the hell out of here. I'm damned if I'm going to share my lunch hour with another man."

As for starlets, I was quite safe from them. Those willing to get parts by prostituting themselves were all snapped up by producers who spent more time on the casting couch than with their films. One famous (or notorious) producer sat at an upper window with opera glasses, scanning the noon-hour crowd for fresh young beauties who had to cross an open space from the sound stages to the cafeteria. A starlet who knew she was being observed made horrible faces and simulated crossed eyes and a spastic twitch so effectively that she negotiated the dangerous crossing successfully. She became so adept that it started her career as a star comedienne.

Aside from the fact that I was no great temptation, neither were any of the many beautiful and sexy actresses I met and worked with in films. Only one, whom I had desired for years on the screen, still had that effect on me when she became the leading lady in a film I had written. In front of the camera she exuded sex appeal, but her performance back stage was disillusioning. She asked the head grip to build her a sort of trough or reclining board against which she could lean quite far back but still remain in a standing position. She told me and a group of concerned actors and workmen that her ovaries were killing her and this relaxed position helped. Her admission did not act as an aphrodisiac. In front of the cameras she now left me cold. It made me suspicious of the sincerity of actors ever after.

30

Not only did Bernice Baumgarten predict that I could never work with Goldwyn, but other writers explained what a mystifying experience I had in store. One, with a string of credits as long as his arm, told me that Goldwyn had hired him to do a rewrite on *Custer's Last Stand.* He found that there were already a lot of screenplays Goldwyn had turned down; so he took several of them home to read over the weekend. When he met with Sam Goldwyn on Monday he told him honestly that he had read some of the plays by famous names that Goldwyn had discarded and didn't think he could do half as well as any one of them. Goldwyn leaned forward and whispered, "You don't understand. I don't like Indians."

I thought as many others did that Goldwynisms such as "Include me out" had been coined by his publicity staff, but after a few conferences with him I realized that he was capable of concocting them all himself.

At first it was a love-fest. He still had a heavy accent. His first words to me were, "Mr. Vatkin, I luffed your letter—and your book. I could have shot your book without a screenplay."

"Thank you, sir."

"And I have read what you have written since, but there is one thing you do not understand: you are changing my story. I always shoot the stories I buy. So you try again. OK?"

"OK."

He favored me with still another production tenet. "Do not write satire. When people can pay two dollars for a ticket, I giff them satire. When they can pay only fifty cents, I *giff* them something *varm.*"

To show that we were still friends he took me down to see some shooting in progress, the beauteous Olivia de Havilland fluffing her lines. The director was patience itself, but there was one speech she simply could not remember, a short simple speech that my youngest daughter could have delivered. During a break Goldwyn led me quietly away to another stage where stagehands were preparing a garden. They had even devised some pigeon droppings, which looked so real I could hardly believe they had been painted on. Goldwyn rubbed his finger over them, remarking with pride at the detail, "Our vorkmen are the best." It was a beautiful set with a fountain and a sundial. Goldwyn inquired of a carpenter what it was, and the man explained that when the sun hit a certain spot it told the time. Goldwyn shook his head, remarking to me, "What won't they think of next?"

When the tour was over, I sought out Max Wilkinson, reporting the conference exactly. "So what should I do now?"

Max was as bewildered as I. "God knows what goes on in that mind. I think you are on the right track. So, for now why don't you just go ahead."

Before I had time to do much more, Christmas was upon us, and the studio might as well have shut down for all the work anybody did. Some did not come in at all and nobody objected. That studio did not hire malingerers, and they let creative people work at their own pace unlike Warner Bros and Columbia, where the top echelons were clock-watchers.

Max Wilkinson had a great idea; he very much wanted Goldwyn to do the Huey Long story, and I told him there was only one man who could give him that: Roark Bradford. Max enthusiastically agreed, so I wrote Brad and asked him if he could come out before the holidays and talk with Goldwyn about it. Brad wrote back that they were tied up for Christmas but might bring Mary Rose to celebrate New Years with us. He would come at his own expense and stay at a downtown hotel where they had been well taken care of in the past. I told him that if he came he must let me find him a presidential suite, lacking which he could stay with us at our huge Malibu cottage, for the weather had been balmy, the beach and the water perfect, our fireplaces burning driftwood logs delightful, with two fine restaurants in spitting distance, and great hotel dining on the cliff above. They did come a few days early and we had a nice visit with plenty to eat and just enough to drink, until New Year's Eve, when we went to a night club and Dot and I and Brad got roaring drunk. Mary Rose, who drank her usual modicum of wine, begged me, as we drove along the coast highway, to pull over and let her drive. I was going much too fast, paying no attention to pockets of fog or red lights. She was an excellent driver, and the like. Finally, Dot turned around and told her with drunken dignity: "Larry is a beautiful driver; if you don't like the way he drives, you can get out and walk." So Mary Rose shut her eyes while the rest of us guffawed at Dorothy's brilliant summation. When I drove into our garage, Mary Rose went straight to bed. Brad apologized as we drank the rest of the night away. "Mary Rose is excitable. She's half wop, you know. That's why she'll only drink wine."

The next day the three of us wished we had, but after a hike along the beach, the usual upchucking, and the diet of aspirin tablets, we were sufficiently recovered to enjoy watching the kids feed the sea gulls, who appeared on the beach at exactly 4 pm each day. I reluctantly drove the Bradfords back to their hotel. We agreed that Max would set up an appointment for him to talk with Goldwyn about Huey Long at 11:00 am on January 3. Brad was sure he would be slept out by then.

On January 3, at 10:00 am, I expected Brad to appear by taxi. When he didn't I called the desk at his hotel. They tried for an hour to wake him. Max apologized to Goldwyn and told me ruefully that Brad had blown it.

Brad called me up about 2:00 in the afternoon. Mary Rose had been out shopping. I told Brad sorrowfully that I doubted if Goldwyn would see him now.

"Hell, Larry, I didn't come out to see Sam Goldwyn. I came out to visit with you, you damned fool."

He said it lovingly. We had a final dinner together that night, and both Brad and Mary Rose said they had had a grand time, one they would long remember, and as soon as I got my bearings in this new job, Dot and I must come and see them. We promised faithfully to do so, but we never found a moment when we could. Mary Rose and I were the letter writers and kept in touch. But it was Bob Taylor who informed me that Brad died in 1948.

Early in January 1946, I had more screenplays ready. Goldwyn had a new idea. He thought I should have a collaborator to learn the ropes, none other than Leonardo Bercovici himself. Our dislike was mutual. I thought that he was a dope and after a week or two with him I was sure of it. He would fall asleep in the middle of a sentence and I would leave him to his siesta. After nicking the Goldwyn Studios for another nice bit of money he departed. Next I collaborated with Bob Pirosh, whom I liked as much as I disliked Bercovici. We couldn't lick the story to Goldwyn's satisfaction. I met a writer who had been hired by Goldwyn. He had had some success with the great one previously. Goldwyn put a script into his hands, saying: "This is a luffly story. It is pure gold. Take it home and make the necessary changes." He wished me well, but shook his head. Bob Pirosh and I enjoyed every minute of our time together, and he became another lasting friend. Our paths diverged, but we met every so often either for dinner at our Malibu place, or at Musso Franks. I asked Bob once where the name Pirosh came from. He said it was Jewish. I didn't know or care that he was a Jew. He cursed the wasted time he had spent in the European theater of war, leading patrols behind the German lines. He knew that if he were captured they would cut his balls off because he was Jewish. Once he asked Dot and me to his apartment for a cocktail party, and we were the only couple there not Jewish. Everybody converged on us, telling me what horrible humiliation they had suffered at the hands of gentiles, especially in college. Finally, I had had enough and blurted out, "Why pick on me, goddamn it! Some of my best friends are gentiles, but now that I'm in Hollywood I don't mind working for Jews. I'm a good nigger. I know my place." They thought that was funny and decided that for Bob's sake they would lay off me.

My next conference with Goldwyn was most pleasant. He thought that I was coming around nicely. "Giff me more of the same," he told me.

Nobody could understand why. I gave him thirty pages more, and he was furious. He shook the pages at me. "You are changing my story!"

I didn't know what to do. Bob Pirosh had departed, knowing that neither I nor anybody else could please Sam. Bob said in leaving that he didn't know what to do just now either. All he knew at present was how Americans fought war, but nobody wanted to hear about that and never would. All the unpatriotic sons of bitches who pretended to hate Hitler had grabbed off all the good stuff while he was away fighting. Bob didn't realize that America would never tire of hearing about that war. In just a few short years he won the Oscar for his original story and screenplay *Battleground*, which may have started the whole thing off, and followed it up with another original, a winner called *Go for Broke,* which he also directed. It told the story of an infantry unit fighting in Italy. Every soldier was of Japanese descent but born in this country. They didn't dare let them fight in the Pacific, but after the record they made in Italy, any American general would have been proud to have them under his command, anywhere.

In the meantime, my conferences continued to be utterly incomprehensible. If one was soothing and congratulatory, the next would be the exact opposite. I would never have found out why if it hadn't been for Dot's flowers. It made no difference whether we were in a rented apartment or not. If there was a few feet of earth anywhere, Dot would have me dig it up to let her grow flowers. If not, I had to build her a long box she could fill with dirt and humus, and she soon had blooms. Roses were her specialty. I always begged a flower for the bud vase of any woman I liked in the studio, who turned out to be the boss' secretaries and the librarians. I liked to talk to smart women, as I did to Catherine McDowell in Lexington, not for romantic reasons but because they were bright. Goldwyn's secretary may have been suspicious at first that I was using her to gain favor with Sam, but when she found that my five-minute visits never dealt with anything about the studio, but concerned politics, education, books, or some philosophical subject, she came to realize that I was courting her brains, for naturally the studio head would have the most brilliant secretaries, and I didn't care what they looked like. So, it was Mr. Goldwyn's secretary who told me what was happening behind the scenes that made Sam so outrageous.

When he had been bidding to buy Bercovici's preposterous screenplay, the smart agent who handled it got Goldwyn and one of Sam's producer friends bidding against each other. Finally, the other producer stopped and let Sam have it. He never really wanted it too greatly, but he loved to kid Sam. Every time he met Sam at lunch or at his famous Sunday morning croquet game he would say, "Sam, how's *The Bishop's Wife* coming? Are you shooting it yet?"

Goldwyn would say, "Great, great. Got some vunerful writers on it now. It should be ready in a week."

Producer Number 2, just to needle Sam, would say: "Sam, why don't you shoot that script you bought? I'll tell you what I'll do: if you'll sell it to me, I'll pay you what you paid plus all your story costs to date plus an extra twenty-five thousand bucks profit and start shooting that marvelous Bercovici screenplay tomorrow!"

Goldwyn thought he meant it, so he would go back and read it or get his wife to read it to him and ask himself, "What does he see in it that I don't see?" Then he would call me in and give me hell for changing his story, which he knew damn well had to be changed.

But I had a secret ally that nobody but the secretary knew about. Ben Hecht, who had written things for Goldwyn which had been hits, and who always offered to buy his time back if Sam complained, liked the Goldwyn studio as a place to work whenever he was in town. In return for a free office he would read a script for Goldwyn and give him his opinion about it, which Sam highly valued.

Goldwyn would feed him my stuff, and Hecht, who had never met me or I him, would say, "Go with Watkin." Then Sam would smile at me. So, it went, Producer Number 2 offering to buy; Hecht praising me. Then Hecht went east and Goldwyn turned against me. I had not finished more than three-quarters of the screenplay when Sam shouted, "Mr. Vatkin, this is childish!"

I had had enough, and I delivered a low blow. "Mr. Goldwyn, the trouble is not with my script; the fault lies in you. You can't read."

Then I walked out, knowing that I would be fired. And I was. One of Goldwyn's less human flunkys came into my office, telling me that I was off *The Bishop's Wife*. They would honor their contract. I would be paid my weekly wage until the year was up, as long as I came into the office as usual just in case they decided to put me on something else, which didn't seem too likely.

I heard later that I was not the only man who ever sassed the great Sam Goldwyn, but was probably the only unaccredited writer. When William Wyler and Sam discussed a script, both slapped down a hundred dollar bill on the table. The first man to call the other a dirty name in a fit of temper had to watch the other pick up his C-note and wait for him to put down another. I never heard how such conferences ended financially, but I know for a fact that a judge in the Deep South fined a countryman $25.00 for calling his enemy a son of a bitch. Whereupon the man said it was worth twenty-five bucks to call that no good polecat by his rightful name. He pulled out his wallet and said he would take another fifty dollars worth.

When I told Goldwyn that he couldn't read, it was cruelly true. His wife Frances, a charming lady, often called on writers in the studio trying to explain her husband to them. She told me that Mr. Goldwyn simply did not react to the printed word that she read to him. She could only go so far and he would sneeze and that would be all for that evening.

"Allergic to my script," I suggested, laughing with her. To tell the truth, not one of the famous studio heads, including Walt Disney at first, could react to a screenplay. They had to see the film. Then they knew. Disney was one of the few that ever learned to judge the written page. He said that the more faults he could detect before it was shot, the less film would end up on the cutting-room floor. But give any one of them a piece of film to play with and he was a genius. They had all learned their trade before scripts were important, and they were remarkable film editors. When Goldwyn saw it shot he knew, and he was courageous enough to throw away a hundred thousand dollars worth of film to make his movie better. All those old studio bosses were tigers. They could take this piece of film and put it here, and that piece there, and tell a completely different story, often looping new dialogue over a shot they remembered, to make it work. They always watched the dailies, and had remarkable visual memories. I didn't know this until later. I wondered how such seeming dopes had anything at all to do with creating great movies. So, I was the dope.

For a while I didn't think I could bear to sit there and do nothing. One thing that made me persevere was meeting an old paunchy writer named Dick Flournoy, who was doing a script for some company not associated with Goldwyn, but renting studio space. Dick called me Watty and when I told him I had been taken off the picture he read my mind. "I can tell you what you'll do," he said. "You fellas come out from New York and you think you can write a movie without learning how. I don't say *you* do, but I have watched them. They come out here for 12 or 15 weeks and find they can't cut it. So, they go into a bar and stay drunk till their contract runs out, then they go back to New York and write a novel which is a scathing indictment of Hollywood."

That was so nearly what I had planned to do that I broke out laughing. "Look, Dick," I said, "I'll be damned if I go back east until I write a good movie. Listen, you could help me. Give me a scene in the picture you're writing, explain it to me, and let me write it. You might find something in it you could use. That way I might be saving you time and I'd be learning."

"I swear to God, Watty, I believe you mean it."

"I sure as hell do."

So he told me about the scene and what bearing it had on his script.

The next day I had it ready for him. "Too fast," he said. Then he read it and looked up. "Watty," he said, "you can write. Tickle it up a little bit, I can use damn near all of this."

"Then give me another scene."

"All right, I'll give you one more to play with, and that's all. Hell, if you did any more, I'd have to give you co-credit or my conscience would hurt me."

I took longer on that scene, since it was to be my last, and when he got it back, he was unstinting in his encouragement. "I don't know how you do with a storyline, but you sure as hell can write dialogue. You stick to it now. Sit down and write an original."

I'll never forget Dick Flournoy, God be good to him. He was a kind of big cynical kewpie doll. "Watty," he'd say, "remember that these bastards out here pay you that big money not for what you can do, but for what they can do to you." He worked hard because he was conscientious. He had saved his money and was wealthy and didn't have to work, but didn't know what else to do with himself. He loved his wife and was too old and fat to chase women. He had started out as a song-and-dance man and could shuffle off to Buffalo even now. In the old days, the troop would take up a collection for the first man to catch the clap. He was full of stories but when he had stayed too long he would take out his pencil and start computing that so many minutes at his pay rate had cost the company, say, thirty-eight dollars and twenty-nine cents. He'd be back the next day, settling down in my easy chair to brag that he had taken the old story of Cinderella and was putting it in modern dress, and so far nobody had noticed the theft. He suggested that if I wanted a sound storyline, I should do likewise.

I was already doing just that, but didn't let him or anybody else know what I was writing in secret. I had dreamed up a fantasy in which a modern moving picture cast is playing out that famous old unfinished story "*The Lady, or the Tiger.*" Dressed in antique garb, my actors are in a coliseum. The hero is facing the two doors. Behind one is a tiger; behind the other a beautiful lady. If he picks the right door, he will be automatically pardoned and be allowed to marry the sweet and gentle lady. He glances up into the stands, where the barbaric princess who wants him for her lover sits beside the emperor. She has learned which door hides the lady and nods to the door on the right. Is she sparing him, or having him devoured? He hesitates.

We come back to modern times. The barbaric princess is a movie queen. A similar but not parallel story unfolds. The movie queen can not have the hero, though she longs to possess him. She can be generous and give him a long and happy life, or be jealous and destroy him. He remembers the look on the face of the barbaric princess. He knows that such a proud woman would see him destroyed before she would share him with another. He has his answer. So do we. So he acts in the opposite manner to her nod and gets the right girl. Thus I answer Frank Stockton, the author of the original story, and our modern hero enjoys a *warm 50-cent* sentimental ending.

I hadn't got far into it before I had to put it aside, for Pirosh sent his agent Al Manuel to me, saying that if I signed with Al he could spring me. I told Al that I was prepared to buy back the remaining weeks of my contract to get out of this intolerable situation. Al smiled at my naiveté. He'd get me out, but before he got through, the Goldwyn Studio would not only pay me the full twenty-five thousand, but some alimony for the way I had been abused. All Al would take was his ten percent of the excess. Then I would have eating money until he could place me where I would be appreciated. I signed and waited.

In the meantime, *The Bishop's Wife* was going forward. Goldwyn had engaged a truly great writer, world-famous, to write an original screenplay. Robert Sherwood, who had already won *three* Pulitzer Prizes for his plays, one of which, *Idiot's Delight,* had in 1936 prophetically depicted the passions that were about to engulf the world in World War II. He was now writing about the humanity that might bind up the nation's wounds after that war. Ten years after *Idiot's Delight* he was here to write *The Best Years of Our Lives*, which won the Academy Award. Goldwyn, or rather Mrs. Goldwyn, for it had become her movie, asked him first to take over *The Bishop's Wife*, almost as a side issue. He used the same theme for that movie, too, not sex, but a social conscience. It made the bishop less stuffy, and a man worth loving, which wasn't too hard to do with David Niven playing the part. Niven had been promised the role of the angel, but along came Cary Grant, who wanted it, and being higher in the pecking order, got it, relegating his friend Niven to the part of the bishop, a happy exchange. Goldwyn was glad to keep out of it. Max said that Sherwood used a little bit of everything, bits from Robert Nathan, and many of my gags such as the angel dictating a sermon to a typewriter, and all the scenes I had written for Monte Wooley, the old professor, typecasting for sure, for Monte had been a math teacher at Cornell before coming to Hollywood as a character actor. I don't think any of Bercovici's lines were used, though as the man who started it, he got a co-credit screenplay. So, this time Mr. Goldwyn *did not* shoot the story he had bought. Max told me later that if he had been better informed he might have got me an *additional* dialogue credit, which would have meant a lot to me then.

Later, when the communist scare hit town and the Screen Writers Guild wanted to rid itself of any subterranean revolutionaries who might be preparing the way for the Russian hordes to march in and take over the Hollywood Bowl, it allowed Secret Service men to enter its convocation and scan the ranks for secret Commie members. Fearing arrest, Bercovici woke up just in time to make a bolt for it. He won the footrace to the door against the government agent, grabbed a taxi, and made it to safety in Mexico, then to Italy. His darling little Jewish wife, cute as a button, and full of life and laughter, promptly committed suicide. So ends that tale.

POSTSCRIPT. I had talked to Robert Sherwood in the Goldwyn private lunchroom, where I was expected to take my midday meal when I was on the lot. I was present when Sherwood asked us all what we thought of *The Best Years of Our Lives* as a title for his screenplay about the crippled soldier. But I was surprised, just before I left the Goldwyn lot for good, to have him enter my office to ask, "Larry, what's a *dissolve*?" At first I thought he was kidding me, then I remembered that Max said he wrote everything like a stage play, leaving it to the director to figure out the camera angles. I explained it to him and he said he was very much obliged. He had always wondered about that word.

31

Late 1946 and the early months of 1947 were times of great secret worry for me. Al Manuel got me an immediate job at Columbia, not at the main studio on Gower, but at the old studio, Columbia Sunset, where the B-pictures were made. Practically all studios had two lots, the good one where only the best and most famous writers, actors, and directors were employed to make the big, expensive, talked-about pictures, the other lot the home of the quickies, the cheap westerns, the whodunits, the tear-jerkers, that were used as fillers for the second feature that the audiences wanted to round out their evening. Some of them were surprisingly good. It was a try-out place for unknowns, like off-Broadway. A strange thing happened to these lots. For a long time, the big-shot movie moguls refused to have anything to do with television. The same with actors. Television had to have a lot of films fast, so it grabbed up practically all the B-pictures. Hence, some of the producers and directors of those B-picture factories got a headstart in TV on their superiors at the A-studios and are in the driver's seat today. One of the writers who worked along with me at Columbia Sunset and never expected to make the big time is presently a top production man at a network where actors who used to look down their noses at him are now very glad to court his favor. The television companies, like the old B-studios, don't wait for the Olivia de Havillands to fluff their lines. They don't allow twenty takes, but grab off the first halfway decent one.

I still got my $500.00 a week, which was no big money for a screenwriter, but since at that rate I was making as much in 6 weeks as I had earned as a college professor in 52 weeks, I didn't sneer at it. Furthermore, my income was steady. Most of the freelance writers at bigger pay worked only spasmodically. Of course, a smart, quick writer might always be writing on the side. Dick Flournoy once told me: "Watty, you know what the real Jewish question is? They're just smarter than we are. Now you take that cute little bastard I just collaborated with. He wrote as much of the screenplay as I did, and he was doin' another one for Paramount under an assumed name at the same time, and Sundays was writing a novel. That's the real Jewish problem. They're wearin' me out."

My stint was to write a screenplay from a sickish sweet old novel called *Keeper of the Bees*. I should have been writing something else on the side, too, but I have a one-track mind and can work only on one thing at a time. What I learned while there was how to set up a screenplay, using the different angles of the camera in photographing the story, even though writers at Columbia and Warner Bros were not allowed on the sets. It was taken for granted that any writer would want to be a director. Those two studios at least wanted their writers to remain writers, not get free lessons in directing. Several writers told me that it was a waste of time to learn when to use a long, a full, a medium, or a close shot, because the director would pay no attention whatever to the writer's conception, but a very wise one told me that the more and better shots a writer's script contained, the more likely he was to influence a director to do it his way.

Any experienced secretary could teach a writer a lot. They warned me not to attempt bizarre angles, through keyholes and between legs, until I was a lot more conversant with the medium.

I wasn't supposed to change the story here either, no matter how much it gagged me. When a sentimental woman sat through the double feature, she didn't want to be robbed of her nostalgia. I don't remember any director or producer there, but I had a cute little secretary with a magnificent sense of humor named Nadine Kennan. There was no hanky panky between us, but she knew all the restaurants in town, and I often took her out to lunch. I remember the fun we had at a particularly staid French restaurant where I suggested that we eat our meal backward, starting with a brandy and dessert and ending with soup. Our shocked waiter finally entered into the spirit of the thing and the management invited us back.

Another writer was Mike Boylan. Malcolm Stewart Boylan and I had more than our Columbia Sunset relationship to count on. My friend Bill Drewry, formerly of Lexington, the man whose insides had been so largely shot away when he was on a Navy support ship covering the Marine landings on a Pacific Island, had met and married Mike's beautiful eldest daughter, Grace. In those early days Mike still owned the luxurious house where he invited Dot and me to dine. He was drinking a full quart of whiskey every day at the studio, which his obliging secretary went out and bought for him, but could yet carry it. The reason for his downfall, for Columbia Sunset was the end of the trail for him, was the coming of sound to moving pictures. Before the talkies, titles were used at the bottom or in preliminary sections to explain the action. They were then used in the occasional foreign import before dubbing in English speech to the foreign actor's mouth had become such an advanced art. When the use of titles was at its height, there were in all of the industry only seven writers who were masters of this art of condensation, known as the Seven Titular Bishops.

Mike was one of them and for years he received $5,000 for a set of titles, which he could knock out in a week. His income was enormous. Women and whiskey had brought him low. His wife was on the point of divorcing him, his daughters were embarrassed, the big house would soon have to be sold.

Bill, who had recovered enough to show no outward signs of his terrible wounds, joined a Los Angeles company and became most successful. Fortunately, they had a fine son before Grace contracted polio, survived the iron lung, and though a helpless cripple from the waist down learned to handle an electric chair. Bill lifted her in and out of the front seat of his car. Like the gentleman he was, he took perfect care of her for the rest of her long life, owned a neat little house in the center of LA, gave parties and never missed coming to one.

When I left Hollywood Sunset in March of 1947 to take a job on a nameless picture backed by Franchot Tone who intended to play in it, I doubted if Al Manuel for all his friendly visits and his cheerful assurances, such as, "Man, are you ever hot at Paramount!" could ever place me. And I rather hated to leave the place, where at least there was a friendly character or two, like Eddie Huebsch, whose name I could never spell, scion of that unpronounceable brewing company. Nobody ever guessed that he was one of the secret communists like Bercovici who had to run from the Secret Service men. He was so quiet and unoffending and heir to all that beer money which he relinquished for the sake of communism. And there was a goof with a soup-straining mustache who was an open and avowed communist. I asked him why, and he said that when Russia took over he would be the czar of Hollywood, but promised to treat us all with consideration. He was insanely in love with his wife and spent every penny he could get his hands on buying her one diamond ring after another. And there was a smart young writer named Bill Sackheim who has become a name to conjure with in the TV industry, more power to him. And of course, I missed Nadine, whose giggle cheered everyone and who knew more Hollywood gossip than Hedda Hopper and Louella Parsons combined.

I can't remember a thing about my new short-lived job. Franchot Tone, whom I do remember, was a well-known leading man who invariably was cast as what he was, a New York or Boston or Philadelphia sophisticate. It was either just before or just after my short meeting with him that his name made headlines all over the country. He had fallen madly in love with a starlet who did all her acting horizontally. When the great Franchot found that she was two-timing him with a younger actor with muscles, he loudly challenged him and was badly beaten up. They were so noisy about it that even in Hollywood it was news. Walt Disney characterized it to me as "three dogs in a gutter." I believe that to the victor went the very spoiled spoils, and it hadn't done Franchot Tone's career any good. There were several story conferences with the elderly so-called producer, Franchot Tone, and me, regarding this piddling story that Franchot had bought. Franchot had been to Yale and had taken a course in the classics. He remembered just enough key words from it to make his pronouncements about this dramatic vehicle ludicrous. It must have the unities, he insisted, and tried to explain them to me, but got so badly mixed up that I wanted to tell him he was talking about Aristotle's *Poetics* and that time, place, and action was what he was getting at, but I didn't dare. He also remembered the word catharsis. We had to have catharsis. I desperately wanted to tell him that if he'd shut up and take a big dose of Milk of Magnesia, he might attain "that calm of mind, all passions spent," that Milton wrote about, but again I bit my lip.

Next day I was on my way to the office to quit when I passed Mr. Tone, who told me somewhat brusquely, "Get your umbrella out," and I think that the producer got in the first word telling me I was fired before I could tell him that I had come to resign. Two years later that man came over and told me he had discovered that I had been on the right track all along. He begged me to use my influence to get him a job. I didn't, not because I was vindictive, but because if I tried to recommend him I wouldn't know where to begin.

I went home thinking that there was nobody in this town who wanted my services, not knowing that even then someone was trying to get in touch with me.

32

Walt Disney seldom attended a play, but possibly because he was in the fantasy business, someone tipped him to see the stock company production of *On Borrowed Time* being put on in Hollywood with Boris Karloff playing Gramps. I met Karloff under his rightful name—William Henry Pratt—in England when he and his wife had come to look over the rented apartment we were vacating. Without his monster makeup, he was unprepossessing, bullied by his wife for being so terribly, terribly British to impress Americans like me. He played a very good Gramps.

The following day Walt called in an assistant and told him to get the author of *On Borrowed Time*. They reported back that they hadn't been able to locate Paul Osborn. Walt didn't want Paul Osborn; he wanted the guy who had written the book. The assistant was confused. Walt asked him if he had looked at the program. The assistant said yes. Then, said Walt, get him the novel. They did so and he read it. So, the assistant called Knopf, who told him to call Bernice Baumgarten, who told him to call Al Manuel in Hollywood, who called me. As Al drove me over to Disney's he said he had never thought of the Disney people because he didn't know that they were just becoming interested in trying some live action. Like everybody else he thought you had to be an artist to make that joint.

I liked Walt Disney immediately and felt that I had known him for years. He told me they had been looking for a writer of fantasy for live action. Eric Knight had promised to come talk with them after the war, but had been killed.

I remember saying, "Tough luck for you. I'd love to write a book as good as *The Flying Yorkshireman*."

"You have," said Walt; "I just read it."

He then related how they had tried to palm off Paul Osborn on him. "Hell," said Walt, "I didn't want Paul Osborn; I wanted the guy who had made up the story, and since I've seen the play, I'd like to know what's in the play that isn't in the book."

Because Goldwyn had said almost the same thing, I'd love to have those—especially Josh Logan—who thought *they* had created *On Borrowed Time*, to chat with Goldwyn and Disney.

Walt asked me how I'd got along with Goldwyn.

"Not at all, but I admire him."

"Why?"

"For two things. I love to see him walk; he has the most arrogant walk. Second, and most important, he always wants to make the best moving picture that he knows how."

Walt smiled. "Yeah, Sam's quite a guy."

When Al drove me back he was grinning all over. Here I'd be able to show them what I really could do. Walt liked me. I had handled myself perfectly. Al couldn't get me a raise, not yet. Five hundred a week was a fortune for Disney to pay, but the big money was just a matter of time.

I went to work the next week in a big, light, end room on the third floor of the Animation building, with a couch, an easy chair, a big desk, a good typewriter, a book case, clothes press, a clean rug, air conditioning that worked, a secretary I could buzz, a view of the mountains, and if I wanted anything in the way of a floor lamp or a Dictaphone, I had only to ask. By comparison all the other writers' offices in town were dirty dismal little cubicles with walls painted a sickly mustard color. Dean Moreland of Washington and Lee had nicknamed that shade "baby's second summer."

My first assignment was to write a story treatment based upon a book called *Darby O'Gill and the Good People*. The "Good" people were the Irish fairies, who could be vicious. The peasantry thought that flattery might mollify them. Darby O'Gill is a canny old countryman who is captured by Brian Conners, king of the Little People, and taken into his cathedral-like throne room inside the Fairy Mountain. The king is captured in turn. But they like each other, and the collection of short stories, written by Kavanagh, is more humorous adventures and battles of wit than real folklore.

To tell the truth, they were so superficial that they came to nothing, and playing along with them thwarted both my attempts and Walt's to make them meaningful, for Walt didn't like a story that was shallow. What we did inherit from the Kavanagh book was the size of the fairies. Walt wanted them to be little people, possibly knee-high to a grown man.

Irish fairies can be any size a writer wishes to make them. In true Irish folklore they were supposed to be a tall, fair, blue-eyed people who came from one of the tiny Grecian Islands in a mass migration in 1500 B.C. They were called Tuatha de Danann, the people of the Goddess Danu. They conquered the Firbolgs, misshapen giants, and the Fomorians, the original inhabitants, in the battle of Mag Tured.

Then along came the followers of Mil, the Milesians, who at first lived with the Tuatha peaceably then conquered them in turn. They made a treaty of peace that the Milesians would occupy all the land above the surface of the earth, while the Tuatha would own all the land below it. They hollowed out the mountains and lived underground on food from an inexhaustible cauldron, ever-bearing fruit trees, and a nectar fit for the gods. Because the actual mounds that existed in so many places in Ireland were small, people began thinking of the fairies that inhabited them as being diminutive, and called them the Little People. One of the great collectors of fairy folklore, Crofton-Croker, calls them elves and obviously considers them tiny, gossamer-like creatures. Keats, in "La Belle Dame Sans Merci," uses the old myth of the beautiful full-size fairy seductress who robs human lovers of their senses before she discards them. Sometimes beautiful young Irish girls become fairy wives and live in their caves acquiring the fairy abilities to make themselves invisible, to dance to irresistible music, to have endless youth and be immortal until the End of the World, when they will be damned to hell, the price paid for ecstasy. Yeats, in his play *The Land of Heart's Desire*, shows a newly married bride being charmed away, though the priest battles for her soul.

Walt, of course, did not know or care about the depth of Irish folklore, but Kavanagh was just too cutie-pie to follow faithfully, as we tried to do for a long time. I wrote a couple of bad treatments, which discouraged Walt not at all. But when Perce Pearce, who was to become my associate as live-action producer under Disney, had completed a movie called *So Dear to My Heart*, a nostalgic story about early America, Walt called me in to help. He thought that the movie might be saved by adding narration, especially over the opening scenes. So, the three of us worked in a small screening room, suggesting phrases that would enrich the dull stuff. Walt liked what I contributed and set out to further my education about moving pictures, encouraging me to watch whatever was being shot, to visit the looping sessions, to see the cutters working on their moviolas to trim the excess fat from the rough-cut movies, to watch the dailies that were being shot. He believed that a writer should be steeped in moving picture lore. He wasn't training me to be a director or a producer, just a better-informed writer. As usual, he disagreed with almost everything that the other producers held dear. He and Goldwyn were nearest alike in that both were perfectionists and neither would make any movie until they understood and liked the story. I learned later that my experience with Goldwyn was not unusual. He took out his frustration over every story by shouting.

I was banging away on my typewriter writing treatments for *Darby O'Gill* when Walt walked in one day in July and asked me how I'd like to visit southern Ireland. Right then. Take Mrs. Watkin along. Put the kids in camps or schools and spend two or three months over there. See it all. Talk to the people, especially the old storytellers. Work with the Irish Folklore Commission, the best in the world.

The Disney company managed to get the last available first-class cabin on the old *Mauretania*, the first American tourist ship to enter Cobh Harbor since the war. On board were 18 Irish-American Catholic priests, the first I had ever talked with, most of them young and, like so many others, going back to visit their parents. A tender came out to the ship to carry the hundred or more passengers disembarking.

An almost toothless young man, sloppily dressed and with one side of his spectacles held on by a piece of twine looped over one ear, sought me out for an interview. He represented the best Dublin newspaper, so he said. I didn't expect much, but could hardly believe what I eventually read. I have been interviewed in many foreign countries, but he was the only one who ever quoted me exactly and with understanding. A girl fell to the deck, taken with an epileptic fit. My interviewer bent down and calmly inserted a pencil between her teeth "so she'll not bite off her tongue," he explained. One of the priests commended him.

On the dock two customs officers tried to handle this whole crowd. A single line was formed leading to an officer at a table; the other man helped people find their luggage and push it along beside them. The second man ahead in the line was a priest; directly in front of me was a young woman, possibly a waitress, trying desperately to hide certain dutiable items. She stuffed them into her bosom, then her handbag, but nothing worked. At the last minute, she thrust a handful into each of the priest's big loose pockets, whispering, "Don't give me away, Father. I'm a poor girl, taking a few small, little presents to my mother and sisters."

The priest did not answer her. The customs inspector asked him, "And what have you to declare, Father?"

He replied in a firm, clear voice: "My right pocket is full of wrist watches, and my left pocket is full of nylon stockings."

"Ah, Father, you're the great man for your joke," the customs man responded, and he passed him through without opening his suitcase. As soon as I had been passed, I asked Dot to wait; I didn't want to miss any of this. So, I followed the priest and the girl to the spot where he was returning her loot. I bent over to retie my shoes and heard it all. He gave her the rough side of his tongue, burdening her with a great number of Hail Marys to recite, *but* he let her get away with it. Possibly that's why Catholicism has lasted down through the ages.

Dot and I boarded a train that took us to Dublin. I reported to Dr. De Largy, director of the Irish Folklore Commission in University College Dublin, who handed me a suggested itinerary for August and September 1947. We followed it exactly, for that closely typed two-page letter was like the orders I had written for my sojourn through the South Pacific. De Largy had a host of workers all over Ireland, usually schoolteachers, who would accompany us as we hired a car and a driver from one center to visit places of interest within that district before we went on to the next. All such people spoke Gaelic, had collected legends to send back to Dublin, and were happy and proud to help a Disney man—and a friend of Seamus De Largy—discover the wonders of their beloved land. Many of them corresponded with us over the years until they died.

At the top of the itinerary it was suggested that we spend a few days in Dublin to see the gold ornaments, the early ecclesiastical art and folklore and the Book of Kells at Trinity College, then to visit by car New Grange and Boyne Valley. I asked for suggestions about a hotel in Dublin and pleased them when I chose the Shelburne, not the swankiest but the oldest and most Irish, Queen Victoria's favorite, which appealed to Dot. It looked out upon a little park, full of flowers; the lift was handled by an antique servitor, who let a rope slide through his gloved hand, for it was propelled by counterweights. When I used the telephone the girl at the switchboard, who gave me the wrong number, cried, "What's the matter wit' me at all; I've been giving away the wrong numbers all day," and before she gave me the right one inquired, "Are you the man Misther Disney sent over to find the leprechaun for his crock of gold?" I said I was and never rang a number thereafter without a dollop of conversation to precede it. I returned to Dublin many times, but nobody could ever persuaded me to stay anywhere else.

Before I started out I had an errand to do for Bernice Baumgarten. Her agency handled a writer very popular in America, who wrote romantic fiction, novels, or long short stories that appeared in the *Saturday Evening Post*—Maurice Walsh. Bernice lived in fear that eventually the manuscript he sent them would have been partly destroyed, because he wrote in longhand, kept no copy, and packaged the script so carelessly that it was usually held together by one strand of kitchen string when it reached them. He had promised to let me deliver his latest manuscript in person when

I returned that autumn. So, we went down to Blackrock to pay him a preliminary call.

He asked us to meet him at his pub and we did so. This, it seemed, was the gentlemanly way to treat a visitor. If you didn't like him, you had bought him a drink and done your duty. If you liked him, you could ask him up to your house. Maurice liked us. His wife had died and he was a lonely man. He had children and a grandson who visited him when they could, but they were away in Scotland at present. He was cared for by a quaint, gypsy-like serving man, with a towel thrust into his belt in lieu of an apron. Maurice had written a book about him entitled *Tomaseen James, Man of No Work*. He lurked around corners winking at us.

Maurice brought out a twenty-year-old bottle of Jameson Irish Whiskey, removed the cork, and threw it into the fire, remarking, "The generous man throws away the cork." He would not let us go until we had emptied the bottle of its amiable conversation. We went home by cab, promising to visit him for the manuscript before we departed in September.

We had one other stop to make. Walt asked us to call upon Bertie McNally, the RKO distributor of the Disney films in Ireland, an amusing man and a good friend. When I walked into his office, I could see by his roguish eyes that I would like him. I said, "Mr. McNally, I have a letter from Walt Disney in which he says what he thinks of you. Now I daresay you have a letter in your files which describes what he thinks about me. Why don't we swap letters?" McNally took a letter from his desk and handed it to me; I handed him mine; we read them and broke out laughing. Bertie pressed a buzzer on his desk and his assistant, a long-faced humorous fellow called John, appeared. Bertie said, "John, this is Larry Watkin and Mrs. Watkin. Come and go out to lunch with us."

"I'd love to, but you'll have to excuse me. I have work piled high."

"Well then, have just one small drink with us. Mrs. Watkin, what will it be: Scotch or Irish?"

"Irish," said Dot.

"God bless," said Bertie. "John, have just one more."

"A small one, then," said John, and he bade us goodnight along with Bertie just before midnight. Bertie's beautiful wife Vogue joined us that evening, and they never visited America or we Ireland for the next thirty years without seeing each other. We were glad to take the train for southern Ireland, for though Irish whiskey makes quick and lasting friendships, my stomach could never tolerate that much alcohol.

The summer of 1947 was the hottest and the driest that Ireland had experienced in 100 years. It was not just warm; it was hot. For us that presented only one problem: everybody at home told us to take mostly wool clothing, because we could freeze in Ireland in midsummer. So, we had to keep washing out the few cotton garments we had packed. The inconvenience was minor compared to the gains; even the sea was warm and for once the deserted beaches crowded. Crops that often mildewed were harvested with ease. Coal and fuel oil and gas and electricity were unheard of in the back country; people depended upon "turf," which is called "peat" in Scotland, for heat from their fireplaces and for cooking. Turf is a kind of extremely low-grade coal found in certain bogs and cut out in slabs like sod. If it rains all summer, it's hard to dry and stack the turf like cordwood, but when it's hot and dry the natives can look forward to being warm in the severe winters. Everyone we met was in holiday mood.

The train ride itself was amusing and the scenery all the way was fine, both the mountains and along the shores of Dingle Bay. In our compartment an English couple was getting a brief respite from the shortages. Middle-aged people, they had gone without essential foods all through the war, and would expect to be rationed for another five years. The lady described herself as overweight and undernourished. It was hard to envision a place where eggs and milk and bacon could be had by everyone. The husband looked forward to the salmon and trout fishing. When I described them to my Irish schoolmaster next day, he nodded. "Aye," he said, "the meal is the Englishman's trout."

The trip from Dublin to Cahersiveen was less than 200 miles, but it took the Irish train a full day to accomplish it. The stops were many and long. I think it was Mallow where switching this car and that took forever, or maybe it was Limerick Junction. Whenever the train stopped, everyone headed for the railroad bar for a beer or a bite, or even a soft drink. It was thirsty weather. At one of these places I decided it wouldn't be worth my while; so, while Dot had a soda I stretched my legs in a quick hike back and forth, then when everyone else was ready to go back to their seats I was suddenly thirsty. As I walked past the engine I noticed that the engineer, called the engine driver, was in his seat in the cab, and so I asked him, "Am I too late?"

"What do you have in mind?"

"I thought I'd like a drink."

"I'll go with you," he said. He came down and joined me.

"I don't want to hold up your schedule," I apologized.

"Faith," he said, "don't give it a thought. We make our own time here."

That was the motto carved on every Irish heart. If a woman hailed a bus, then told the driver she had forgotten to put the cat out, he waited good-naturedly.

I asked the engine driver what he would have, and since I was a rich American, he chose a bottle of Guinness Stout. I had a draft beer. He was in a golden mood, remembering the good old days when he drove an engine on a thirty-mile experimental monorail. Weights had to be balanced. If a man shipped a bull to market, he had to supply two yearling calves to put on the other side. On the return journey, one calf on each side. Walt was pleased to hear about that, for even then he was thinking about a monorail for the park, as he called Disneyland, though he didn't share that confidence with me then.

Eventually the train reached Cahersiveen, where we took a bus for Waterville to pick up our reservations at the Butler Arms Hotel, one of the finest hostelries in all the world. We were put up in the annex across the road, where the great Mr. Disney himself had slept the year before. Though every guest was expected to use the bar, the lounge rooms, and the dining room in the hotel proper, the fine rooms in the hotel went to those who had reserved them every season for the last quarter of a century. Only by the demise of an old client could you expect to move up. But even the lowliest guest was made to feel the warm hospitality of Martin Huggard and his wife. In the dining room every table had its vase of beautiful flowers. Over twenty years ago, around 1927, that is, Colonel Knaggs, an English gentleman who loved flowers, first came to the Butler Arms, and liked it so well he decided to retire there. He asked the Huggards if he might dig some flower beds around their hotel and they gladly gave him permission. His planting added to the beauty. The owners consider them to be his flowers and always ask if they may have some for decoration. He is proud to supply them. The success of the Huggards is the old story of doing what you like to do best and continuing to like it. Their daughter has a similar hotel of her own at Killarney.

Waterville became our headquarters for story hunting because of its central location in the Kingdom of Kerry and because of Tadhg Murphy, the schoolmaster and his wife, who had long been collectors for the Folklore Commission. Tadhg, himself no spring chicken, knew the history of every standing stone left by the prehistoric people and was intimate with all the fine old Gaelic storytellers. They were called shanachies, and though they may eventually be replaced by the American moving picture, they were still in evidence when I was there. The shanachie told traditional folk tales that he had learned word for word from his grandfather. Many of these old stories had been brought back to Ireland during the Middle Ages by the doctors, who went to Rome for their medical education. Such tales may be heard in many European countries because of their common source. Some include the old hero tales about early warriors and the high kings of Tara. The tales about the good people are legend, and there are even modern stories about farmers who carelessly plowed the fields that belong to the little people and of the terrible retribution the fairies took against such men and his children. The shanachies were not so much the creators of tales as tellers. They acted out certain parts. If you were a peasant leading a dull, toilsome existence, an evening at the shanachie's house brought excitement into your life. Late at night on the way home you imagined the terrifying beings the storyteller had described behind every bush and ruined abbey or cromlech or dolmen, burial chambers or standing stones to mark the grave of some prehistoric king. They are to be found everywhere with their ogham inscriptions from the second or third centuries. The early monks, centuries later, defaced them, trying to turn the characters into church Latin and force the old figures into crosses, but they still retain their ghostly nature. I sat down to rest on such a stone and Tadhg said, "That's where my grandfather first saw the banshee." I got up in a hurry. I thought he was kidding, but he wasn't; he was dead serious. It gets to you after a while. A sophisticated Dubliner who laughed at the folk tales suddenly lowered his voice: "But I wouldn't want to be crossing a graveyard at twelve o'clock at night, would you, now?"

Loch Currane, originally Loch Lee, is just across the road from the hotel, so near the ocean that it seems almost a part of the long curved bay. It's full of trout and salmon, and so are the smaller separate lakes above it. Late every afternoon that flat slab in front of the hotel would become the case where the anglers displayed their big ones. But we were after other fish. Every day we would hire a car and driver and set out with a case of Guinness Stout in the back, which the fine old scholars liked better than gold, and head up a country road to visit, let's say, the delightful schoolmaster-historian Donal O'Sullivan of Caherdaniel. Every day I'd fill a clean notebook, jotting down scraps, sayings, stories. We traveled to places with names like Bolus Head, the Glen, Bealach Oisin, Derrynane, Dunquin. We went north to Dingle and south to Parknasilla, where we saw bamboo growing and plants whose seeds had washed over from Spain. I can't begin to remember the names, nor can I find them on the maps, but many things stand out. In a bay whose rocky headlands jutted out so far west they seemed to be headed for America, we went with a lobster fisherman while he tended his traps. He told how his grandfather had fished this bay and caught a fish which was no fish but an enchanted thing that pulled him out of his boat. The line was tangled round his leg and he was being pulled down to his death. He had only one tooth left in his head, but that tooth was so strong that it sawed the line in two against his gum and let him swim up to his boat.

On another occasion a Gaelic storyteller (translation for me by Tadhg) related the basic story of *On Borrowed Time*, of an old woman trapping Death in her apple tree. I didn't mention it to Tadhg, but when I returned to Dublin I asked De Largy if they had that story. Almost every other country had written me claiming it as *their* legend, but I hadn't heard from Ireland. The Folklore Commission had 22 different versions of it—retentive bag, retentive chair—everything.

We hated to leave Waterville but had to. Before doing so I must mention two more things, the first Killarney. Everything ever written about Killarney in song and story is true. Since it is indescribably beautiful, I will not attempt it. The best passage to understand the spirit of the place is in that magnificent book by Richard Hayward, *In the Kingdom of Kerry*, written in 1946, and dedicated to my friend Maurice Walsh. No, neither Dot nor I kissed the Blarney Stone. Some particularly obnoxious American tourist types had just desecrated the place as we arrived. God knows how they could have become any more shriekingly verbal after doing so than before.

The other wonder is Staigue Fort. We went to the Aran Islands and saw the great stone fort called Dun Angus, often called the greatest barbaric fort in the world. These forts were built a thousand years before Christ and nobody knows why or what they protected. Dun Angus is on top of a three-hundred-foot sea cliff and has more height and more interior barricades than Staigue. But some stones have fallen off into the sea and a small amount of restoration has taken place. It has another feature, an *abattis*. That word isn't even given in many dictionaries, and when it is, it usually is given as *abatis*. But scholars who write about them use the double "t". Originally it meant to fell a tree to slow down an attacker by cutting the limbs down to points that would stab him if he ran into them. Here at Dun Angus they are standing stones with sharp edges placed higgledy-piggledy into the ground to stall a man charging on his horse. They were used by the English at the battle of Yorktown, sharpened sticks pointing outward to make it hard for the besiegers to get close enough to the two redoubts the British built as a final defense. They were stormed in one night by the combined troops under Generals Washington and Rochambeau. The American charge was led by Lafayette; the French took its twin.

Staigue Fort is reached by a rough mountain road three miles from Castlecove. You get out and walk across a rough field to reach it. It is a perfect circle 114 feet in outer diameter, 88 feet inner. The walls are 13 feet thick at the base, tapering to five feet on top and roughly twice the height of a man. Like all such forts it had only one doorway. No mortar was used, only smaller stone spawls to make it smooth and tight, but it seems as perfect as the day it was completed roughly two thousand years ago. Staigue means the Fort of the Bleak Place, and it certainly is that. Nobody guards it, nobody touches it, and I hope the fairies will break the arm of the man who does.

I keep remembering things. Tadhg asked me how I'd like to have dinner with some country friends of his. Dot and I accepted gladly. The sweet little old lady who cooked for us and her equally kind husband had never been out of the county, nor aboard a train, but they knew all about America and asked some searching questions about its politics. They had seven sons there. She asked us if we knew her boy John. Had we ever been to New York City? We had. Then we should know John, who was on the "force." I explained that New York City was very large indeed. So, she said, was her John. All the cooking was done in the open fireplace. Suspended pots and kettles hung down from cranes into the glowing turf fire. A hugh dish held a mountain of boiled potatoes, enough for a dozen people. Tadhg explained to us that this was a gesture of hospitality and that they would be eaten in a variety of ways by the family in days to come. I liked them with the lovely fresh churned butter. The main dish was a mixture of brussels sprouts cooked in the same pot or Dutch oven with tender lamb chops. Everything was delicious. I whispered to Tadhg after dinner that I needed to go to the toilet. He looked blank. I took him outside and asked where they kept the bathroom, the convenience. He continued to look blank. In desperation, I said crudely, "I've got to take a piss."

"Oh, faith," said Tadhg with a wide sweep of his arm."Go abroad in the fields and pee to your heart's content all the way from here to Tralee."

In Galway, we stayed at the Railway Hotel and our historian there, District Justice Sean Forde, told us what the Claddagh, the old fisherman town, was like before it became empty warehouses, and about the Claddagh rings, with two hands coming together holding a heart with a crown on top. You must never buy one for yourself. They must be given to you and will bring you good luck. I got one for Dot. We went out to the Aran Islands to the Isle of Inishmaan, the setting for Synge's *Riders to the Sea*. I genuflected but was more interested to watch the natives using currachs and ropes skillfully to load recalcitrant cattle aboard a big trawler.

We attended a horse show in Galway and watched a 60-year-old priest with shiny black boots taking the high hurdles on a beautiful horse along with the best of them. I didn't like the arrogant priests in America but loved them in the little towns all over Ireland. They were the preachers, the teachers, the doctors, the magistrates all rolled into one, dedicated and hard working. They kept the peace. Usually gentle, they would bawl out a man for getting drunk and beating his wife, saying, "You do it again, and I'll break your back—and you know I can do it, too."

I don't remember much about Mayo and Sligo, but in Donegal we got a bus for Ardara, where the national teacher Patrick MacGill was full of hero stories. I'll never forget the hotel, a fine one. The Irish never say no to you. I asked the lady at the desk if we could have a bath. "Of course you can," she answered; "you can surely... whenever it rains."

Patrick MacGill told us about an early hero, a great warrior, who finally was run to earth with some of his men and their wives in a cave along the ocean shore. The force against him was overwhelming. Their leader called in to him that if he would give himself up, they would spare whoever he could carry out in his two hands. He gathered all the women together in two groups on either side of him and led them all out, holding to one strand of the long hair of each of them in his two fists.

I remember nothing about returning to Dublin cross-country except stopping at a fair. I ordered a beer for me and an orange for Dot. They poured both the beer and the orange crush together in a big carton. I explained I wanted separate drinks. Somebody else took the carton and drank it down thirstily. I tried one later. They called it a shandy, and strangely it was excellent. I had one in Paris years later when I met an Irish friend outside a nightclub.

We took a plane to Edinburgh. Dot had never been on a plane before, and the weather was so foul we could scarcely see land, but though she clung to me, having given herself up for lost, she was not sick. Our stay in Edinburgh was too brief to mention. We saw it under pleasanter circumstances a few years after that. One thing only stays with me. At a fruit and candy shop on a side street we beheld three of the hungriest looking small boys, their noses pressed to the outside of the store window staring at two large bunches of luscious grapes. I went inside and bought the grapes with my own money. I figured that Walt had bought barrels of Guinness Stout. It paid off in the end, but I funded the grapes. The boys moved only their eyes, somewhat reproachfully, but when I gave them the grapes, those eyes opened volubly. No word was spoken or needed to be.

I didn't mention that Scotland wanted American tourist money so badly that the airport custom officers took us into a side room and though I had made a list of dutiable goods, they didn't want to see it. Nor would they open our bags. From the same plane these Presbyterians were gleeful in taking two of our fellow passengers, Catholic nuns, into another private room and removing from their voluminous robes a great quantity of Irish linen they were smuggling into the country.

London was a bust. Tourists at their hotels would not give up their rooms as they waited for delayed ships. We had to stay at the apartment of the Disney office manager, and disliked the imposition. But we had a fine cabin on the *Queen Mary* returning to America, which was the highlight of the trip for Dot. We could not have guessed that very soon we would be taking it back to London.

33

Returning to the studio, I was attacking the Irish story with new zeal when Walt walked into my office one day and asked how I'd like to write a screenplay for *Treasure Island*. I dropped the Irish story like a shot and whipped out an excellent treatment in no time at all. Walt read it and called me into his office, saying that this was very good indeed, but that *Treasure Island* was a classic and that its admirers in whatever country would not allow me the changes I had made from the time the boy meets Ben Gunn to the end of the story. I said it had to be changed because Stevenson, who wrote with such romantic charm that he carried his reader along with him however shoddy the plot, had first written it for a magazine in great haste and hadn't been too careful about what happened. I said that if we saw the story enacted, we wouldn't believe some parts of it, and that we had to save Stevenson from himself. It was no conceit on my part; I'd give an arm and a leg to be able to write even the indifferently good parts as well as that man had.

Walt shook his head, and said to try again.

I went back to my office and took three sheets of pink paper and ruled them down the center. In the left column, I wrote: "*This is what happens in Treasure Island.*" In the right column, I wrote opposite the other action: "*This is what I propose to have happen.*" I outlined the whole story and sent the letter in to Walt. The following day he called me in again, saying, "I don't believe that's what Stevenson wrote."

I answered, "Walt, about most things your memory is three times as good as mine, but when it comes to *Treasure Island*, I know what I'm talking about."

Walt said, "I'll read it again."

Two days later he called me in. He grinned and handed me my outline. "We will do it your way. Bring Perce in on it, but stick to what you showed me. When you have the screenplay, let me read it."

Perce Pearce was a nice little man, short and stocky. Like Walt and so many of the Disney men, he had little schooling though he had read enough to pass as an educated man unless he used some particularly atrocious grammar. He was conscious of it and once said to me, "I guess it's obvious I never got by the 7th grade." I told him it was not and that all learning was not in books. If he used a hideous mispronunciation I would wait a week and then try to work that into our conversation so that he could hear it said. Several of the artists were that way. They saw an unfamiliar word in their reading and tried it out the way they thought it might be spoken. I understood because if I was taking a medication, say epifrin, I didn't know whether it was épífrin or e-pif-rin. Perce was a bit too folksy sometimes, but he had a sense of humor and we enjoyed working together. He was so slow it drove me nuts, but that was good for me. I worked too fast. It never occurred to me that he was an artist, too, but one day when we were having difficulty mentally framing a shot of the coach going over a hill, he grabbed a pad and did a quick, excellent sketch of it. I remarked about it and he told me that in his late teens he had been in the Navy in World War I and had done a cartoon character called *Seaman Si* which, while not quite up to Maudlin, had been popular enough to make him a lot of money. He formed a company and took bankruptcy at age 22. He had been with Walt for a long time and had done his best work on the seven dwarfs. He had one rather pathetic problem: he wanted to *be* Walt Disney. He was very liberal with Walt's money, penurious with his own. He had married a lovely woman, June, whom Walt admired and so did Lillian, Walt's wife. The two couples had taken a few trips together. June had one daughter who was married to Stanley Kramer and she and Perce had a teenaged daughter of their own. We all became very good friends, and either because Walt had told him to or because he needed my help, he wanted me to be a part of everything, not just the writing but the casting, working with the director and cameraman, every single phase of the making of a moving picture. It was taken for granted that we would both be on the set to watch the shooting, and if he wasn't, I would be. No writer was ever before treated with such respect. Perce, of course, was in seventh heaven. We made those pictures in England without Walt's controlling hand. On *Treasure Island*, he visited the set only one day. Perce kept him advised of everything, but Walt was glad to let us carry the ball.

From Walt's point of view, it was a good deal financially. His cartoon features had accumulated a tidy fortune in English pounds, but he could not take the money out and convert it to American dollars. But if he made the pictures in England, using English stages and actors and camera and technicians, he could take the film out, and if they were hits in England, too, he was way ahead, piling up more pounds to finance the next picture. I believe that the British government even kicked in some pounds: if 90% of it was made with British facilities, it was then called a quota picture.

Perce and I welcomed it because we created the films. We had a nice little stock company going. Also, thanks to fine art directors and usually superior cameramen, and best of all, thanks to the casting director Maud Spector, we had actors of a caliber we would have been denied in America. We caught all the future great English stars on their way up. We took it for granted that we could use Geoffrey Keen and John Gregson and Peter Finch and Robert Newton for actors and Guy Greene as a camera man before he became a director, and James Robertson Justice for Henry VIII. I didn't care for that fine comedienne Glynnis Johns as a leading lady, but she was a good actress. Steve Grimes, who subsequently teamed up with John Huston, had no equal as a sketch artist, and Peter Ellenshaw was and is the world's best matte artist. Carmen Dillon, a knowledgeable person to work with, gave us delightful sets.

Working for Walt had its disappointments. I worked just as hard on Kingsley's *Westward Ho!*, and even harder on *Don Quixote*, doing a screenplay on the former and a treatment on the latter, as I did on *Robin Hood*, a big hit and a moneymaker, and was disappointed when he turned them down. Furthermore, Richard Todd was forced on us as the leading man for the last three of the four moving pictures we did in England. He wasn't my idea of *Robin Hood* or of *Rob Roy*, though we might have done worse, but Walt's daughters had decided that Dickie was the "cutest" thing that ever lived; so, Dick was it.

One reason that Walt gave us so much latitude in making the English movies was that I usually wrote the first draft screenplay in Burbank, and he knew pretty well where we were going. What's more, I had been right about saving Stevenson from himself. Every single critic in England had something nice to say about *Treasure Island*. The consensus seemed to be:

> Thank God for an American moving picture company that has enough respect for our great writers not to change a single word of their classics. Furthermore, they seem content to use our famous castles and existing background with taste and discrimination.

Peter Ellenshaw and I got a kick out of that. Research provided some old sketches from which Peter re-created a castle that had been destroyed a century or two before. *Matte* means *match*, and Peter could paint a castle on glass so that some present-day action could be superimposed upon it that would fool almost anyone. If we wanted something of the sort, we always called it Castle Ellenshaw or Mount Ellenshaw. Furthermore, we discovered that the British newspaper critics were not very knowledgeable. I'm sure that Dorothy knew ten times as much about their royal families from 900 A.D. to the present as all the newspaper men put together. *Treasure Island* did for me as a movie what *On Borrowed Time* had done as a novel. Even *The New Yorker* gave it what amounted to a rave review. When I showed it to Walt, he said, "I wish they'd be a little more consistent."

Walt was incapable of saying "well done" to anybody. When they ran *Treasure Island* for the studio workers to get their comments, he was so obviously pleased, but he said to Perce and me, "I've seen worse movies than that saved by a little judicious editing." So, he went to work. When we ran it again complete, he said about a scene in which Robert Newton was looking up and listening in the jungle, "I shouldn't have cut that. He was great there. I went too far."

Robert Newton was a magnificent actor, but he was an alcoholic, and under the influence a Mr. Hyde. He could turn from the charming gentleman to a wild maniac. He loved the role of Long John Silver so much that he stayed stone-cold sober all the way through except for the one day that Disney visited the set. Perce and I told Walt that he had the flu. Walt said, "Yes, I know; he's drunk." But he never was again. Everybody loved Bob Newton. He was considerate, helpful, and his enthusiasm was so genuine that it kept the whole cast excited. Byron "Bun" Haskins, an old-timey director, felt the same way. He too was an alcoholic, but he and Newton drank nothing stronger than ginger beer until the shooting was over. Then they went on a two-day drunk that London still remembers.

I heard this story about Newton and believed it. He was in the process of divorcing his wife, who sold the lovely little London house with its geranium window boxes against Bob's will. He rapped on the door. The new owner, a pleasant lady, was charmed when Mr. Newton doffed his hat and said he hoped she loved the dear little house as much as he and his wife had. She invited him in, and found him such a gracious gentleman that she served him tea. Bob waxed sentimental. Would she...uh...understand if he just went up and had a last fond look at their bedroom? Not at all, the lady said. Bob smiled gratefully as he climbed the stairs, but in about three minutes their old bedroom bureau came crashing down the stairwell, then the bed, the chairs, the pictures, and the crockery. Then Newton himself, face red and distorted with hate, climbed over the shambles he had created, shouting, "Divorce me, will she, the flaming bitch!" and slammed the front door. He sneaked his child by the former Mrs. Newton aboard a ship and took off for America.

I was told that the drunken parties in his Hollywood house were too much for that sink of iniquity and that he died of a fever which laid him low, while invalided from reaching for a glass of water. But I still see him between takes, congratulating a fellow actor, or spying me to remark, "Lovely line, Lahrry."

Walt wasn't inclined to give actors too much credit. They would never behave the way his cartoon characters did. They were vain and unpredictable and sure that they had a good side and a bad side to their faces, which was hard on cameramen and directors, and they all wanted too much money. It was a long time before we got another Robert Newton.

I was very proud of *Treasure Island*. Walt wanted me to sign myself Larry Watkin. "That's a good movie name," said Walt. I insisted that I had always used my full name, even on a short story. "Look, Walt, it means a lot to me."

"I know it," Walt kidded, "and I'll tell you what we're going to do; when your name comes on, we're going to have a flashing red arrow on each side of it."

I had an inspiration. "There are twenty letters in my name and there are 20 letters in Robert Louis Stevenson. I'll gladly accept screenplay by Larry Watkin if you'll say, based on the novel by Bob Stevenson."

Walt threw up his hands and walked away, muttering, "Goddamn prima donna." But he was grinning.

I had done another small thing in Hollywood that gave me such credit that, along with *Treasure Island*, Al Manuel was getting offers for my services all over town. A Warner Bros producer, Jerry Wald, got the Navy to let him use footage the Navy had taken of the great Mariannas "turkey shoot," as it was called, in which the Navy flyers broke the back of the Jap carrier force. A director, Delmer Daves, who also wanted credit for writing it, started to put together a screenplay for Gary Cooper. The trouble was that as usual they started at the wrong end and were then realizing that they needed a story to hang the footage on. The producer heard about my Navy experience and begged Walt to lend me out for six weeks. I thought up a good plot: Gary Cooper, a young Navy officer, fights for Navy air, succeeds, leads an invincible fighter squadron, gets too old to fly (as Cooper would be), and is put in command of a carrier. He doesn't realize it at first, but a carrier is a ship, and he loves his ship and comes to hate the only thing that can destroy it, the enemy airplane. He begins to hate all airplanes. He has become like a battleship captain. His carrier gets creamed and he barely manages to get her into port, where she will be used for scrap. His emotion-filled voice calls upon the dead men at the mangled battle stations as the story ends. It was called *Task Force*.

Marty Rackin, one of the wittiest writers that ever lived, also represented by Al Manuel, was then working at Warner's. He brought in a writer I greatly admired, Ranal MacDougall, saying, "I think it's time you two fellows met each other since you're both writing the same screenplay." We swapped scripts and both liked what we read. Ranal bawled out the producer, since he had wanted to go to New York, and since he thought the script was in good hands, he did so. The director, Delmer Daves, got credit for the screen story and screenplay, though I very greatly fear that he took my stuff and had his typist retype it and turn it in as his. I got an additional dialogue credit, but enough people knew what I had contributed so that Al could have got me employment on war pictures if he could only persuade me to leave Disney.

I was even more greatly surprised that Walt had found out what I had written because he said to me one day, "That was good, gutty stuff you wrote for Warner's. Why don't you write for me like that?" I could have told him, but I didn't. I could very definitely have told him when he saddled me with that old Midwestern moth-eaten phony, *When Knighthood Was in Flower*. Walt, who had seen Marian Davies do it when he was at an impressionable age, went for all the corn; before that he had participated in the creaky classic in a school play when a girl he fancied was the heroine, and he never recovered from the impression it made on his adolescent mind. Neither did we. The players "camped" the parts, reciting their lines with a pretentiousness just this side of satire. If it had been played for satire, it would have been great. Henry the VIII's sister, in love with a court follower, was betrothed by her brother to Louis, the aged French king. She disposed of him by making love to him excessively until the old man succumbed, but under the stern Disney rule of no sex I doubt if the audience ever got the point, but thought she danced him to death. Anyway, after much swordplay with a hokey villain, the two lovers are reunited.

Bill Walsh at the studio suggested we call it *The Sword and the Rose*. Walt thought that was a mistake, but he went along with it. The English reviewers wrote in letters Headline High: "OH, MR. DISNEY, THIS IS AWFUL." I did the best I could with it and at least succeeded in presenting an excellent and honest picture of Henry the VIII, portrayed with gusto by James Robertson Justice, for the notorious monarch with all those wives was not the king that Charles Laughton pictured throwing chicken bones over his shoulder to the floor as he exclaimed, "Delicacy is a thing of the past."

There were so many sonnets following the Shakespearian rime scheme written off the cuff in the Elizabethan court that a chronicler of the day remarked that a courtier who could not produce a sonnet upon demand would have a thin time with the ladies. Now it was taken for granted that if Walt had okayed a shooting script, no director would change a word. That kept a great many fine directors away. I heard Walter Huston once say to Walt, "Walt, how in hell can you make such good pictures with such awful directors? Neither I nor any of my friends have ever heard of any of them."

"Storyboards," said Walt.

I liked Walter Huston. He once said to me: "Larry, is your mother living?"

"Yes, indeed."

"Where does she live?"

"Upstate New York."

"Does she love you?"

"Yes, very much."

"Well, as long as she lives in upstate New York, you can believe her, but if she ever comes to Hollywood, you'd better get it in writing."

When Ken Annakin, who was directing *The Sword and the Rose*, came to the sonnet, he stopped and came across to me.

"Larry, I can't ask an actor to say that."

"Why not? It's a traditional sonnet, very much a part of courtship at that time."

"But it just won't *play*." He spread his hands despairingly.

"The hell it won't play. Look, let me take over this one scene for you."

"No, but if it means so much to you..."

"I don't give a hoot in hell one way or another, but I happen to know that Walt does," I lied.

Ken returned and told Dick and Glynnis they'd try it in one long two-shot, and to keep it low key and for Dick to pause a few times as if composing it.

Dick did well by it. Ken let the single take stand.

Walt invited us over to his house one evening to see it all put together. He had a game room filled with theater seats, where he often ran movies. In the back of the room was a soda fountain, where Walt acted as the soda jerk. He'd give you a real drink if you insisted, but he loved making his guests big gooey sundaes with any kind of syrup they wanted before taking their seats. During the showing I heard someone sniffling. I turned around and sure enough it was Walt crying over that sonnet. I couldn't believe it.

Walt said, "Watkin, you should write more poetry. I never hear that without it bringing a tear to the eye."

And he had turned down *The Mudlark* with these words: "Let Fox do those subtleties!"

"What subtleties?" I had asked one of his oldest employees, a man who should have known him if anyone did.

"If you try to figure out how Disney's mind works, it will drive you crazy. Just take it for granted that you're going to win some and lose some, and they'll never be the ones you expected."

The follow-up to *Treasure Island* was *Robin Hood*, and it was even more successful in its way. It was high spirited. It seemed that I could do nothing wrong. Perce and I had taken in one of the London plays, and a very good actor with a pleasant voice came out between scenes and played upon an ancient mandolin-like instrument a tiny scrap of verse that set the next scene. I suggested that we add that actor to Robin's merry men and let him do the same for us, helping cue the audience into the next section. He joined us. I would compose a jingle:

> Now Robin, who is called Fitzooth,
> Is dwelling in the wood;
> His cloak is changed to Lincoln green
> His name to Robin Hood.

Then the singer, Elton Hayes, would dig up a tune for it from the British Museum, and we had a substitute dissolve. One that Walt particularly liked was:

> He robs the rich to pay the poor,
> A most unusual practice,
> And what is more remarkable
> He doesn't pay his taxes.

From the very first Walt invited me, as he did any other of his American live-action team, to bring their wives along and their children if they so desired. He thought an employee did better work with his family at hand. Sometimes I came early to work with Perce, but Dot and the three children would follow as soon as their schools closed. We had no trouble renting our houses for the summer, and once we brought out a couple from Lexington to act as house sitters. This was the time of greatest popularity for the *Queen Mary* and the *Queen Elizabeth*. A beautiful first-class cabin became the highlight of the season for Dot and the kids, but the only trip I thoroughly enjoyed was the one during which I worked with Perce on the screenplay all day long. Ships bored me and latterly I took to flying. One pleasant aspect was a stopover to see my mother and sisters both going and returning. These were hurried visits, but they let me keep in touch.

Walt, who was tight about salaries, was more than generous with expense money for our families. I never asked him for a raise, but after a couple of pictures he raised me to $750 a week, then a couple of years later to $1000 a week. While we were abroad the salary piled up in the bank. All workers with families got 100 pounds a week for expenses and sometimes 125, which meant we could take a suite at the hotel of our choice, which always was the Dorchester, usually on the second floor looking out on Hyde Park. Three times we rented luxurious apartments with cooks and dailies, and once a three-story house on Trevor Square from a member of the House of Lords. We were all supposed to spend every cent of that expense money, not return any of it, and after *Treasure Island* the Disney company in London, without Walt's knowledge, paid me an extra 500 pounds (around $2,000 then) to write a 127-page novel entitled *Walt Disney's Treasure Island*, the story of the screenplay. I said I would do it if they let me write a disclaimer opposite page 1. This was granted:

> Because of the wide interest in the Walt Disney screen version of *Treasure Island*, this novel was prepared for those who wish to recapture the essence of that film.
>
> The intent has not been to *edit or revise* the Stevenson classic. Rather, the purpose of this book is to recapture the dramatic form of the screenplay.

It was beautifully illustrated with color stills from the film with tiny pen-and-ink sketches of the actors by an unsung artist. It read very well indeed and was several cuts above the usual god-awful Disney kid's book. Sometime in 1950 I was in Walt's office. He had the book in his hand. I quailed as he shook it at me. He said, "I'm telling you this is one hell of a piece of merchandise. We should have had this over here, too. Somebody missed the boat." I felt better about that solid silver tea set and coffee service we bought from a store on old Bond Street and that extra set of Wedgwood we shipped over with that 500 pounds.

Walt and his family always had the penthouse atop the Dorchester, and sometimes if his family was away, he would come down to visit us and take Anne, about the age of his youngest daughter, on his lap. Then he'd say, "Better get down, Anne. You're making me too lonesome for my own kids."

If he took us out to dinner, we had to wait till the autograph pack would pounce on him just outside the door. He wrote fast, and once spied Tyrone Power heading for the Screen Writer's Club across the square. "Hey," he told the kids. "There's Tyrone Power.

One autograph of his is worth three of mine." They'd make a dash for Tyrone and Walt would would slip us into a cab.

Anne, who was 10 or 11 at the time, wanted an autograph book, too. I bought her one, but said, "You know yourself how rude it is to stick your book into somebody's face and beg them for their signature just because they're famous. Now you'll be out on the set and the still photographer will probably grab you and Maggie and take your picture along with some well-known actor, and you can keep the picture. If you see enough of that actor or actress, and he comes over and talks to you enough so you can consider him your friend, it's quite all right to ask for his autograph. But keep it for your friends, not just to show off. OK?"

Anne understood. We talked to our room waiters and when we were being driven home at night, I talked to the drivers, who had interesting tales to tell. I learned a lot of Cockney that way. No Englishman would talk to a servant; they wouldn't know what to say. Not so with Americans. At the end of the season I asked to see how many signatures Anne had collected. I know that she had Disney's name because I heard the interchange. Walt, when asked, said he'd be honored, adding, "Anne, for you I'll do something special. I'll spell my name backward." So he wrote "Retlaw Yensid." Anne was gratified because she considered him a friend. She had the names of only two other friends, the room waiters. I heard that conversation, too. One of them said, "I think, young lady, it would be more fitting if you gave us your autograph," but Anne insisted that she wanted theirs. I congratulated her on her discrimination and the catholicity of her taste.

My curiosity led me into less savory conversations. Whores abounded, especially in Shepherd Market. I cut through it as a shortcut to Regents Street and was accosted. I seldom bothered to answer until one day two bobbies signaled a prostitute to accompany them. They took her away in a cab. I was so surprised I asked two whores why. They said she was paying her income tax. Since they were usually standing together at a certain station I stopped from time to time and got from them a sort of continued story of how prostitution worked in London. Usually when they had spent what they considered ten shilling's worth of time they charged me that and asked me not to linger, for I was interfering with Johns who might want something more lucrative, such as a show. They admitted that they were lesbians. It would have made a great magazine piece, but I didn't think a Disney writer was the one to do it.

All prostitution was handled in London by the four Messina brothers. They got a cut of all earnings and gave protection in return.

One day a member of the House of Commons arose and said that the prostitutes constituted a great source of untaxed money. Some of those girls made a hundred pounds a week. (I felt less compunction after that in taking Walt's hundred pounds a week for prostituting my art.) So they issued tax forms for all the whores to fill out. The first one to hand back a form was a great heroine. Under occupation she wrote *"prostitute"* and the whole House of Commons fell flat on its face. They couldn't pander to vice. They had tried before to get the girls off the streets and couldn't; so thereafter a police detail took in each girl separately for a judge to fine them for loitering. If the girl was polite, she paid only two pounds ten a month; if nasty, she was fined five pounds. Most of the whores had pimps because they were lonesome; these two girls had each other.

One day I was walking past the pair accompanied by Fred Leahy, the general manager. He and his wife were over for the summer. I said, "Hello, girls," and they said cheerfully, "Hello, Mr. Watkin."

Fred was scandalized. "My God," he said, "what if you were walking along the street with Mrs. Watkin, and they hailed you by name?"

I told him, "First of all, Dot knows me too well to think I would patronize two such bags. Second, I've written her all about my street historians. Third, all English whores think most Americans are unmannerly, especially our noisy young college boys. They wouldn't think of addressing me if I hadn't spoken first."

Dot and I and our two daughters did walk past them. They did not look in our direction, but I whispered to Dot after we had passed, and Dot laughed and Maggie asked why so many girls stood around like that. I told Dot to tell her, so I walked with Anne while Dot told Maggie the drearier facts of life.

Maggie was the sweetest little girl that ever lived. She was born good. She was beautiful and quiet, loved everybody and was loved in return. Unlike the other two children, she was not bookish, but she could manage anything, was president of her sorority, Alpha Phi, and could handle problems. So when she got the lowdown, she was shocked. Fair-haired and with a delicate complexion, she was furiously blushing now. "Well," she exclaimed, "I must say, I thought better of the ladies of London than that!"

These junkets abroad were wonderful for our youngsters. London is the one city that could never bore me, and I think that after a while our children learned to love it, too. The girls were never bored, for in addition to the music and the painting and the plays and the four o'clock teas in the hotel where all the American movie stars foregathered, there were the flower shows and the river boats and Kew

Gardens and Sunday trips into the lovely countryside. Parke wanted to stay home one summer and play baseball. He was sulky and stayed in until he saw an American sailor teaching a parcel of English kids how to play American baseball in Hyde Park, so he joined them and they had two teams. Parke picked all the younger ones because they hadn't learned bad habits like stopping the ball with their feet. They had regular matches. I couldn't make him visit the British Museum. But he met a cute little Irish secretary at the Disney office and she wanted to see all the things on weekends that I had been imploring him to study. He could easily pass for the extra three years he tacked on his age to give him man-of-the-world status. He went to Foyles and bought books to show her his knowledge of English antiquities. I gladly upped his allowance. I couldn't have hired a tutor for ten times the money. I no longer had to beg him to see the British Museum or the Tower of London. Katie saw to that.

Somewhere Parke met a young French nobleman who said that if we visited Paris we should go to a real French hotel, the Hotel Baltimore on the Avenue Kleber. Dot and I and the two girls flew over one Saturday and got settled in. The place was unpretentious but clean and charming. Each room had a little grilled balcony and the food was superb. It was only a little way out of town and taxis were cheap and plentiful. The bartender bragged that he made the third-best martini in Paris. The old doorman was taken with Anne and Maggie, and when he found that they knew no French, he said he would teach them a useful expression every morning and every evening. He asked them their room number, which was eighty-eight. Maggie, who had taken two years of French in high school, didn't know, but she said she knew that 8 was *huit*, so she thought 88 would be *wheatywheat*. I asked her how she had made Bs. She said that the teacher, a practice teacher from the UCLA Education Department, didn't know any French either, but taught them what she had learned, which was *how to teach French*. That fall I yanked both daughters out of the LA school system and sent them to Westlake School for Girls, where they received a decent old-fashioned education that prepared them for college. After two days, I asked for the bill which, thanks to my American dollars, was only $7.00 a day. I thought they meant apiece, but they said no, the $7 was for all four. I asked Dot if she'd like to stay another week and they did. Both girls mentioned that they didn't realize what it meant at the time, but later when they studied about the *Venus de Milo*, they had seen it.

Even though I was so busy I couldn't always be with them, I missed my family. Once, when I had to leave for London a month before they could come, I got a cable that my work permit had been delayed and that I should stop off in Ireland. I settled in at the Shelburne Hotel. Perce flew over and worked with me Saturdays and Sundays. Once we were beside a window during a long twilight and could see to typewrite before we noticed that it was 10 pm. After two weeks, my permit came through. I would take a plane for London on Monday morning. Bertie McNally's wife Vogue and her sister Joan, married to a dear man named J.P. Roughneen, who had collected for export every other egg in Ireland, were entertaining an Englishman named John, a breezy type in the manufacturing business with his father. The two ladies wanted to take a trip to the western seacoast. I had to go along; John would drive J.P.'s new Ford. Neither J.P. nor Bertie could go, but the girls felt they had to get out of Dublin and see some country. It was sparkling weather. We had a nice drive, a good lunch at a country inn, and were returning early. It suddenly began *pouring down with rain*. We saw another inn and went into it. The place seemed deserted and very cold. Finally, we called up a slatternly spirit from the rear, who sold John a bottle of Irish whiskey and disappeared, never to return. There was no fire. The girls set up a bar on a table and served whiskey and water. We drank to keep warm. I challenged John to a steeplechase race. We jumped over chairs as obstacles, which amused the ladies. I got warm and John got dead drunk. We decided to load him into the car while he could still walk after a fashion.

Neither lady could drive, so I was elected. I found the right-hand drive strange but could manage it. Suddenly around a bend came a pack of bike riders. They took over the whole road. Fortunately, I wasn't speeding, not in that rain, but in order to avoid them I pulled out on the shoulder. Not too far to be dangerous. Not in America. But in Ireland the grass of the shoulder hid a drain. A drain is about a foot deep and not much wider than an automobile tire. Once your front wheel is in it, you can't possibly get out. This drain directed us straight toward a huge boulder, twice the size of the car. No doubt the drain went around the great rock, but the front end of the car did not nose its way around to see; it struck with shuddering force against the immovable object, sending the front of my face to the steering wheel. My two front teeth were snapped off and cut a hole through my lower lip. The girls in the back each received a broken leg or arm; only John slept peacefully. My memory of the next hour or two is a little blurred. I believe the cyclists brought J.P. and Bertie out in another car. I have no recollection of the constabulary. My greatest concern, when I was safely back in my room in the Shelburne, was about Vogue and Joan, whom J.P. said had only minor injuries and were concerned about me. He would not listen to my insistence that I buy him a new car; he had full insurance that would provide him with a brand-new one tomorrow and not cost him a cent. He named the number of people in southern Ireland including the magistrates, and he knew every one of them by name. John was already on his way back to England, where he belonged. It was in no way my fault. The cyclists said I did well not to hit one of them, and the road men were supposed to keep that long grass cut which had obscured the drain. The telephone rang. It was for me. The best surgeon in Ireland, Bouchier-Hayes, whom everybody called the Butcher, was on the other end, asking to know when I wanted my lip sewed up. Right now, I replied, if he could make it on a Sunday afternoon. He promised to be right over. J.P. assured me he was a wonder. I'd like the Butcher.

It was 4:30 in the afternoon when the Butcher called, seven o'clock before he arrived. His first words to me as he examined my lip were: "I meant to come before, and I planned to come before, but you know how we Irish are: I went to the races, God forgive me."

"Could you still do it now?" I asked him.

"Of course. We can't be letting you walk around with a hole in your lip you could put your finger through."

He called a nurse who had opened up a tiny dispensary by the time he took me there in his car. I was slightly apprehensive, for he obviously was a little tight, but that didn't stop him. He took X-rays of the lip and held it up against a light, then proceeded to remove particles of cracked teeth, dentine, out of my lip. This took a long time before he was satisfied that he had it all. When the Novocaine began to wear off and I winced, he said, "Faith, I know you're prayin' for me now."

After he sewed up the lip, I told him I thought I had broken a rib. He felt them and said though one may have been cracked it was not separated. "As long as it's touching it will grow together; it will even be stronger than before. Try to forget it."

He took me back to the hotel and I thanked him and asked him his charge. He said, "Would two pounds ten be too much?"

"Not half enough for all you did."

"That's my charge."

I paid him and thanked him sincerely. He said I had been a good patient. Not one yelp out of me. We shook hands. The next time Bertie and J.P. Roughneen were in England, we entertained them. The two of them held up the plane while they examined my lip, which had healed. "Lovely," said J.P. "Smashing!" said Bertie.

A striped-pants dentist gave me a couple of temporary caps for my teeth which were so excellent that my own dentist remarked: "We were taught in dental school not to make the temporaries too perfect. I swear it's a pity to take these out." I thought I'd have the lip checked just to be sure there were no particles of dentine left in. The X-ray showed nothing. The American doctor charged me twenty-five dollars to say that it was one of the slickest jobs he had ever seen.

During that hiatus, I managed to visit Maurice Walsh again and asked how he was keeping. "Not too well. I miss my wife. The doctors have a name for it, but it was the drink. Yet I would do so again." He asked me if I would like to meet his old friends who were distillers at Jameson's, where he had once worked.

They were two handsome old men, each with a ruddy face and a shock of white hair. One of them said, "Did you bring your cup, Maurice?"

"It slipped my mind."

They had only the one tin cup to serve the 20-year-old John Jamesons in. They rinsed it out each time they poured a drink for the next man, not at the water spigot, which was ten feet away, but with a slosh of the 20-year-old whiskey which they threw out on the dirt floor before serving a visitor or themselves.

Dorothy was with me when we stopped later in the fall to pick up from Maurice the hand-written novel we took to Bernice, and Dot was much taken with his grandson and sent him in a Christmas box the one thing every English or Irish kid craved, a big supply of chewing gum. I received this letter from Maurice:

> Dear Larry Watkin,
>
> Your book and the box of chewing gum have come to hand. For "On Borrowed Time" I am all gratitude, but for the chewing gum my gratitude has worn a bit thin. Should I blame Mrs. Watkin? My grandson is not yet an adept at disposing of the insoluble residue, and twice I have sat on particularly adhesive pieces. In a country viced with chewing, how do you get rid of the residue? Does a municipal scavenger come round with a barrow?
>
> Your book is a delight, and I heartily congratulate you on it. It is a unique combination of modern sophistication and the true naturalness of the folk tale. And it is beautifully and delicately told. Keep on working, or are you going to let films work you to death? Still I hope your visit to Kerry supplied you with material for Walt Disney. I'm thinking of going down to live there, and if you and your woman-of-the-house are over again we'll foregather and talk some with oiled throats.

My regards and thanks to yourself and Mrs. Watkin, and hoping your Parke is fit and fine.

Yours Aye

Maurice Walsh

Dear old Maurice. We did see him again in Dublin after *The Quiet Man* came out. I could not tell him that I thought it a fine and rollicking movie, for he was so greatly disappointed in it, he said he would not sell anything of his to the films again, unless I wrote the screenplay. He gave me several of his novels, should I care to do them, but Walt went instead for *Rob Roy.*

34

Rob Roy came off well enough. It was the sort of thing that Richard Todd could do well. He was no taller than Alan Ladd, but like him in being athletic and stout-hearted. We were lucky enough to have the loan of a regiment of Scots back from duty in Korea, and most of them were tough little men who could trot up a mountainside with a pack on their shoulders that weighed almost as much as they did. I remember hearing one remarking to another when he first saw some of them in costume: "There go our fookin' old ancestors." Dick had a good record as a fighting man in World War II and he seldom used a double. He spent the best part of a day doing take after take in icy water. At the end of it the crew burst into spontaneous applause.

I felt sorry for him one time. Because he was small, he surrounded himself with everything large. He owned a big house, a huge black dog, a monstrous big car. We were on a mountain top in the Highlands. Richard was to lead his embattled MacGregors down the slope to meet the enemy in the glen. He drove up in his car, stepped out in full makeup, tossed aside the scarf that kept it off his shirt collar, and said to his dog, "Down, King!" Drawing his gleaming claymore, he said to the director, "Ready, sir?" then to the soldiers, "Ready, men?" I can't give the Gaelic, but I can supply it phonetically. He shouted the war cry of the MacGregors, "Ard hoi-la Mac-Gregor!" Then he sprang forward, tripped on a rolling stone, fell, and sprained his thigh so that we had to shoot around him for two weeks.

As I recall, we had a very uninspired director, which was all right with Walt. He didn't want a big-name director. We would start out talking about John Ford, but end up with an unknown. I don't think Walt wanted it to be called John Ford's picture, but Walt Disney's picture. Bun Haskins ran so many puffs in *Variety* after *Treasure Island* that Disney didn't hire him again. They always called me to take a page ad, but I always refused. I liked the fact that I didn't have to fret and scheme to make money. I gave Dot the money; she did the banking. I was free to think about the story, good or bad. Sometimes I was so disgusted with Walt for being sure to pick the second-rate rather than the best that I swore I'd quit, family or no family; then something tempting would come along. I asked Walt to let me write about the American Revolution, like the events leading up to Yorktown, but Walt was afraid to touch it. I wanted to do Robert E. Lee, but Walt didn't understand him. I begged him to let me take a crack at the Arthurian Legend, but Walt said, "Larry, when I was a kid I read Mark Twain, but I never did understand what the hell those old knights were doing banging each other around."

It was probably just as well that I didn't insist. I later realized that I could no more have explained chivalric love to Walt Disney than General Haig could be made to comprehend the romance of the Holy Grail. In all fairness, Walt could never have made me understand the working of his multiplane camera. I was lucky to have figured out that engineering marvel, the safety pin. *When Knighthood Was in Flower* was more Walt's dish. And where could I find a smarter producer? What if I'd been asked to put that happy ending on *The Snows of Kilmanjaro*? I had worked with Goldwyn, I had worked for six weeks at Warner's. At that very moment Jerry Wald called me up saying they were sneak-previewing *Task Force* at their downtown theater, and I was invited to sit with its creators, also to attend the banquet that took place at 7:30 in a certain room at the studio. I inquired my way and when I arrived at 7:30, there was a great long table set up but only a handful of men at the far end engaged in loud conversation. They paused and looked at me. I inquired: "Is this where the *Task Force* banquet is being held?" They said no, so I said "sorry," and walked out. I went to Jerry Wald's office. He said they were great kidders, grabbed my arm, and led me back. Magically, almost every chair had been taken. Jerry took the seat next to the end; I took the very end seat. The steaks were great; so was the champagne. There were no speeches, but just before time to leave, the man at the head of the table looked up and called out, "Hey, you down there at the end of the table; what's your name?" I actually didn't know who he was, though I suspected that he was one of the Warner Bros, so I arose and said very distinctly, "My name is Larry Watkin. What's *your* name?"

He didn't answer, but he gave out with a tremendous guffaw, and so did everybody else. Jerry whacked me on the back. "Jack will love that," he said. There was great confusion. I was soon separated from Jerry and from everyone else I knew. Dozens of limousines were lined up. A very busy factotum grabbed my arm and pushed me into a limousine. There was one other passenger seated there, the star of the show, Gary Cooper. I introduced myself and told him briefly why I was there, for he had not been at the banquet. He was friendly enough, but not glib. He said he had liked the part, but hadn't seen any of it. Had I? No, I said, but heard it had come off well. I was struck with the fact that if the nice ones looked nice in everyday life, they looked nice on the screen. If an actress was hypocritical and mean like a girl we knew, the camera would show it up every time.

When he reached the theater the kids spotted him, but he could move those lanky legs fast and slipped into the safety of the theater before the brats could mob him. Jerry Wald steered me to the section reserved for those who had come to evaluate the show. He hadn't got far before Jack Warner spotted me and told the man sitting beside him to move. He wanted the admiral to sit beside him. He had dubbed me the admiral and never called me anything else. He made puns constantly, terrible puns, and knocked himself out with them. I was not only the admiral. I was Admiral Television, he, he, he! He talked to me through the first part of the movie, then got interested and watched it as I was doing, critically. When it was over he told me, "Come on; we're going up to my office and talk about it."

Only ten or twelve people had been invited. There was one easy chair behind a big desk. Jack sat. Everybody else stood. The discussion started and never stopped. Jack just listened. Some of the debaters got heated. Finally, Jack, who had been smoking a big cigar, removed it from his mouth, spat resoundingly into the empty waste paper basket beside him, and delivered himself: "What this picture needs is an eerie sense—Erie, Pennsylvania, he, he, he." There wasn't much more after that. As we were breaking up, Jack said to me, "Admiral, you've been awful quiet. Haven't you any criticisms?"

"Dozens of them," I said. "I'd write them down and send them to you tomorrow if I thought you'd read them."

"You're damn right I'll read them, every one. You send them to me now, OK?"

"OK."

I sent him a twenty-page critique, tactfully written, I thought. He called me at Disney's in a day or two. The operator said she thought it was Jack Warner and she thought he meant me. He did. I was the admiral, wasn't I? He thanked me very nicely, saying he appreciated everything I had done and that I was a smart cookie. And thanks.

Wat kin you do about a guy like that? He, he, he.

The time that Walt really broke my heart was when he mentioned in passing that Perce wanted to stay in England the better part of a year, not only to prepare for some big sets but to work on the next story. He couldn't do that without me. Walt made it clear that he wasn't pushing. Could we settle our daughters in happily at Westlake School for Girls? It was entirely up to us. Dot was all for it. In that case, said Walt, I'd like to have you give some thought to *Don*

Quixote. Ever read it? I said I had and thought it would be wonderful. Walt then told me something that had my tongue hanging out. Cary Grant and Cantinflas, the little Mexican comedian, had put their heads together and come to him. Cary wanted to play Quixote; Cantinflas wanted to do Sancho Panza.

Walt himself suggested that if we found an appropriate time, Dot and I should both visit Spain, rent a car and chauffeur, drive all over the damn place, find the old windmills, visit the castles, the museums, see it all. That of course is exactly what we did, after I had read the monumental work twice more. Every time you read *Don Quixote* it's a different story. We picked up an Englishman named David Ley in Madrid. The Disney office knew about him. He taught English at the University of Madrid, was as excited about the project as I, mapped out the essentials, and stayed with us until nearly the end. We loved all of it: Madrid, where nobody gets up until noon. We saw some movie-making. To avoid the worst heat of the day everyone has a siesta. The movie studios opened about 2:30 or 3 in the afternoon and worked through our dinner hour. Dinner is at midnight or just before. I recall that a bull fighter of some reputation was playing a role and that he dined with us, a charming gallant, who, when he kissed Dot's hand, kissed it all the way up to the elbow. I asked her later if she disliked his ostentation. I expected her to say yes, but she didn't; she had to admit it gave her a certain thrill.

It gave Ava Gardner one, too. She was having a heavy romance at the time with Frank Sinatra, but was falling for the bullfighter. Frank appeared in town without warning. The publicity girl in charge of La Gardner, a clever Scots lassie, managed to steer the bullfighter down one street, Frank up the other into Ava's hotel. It was reported that Ava was so glad to see Frank and so contrite for her aberration that she couldn't wait to open her door but took him to bed on the hallway carpet outside. A likely story. The Scots girl also told me that women adored Frank not only because he was a great lover, but because he was so thoughtful. He remembered any small nicety that pleased them and worried about their well-being. When he unpacked his bags, he had carefully packed away a syringe with some medication that relieved Ava Gardner's stuffy nose. Maybe the publicity girl made up that one, too, but if she did, it worked with me. I had never liked him before I heard it, but have been a devoted fan ever after.

I loved the primitive LaMancha plain. In the heat of the day when only mad Americans and an Englishman would be driving around in the glare of the midday sun, we would pass a newly plowed field with perfectly straight dark brown furrows which ended when we came upon the plowman, stretched out upon the ground with his sombrero covering his face as he took his siesta in the shadow cast by his patient mule. To reach the tiny town of Camp de Criptano, where the traditional three windmills charged by Quixote stood on a rise above the town, we had to drive across fields where there was no road. The children were so shy they did not even beg. In Madrid, you had to carry a pocketful of very small denomination aluminum coins which you scattered as a sower sows his seed to escape the more vociferous packs, but not here. They had never seen a motor car. We had come straight from Mars. We were warned when photographing the windmills to pick our way with care, for the whole town used the mesa as an outdoor privy, there being nothing resembling the wash-down water closet named after Thomas Crapper, whose plumbing vans bearing his name were everywhere in London.

We did not tarry in Campo, but drove on to Tobosa, Dulcinea's town. These little towns seemed bare and deserted. Doors would be open, but everybody must have been sleeping. We liked the primitive open countryside. Irrigation was from chained buckets lowered and raised from deep wells, a mule walking endlessly at the end of a long pole supplying the power. Often they were blindfolded, whether to avoid dizziness or to let their imaginations roam, I do not know. Thurber said that once when he experienced all but complete blindness, he used to gaze out a certain window and see the most entrancing sights. His sight restored, he drew the shade and never looked out of that window again. Could not blindfolded mules have visions of green meadows and still waters to quicken their dull lives?

Dorothy and I wanted to have a brief look at Sevilla, so we took a plane and flew down. I'm sure David was invited but did not go along. We had two days of pleasure and admiration in the lovely hotel, the parks, and the cathedral. The flamenco dancers in the supper clubs were the best we had seen. I called Dot's attention to the girls' symmetrical bosoms. She barely looked up, and when she did, said dryly, "You can hardly expect me to go into ecstasies about some other woman's front."

I argued, "But these are works of art. They are superb."

"So is this soup. I wish I had the recipe."

We rejoined David and took in the castles and the museums. We thought we had covered everything until he told us that we should make one final stop, fly to Palma in Majorca, where folk dancers from all over Spain were holding a festival. They'd bring the gigantic cardboard figures out of the town hall, and we would see and hear native singing and dancing groups we'd never forget. From there we could fly to Barcelona and get a plane for London. The only trouble was getting a reservation. We must stay at the Hotel Victoria, but hotel managers were unwilling to take Americans. Too many failed to honor their reservations. He'd leave it up to the telephone operator. David listened in, smiling. "This girl is *very* good," he reported. "She is saying: 'Mr. and Mrs. Watkin are very quiet, inoffensive Americans. Just tuck them away in a little corner somewhere.'"

That's exactly what the manager did. He gave us what must have been the maid's room with an old brass bed. The single window looked out on a rock cliff. I saw him watching us at tea and at dinner. Evidently we were being hazed to see how we bore up. Next morning, I sought him out and said that we loved his establishment, but if something just a shade more luxurious became available, we would be grateful.

He signaled for us to follow him. He opened up two of the most delightful suites, a hallway, a capacious bathroom tiled every inch, followed by bedroom, sitting room, and a screened patio-porch with awnings on three sides for perfect privacy. The view was across a sparkling bay with sailing ships to a 12th century cathedral, rose-colored. The food was delicious, the wines mellow, the water of the Mediterranean warm and so clear that a swimmer could see the bottom twenty feet down. The clientele was largely English; hence the name Victoria. Taxis were abundant to carry you to the promenade in the city park, where everyone went walking of an evening. Then the folk groups arrived and followed their bands through the city streets. When I looked wishful, they would motion me to join them, and I sang along with them, as I did with the Welsh singers outside Hyde Park. Dot laughed at me but never reproved me when I was having fun. We saw a bullfight, our first and last, took the bus trip the hotel sponsored that drove through vineyards and twisty olive trees, lovely against the dark red soil. We visited the house once owned by George Sand, though I don't remember whom she was living with at the time. I think de Musset, not Chopin.

We hated to leave that place. When we did the bill was negligible, and the manager said to come back at any time. We were in the club. I never had a second chance but Dot took the girls, and Parke went once alone. When I called the manager from London, he said of course he remembered me and he would take good care of any members of my family.

I worked like a dog that year, not slighting the current screenplay, but writing what I thought was the best treatment I had ever done. I kept seeing Cary Grant with his haunted eyes, driven sane by ridicule, not to be comforted even by his loyal but unromantic squire Sancho Panza. My hopes were soaring. Walt dashed them with a single sentence, the only remark he ever made about the project: "Larry, we've got to get ahold of the horse."

Neither did I say anything more to him about it, but I said a great deal to Dot that night. "I've had it," I said. "I have read a 766-page book twice, a book of fine print. I have worked my ass off to do a treatment worthy of the best acting team any producer in the world ever had thrown into his lap. Think of it: Cary Grant with those deep-set eyes and that marvelous little Mexican born to play Sancho Panza. This is one of the world's few great books. It has lasted for hundreds of years because it's been loved by great and small. And all that goddamn moron can see in it is how to animate a bony old horse! There should be a law against such stupidity."

Dorothy tried to calm me down, but I was sick of the whole illiterate mess. She told me to sleep on it. I still said no. She said, "You love Walt; you know you do."

"He doesn't love me."

"He's our friend. When has he shown you or the rest of us anything but kindness?"

"He's incapable of friendship. Remember that dinner party he had us to when that clueless clot, the overage actress, and that bag of worms she called her husband kept murmuring the whole damn evening, 'Genius...sheer genius?' Walt pretended he didn't hear it, but he was eating it up. That's who his friends are."

The next day Dorothy told me some home truths. I was not ruthless enough to be top dog. I would always be fighting the president of a college, or an admiral or general, or a producer because I really didn't want to be one. To be a king or a president or the chairman of the board I would have to be a bastard, so self-centered that I'd dump my family or climb over the backs of my friends if need be, because I wanted to manage other people—and I didn't. I wanted a certain independence: I would not kowtow to inferiors and did not want them to bow to me. Finally, I had already achieved more fame and had more reason to be proud than thousands of my peers. I was having a lot of fun. I had the world by the tail and didn't know it. She might have added that she was tired of hearing me belly-ache, but was too kind to do so.

As usual, she was right; so I simmered down. We went back to California where I tackled *Rob Roy* in earnest. So far I had only scratched the surface, having read two biographies reputed to be factual, and, of course, Sir Walter Scott's romantic novel *Rob Roy*.

I had also explored the Highlands and learned that Highlanders were a breed apart, Catholics and Gaels like the southern Irish. They were Celts like the Bretons, the Welsh, the Cornish, and the southern Irish, pushed back to mountain fastnesses to escape the Roman legions in 55 BC. They were not Presbyterians like the northern Irish and the Glasgow and Edinburgh Scots.

I had bought a Scots-English dictionary, thinking, like most Americans, that all Scots talked like Bobie Burns, and that "The best laid plans o' mice an' men gang aft agley" would be the speech of the Highlander, too. But the Highlander learns English as he would any other foreign language and Rob Roy was a true Gael, possibly the last great chieftan of his clan. He told the piper that when he was dying he wanted him to play the old Celtic air "Cha teil mi tulidh" (I will never return). Rob is a shadowy person, thought by many to be a pure cattle-thief and outlaw, by others as a Robin Hood of the Highlands who took from the rich to give to the poor, and by still others as a brave man fighting against terrible odds to regain possessions which earlier injustice had given to rival clans, especially the Campbells. He seemed a grim, cruelly proscribed figure, who had to be lightened for a Disney film. There are so many conflicting legends that once I had satisfied myself he was a brave man more sinned against than sinning, I had few compunctions about putting the best possible interpretation on my storyline.

Somebody had told Walt that Rob, while still an outlaw with a price upon his head, had marched a little band of followers into London. Walt wanted that so badly that I didn't fight him over it. I believe that Rob had been captured and sentenced by the English throne to be outlawed to Barbados, but that his sentence had been lifted. So, Walt had his big production number, and Richard Todd had never appeared more valiant. It was a darn good romantic film, but badly promoted in both countries. Few people in America appeared to have heard of it. Maybe they confused it with *Robin Hood*, and thought it a re-release.

In England, the film won high honors, chosen for the 1953 Royal Command Performance and without a dissenting vote, which was unusual. At such a screening, I would have been one of those to stand in line and meet their royal majesties, but chose not to attend for a very good reason. I had barely put the final polish on the shooting script in early June and was working out a storyline for the next one Walt wanted to do (or let's say explore), *Westward Ho!* by Charles Kingsley. I had moved into a delightful apartment in Knightsbridge, and I was sure the family would particularly like it, when I was taken with stomach cramps and nausea which actually floored me. I could just crawl to the telephone and call my secretary to bring a doctor quickly.

That was late afternoon. It was night when a strange but kind medical face bent over me, saying I appeared to have suffered a ruptured appendix. Could I give him permission to operate? I said yes and remembered nothing more until I woke up next morning in a quite different place.

35

It was not surprising that when I came to I was at first unaware that I had been moved to a medical facility, for the London clinic was too swank to look like one. My room was large and well appointed, my bed wide and comfortable, and I was attended by two nurses, one an Irish beauty named Mary O'Reilly, who had upper-class Dubliner written all over her, the other a fine happy person and an excellent nurse. It hadn't been appendicitis at all, though the pain had been localized on the right side, a characteristic of diverticulitis, which means a perforation of the large intestine on the left.

My doctor, John Hosford, one of the top surgeons in England at the time, had inserted a drainage tube and put me on a course of antibiotics to cure the infection and make it safe to operate. They had no effect; so, a temporary colostomy was indicated. That called for three more operations: one to install the colostomy; one to remove the infected section of colon, called a resection; and one to close up the colostomy. All four operations were accomplished in ninety days, with much head-shaking by the surgeon, who thought all Americans mad in trying to hasten nature. He would have expected an Englishman to take a year for such protracted surgery. I asked him if nature was so great, why had he been called in, and quoted his countryman James Hilton, who had written that no self-respecting plumber would have made such an inefficient valva as the male prostate.

He thought I might have a point. So did the anesthetist. Both were droll, straight-faced men with that marvelous English sense of humor. They use understatement and seem happiest if they can slide one past you. Americans use overstatement, as in Mark Twain. Walt himself used it when he visited me in the hospital and said he was sorry to hear that the colostomy had been closed up. He was hoping to fit it with a bagpipe and use me to plug *Rob Roy*.

Dr. Hosford was the top surgeon at St. Bartholomew's Hospital in London, and his operations were watched by a gallery of eager young practitioners, who hoped to copy his skill. When a doctor reaches that eminence, he is no longer called doctor, but mister. He was so fundamentally kind that when I was nervous and worried just before my fourth operation, the nurse called him at a cocktail party in the country and he immediately drove all the way in to cheer me. I told him I did not wish to impose on him in such a fashion, and he said it was a pleasure to discuss the human body with me, my ideas about how it worked were so bizarre. After the operations I pointed to one contusion and said I didn't remember which operation had caused that. He said in his rather high-pitched voice, "I never did think too highly of an American's perspicacity, but I do think one should remember one's own belly button." He was as casual as an old country doctor, and as genuine. He charged only 100 pounds for each operation, which I said was not enough. My Disney insurance, which I didn't even know I had, more than paid for his fee and all the other hospital expenses. I said that if we had any money at all, we expected to pay a little more so that our doctors could afford to devote a bit more of their time to charity. He replied that if I were a multi-millionaire, that still would be his charge, and that he would be happy to compare his charitable contribution with that of any American doctor. He did, however, accept my offer to put the whole sum to his account in dollars in the Chase Manhattan Bank of New York. He could not take enough money out of the country on his forthcoming visit to the Mayo Clinic to permit him to take his wife along, without some such contrivance.

I had fun in that hospital. Wally Simpson, the Duchess of Windsor, had a room three doors down. She was having one of her many face-lifting ops, but told the newspapers that on its last trip over, the *Queen Mary* had lurched violently, throwing her against a bulkhead, which caused the need for surgical attention. My wife and daughters, on the same crossing, said the Atlantic had been as smooth as a millpond. When I could be wheeled around, I peeked into other rooms and saw that as my secretary had done in mine, every room had its corner table with a variety of liquors set up for guests. My "mister" inquired, when my colon did not respond to antibiotics, if I was drinking considerable alcohol. I was shocked. I said I had never had a drink in a hospital, and he had expressly forbidden it. He replied, "Yes, I know, but I didn't expect you would pay any attention to what I said."

On the last operation, I played a little game. I had two large moles, one in each crotch, and asked Dr. Hosford if he could not snip them off in the course of an operation. He said of course he would, but each time he forgot. So, I asked my nurse to let me shave myself and put on the sterile bandage preparatory to the surgery. Since I promised to do nothing dangerous she permitted it, and agreed to attend the operation, as I requested. I scissored out two arrows from white adhesive tape and outlined them in black ink to show where they were pointing. Now, it is insulting to a top surgeon to suggest that he join the National Health, or socialized medicine, which Great Britain had in 1953. So, I pointed an arrow at each mole and wrote on the twin tapes: "If you don't remove the moles this time, I will take my business to National Health."

When I came to next morning the nurse was laughing. She said that in the middle of the operation, with my guts spread out on the table, the head nurse had uttered an involuntary gasp, telling the surgeon that there was a black bug on me. He said, "Well, take it off." The black bug was the tip of the inked tape. She read the message and everybody had a big laugh. The surgeon not only cut off those two moles, but the operation was suspended while a mole hunt ensued. Somebody would say, "There's another one." And they say the British have no sense of humor.

My anesthetist always paid a social call on me before and after each operation, so this last time I said to him: "Houdini says he can get through the spirit world to send messages after he is dead. So, shouldn't I be able to get through the ether to you during an operation?"

"Sounds reasonable," he said.

"All right, then. During the operation, I will say to you, 'The thick, sweet mystery of chloroform.' OK?"

"I'll be listening."

"Then shoot in your pentothal."

He was sitting on a straight chair the next day, waiting for me to come around. He looked grim.

"Do we go along with Houdini?" Sorrowfully he shook his head.

"I didn't say 'the thick, sweet mystery of chloroform?'"

"You did not."

"Did I say anything at all?"

"You talked incessantly."

"Like what?"

"It doesn't bear repeating."

"Give me a sample."

"You kept saying, 'God, I'm so hot; I'm so goddamn hot!'"

After that fourth and final operation, I regained my strength in an amazingly short time and worked harder than ever on a screenplay for Kingsley's *Westward Ho!*. Walt had said that it *might* be our next one. I always worked during an illness. My secretary, a prim, proper, and most efficient English girl, came in every day. I dictated from notes, and she took them down not in shorthand but on the typewriter. An unused commode under the bed with a crocheted lid made a perfect typing stand. I tried to keep her busy, for if I paused too long she would try to convert me to Catholicism. I might have died and would some day. I said why condemn me to a fate worse than death, but she would merely shut her eyes, probably praying for my blasphemous soul, and wait for another opportunity.

One reason for hurrying was that Walt had at one point almost canceled *Robin Hood* until I had given him seventy pages of screenplay. He was surprised that I was that far along and that the screenplay was that good. So, he had let us go forward with a happy result. I was less sanguine about *Westward Ho!*. I knew that he would love all the adventurous parts, especially the fight with the Spanish Armada, but suspected that he would not follow the hero Amyas to the bitter end, when, blind and helpless, he must accept the love and pity of the Indian girl Ayacanora. But I must try.

It was really hard on me to be used that way. If Walt was unsure, he'd have me experiment with a screenplay, maybe with two in a row before he settled on something. He had me whipped up about Robert Nathan's *The Woodcutter's House* and about the Irish story again, then told me to drop them and go after *Robin Hood* full tilt. He would let me work long enough to become engrossed and enthusiastic on a story, then drop it. I much preferred his immediate no on *The Mudlark*. "Let Fox do those subtleties," he said. And by the way, 20th Century Fox did just that in 1952 with Irene Dunne and Alec Guinness. Fox used Alec; we used Dickie.

There was another reason for not making *Westward Ho!*. Walt fired Perce Pearce. That put an end to our British movies. Walt himself visited me to tell me what he had done. He explained that he was firing me, too, but he was rehiring me after I returned to America, and that I would be paid a bonus so that there would be no lost salary. He didn't tell me why he was firing Perce, but he did ask me, "What did you ever see in that son-of-a-bitch?"

I refused to curse out Perce, as he invited me to. Instead, I said, "I might ask you the same question. You knew him long before I did. Perce has always been very helpful to me."

"Hell," said Walt, "it's the other way around. You don't need him. He needs you."

That's all he would volunteer. Perce didn't explain anything either, except to say that he was staying in England and when he got set he would present me with an offer that would make Disney's wage look small. He also urged that I attend the command performance. I told him I doubted very much if I would do so. Dot wanted to go home.

Perce accepted that. I waited for him to tell me what had caused the break between him and Walt, but he didn't explain it.

His wife June did. She called upon me and spelled it out very directly. They had entertained Walt for dinner at their rented house in the country and Perce had got stinking drunk. The drunker he got the more abusive he became, damning Walt out for not backing him in a venture that had happened years ago. I think it was some toy or gimmick that Perce wanted the Disney company to promote. It would have made millions for all concerned, Perce thought. Walt had only to speak the word, but had refused. Walt tried to explain, but Perce would not stop berating him for his ungenerous behavior. It had festered in Perce's mind over the years until the molehill had become a mountain. June did not assess the blame. Rather, she was saddened that a long, friendly relationship, during which the two couples had taken pleasure trips together, had been so abruptly halted.

The following year Walt came to me, saying he had decided to do *Westward Ho!* after all. He might get the financing from his funds piled up in México. Would I like to work with Perce Pearce on the project? I said yes, but before Perce could wind up his affairs in England, he had died in his sleep. So once again, and for good, Walt shelved *Westward Ho!*. He was pleased that Perce had been returned to the payroll just before he died, for it meant that June would get the $36,000 insurance money that the Disney company automatically paid a widow upon the death of any high-ranking employee. "That June," said Walt, "is great—far too good for that son-of-a-bitch she married." If Walt had ever heard that Perce was sorry, he did not care. Once he had decided that a man was a son-of-a-bitch, he would always be so, even beyond the grave.

The insurance money did June little good. She had money of her own, and Perce had scrimped and saved all his life to leave her a million more. She died the next year.

When wise men cautioned me to put away something for my old age instead of spending my money going through life first-class, I told them about Perce Pearce who stayed in lousy motels and ate greasy hamburgers unless he was on an expense account. He had plenty in a sock for the golden years, not realizing that the golden years were when he could have enjoyed them.

So it was that in October 1953 I was aboard a BOAC plane flying non-stop to New York, occupying one of the two forward berths reserved for passengers who could not sit up. I stretched out most comfortably in my pajamas and bathrobe, napping when it pleased me and well attended by two bonny stewardesses. I never expected to see England again. Only the year before, on June 10, 1952, eight days after his 22nd birthday, my son Parke had married Barbara Burr, a Vassar girl he had met while he was at Yale. I had flown over to attend the wedding and flew back to England the next day. I tried very hard not to let my work completely divorce me from my family.

During one of my trips back to California, when we were all beginning to think of England as home where the interesting things happened, and California a place to visit, my daughter Maggie wanted to celebrate her graduation from junior high school by having me take her and her sixteen-year-old friend Susan to a night club on the Hollywood Strip. The old Mocambo was then the place to go. In a weak moment, I said yes.

By degrees I learned what I was in for. There was a hot polka band, which was bringing all the stars out. I said I was a lousy dancer, and I would not dance the polka. The young ladies had other ideas. Every night for a week when I came home tired from the studio and wanted to talk to Dot while she was getting supper, Maggie put on a polka record in the living room. The rug was already rolled back as I entered the front door. Maggie and Sue, a football coach's daughter, and a really powerful child, would grab me and fling me across the room. At the end of a week they pronounced me ready. When the great evening arrived, they had decided that we would first dine at the night club, though at such an early hour that office barflies were still downing that last one after work when we arrived. Plainly nobody ate at the Mocambo; nevertheless, in a curtained-off alcove at one end of the bar, two tourists, as ignorant of night clubbing as I, occupied another table. I immediately ordered champagne, forgetting that I was not in London or aboard the *Queen Mary*. The waiter said he feared the young ladies were not quite old enough to partake of that beverage legally. Maggie was disappointed, but not Sue. She whispered to me that she would rather have a cup of coffee. So we had a potful. Sue almost got drunk on it. This was the first coffee that she had ever had. The coach didn't allow it on their training table.

We stretched that meal out for a long time, for nobody had yet appeared to enter the ballroom, but finally we heard the strains of the band. I believe that they would have asked for a table on the very edge of the dance floor, though I wanted one well to the side, reasoning that it would take some time to push through the crowd which was sure to come later and thus cut down the dance torture. Fortune favored me. The only early arrival was Anne Sheridan and two gentlemen, sitting at a secluded table to indulge in a night of quiet drinking. So naturally the girls wanted a table near Anne

Sheridan. I chose one near at hand, but not so close that Sue could actually touch the great star. I liked Anne Sheridan. She drank like a gentleman, owing her vibrant good health to the glasses of tomato juice she consumed on the set. The tourists put her down as a health nut, not knowing that they were Bloody Marys. Here among friends she had a quart of whiskey on the table. Probably she had brought it herself, knowing the amount of water the Mocambo put in their drinks. Before the night was over I was so pooped that I begged the waiter to bring me a double or a triple or at least a straight, but at last I gave up. Though I was drinking very little those days, I am sure he put me down as a lush, and I got the same pale amber glass of water every time. I tried to keep smiling, because Maggie and Sue were so pleased. I'm sure Maggie must have been bragging to Sue, and was proud to be able to deliver.

The celebrities kept coming. The small oblong dance floor was so crowded that I needn't have worried about the polka. If I had cut loose as directed in my living room I am sure I would have accidentally kicked somebody, and by midnight the girls didn't care whether I danced or shuffled as long as I allowed myself to be steered close enough to an idol to let them brush arms with him. I would just have done my duty by Maggie and sunk into my chair when Sue would whisper, "There's GEORGE RAFT!" She would snatch me into her muscular embrace and draw me into a CLOSE TWO SHOT—RAFT & SUE, WATKIN IN B.G. I couldn't care less about the beautiful people. I was hot and tired. But I did enjoy one bit of Hollywood snobbishness. Rosalind Russell had come in unattended. Though limping badly and leaning heavily on a cane, she had recently scored a triumph, and could not resist being seen if her leg had been broken. She was immediately given a chair not only on the edge of the dance floor but at least two feet out from the edge. Here a steady retinue of dancers would pause and have a flattering word for her before dancing off again. Her glory was rudely eclipsed when Jane Wyman entered. I don't know if she had already dumped that B-actor Ronald Reagan by this time, for she was a truly fine actress, and I don't know what performance had elevated her. It might have been *The Glass Menagerie*. Anyway, the management understood how the world was run. They put a chair for her two feet farther out on the dance floor directly in front of Rosalind Russell. Jane nodded prettily to Miss Russell, who rose, glowering, and limped off into limbo. Now the true friends mobbed Jane Wyman. I don't know how long the adulation went on, but I know that Maggie and Sue and a most insignificant screen writer closed up the joint at three o'clock.

Driving home, I thought how wonderful it was not to be an actor. To be always on display must be very galling at times.

My other daughter, Anne, four years younger than Maggie, wanted me to take them out one night when we were in London. "Sorry, honey," I told her, "but I'm afraid that tonight I will have to stay in and write a love scene for Richard Todd."

Anne looked shocked and couldn't restrain herself: "You're writing a *love* scene?"

"Why, yes. Did you think that Dick made it up as he went along?"

"I guess I really knew better, but I like to think he's making it up. Besides, I don't think of you as the *lover* type. I think of you as the *father* type."

In Paris, when Perce and I and Ken Anakin were interviewing French actors for parts in *The Sword and the Rose*, I took Maude Spector, our casting director, out to dinner one evening. Maude appeared to know actors not only in England but all over the Continent. Her taste was unfailing. I guessed that she knew about quaint Parisian restaurants, too. She did. She guided me down some steps below the book stalls on the West Bank of the Seine, not far from Notre Dame Cathedral, for we could look up at it. This was the real thing. Hams and baloneys hung down from the rafters in their casings. At the entrance the pug-ugly bouncer was playing a gambling game with a customer. I wanted to have a go at the dice, but Maud said he was a gentleman and friend and since he always won in the end, wouldn't let me play. No English was spoken and I knew very little French, so I told Maude to coach me. After the waiter took our order and came back with our wine she told me the French expression inviting him to have a glass with us. I couched my offer in my best Julia Child French. He accepted, standing beside the table, drank my health, and said something with a flourish. I nodded and smiled. The owner was on the way over for a word of greeting. Maude quickly murmured what I should say to him and I did so. He was pleased, and again I nodded and smiled. Maude quickly engaged him in a torrent of French, knowing that I had given my all. He left shortly, saying a final word to me. I gave him a "M'sieu," and a little bow. The dinner was great. I excused myself to go to the toilet, and when I came back Maude said the whole establishment had complimented her on her escort. They said they had never met a more charming American. "You big ham!" she said with a certain indignation.

I told her, "Now you know what it's like to be a screenwriter, and how it feels to have some actor get credit for the lines that you have put in his mouth."

36

I returned to California for good, not yet perfectly recovered from my operation, in late October, and I must have worked like a madman to tackle the story of "Powell of the Colorado" and have it ready for Walt to shoot by February 1, 1954, but I have a letter I wrote my mother to that effect. Fortunately for me, she not only kept all my letters but the envelopes they came in, and the postmark gave me the month and the year in which they were written. I had the bad habit of omitting any inside home address. They all were on Walt Disney Productions envelopes, and I never jotted down more than the date of the month. To a late letter which I had written in long-hand my mother answered that it was so nice to get a purely personal letter, not one that I had dictated to a secretary. I promptly informed her that I had *never* sent her a letter first shared with a secretary and that I had typed every one myself. They are the only guide I have to the bewildering stops and starts I encountered in working for Disney from 1954 to 1960. I never kept a scrapbook or a diary, and in rereading these old letters I'm continually surprised. For example, in this first letter to my mother I mention that my screenplay for *The Sword and the Rose* was one of the few chosen to compete for a thousand-dollar price put up by the Heritage Press for the best screenplay based upon a novel in 1953. I said that it didn't deserve to win, but why it was even nominated I'll never know. I hadn't submitted it and was anything but proud of it. I also mentioned that *Rob Roy* had received a fine review in *Time* and that I was appearing tonight on a local TV program, which she could not get in Utica, to plug *Rob Roy*. I'd talk about production in England and in Scotland.

Because my mother was apprehensive that I might not continue to earn the thousand dollars a week Walt was paying me—to her an unbelievable amount of money—until I had seen my children through college, I was constantly reassuring her that I was earning my fee. For example, in this same letter I started off by telling her that Disney had come into my office and asked me if I liked science fiction. I answered him truly that I had no great enthusiasm for it, but I would not have said so if I had known that he was offering me the chance to do *20,000 Leagues Under the Sea*, and that he planned to hire a cast with James Mason in the lead, supported by Kirk Douglas, Peter Lorre, and Paul Lucas. I had never had a chance to work with stars of that caliber and kicked myself that he took a casual remark of mine so seriously, saying that if I didn't like science fiction it would be like pulling teeth to get a screenplay out of me. He hired a writer, Earl Felton, and a director, Dick Fleischer, and I was sure that meant the end of my predominance as Disney's top screen writer. In subsequent letters, I was able to inform my mother that such was not the case, for he came to me once asking if I would help if he got really stuck. I told him of course I would, but he decided to fight it out with the two of them. Though the picture was a very big hit, Walt told me that it would have been better if I had been on it, and that he certainly would never hire that writer or director again. Nor did he.

He never lost faith in my ability to write, but he drove me nuts with false starts and stops. Three times he had me tackle *Westward Ho!*, but with the death of Perce that was permanently shelved. I finally worked out a version of the Irish story, *Darby O'Gill*, that he liked and we were all set to do it in England, the live-action part at least. But he had determined to do the little people in animation, for that was a long-held dream of his—to combine live action smoothly with animation. Then he discovered that if he did the animation at his studio, he would lose the financial backing of an English quota picture. He dropped it. So many times I wished I was back in England, where we were committed to doing one picture and saw it through. We were so far away that Walt could not continually heckle us.

The reason Walt postponed shows was that he was doing the work of ten men. He liked to say that the ability to delegate authority was the mark of a good executive, but he felt a compulsion to have a finger in every pie. It wasn't a case of spurring his employees on; rather, it was a case of all of the different people clamoring for his attention.

He was up to his neck in True Life Adventures, as he called his nature pictures. Before I went to England to work on *Treasure Island* in 1949 he called me in to "save" *Beaver Valley*, his second nature film. I rewrote a narration to his liking and got a first credit on that thirty-minute movie, which was so much liked by the public that it was often billed as the first feature on a double bill. He continued to work with the nature films, which would have been quite enough to absorb the average producer's interest. In 1953, when he was working on *The Living Desert*, deciding to put it out as a full-length feature against everybody's advice, I was in his office giving him my final ideas for *Rob Roy* before departing for England. He answered the phone. Louis B. Mayer called to advise him not

to try to stretch his nature shows into an hour. Since he shouted,
I could hear every syllable. He said they had made tests at MGM and
discovered that the public wasn't that much interested in nature,
and he didn't want Walt to lose his shirt. To every well-meant bit of
advice Walt kept saying, "We'll see," and when he had thanked the
great Mayer and hung up he turned to me and said, "Those fellows in
Hollywood haven't the foggiest idea what people want. The public is
starved for entertainment—starved." Of course, he got an Oscar for
The Living Desert, then had to follow it up with another and another.

He continued to make animated films—a big one every three years
and innumerable short subjects. Experimentation was constant.
Geniuses like Ub Iwerks were constantly inventing new cameras and
new and better processes, while various members of his art staff were
introducing new characters as comic foils to Mickey, the straight man.

For years he had been working in secret on Disneyland. Most
weekends were devoted to it. Every tiny detail of it came under his
scrutiny. It was never finished. From the day it opened in 1955, it
had just begun. Every day he worked to make it more perfect. When
he went abroad in the summers it was not a holiday in the ordinary
sense: he picked up an idea from the park in Copenhagen or an engineering skill from Sweden or Germany.

And finally, long before any other producer would humble himself
to make use of television, he was into it both as a new outlet for
his product but also as an advertising medium. The underwater
photography he used to show how *20,000 Leagues Under the Sea* had
been made not only advertised the live-action show but became an
award-winning show in its own right.

In addition to all this he was always scheming where he could
get the financing to do a show or a series for the park, as he called
Disneyland, then schemed how he could buy it back and have full
control. I did not realize at the time just how burdened he was
trying to keep three things going and side-stepping the fourth and
the fifth until he had time to fit them in. It seemed to me that he
was constantly using my talents as a way of testing out a show on
the off chance that I might give him the answer. Some of that may
have been true, but usually it was a matter of keeping me happily
employed, so he thought, until he could tackle any one of the many
shows that I had hanging fire.

It made me dizzy.

There were two properties he owned that I spent a great deal of
time trying to bring off, and failed in both: Robert Nathan's *The
Woodcutter's House* and Victor Herbert's operetta *Babes in Toyland*.

Walt was never able to explain what he saw in *The Woodcutter's House*, except that when a man falls in love it makes him ambitious. I felt that Nathan's symbolism had Walt in a little over his depth. As for *Babes in Toyland*, I worked with artist Bill Peet on this one. I think it was a good collaboration, for we both had ideas and admired each other's abilities. Bill was not only a marvelous artist but a fine story man. We gave Walt at least two different stories, using both the music and the spirit of Victor Herbert, that we knew were good. But Walt didn't like either, for no particular reason that we could tell. I would have sworn that *Babes* was a lost cause, and it should have been, but five years later Walt gave it to another writer and one of his artists, and brought it out in 1961. It was so embarrassingly bad that I think it had a mercifully short run. I believe the fat clown in *Zorro* was unearthed to provide the menace, which is all I can remember about it.

In the meantime, he had me working again on *The Great Locomotive Chase*, which I had started in 1951, then shelved for years. Now he was hot to do it, and he wanted me to produce it. I said I had no ability in that regard and as an associate producer under him would have so little authority that by the moving-picture code a director could order a producer off a set. "Not," said Walt, "if you pick the director. Go out and pick one." I would be given plenty of backing with a couple of experienced assistants to handle leasing and construction costs. They had already located an antique railroad which didn't even have modern cross pieces on its telephone poles and ran only one train at night to keep its franchise. We could tear up track as long as we replaced it before nightfall; they already had two locomotives that could pass for Civil War vintage. The actual site of the chase took place between Big Shanty, now Kennesaw, Georgia, and Ringgold, now a part of the Nashville, Chattanooga, and St. Louis Railway's high-speed steel straightaway, which bore little resemblance to the winding route that Andrews and Fuller fought over. Historically, the daring raid, led by a Northern spy, a Kentuckian named James J. Andrews, wherein a handful of disguised Union soldiers stole a locomotive called *The General* and drove it northward to burn a dozen wooden railroad bridges along the Western and Atlantic's main line route, might have ended the war had it succeeded. It failed because a Southern train conductor, William A. Fuller, chased him by foot, by hand car, and finally ran him down with a locomotive called *The Texas*. The South's main supply line between Atlanta and the central front stayed open.

The old railroad that doubled for our movie was the Tallulah Falls Railroad, which ran by Clayton, Georgia. The little village became our headquarters. For actors, I could have Fess Parker for Andrews. For the Southern hero, almost equally important, Walt had the promise of a man ready to sign on, that fine actor Jeff Hunter. Knowing that Walt would not go for a big-name director, I picked the best I could find for the money, a very sincere, affable man, and a hard worker, Francis "Pete" Lyon. Together we chose a good cast of young aspirants, some of whom made names for themselves. I wrote in many fine little vignettes for them to humanize the piece and add to the tension felt by these youngsters, but Walt with his motto of "stick with the money," which meant milk the lead actor for all he's worth, edited out all such. The movie was the worse for his doing so.

There wasn't enough money in the budget to hire suitable actors to go around, so I turned to local talent to fill in the gaps. It was like coaching a Troubadour play. The mayor of the town, also the local bootlegger, sold us half-way decent corn whiskey which had been accidentally aged in a charred keg for seven years, for he had been so drunk when he buried it he had only recently stumbled upon its hiding place. I coached him on his lines until he had them letter perfect. Harvey Hester, who owned and operated a magnificent restaurant on the outskirts of Atlanta, was a man of the world and did yeoman service. He not only was a good actor, but dropped in on us from time to time bearing gifts. He later visited me in Los Angeles, walking in casually with a hamper of cracked crab he had carried all the way from Atlanta on dry ice. Known to many of the Hollywood stars, he achieved a fortune by asking an oil tycoon who patronized his restaurant how he could get into the oil business. The prospector answered, "By writing me out a check for twenty-five thousand dollars." Harvey did so, and heard nothing more from the man for a long while. Then, just when he thought he must have been taken, he received a letter that eleven wells had come in, and thereafter the money rolled in so rapidly he was hard put to it to bag it all.

An amusing thing happened in a scene following the jail break. The second unit director lined up the actors at strategic points and told them that when he gave the signal he wanted them to run for the woods as fast as they could. One actor kept disappearing from view before the director wanted him to, so he hauled in the young fellow and asked him why he hadn't waited for the signal. The actor, Claude Jarman Jr., who as a child star had made a name for himself in *The Yearling*, said he hadn't cheated. One of the other actors explained the problem: young Jarman had been a track star at college.

Time gave us a fine review, though the reviewer mentioned in passing that some parts had been played by amateurs. Walt was grumpy that I hadn't kept in touch with him enough by telephone. The story was authentically told by Pittinger, one of the men who lived through the ordeal. Andrews and some of his men were hanged; some escaped after a jail break; two followed a river all the way down to the sea, traveling at night, stealing food from plantations and often aided by Negroes. They rode a raft out to sea beyond New Orleans; instead of running the blockade, they ran to it and were picked up by the Yankee warships that encircled all Southern ports. I wrote an apocryphal (but possible) scene in which the two strong men, Fess Parker and Jeff Hunter, meet while Fess is behind bars. Facing an ignoble death, Fess extends his hand and Jeff reluctantly takes it. When Dorothy saw it as a TV rerun some years later, she said as if surprised, "Why, Larry, that's very good."

I have often thought how ridiculous the whole thing was, but dynamite was little used during the Civil War. Fire was the only sort of destroyer that entered the heads of the saboteur. Not until Andrews' raid did the South mount guards on those bridges, which were in the wildest sort of country. Even using fire, a quiet, concerted effort some night by a few picked men would have more successfully accomplished the task which the hidden contingent in a box car on the stolen train could not perform.

I then did a lot of things in a rush. The next was *Light in the Forest* based on a novel by Conrad Richter. It was the story of a boy taken as a baby by the Indians and brought up as one of their own. By a treaty he must return and live with his white parents in Pennsylvania. He escapes, returns to the Indians. But when he is used to decoy a boat-load of whites to the Indians hidden along shore, he cannot do so. He is tried by the Indians, and shunned thereafter as a traitor. Nor can he go back to the whites. Richter leaves him standing in the middle of the river, a boy without a country, but that was not possible to portray in a movie in those days. I gave fair dealing to both whites and Indians, but worked out an ingenious way in which he might return to the whites and depose the leader of the gang of ruffians and Indian haters that infected the otherwise decent community.

In the flyleaf, Richter quoted Wordsworth:

> Shades of the prison house begin to close
> Upon the growing boy;
> But he beholds the light and whence it flows
> He sees it in his joy.

Walt didn't understand what Richter was driving at when he quoted Wordsworth's "Light" and asked me what it meant. It was quite a task to give Walt a quick, easy answer. I have always thought Wordsworth the greatest poet in the English language and "Intimations of Immortality" his grandest poem. I should have liked to take a week explaining Wordsworth's philosophy to Walt, but he always wanted a summary in a few words, and I gave him one that satisfied him, keeping it as free of religion as possible yet as deeply reverential. Then I sent him in a page and a half to round it out, and he was pleased. It's always difficult to educate the boss and not sound pompous, but unlike so many of the moguls in Hollywood, Walt wanted to learn and picked up scraps of erudition from whatever source. He often bewailed to me the fact that he had no education when the two of us were riding back from one of the English sets. I told him that he was an educated man, though he equated education with college. He learned something daily; furthermore, he read, unlike Jack Warner or Harry Cohn. To compare himself to some students that I knew, who had coasted through four years of college untouched by ideas or human thought, was highly ridiculous, and I wasn't saying so to gain favor, just stating a simple fact. I told my son when he went to Yale I would be quite content if he made C grades provided he spent a large part of each day in the Yale library, one of the greatest in the world. He did so and came out a highly educated man.

My explanation about Wordsworth's "Light" led to a much greater embarrassment. I often wrote the lyrics to a little song if one was needful in a show we were doing. For example, in *The Great Locomotive Chase*, when Andrews and his spies were riding a train as ordinary passengers going south, I figured that a Rebel song sung by the Confederate soldiers aboard would lead to embarrassing complications if everybody didn't join the chorus; so, I composed on the spot a song:

> We are sons of Old Aunt Dinah
> and we go where we've a mind to
> and we fight if we're inclined to
> as long as we have fun.
> We licked the Yanks at Shiloh
> Oh me oh me o-my-o
> Yes, we licked the Yanks at Shiloh
> Just to see how they could run!

A musician in the group worked out a tune on his guitar, and we used it and it fitted in beautifully. So now the studio nurse had teamed up with one of the studio musicians to write a song, which concluded, "But the light in the forest is love." Since the nurse did consider herself an educated person, I was quite unprepared when she entered my office and presented me with the song, saying, "I took it to Walt and all he would say was 'Take it to Watkin.'" He had thrown me quite a curve. I couldn't tell her that love didn't belong in that title, so I said that Walt shouldn't be sending her to me; her boyfriend knew ten times as much about songs as I did. I had written a few comic jingles. Maybe he thought her song was too sentimental. That was my only guess. It satisfied her and got me out of my predicament. I much preferred having her consider Walt insensitive to beauty, than to act as the heavy, delivering her a lecture on poetry.

The Light in the Forest came out in 1958. Though I wrote it, I did not produce it. Walt sent me to New York to see if I could find a young actor from one of the Eastern drama schools or from New York City. I brought back a couple of tests and made others in Hollywood, but those I picked were too physical to suit him, so he chose young James MacArthur, the adopted son of Helen Hayes, and I think Helen charmed Walt to make the choice. He was a nice kid and played well enough paired with Carol Lynley. She was a young teen then and seemed innocent enough to play the part of the indentured servant, whom True Son thought of as a slave to the brutal white people, but she was a pig about candy, and always had her hand in a bag of chocolates. Her face was so pudgy when we got around to shooting that the cameraman could hardly find an angle in which she didn't look fat. Much later, when she posed nude for *Playboy*, I could summon up no lust for her beautiful white body. All I could see was that little pig with her hand in a candy bag.

I did not follow through as a producer on *The Light in the Forest*, for in February of 1957 I was the victim of an accident that almost killed me.

A year or two before we had bought a lot for fifteen thousand dollars in a very posh section of Encino called Royal Oaks and after a couple of years got a fine architect and built a house on it exactly suited to our needs. We had utter privacy, views of the lights of the valley and the mountains beyond, a swimming pool just outside my study. We missed the view of the ocean we had in Pacific Palisades, and I missed saying good morning to that magnificent writer Thomas Mann as we passed, taking our constitutionals, but it was just too cold. We loved the warmth of the valley. Though we did not consort with any of them, we were surrounded by movie stars. My next-door neighbor was Shirley Maclaine. Her small daughter stuck out her tongue at me every morning as I set out for work. Her mother joined her in sticking out her tongue in a mother-daughter photograph on the cover of *Life* magazine. Just across the way was

Steve Allen. Above us was Andy Devine. I hired the same man to build my pool that all these wealthy stars hired. He asked me how I wanted to pay for it. I said, "By check."

"You mean the whole amount?"

"Of course. I wouldn't order it if I couldn't pay for it."

He shook his head. "I never heard of such a thing." I mentioned a few of my neighbors who certainly were making a quarter of a million a year. "You mean they buy on time?"

"Hell, yes, and most of them can't come up with the payments. They may drive Cadillacs tandem, but they are always in debt to the car dealers, too."

We loved that house. It was much more livable than Castle Hill in Lexington. Dorothy was a confirmed gardener. We grew roses all along the bank that could have won prizes. I would take a bud or two into the studio almost every day, for the librarians, for my own secretary, for Walt's, for the nurse, for almost anyone who admired them. I was still enough of a farmer that I enjoyed digging beds for flowers, planting fruit trees and the like a part of every weekend. Golf was so time-consuming that I preferred getting my exercise that way. I soon had the banks planted in ivy and ice plant, but the section was so new that gophers and ground squirrels were in everywhere and fought me for every bulb. I had to dig the beds deep and line them with hog wire at the bottom or lose half our plants to the gophers.

I had no luck trapping them nor did they seem to touch the poison grain the nurserymen recommended. So, I took their advice and bought what they called gopher bombs. These were large firecrackers filled with a lethal gas. You cut a sizable sod which you had ready beside a freshly opened hole the gopher had dug during the night. You lighted the wick, tossed the bomb down the hole and covered the opening with the sod and pressed it down with your shoe. The bomb exploded underground and shot its gas into the intricate network of tunnels the gopher had dug, and unless he could detect the gas and close off a partition with dirt, it got him. They seemed to be working.

One morning, though I took all the usual precautions and had the sod ready, the bomb had a short or defective fuse and blew up in my face as I knelt to toss it in. I inhaled a lungful of the gas and immediately ran into the house, stretched out on the bed, told Dot to get an unused bomb and read the antidote, and also to call our son Parke, who lived not too far distant. The directions said to swallow a lot of warm salt water, induce vomiting, and call a doctor. I did so, threw up repeatedly, stretched out and barely retained consciousness. My son arrived quickly, called the nearest hospital, and asked for an ambulance, which arrived in due course. He and Dot followed but the ambulance arrived first, dumped me in the emergency room, where somebody wanted the name of my doctor. Parke had already called him, but he was playing golf and could not leave his foursome. I couldn't speak, though I tried. When Parke arrived, the attendant wanted to know about my insurance and ability to pay. I believe Parke gave them a little legal hell, explained about the bomb, and asked them to get a doctor who understood poisons. Somebody mentioned a Doctor Hertz, who arrived in time to save my life though he had to tap many hospitals to get enough of the medication that pulled me through. As it was, my blood pressure had been lowered for so long a time that much of the heart muscle had been destroyed.

The reason Dr. Hertz had an inkling of what to do was because he had been studying poison gases on the side. He figured that in case of an atomic attack the average doctor would be as helpless about procedure as the ordinary citizen; so, he set about to inform himself. Slowly I adjusted and started to recover. Soon I could have visitors. Among the many was a character actor, an excellent animal trainer and rodeo man we used on *The Great Locomotive Chase*, named Lennie Geer. We had become fast friends. He noticed that my roommate was a teenaged boy who was recovering from some frightful burns inflicted when an airplane crashed and exploded in a local high-school playing field. The boy had a bed which was placed under a window. He lay and looked out of it all day. Lennie's generous heart was touched. Since the kid was not moaning or making a sound (for the very good reason that he was almost entirely cured) Lennie said, "How brave can you get!" He told the kid he was going to put on a rodeo show just for him tomorrow afternoon. The boy nodded acquiescence. Sure enough, at two the next afternoon Lennie appeared with a truck carrying rolls and rolls of old carpeting, which he spread out upon the hospital lawn outside the boy's window, and with his trained horse proceeded to do all sorts of tricks and acrobatics. He even had the horse counting to ten, first by pawing with a foreleg, then by nodding his head. The kid as usual was eating chocolates. His mother brought him box after box, which he devoured, refusing all other nourishment. Lennie told him to pull down the window, which the boy was quite capable of doing. Then Lennie said for him to hold a chocolate in his palm and the horse would take it. The kid started to hold the chocolate, then at the last minute pulled his hand away, telling Lennie to get that horse out of there. Lennie did so, but explained to the boy that the horse wouldn't bite. He wanted to be friends. For answer the boy shut the window and popped the candy into his own mouth. I explained to Lennie later that city kids didn't always understand about animals, but Lennie was not offended. He had tried. I thanked him profusely. I thought it was a wonderful show.

I watched that boy for a day or two. He could move about quite freely and easily unless a nurse, a doctor, or his fat mother was in the room. When the nurse gave him a very gentle bed bath, he yelled bloody murder. I heard her talking to another nurse. She couldn't understand why. He simply should not be feeling that much pain at this point. It must be very deep. Nobody could comfort him until his fat mother came and crooned over him, asking if the pain wasn't better today. The only thing that relieved it was more chocolate creams, which he munched with tiny groans while she stroked his forehead. Finally, I got sick of it. He had never looked in my direction, nor had I spoken to him, but at last I said that I was fully aware of the game he was playing. He had gone through a hellish experience, but that was all behind him now. He was not in pain. He was yelling to get sympathy and candy because he was a spoiled brat who would soon ruin his liver if he didn't quit eating those damn chocolates. He was such a fat little pig he wouldn't even share one with a horse who had spent an hour trying to entertain him. Now today when the nurse gave him his bath, if he let out a single yelp I was going to write him up in the local paper. I was a writer and the paper would be happy to print anything I sent them, and I swore that if he bawled today, I was going to let the whole valley know the kind of phony cry-baby they thought was a hero.

He still didn't look at me, but when the nurses gave him his bath, he cooperated fully, turning over of his own accord and uttering no sound. The two nurses stared at each other. They simply couldn't figure it out. He went home in a day or two, where he no doubt grew fatter and fatter, eating chocolates from the pudgy fingers of his mother. I'm sure she had him in pin curls. If that boy had met Carol Lynley, the two of them would have been supremely happy.

Very soon thereafter I went home, too, and though I couldn't stand up alone, I phoned the studio saying I could work in bed. Walt had me try out a modern novel, a spy story about the Revolutionary War. Though I was pretty sure Walt wasn't serious about making it, I had researched that period backward and forward and I knew exactly what happened at the Battle of Monmouth, where the traitorous American general Charles Lee countermanded Washington's orders and let the British escape just when he had them dead to rights. I remember a bulletin Washington distributed to his army, which starts out like this "The general is sorry to be informed that the profane habit of cursing and swearing has become commonplace among our troops. How can we expect the blessing of Almighty God upon our endeavors if we loosely take his name in vain?" At least that is pretty close. Yet all competent historians report that before Washington sent that cockroach to the rear, he cursed him out so roundly that the leaves on the trees trembled not from the explosion of the cannon but from that great man's wrath.

Anyway, Walt sent Yakima Canutt out to work with me. Yakima was not only the greatest stunt man that Hollywood had ever seen, but became a second-unit director responsible for such spine-tingling scenes as the Chariot Race in *Ben Hur*. Yakima had no particular respect for the truth of history, thinking that history was made in Hollywood, and he also believed in blowing things up. Had he been working with me on *The Great Locomotive Chase*, he would have dynamited those bridges on day one. As it was, we had a most enjoyable two weeks setting land mines and sending both Hessians and redcoats high into the air. I think when Yakima got through, Washington had won. If the general had had Watkin and Canute on his staff, he'd have blown the British into the sea right then, making all that cannonading at Yorktown quite unnecessary. Yakima was worth a dozen nurses, an exciting man of thunder.

When I went back to the studio in the spring, shaky but ready to hit it, Walt trotted out "Powell of the Colorado"; and this time I completed that one. John Wesley Powell was a man largely responsible for bringing water to the West. As his name implies, he came from such a religious background that he had been named after the founder of Methodism, but as a geologist, the undisputable truths in which the fossils show the different ancient epochs of the earth discredited the more ignorant claims of the religionists about creation and made him quietly irreligious. While participating in the Battle of Shiloh, he became so greatly interested searching for a specimen along the river bank that he exposed himself to Confederate fire and lost an arm. In spite of this drawback, he led an expedition of nine men down the unknown Colorado River for some 900 miles, losing several of the boats to the raging rapids, the falls, the submerged rocks, the heat, and the dwindling rations that taxed the strength of these hardy explorers. All sorts of legends by the Indians warned of the river plunging underground and of cataracts ahead that no boat could survive. He made precise notes as they made their way through the mile-deep gorge, where the water had cut through to disclose layers of past ages piled on top of even earlier ones. Often he climbed out on narrow rocky paths for a better view of some geologic marvel where he could not turn around to retrace his steps because of his missing arm. His men rescued him in ingenious was, sometimes using an oar to pinion his body against the cliff until he could return. Since many were mere adventurers, they resented his constant surveys and when they reached Separation Rapids where only a narrow raging tunnel of water faced them, three decided not to risk it, but climbed out taking a chance against the desert. Powell was certain that they were almost through the wild part of the river, but he could not persuade these three. That night he prayed, and not believing conventional religion, prayed to the Bright Angel of Immortality. It was not the equivalent of the death-bed repentance, but it came close, for here was a soul in torment. I used it, not cheaply, but Walt cut it out. He also cut out the fate of the men who walked out. In actuality they were lucky, so they thought, in reaching a party of friendly Indians before their water gave out, but it so happened that on the previous day some white men had killed a squaw. The Indians mistakenly reasoned that the men who told the unlikely story of walking out from the bottom of the canyon had done the deed, so they took revenge by murdering the explorers in their sleep.

Powell was proved right. His boat had a wild, tumultuous ride to the safety of calm water not far beyond. He made the trip twice more, feats that gave Powell not only the meager backing of the Smithsonian Institute, but persuaded Congress to make him the director of the Far West Government Survey of all the rivers and tributaries as well as head of the Department of Geology. His reports and books on the subject undoubtedly led to irrigation and the great power dam that harnessed the Colorado.

Walt wanted the conflict to stem from the fact that the volunteers thought that Powell, chipping away at rocks, was prospecting for gold and that their disappointment led to bickering and final mutiny. I thought that Powell deserved to be named in the title and wanted to call it "Powell of the Colorado," but some giant intellect in the advertising department, possibly Card Walker himself, entitled it *Ten Who Dared*. It took awhile before Walt found a director tough enough to follow in Powell's wake down that treacherous river, so *Ten Who Dared* did not come out until 1960.

Before that I had an inspiration about the Irish story, started way back in 1947. Now ten years later, after near misses and false starts, I knew what to do. As I have already mentioned, the book of episodes about Darby O'Gill in his friendly war with King Brian of the Little People had no basic plot. There was no real conflict; Darby was under no constraint to prove anything. I had, while teaching at Washington and Lee, written a story called "Steady Job" for *Colliers*. It was half true. The night watchman at the college was fired because he was 65. Considering himself right in his prime, he was ashamed to tell his wife he was fired for being an old man, so he came every night as before and accompanied the lazy young man who replaced him on his rounds. The loafer lets the old man make the rounds alone. His vigilance surprised thieves after incunabula in the library. Now the young man is fired and the old man gets his job back.

I suggested that Darby O'Gill is the caretaker of an estate owned by a wealthy but benevolent Englishman named Fitzpatrick. He seldom visits his Irish preserve, but when he does he wants it spic and span. Darby's daughter Katie does more than her part keeping things ship-shape, but Darby would rather tell stories about the Little People in the local pub. Fitzpatrick appears without notice, bringing a fine young man to take over. Darby is too old to do the hard work; he deserves retirement with a generous pension for life. Fitzpatrick'd like Katie to stay on to clean the big house and cook for them when he comes over for the fishing. Possibly Katie could even find a place for the young man in the caretaker's cottage. He'll ask her. Darby says no, please let him do that. He'll speak for Katie.

After Fitzpatrick goes, Darby asked the young man if he would mind playing a little game. Would he pretend that he is Darby's assistant? It's hard for a man to tell his daughter, who has always looked up to him, that he has been discarded. The young man obliges. Katie soon learns the truth, but she feels very kindly toward the new caretaker for being so generous to her father. Now Darby, to prove himself, lets it be known that he's going to capture the king of the fairies and all his crocks of gold.

At this point Walt said, "Say no more. Write it up. We'll shoot it."

Along the way he decided not to animate the Little People but miniaturized live actors to make the fairies more believable. Walt liked everything I told him about Irish folklore. Some of them he had heard mentioned, but didn't really understand them. So if I described the pooka, the banshee, the Costa Bower (the death coach), he wanted them all used. We ended up with a story that was funny, fearsome, and appealing. Barry Fitzgerald, who had previously been mentioned as Darby, was unavailable, but Walt took a casting director and went to England and Ireland and rounded up a first-rate group of actors. To play the part of the young caretaker he signed a young Scot who passed for an Irishman. This was the first American role for the famed Sean Connery. Everything worked.

The trick photography that brought the fairy men down to pint size was realistic. The color was beautiful. Ellenshaw's special effects and mattes were flawless. The picture was a critical and financial success. Before it opened I asked Walt for a two-week vacation. I had taken other respites, but no matter where I had gone I was always hunting a story or devoting half my time to a screenplay, even when I was hospitalized. I wanted to take my wife to Denmark and the surrounding country and spend a few days in London, at my own expense, of course, and with nothing on my mind but sightseeing. Walt agreed, and we were off. This was in the summer of 1959.

37

Dot wasn't too sure that we could go anywhere and not have the trip end up in my researching a story for Disney. I had spent only one day at my son's wedding before I felt that I must fly back to England. Recuperating from that gopher bomb had left me too sick to attend my older daughter's wedding, and though I had flown with our youngest daughter to Tokyo with Dot and the mother of the man she wanted to marry because he would be stationed in Tokyo for another two years, even there I had not escaped hunting down a story. Once I had seen my daughter married and banqueted, I wanted to meet the son of the famous writer Lafcadio Hearn to learn what I could about his father. By hounding the American Embassy, I met an enthusiastic young Japanese student who was a friend of Hearn's son, then an old man and unwilling to meet Americans. He made an exception in my case because my intermediary, George Saito, read him something I had written about my philosophy of life that struck him exactly right. Furthermore, when his father was living briefly in our Midwest a man named Henry Watkin had kept him from committing suicide, and he liked anybody of that name. The son invited me to his house.

Though he understood English perfectly well and could write it, too, he considered himself Japanese in spite of his paternity. He was fearful of making mistakes in pronunciation, so he spoke only Japanese to George Saito, who translated it for me and did the same with my reply. His darling little wife served us tea and cakes as we sat upon the floor shoeless in the custom of the country. He not only presented me with the book he had written about his father, but told me his romantic story.

Lafcadio's father was a titled Irishman owning a castle, who occupied high rank in the English Army. He married a beautiful Greek lady from the island of Cytherea, the Land of the Lotus Eaters, but separated after Lafcadio's birth. Both Lafcadio and Hearn mean a rover or gypsy, and that's what Lafcadio became after being brought up by an aunt who frightened him with the Christian god whom she thought of as a vengeful ogre. He lost his left eye while playing a game with a knotted rope, which caused his one good eye to be enlarged. He could see things clearly only at a distance of six inches. It made him shy and introverted, and though his profile was beautiful he thought himself deformed. Coming to America he attempted journalism, wrote some lovely, delicate, imaginative things, which he sometimes merely left on the editor's desk, nearly starved, gravitated to Japan and became instantly in love with the country, trying to explain its sensitivity to Americans. He taught at the University of Tokyo; his lectures were so wonderfully simple and clear and intelligible and so full of the best literature the world provided that they became copybooks. He disliked Christianity and communism equally, writing early warning tracts of how communism would ruin all the lovely Far East, denying freedom of thought and expression. Sometimes he wrote so continuously that he neither slept nor ate nor stayed warm, until the president of the college said he must take a Japanese wife or he would die. He said that they would select a lady from the most aristocratic class. Lafcadio agreed and fell in love with her *after* they were married. They had four children. He took his wife's name, Koizumi. He very much wanted to take his son Kazuo to the United States, for Cornell had offered him a summer lectureship, but when it fell through, Lafcadio proceeded to teach the boy everything about the West, especially its idealism as compared to Eastern mysticism. He drew and painted very well, depicting for the boy Western animals, houses, bridges, ships, birds, and commonplace things like pets. When he was dying, his wife asked if he minded being buried in the Buddhist manner. So they cremated him, put his ashes in a tiny boat with one lighted candle for a mast, and sent it out to sea from a river's mouth.

Kazuo Hearn Koizumi, Lafcadio's son, gave me a copy of his precious book *Re-Echo* with permission to write the story he had told me for the screen as long as Walt did it. I devoted a large part of my two weeks writing it, but Walt gave me a loud *no*. He couldn't see anything special about a writer teaching a little Jap kid about America, or not being buried in a proper graveyard. It's true that I took Dot to Kyoto, but I wished then that I had paid more attention to the temples, rather than try to communicate as delicate a spirit as Hearn's to a man like Walt. Maybe I was wrong; maybe a college education in the humanities would have helped.

Anyway, Copenhagen, un-shadowed by Disney, was so delightful that while we were being coddled by the Hotel Angleterre, we decided that I'd work hard for three more years, save every penny, then retire and travel. We wouldn't start saving just yet, not until we had bought things in den permanente.

We had so completely forgotten about Disney that we were surprised when we checked into the Dorchester in London to find Walt and Lily and entourage ready to depart the next day for Dublin where *Darby O'Gill* was opening shortly. Walt said he'd been trying to get in touch with me; of course, Dot and I would have to attend the opening. Big deal. So he called the London office to add us to the plane reservations, the hotel, and all the rest of it.

Arrived in Dublin, we relieved the mind of the man in charge. Everybody wanted to stay at the Gresham, but we loyally chose the old Shelburne. There was a great deal of riding around the city the next day to the blaring of sirens by a motorcycle escort and a great deal of picture taking on the steps of government buildings. In the evening a banquet without speechmaking was followed by showing the film in a theater where Walt was to make a speech. Dot and I sat in the balcony with Walt's wife, Lily, no great favorite of mine, but I felt sorry for her, for Walt had been downing Scotch whiskey pretty freely and though not obviously drunk was right on the edge. Lily was so worried that he'd make an ass of himself, she gripped Dot's arm and pinched it black and blue. Walt rambled a bit at first, then got going and did very well, receiving a nice hand. Just before the speech he came to me and whispered, "What's the name of that guy who runs the Folklore Institute?"

"Seamus De Largy."

He nodded and went off murmuring, De Largy, De Largy, De Largy, but never mentioned him in the course of his speech or anybody else for that matter.

What he did do that made me squirm was use atrocious grammar, far worse than ordinary, but that didn't bother Lily. Nor did it worry Bertie and Vogue McNally, or J.B. and Joan Roughneen. Walt couldn't fall overboard and not come up with a pocketful of fish. "Now wasn't he the gracious man to use that kind of speech to put the most ignorant one in the audience at his ease?" one of the girls exclaimed. I agreed; he certainly did have the common touch.

For the rest of 1959 he kept me busy writing a long television plug for *Darby O'Gill*. There was a lot of ham in him and he used up a lot of footage imagining himself in Ireland stalking a leprechaun, transfixing him with one eye open, one eye shut. In 1960 the Writer's Guild kept me away from the studio for a long time, calling a writer's strike against the producers. I attended most of the meetings but made no impassioned addresses for the pre-1960 residuals on theatricals. Walt wanted me to sell him my kids book, *Marty Markham*, an excellent boy's story about a spoiled rich kid at a dude ranch, attended by the butler that his doting grandmother sends along. The other kids whip him into line; he falls in love with a horse, who returns his devotion. The staid butler also becomes a favorite, for he can do handsprings. Walt asked me not to demand residuals, as he simply couldn't afford them.

Spin and Marty, as the television adaptation of the book was to be called, brought me huge royalties. Walt promised that at every showing of the serial, they would hold the book right up to the screen and say, "This is the book the series is based upon. You'll get all kinds of royalties." Of course, the book was never advertised on the screen or elsewhere and only a very sharp-eyed kid knew it existed, the credits rolled by so fast. If the writers had won the strike, all the movies which Walt constantly re-released would have paid me a fine pension as long as I lived, but I received no pension nor did I receive one share of stock as long-time employees invariably did from the companies they worked for.

Walt wanted to do one more picture, *Mary Poppins*, featuring live action and animation. When he finally got the rights from the author, Pamela Travers, such stars as Mary Martin and Bette Davis wanted to do it, but Bill Walsh, who produced the film for Walt, said he thought he gave it to Julie Andrews because she could whistle. It was a magnificent hit and deserved to be. One of the heroes who received no mention was Walt's old partner and now his silent but brilliant inventor, Ub Iwerks. It was Ub who had developed the traveling matte when all the other special effects men both in America and England said it could not be done. He quietly did it. The hit of the show, the dance of the chimney sweeps on the rooftops, could not have been done without Ub's traveling matte, but his name was not bandied about. Who realizes when they are watching a continuous show in Disney World that the best projection camera Disney could buy from Eastman would go for less than 200 hours, but the one Ub developed would run for 5000 hours?

A year or so before the writers strike, Walt took me to lunch and asked me if I didn't want to be a producer. I told him no. I knew that in offering me a producership he was paying me the greatest compliment he knew how to give, but I knew I'd be no good, for my heart wasn't in it. Somebody said the only hard work in the world is doing something you don't like. He said, "You mean you just want to be a goddamn writer all your life?"

"Yes," I said, "that's all I ever wanted to be."

That wasn't quite true; if I had been younger, I'd have liked to direct.

The truth of the matter is that around 1960 Walt had decided he didn't want to do any more moving pictures, and after *Mary Poppins*, which was a great one to quit on, he gave more and more control to co-producers like his son-inlaw Ron Miller, a former college football star, and Winston Hibler, Jim Algar, and Bill Anderson. They all made small fortunes making small pictures. There was one, Bill Walsh, who deserved to be a producer, who had original ideas and a lot of natural ability. He was a master of the zany, using an old story of Flubber, a rubber that turned ordinary basket ball players into giants when wearing Flubberized sneakers, and of a Volkswagen that could all but talk, a dog that could drive a car, and the like. Had he lived he might have been the man to take over the creative burden of film that Walt wanted to be rid of. That was the trouble with the studio, once Walt let surrogates handle it. There were cartoonists with all the talent in the world, but though they all admired each others' expertise, Walt didn't say to any one of them: "*You* run it. *You* tell the rest what to do. *You* plan the whole thing. They can't all go their own separate ways."

Walt used to say to me, "Don't ever grow up, Larry." He said the same thing to others. Then *he* grew up. He became so greatly interested in creating the perfect city state, Epcot, that he robbed his own organization of some of its best men to plan a city, a miniature world in Florida where he would build a town in which movable sidewalks and people movers and monorails for the longer haul would make the stinking automobiles passé, their houses warmed and cooled and cleaned by efficient central devices, music and entertainment of a high order, cookery simplified, furniture and gadgets so improved that comfort, convenience, and cleanliness would always be 25 years ahead of their time, poisons eliminated, diet improved, medicine updated. Such people would work in modern industrial plants owned by General Motors or Monsanto. They would be inventors, technicians, artificers, mechanics, machine operators, and skilled workmen, making the products that would be tried out in the laboratories their own houses provided. Walt would supply the showmanship that led the public to view and want and order these marvels for their own homes in their own cities.

Before he died he had made a start in that direction. The Magic Kingdom that people came to gawk at was only the frosting. The real magic was in the basement underneath where the engines and communication systems made the kingdom above operate with smooth efficiency. There were dynamos and replacement parts and offices down there which few above knew about. They did not realize that Walt had bought enough land to house dozens of amusement parks.

He had connived with the politicians to make his own building laws, not to skimp on sewage and water and electrical pipes designed to make shoddy contractors sink them three feet underground. He might want a system so much superior that he wanted huge pipes twenty inches in diameter sunk ten feet underground. All the trash that cleaning men were constantly collecting would be sucked into a conveyor system and travel to an incinerator site several miles out of town. The same with sewage. It was purified until it was almost drinkable, then used to water a forest of young trees. There were real lakes and man-made lakes, a monorail so quiet that it ran right through the middle of the A-frame hotel, the prefabricated rooms of which were built not far away and lifted into supporting steel frames by giant cranes. In the center of the tract was a preserve not open to the public where birds and endangered species of animals were brought for regeneration. If Walt had only lived another ten years, he might have had his Epcot going full tilt. As it was, he created life-like figures who could walk and talk built in a factory in Burbank where men that he had trained performed wonders that the engineering schools at the great centers could not approach. He stopped hiring graduates of MIT. They would say, "That can not be done. It defies the laws of physics." Walt would say to one of his own men: "Forget the laws of physics. Do it." And they did it.

Of course, I did not know any of this when he called me in to fire me after the writer's strike. Though he didn't say so, he fired me because I had refused to be a producer.

I think he was embarrassed to do so; we had been together so long. He started out by saying, "We just don't have anything for you to do," which of course was untrue. I said nothing. I looked at him all the way through the conference, but he never looked at me. The next remark was one of the strangest I ever heard from him. He referred to the four British pictures as if they were the sum and substance of my whole contribution to the Disney fortunes: "Those first two you did were OK, but those last two were just trading dollars. We suffered from your enthusiasm!" He paused, possibly expecting a reply, but it was too asinine. The first two had been pretty much all my doing; the last two had been suggested by him. He insisted on doing that god-awful Midwestern insipid *When Knighthood Was in Flower* out of his corny past. God knows I didn't, but I worked like a Trojan to make it palatable. So I still said nothing, but that was all. There were things that I might have said. Not so long ago I had met Bill Walsh in the hall, and he said, "I hope you're enjoying your residuals from *Spin and Marty*. It looks like that is going on forever." I didn't tell him that I was the only one who was *not* getting residuals and not enough royalties to pay for the books I bought to give to young friends. I might have reminded Walt that less than a year ago his secretary Dolores had called me up and said, "Larry, I think I should tell you this, because Walt is constitutionally incapable of telling anyone that he has been pleased; but when he finished your final script for *Darby O'Gill* he told me, "That's the best screenplay I have read in thirty years."

When it became obvious that I had no intention of arguing, he softened his tone and said, "I'm sure you'll make just as much money as a free-lance writer as you will working for me." Whereupon he picked up a script on his desk and opened it. I got to my feet and said, "Well, Walt, it's been nice."

Yeah," he grunted, not looking up from the script. Dorothy, who seldom showed emotion, cried when she heard about it. I tried to comfort her, saying that we would be all right. "It isn't that," she said, "but you've worked so hard, and I thought he was our friend."

"He's incapable of friendship, and I think there are only three things he loves: his two daughters and that goddamn studio."

"What about Disneyland and the Florida one?"

"Those are his playthings."

"Which he talked you out of investing in."

She referred to the fact that when Disneyland was doing well in the stock market I went to Walt and asked him if I shouldn't buy in. He advised me against it, saying it was far too risky. It could be a flash in the pan. If I wanted to buy a stock, I should buy General Motors. So I went to Roy, supposedly the money man in the firm. The stock was then 16. He said it might go to 25 and then take one hell of a nosedive. So I listened to them. It was not until later that I found that the Disney brothers were even then buying back every share of Disney stock they could get their hands on. But I knew nothing about money and let it climb out of my reach.

I lost out in another attempt to make a killing. Like others at the studio I had seen the drawings and the plans for Disneyland and I was sure that it would be a success. So I went to a friend who was in the real-estate business in Anaheim and gave him a check for $5000. "Now if you will put another five thousand with this and buy whatever land is available along the peripheries, I think that in a year or two it will become very valuable. I know this thing will be different enough to be a winner, and a piece of land big enough to build a motel or apartment on will be in demand. I've got to go to England, but I'll be back in the fall and I hope we'll be partners."

When I saw him again he handed me back my check, saying, "Do you know how much ten thousand dollars would have bought: ten acres! Think of it, a thousand dollars an acre! Well, I'm not that kind of a fool and I didn't think you'd want to be."

I bowed to his wisdom in real estate. Two years later our ten acres would have brought us half a million dollars, and was still going up.

Walt's prediction that I would do well elsewhere did not come to pass. My agent, who had been decent enough several years back not to demand his 10% when he found that I did not want any of the jobs he could have secured for me for more money, found that producers did not want a sixty-year-old cast-off from the Disney studio. So I faced the labor market without a pension, without insurance, and without recommendation from a previous employer. I was not greatly concerned, except for hurt feelings. But I could sympathize with other employees Walt had shrugged off who had worked most of their lives for him as cartoonists. Animation was a very narrow field. Those men were really hurting.

For a man who didn't believe in saving money, I was in good shape financially. The lot upon which we had built our house in Royal Oaks had not been recompacted deeply enough to break up the flat shale rock it rested on. The whole hillside was held up by the toe of the bank below. The city geologists knew this, but when a man wanted to cut it away to give himself a bigger lot, replacing the earth with a flimsy wall, he was warned what would happen. He asked if he had the legal right to cut it away. The answer was yes. So he said to the bulldozing crew, "Go ahead and cut."

The first torrential rain was deep enough to reach the slanting shale underneath and brought half the hillside down on him and his next-door neighbor. For a year, our swimming pool stayed intact but dry while lawyers argued the blame. My son's firm protected me. The three of us all paid the cost of proper re-compaction, which cost me only a few thousand dollars. With the lot restored better than before I might have continued to live there, but the pleasure of the place had departed. Our children had all been given the best of educations, had married well, had children of their own and their own houses and families. We decided to find a place where we might eventually retire and found it in the Back Bay section of Newport Beach. We sold our Royal Oaks house for a big profit and bought into a delightful small community of not more than a dozen fine houses built in a circle around a central lot big enough to hold a nine-hole putting green, a shuffleboard court, and a swimming pool. For the upkeep of the pool and the green we each paid a very reasonable fee. None of these amenities was ever crowded, but led to good fellowship. About once a year we all got together, covered the putting green with ruggings, set up tables and Chinese lanterns, and had a catered dinner. I found that the commuting on the freeway was not too difficult, for I had a fine car and loved to drive.

The climate was even better than that in the valley and smog free in the 1960s. Except for the enforced retirement, I began to enjoy myself. Actually, it was a relief to be away from Walt's moods. Walt and Roy had two brothers. One was a lazy bachelor who dabbled in insurance; the other was a postman. He was the one I admired. He and his family lived frugally, but were happy. He did not thrust himself upon his brothers, though he occasionally visited Roy. He thought both Walt and Roy were crazy sitting up nights worrying about this million dollars or that million dollars. He said that very soon now he would have a fine government pension for life and could put his feet up and watch the silly world go by. I began to feel a little like that. For a while I took out my frustration making our house more perfect, though it was very well built and commodious. I put in a smooth, weed-free lawn both back and front, extended the patio, built raised flower beds, planted fruit trees and a few bottle-brush plants which I trimmed into small trees. Those bottle brush attracted tiny birds, who, like the humming birds that got drunk on peony juice in Castle Hill, would burrow their bills into the bottle-brush blossoms, get high, and fly against our living room windows before coming out of it. And I built a workbench and a myriad of cupboards in our garage. Hannibal Coons used to say, "Watkin, I'd love to buy one of your houses just to get the garage."

We hated to leave that place, but I soon became restless and knew at the bottom of my mind that the time to retire had not yet come and probably never would. Many a fine old gentleman like some of my neighbors were quite content to head for the golf course every day and sharpen up their putting on the centrally located green, but like the average military man their minds had never been troubled by thought. Swift said, "There is no such thing as a fine old gentleman; if he had a mind or a body worth a farthing he would have used both up long ago." People like Eisenhower and Ford were happiest on the links, but Truman knew his way around a library.

A writer can be happy in his study, but once he had been spoiled by life at a studio or a college, he misses not only the companionship of kindred souls, but the walking dictionaries. No matter what he may be working on, at such places he can pick up the phone or open the door where he can talk to an expert on almost anything he may need to know. The lawyer, scientist, historian, linguist, philosopher, mathematician usually is pleased to give you an answer that's worth hours of book research with additional highlights thrown in, and will come to you in return.

Temptations occurred, but they were or would be stop gaps. We ran into Andy Devine in a Newport Beach restaurant. He had just finished playing Gramps in a stock company doing *On Borrowed Time* in the Midwest. He begged me to write him another part like that to take on tour. A producer at MGM was butchering Taylor's Jaimie McPheeters, and a ten-minute chat with him told me why, but there I ran into another producer who was doing a farm program. I did an excellent TV show for him about an Irish hired hand and the farmer's small son. The producer loved it and asked for another. When it came out, the ending had been changed, not for the better. I did not go back. The producer called me. He wanted another. I told him I wouldn't work for him again, for he had changed my story. "So what? I'm the producer," he said.

"But you can't write. If you had wanted changes, you should have called me. I'd have made the repair without charge if it made sense to me."

"There wasn't time."

"So to hell with television."

"I never heard of such a thing!"

"You have now."

When I told Coons about it, he doubled up with laughter. "My God, Watkin, I always look to see if my name is still there. That's all I care about. That and the check."

Coons was one of the most outrageously self-confident, funny fat men I have ever met. He was always in debt, sometimes even when he had a series going in a magazine such as the "Dear George" stories, from living too high on the hog. Then when the series folded, he would almost starve, literally. When that happened and they had exhausted their friends' hospitality, they would tour LA at night until they ran into, let's say, the Rolls Royce Agency, which was having open house in their showrooms with free punch and hors d'ouvres. His wife told me that nobody else even bothered to speak to a salesman, but Coons always put on a show as a large corporation executive to pay for the free food. He would take out a notebook and get the salesman's hopes sky high, jotting down the extras he did and didn't want on his next Silver Cloud. He had a great run of luck on the series *The Addams Family*, for the writer he collaborated with could contrive a plot and Coons couldn't. All he cared about were the gags. He tossed them off at all times at random and would have been worth a fortune to someone like Bob Hope with his stable of gag writers. When he was making steady money, he built a palace for the two of them, saying a big writer had to have a baronial mansion to write in. Then his collaborator quit and he was back to a dingy apartment, but was such a superlative salesman that when he showed it to you he almost had you convinced that he liked its convenience and trouble-free perquisites better than the gigantic study with its pool table at the far end for the relaxation of friends talking story. It's hard not to write about Coons. He decided to tour England and the Continent to do a travel book for the "little guy"—tradesmen and carpenters and people like that. I told him that those little guys had all been to Europe first class, but Coons didn't believe me. I read some of his pages (it was never published) which were a lordly jumble of hilarious misinformation. He described Oxford as the dirtiest town in England. He had never left the train station (riding third class to let the little guy know what he was in for), saw some newspapers blowing down the street, and postulated his condemnation of that seat of learning without the drudgery of further research. Nobody will ever know how I loved that big happy man or how much I miss him.

I was discussing TV and at last found something that I thought made sense. Bruce Geller, writer turned producer, was starting a new series in which Robert Taylor is sent out by the government as a sort of investigative troubleshooter. He goes to the Amish country in Pennsylvania to see if he can't persuade the leaders of that stubborn religious sect to meet the federal regulations about signing papers and meeting minimal regulations which will not force the authorities to sell their beloved teams of horses at auction to raise the few dollars to meet social security standards. The strength of their community had always been that the group succored any member in trouble. To depend upon government would destroy them. They had left Russia rather than bow to government interference in their religious principles. Soon many of them would be heading for Canada to practice their religion and hold to their ideals. It was growing harder for the elders to keep their children uncorrupted by the world around them. It was hard to remain agrarian when other children read exciting books by electric lights not candles, and listened to radios and drove cars, not buggies. Airplanes soaring overhead came from exciting places in a big world. The conflict centered on a son who wanted to expand his mind and a loving but stern father who believed in his god and fought to keep his children. I knew these people and admired their thrift and honesty and self-control in a cheap, undisciplined world, even though I could never follow their precepts, and I wrote a truly affecting screenplay. I had every right to be proud of it. It was being readied for shooting when network politics canceled the series. I wrote one more for *The Virginian* series, collaborating with friend Tom Blackburn, before I found a job that taxed all my energies and made me feel of some use in the world. I went back to teaching and had a ball.

38

I said that I found the job, but the job found me. Ed Caron Jr., the husband of my daughter Maggie, was taking a special course in the Commerce Department of Cal State Fullerton. He mentioned to his instructor that he had married a girl whose father used to be a college professor. The fellow repeated it to a professor in the English Department, which promptly sent out a professor to look me over. The English Department was understaffed and recruiting teachers. I was all but implored to take one class in the second semester to see if I liked it. I enjoyed it tremendously. The students in that class gave such flattering reports about my instruction that the head of the English Department, a man whom I never ceased to like and admire, asked if I'd like a full time teaching position in the fall. I said I would.

He asked in what capacity—as a writer in residence? I said no. I couldn't be a stuffed owl. I was a teacher. He smiled, saying he had heard reports to that effect. I told him that ideally I would like to teach three seminars for advanced and interested students, all writing courses with a maximum of twenty students in each: Screen Writing, Short Story Writing, and Novel Writing. I would start with a few general lectures in each class, then begin conferencing, short individual meetings at first until they picked a subject and got started, then longer ones. I would meet with every student once a week, would drop my malingerers, would read every word they wrote, and hold infrequent class meetings to read and discuss the best results. I planned to pattern my classes on those of Dean Briggs. At first I'd depend on other English teachers to send me their most likely students, for I couldn't teach students like those I had had in that one class. I had to spend half the semester telling them how *not* to write. He grinned. He had heard about that class and thought that I had done wonders with them.

That had been some class. It was a big class composed almost entirely of older women who had been teaching English in grammar schools around the county with disastrous results. They were all in the Education Department, where teachers of education had indoctrinated them in that special brand of incomprehensible gobble-de-gook used by all teachers of education, sociology, and psychology.

Not knowing their backgrounds, I confronted them after reading
their first themes, and said that only once before during a fairly long
life had I encountered English as bad as this. That was when a group
of professional writers in the Navy had to interview flight engineers
about their manuals and make them explain what in hell they were
talking about so that we could translate it into English that combat
flyers could understand. I read them a few examples from the themes
and wrote out what I thought they meant. They grinned sheepishly.
"No wonder they want you to take a refresher course in English:
just where did you ever learn to write this outlandish gibberish?"
One man, smarter than the rest, and braver, said, "Mr. Watkin, we
get it from our education textbooks. They're all written this way."
I sympathized with them after he had pointed out several passages.
"You have been reading drivel by so-called writers who could not get
one passage accepted by the editor of a Sunday School newsletter.
Only in a book on education would such pedagese be tolerated. I'll
guarantee that if all the phony ideas in any one of these books were
boiled down by a professional writer, then polished by metaphor and
symbol to make it appealing, it wouldn't take fifty pages." I wrote
one of the passages from his book on the blackboard and asked for
volunteers to tell me what it meant. "Take your notepaper; work on
it for a few minutes. Imagine that I'm a French student just learning
English. Try to find a way to make me understand it. First just try for
simplicity." They came up with some very good substitutions. "You
know," I said, "I thought you were dumb. You're not dumb; you're
brilliant. I couldn't even translate that stuff."

The next hour I read them parts of Sir Arthur QuillerCouch's
essay on jargon, and H.L. Mencken's satire on Veblen's *Theory of the
Leisure Class*, and Stuart Chase on windy and pretentious writing,
and Samuel Williamson on academic talk and how to write like
a social scientist, and Stephen Leacock at his best and funniest, and
Aldous Huxley and George Orwell. By the end of that hour I had
made a good many converts. Two of those students took my short-
story course and did good work. One boy told me he was going to
try an experiment. On his first education test, he planned to write
simple, good answers. He showed me the F he received. On the
next test, he was going to write it the way the textbooks wrote. He
showed me the A he was given. He told me something that I never
forgot. "Mr. Watkin," he said, "I'm going to be a high-school principal, and I'm going to teach every teacher under me how they should
be teaching the kids to write. Those kids will owe a lot to you." It was
one of the finest things any student ever said to me.

Having made them conscious of the pomposity of the academic writer who covers up his basic ignorance or unoriginal thought by big words that seem profound but are not, and the corresponding frenetic glitter of advertising copy, which keeps its Christmas lights burning all year long, I tried to show them true eloquence in some exalted passages from the jurist Oliver Wendell Holmes.

Returning to the conclusion of my chat with the department head, he inquired what rank I expected. I told him that the masters degree from Harvard gave me academic respectability and that my long experience as a professional in the fields in which I would teach more than made up for my lack of the Ph.D., and that at my age I would be a full professor or nothing. He responded: "You are now a full professor."

Dorothy, who was very proud of me, suggested that we look for another house near the college, which had now reached university status, had almost tripled in size, and was housing the English department in a fine new building, where I could have an office I didn't have to share with another professor. That meant a lot to me, for I wanted to work with students individually. I could pick more truly interested writers now, and though my teaching took my full time, if I didn't live so far away, I could see more of Dot. Also, I think she had got in the habit of moving and it was fun to decorate a new place and landscape it. We found the perfect house, with a sizable, well-compacted back lawn that looked off to mountains in the distance and a new freeway below but far enough away to send up no noise. It was on the outskirts of Yorba Linda. Again, we had good neighbors. One was Mickey Clark, who had been with Walt Disney from the very earliest days and now because of his business sense, handled many of Walt's private financial accounts. Another neighbor besought us not to build a pool but to use theirs. We bought the house before it was quite finished and added an extra here and there like the window I wanted over the desk in my study and another over the place for the workbench in my garage and certain cupboards and built-ins Dot wanted. We never had dirty window curtains. Before they needed cleaning, we moved. We always made money on a sale. I think we enjoyed that house more than any we had ever had. The surrounding country was wild enough so that we were often visited by the fussy, old-maid roadrunner birds. I didn't tell Dot that I chased a tarantula out of our garage one morning, but since I knew that their bites were not fatal and that Indian kids made pets of them, I wasn't much concerned, and never saw another.

I remember that when we sold Castle Hill in Lexington because we were going to California and in all probability would never live in

Lexington again, a "friend" quoted the old saw, "Fools build houses for wise men to live in." In our many moves I heard the old chestnut murmured again. But whenever we built or made additions to our houses, neither my wife nor I regretted the money we had spent or the time and thought we put into them. What the new owners who think they have made such a smart deal don't know is that the fools have all the fun. The wise men, who never take a chance, miss the joy of creation.

I think that Dot knew when she suggested closer proximity that I would be bringing students home to the new house and that it would be more like Washington and Lee again. And so it turned out to be.

I became a friend for life with several of my students, as I had done with many at Washington and Lee, only this time there were girls or young women as well as boys among them, for the school was co-educational. Two of them suggested that we have affairs, but I told them that though the temptation was great and the compliment to me extraordinary, I never had and never would have an affair with a student. I was in love with their minds. Furthermore, though they never seemed to think of me as an old man, I told one of them I was old enough to be her grandfather. It startled her, but she remained my fast friend. I had a private laugh one day when a girl told me that she wanted to write a story about a young girl and an old man. Not sex. The girl would be only six or seven, the man very old. "How old in years?" I wanted to know.

"Oh, way up in his fifties."

I kept a straight face. I was sixty-six at the time.

Their first stories were almost always about themselves. Someone said, "Catholics go to confession; Jews have psychiatrists; everybody else has to make do with Larry Watkin." They would write about their own problems, then break down and admit that it was their true-life story and they didn't know how to end it. So many of the young girls were either recently divorced or deserted, their tales became a kind of therapeutic exercise. When my wife was invalided, she wanted the TV on while I was getting her lunch, and I was forced to listen to a soap opera that she was following. I heard it all before from my students. It was hard to believe how many of them had married young, taken secretarial jobs, postponing their own educations until they had put a husband through college, whereupon he had divorced them for some other girl, often leaving them with a baby to take care of with no, or dwindling, alimony. These girls were invariably nimble-minded, sensitive, and often beautiful. I remembered something and had a closer look. No, not one had enlarged pores. If they had,

I could not understand how the young pups who had used and discarded them could blithely walk away and not repay the remaining three years of college the girls had sacrificed in their behalf.

I got on well with the other teachers. I even attended faculty meetings. When I went into moving pictures I promptly joined the Screen Writers Guild and paid full dues, responding to all requests for benevolence, but I went to the first guild meeting and found it was just like a faculty meeting, in which certain members in love with the sound of their own voices would spring to their feet, make motions and talk to them, using the same old clichés the professors had used, especially that time-honored one about being very careful not to pass anything that made sense because of the danger of establishing a dangerous precedent. Some of them knew the rules of order and as in faculty meetings challenged each procedure until another had been fulfilled. I decided that I would never go to another guild meeting and attended very few. Now I thought I should go again, but sat quietly and listened. Nothing had changed very much except the vocabularies. Pedagogy, in whatever department, never used the word *subject* any more. English and French and sociology were not subjects but "disciplines." The less discipline in teaching them, the more certain they were to be called disciplines. If a teacher wanted to combine English and sociology, which meant a watering down of both disciplines to the glory of neither, he described his aim as "Interdisciplinary." That was the summit, as far as human ingenuity could go. Such a man was regarded with awe and would go far. Like John Wesley, who took all the world as his parish, so this teacher hoped to mingle all disciplines in his province.

The other word heard at every faculty meeting was the Latin phrase *ad hoc*, meaning special. Someone would suggest a simple question that could have been decided in about two minutes by a show of hands, but there was always an old dependable obfuscator on hand who could be relied on to jump to her feet and say, "I move that the chairman appoint an ad-hoc committee to meet and study the matter in detail and report back to the full faculty at the February meeting." Whereupon Professor Wynken, Blyncken, and Nod would be appointed to get together and argue the matter out. I always refused to take part in such idiocy, saying that I was far too busy.

Another thing I tried to avoid was college politics where certain groups were always canvassing members to join their clique to oust the incumbent department head to put in a friend. I really *was* too busy working with kids to play these spiteful little games. Several students in my classes became professional writers and many of them, fatally bit with the compulsion to write long before they met me, took advantage of my offer to read and criticize anything they wrote. At least half of my extensive Christmas card list is made up of students I knew at Washington and Lee and Cal State Fullerton. One writes me at least once a month. She writes like an angel and is bound to be published sooner or later. She has a tough exterior but is so fundamentally kind that for the four years during which Dorothy was a stroke patient, she never failed to add a tiny envelope inside with a beautiful card in the color of a bird or a flower which she had photographed herself or hunted down for its message of fun or beauty. She was cruelly crippled from polio but presented a challenge to the world not to pity her. Her father had taught her to swear, as therapy, I think. One day on her way to class in crossing the square after a rainstorm she slipped and fell. She was struggling to get up, but had fallen on her bad side and couldn't make it. Scowlingly, she addressed a group of boys who stood nearby: "Would one of you dumb bastards help me up?" When they all rushed over, she ordered: "I don't need all of you. Just one dumb bastard will be enough." When he had done his duty, she thanked him and explained, "It's these goddamn new shoes my parents sent me. I told them not to."

The boy who had helped her up knew me and knew that she was going to my class. He said that he thought the new shoes were quite nice, but she threw them into the nearby trashcan and limped along barefooted. I told him what happened next. She came to class barefoot and seemingly unembarrassed. The class sat in a circle and some of the others were sniggering at her. She was a tiny little girl, and had the cutest little feet. To relieve the tension, I grinned at her and quoted:

> Her pretty feet
> Like snails did creep
> A little out, and then,
> As if they played at bo-peep
> Did soon draw in again.

A boy across the room, to show his erudition, called out "Lovelace!"

She threw him a look of scorn and said, "No, Herrick! He was an Episcopalian rector and therefore exceedingly horny."

After the class stopped laughing, I informed her: "Not in that verse. He had all his affairs with a dozen beautiful women when he was a student at Cambridge. When he became rector of Dean Prior in Devon, a little town near Plymouth, he didn't find any country lass that compared to his Julia in London, so he wrote mostly pastoral verses and graceful poems to little children."

"Oh, I thought maybe he had a foot fetish."

"Maybe he did in times past. He wrote the famous couplet: 'I love to kiss my Julia's leg / Which is as white and hairless as an egg.'"

That got a guffaw, too, but I continued. "He wrote a great many epitaphs for little children. Childbirth claimed a lot of them:

> 'Here a pretty baby lies
> Sung asleep with lullabies;
> Pray be silent, and not stir
> The easy earth that covers her.'"

Though I didn't mingle in faculty or in student affairs as I had done at W&L, I could not resist writing one letter to the editor of the *Yorba Linda Star*, who belonged to that pious group of southern California idiots who were always searching out some minor indecency and taking it to the state legislature. A few years previous a religious student, a born bigot, had discovered that the *Dictionary of American Slang* had a slim little cluster of dirty words which took up possibly a fifth of one page. He stirred up a former Navy chaplain to action. They became organized and kicked up a tremendous fuss about removing that very excellent and erudite book from all the public libraries. That bellowing demagogue Max Rafferty joined them, and Governor Reagan who wanted their votes as he later courted the Moral Majority ostensibly implied his approval. These people printed a thousand copies of that list and even were vicious enough to thrust a copy in the blouse of the teen-aged daughter of the senator who opposed them. When the librarians won and the book-burners crawled back into their decayed logs, they emerged again when the drama professor at Cal State Fullerton permitted a private showing of an off-color play called *The Beard* to be privately produced and directed as a class exercise. No tickets were given out unless signed for and limited to students of the class, but some sneak put three of them into the hands of Bill Drake, the local yokel who edited the *Yorba Linda Star*. In turn he got Senator Whetmore embroiled, and the senator introduced a bill to control such filth.

I wrote a satirical letter to Bill Drake for his stout defense of morality against college "freedomists" as he called them and for his most recent campaign against glue sniffing. A lady had shown him a discarded glue tube which her dog had nosed out of a gutter while relieving himself. On the strength of that he warned his readers not to let their children buy one of those assembly kits with its viperous tube of glue unless attended by an adult. The students thought my letter funny. Maybe it helped. Senator Whetmore's bill to fire the drama professor and let the taxpayers decide what books the students should and should *not* read was voted down overwhelmingly.

One of my writers wanted to apply for a teaching job and picked up one of their application blanks. She brought it to me. I took it to the head of education and asked for a translation.

Since he seemed incapable of putting it into English that anyone might comprehend, I asked politely if he could direct me to the teacher who had written it. He said he thought that the teacher was no longer with them, that these were forms that had been around for some time. He managed to keep his voice from trembling, but he wanted to slug me. I might have known I would get no intelligent response from him, but I sent a letter to the Placement Bureau of the college, for they were not supposed to be allied to any department, suggesting that such questions as *"What is the candidate's understanding of the learning process?"* belonged at the bottom of *The New Yorker*, not at the top of a college making any pretensions to intelligence. But I never got an answer from them either.

Even though it was more confining and did not seem as important as screen-writing, teaching was a lot more satisfying than working for Disney. My wage was more than enough for our needs; I even started saving something. And I know that I was appreciated. After they had graduated so that they would not be considered flattering me to get a higher grade, students sent many kind letters of thanks. One which was embarrassingly kind went to the president of the university with a copy to the chairman of the English Department, not to me, but both of those men honored me with a copy. The boy said that in getting his B.A. degree he had had few bad instructors and many good ones, but that one professor stood out from the rest:

> Mr. Watkin's classes are not dry rehashing of the same lecture prepared sometime just after World War II. Mr. Watkin injects into each hour his own enthusiasms and warm sense of humor. ... What makes Mr. Watkin an outstanding instructor? From my own experience, I can say that he spends more than just classroom time when a student needs it. His efforts in my behalf, often in his own home on his own time, have helped me to become a published writer. Mr. Watkin does not preach down to the students; he talks to, discusses with, and works along with people.

There is another whole page of it. I received shortly thereafter an inscribed copy of *Ellery Queen's Mystery Magazine*. This student, under the pseudonym of Len Gray, had sent them a pair of stories.

The magazine gave them the heading "Department of First Stories," with this note:

> The author submitted two stories simultaneously. We couldn't decide which one was the first "first" or which one we liked better, a thematic dilemma you may find yourself in. So we ducked both decisions by deciding to publish both firsts at the same time.
>
> Len Gray (a pseudonym) is in his mid-twenties. For two years preceding his double submission he studied under Lawrence Edward Watkin, author of *On Borrowed Time*, at Cal State College Fullerton.... We thank Mr. Watkin for his knowledge of EQMM and even more for his recommendation of *Ellery Queen's Mystery Magazine* to one of his students.

Another student became a screenwriter; two others dedicated first novels to me; a fourth credited me on the flyleaf of her book on organic makeup. My cup was brimming but did not quite run over, because the most publishable novel of all, after it had been completed and ready to submit, suddenly became distasteful to the author. She consigned it to the fire and will not write another. Her frequent letters, all fascinating, have taken the edge off my disappointment.

39

It was in 1969 that I realized I was considerably over 65 and should sign up for Medicare. At the same time, I decided to investigate what I might have in the way of a screenwriter's pension. I found that I could have been receiving a small pension from the Writer's Guild. If I wrote anything for the moving pictures, the pension would stop for six months, then start up again whenever I had failed to write another. The director of the pension plan told me that I had qualified for 19 years of sufficient dues paid to the Writers Guild. If I wrote one more script, even a TV hour show, I would be a twenty-year man which meant everything when I eventually stopped writing. Both my wife and I would get free medication for the rest of our lives. We had not had any serious illnesses, but should we have such, that medication, as well as other perquisites, could mean thousands of dollars to me and to my wife. He urged me to do one more script.

Walt had died in 1966. I had long since forgotten any irritation I had suffered at his hands. I sent him a get-well message the moment the newspapers told of his hospitalization, but I don't think it ever reached him.

So I wrote Bill Anderson, one of the crop of producers, to tell him of my need and my sorrow at Walt's death. He immediately sent me a ten-page story by one of my heroes, James Street, called *The Biscuit Eater*. I did not know then that the story had already been done before, badly, by one of the big studios, nor that Bill had vainly tried to get a script out of it since the Disney studio had recently bought all rights to the property. I would not have read anything that had gone before anyway, not wanting to be influenced by other people's mistakes. The story was a natural for me. I had a notebook full of Southernisms I had never used, and I wrote a script I knew was good. He immediately sent me a big check for a TV two-parter, and wanted more. I wrote back and said that I had for some time thought what a wonderful movie could be made on a Disney biography. There was so much footage of him in the vault and he was so much an actor anyway, as I discovered in doing the TV plug to advertise *Darby O'Gill*, that I was sure it could be done. Furthermore, I told him truly that when Richard Schickel had brought out his insulting biography of Walt in 1968, going out of his way to depict Walt as a plain vulgarian interested only in making money, it had infuriated me. I had worked closely with Walt for a long time; he had confided all sorts of intimate things to me, and though like everybody who worked with him he had often bewildered me, I held him in the highest respect. Bill asked me to come up to the studio for a chat.

When I got there, Bill told me that they didn't want a movie about Walt but a biography, that he had discussed it with Roy, who was now running the studio, or at least was its titular head, and both Roy and other top personnel agreed that I was the man to do it. My son Parke and the Disney lawyers worked out a contract. There was no pressure on me. They wanted a thorough job. I would have access to all papers, tapes, could run any of the films I wanted to study, even from the earliest days. I would be well paid—not my old rate, but enough. I estimated that it would take me two years. If they accepted and published it, I would make a great deal of money. I suggested that I would turn in a section to Bill Anderson, as I completed it. He could give it to anyone who might be interested in that particular part, and that anybody could stop me and give me specific criticism or suggestions for improvement. I would not pause to request a critique unless it was offered, but would press on to the end.

I hated to tell the college that I would have to stop teaching at the end of the first term, but they quite understood; so after the exams at the midyear I began commuting to the studio. If my neighbor Mickey Clark could do it every day, I could certainly drive up every few days or so, make research notes, then write at home. Those students of mine who were embarked on something pressing I carried on the side.

I had never known Roy Disney intimately, but since the earliest papers relating to the family were in his files, I soon made his acquaintance and discovered that he was anything but the figurehead so many people thought him to be. He was a balance-wheel for his impetuous brother. He read the earliest stuff I had written and highly approved. When he died before I had completed the book I lost a good friend.

I was going great when I suffered a setback. I had been consulting a doctor in Anaheim for nausea and stomach trouble. Fairly late one night I knew my heart was failing me. I called the doctor at his home and told him I could drive down if he would be ready to meet me. He directed me to Saint Joseph's Hospital. He was there and saw that I was just about gone, so he got out the electric shock machine. The damn thing was balky, but just before my heart stopped, it worked. That charge went through me and started my heart pumping again.

Dot who was with me asked that doctor to dig up another heart specialist or so. I was admitted to the hospital, and my son Parke determined from several specialists that the damage from that gopher bomb had so affected one side of my heart that an operation was necessary. Parke investigated a team of local heart surgeons, heard only good reports about them, and we all decided to let them do the job. They proved to be excellent.

What they did roughly was this: A part of the heart muscle had calcified, or hardened, if that's a better word, and the blood hitting it regurgitated. After the obstruction had been removed and the wound sewed up, I was still bleeding. The surgeon asked everyone's permission, including mine, to open me up again to cauterize the ends of some tiny blood vessels that had been freed. He did so, but nobody except Dot expected me to live through this double operation. She said, "He has no intention of dying," or "He will not die. He hasn't finished his script." She was not being flippant, and indeed it never occurred to me at any time during any operation that I would die. That surgeon was great. He stayed beside me all night long. He also listened to me. I could not take the oxygen tent. It smothered me. They could give me the oxygen in some other way, and they did, and I survived. As a matter of fact, I was soon out of intensive care and kidding with those wonderful nurses again. St. Joseph's was a Catholic hospital and most of the nurses were religious. I was nervous just before the operation and called continually for the urinal; so just before I was to go into surgery, they scotch-taped a note to the can. It read, "We are all praying for you," and they signed their names. I didn't believe in the power of prayer, but I strongly believed in the power of kindness and love, and that note smoothed me out better than any analgesic.

In no time at all I was working on the biography in my hospital bed. The Disney lawyers ruled that the interruption would not invalidate the contract, so I went to work again.

Another move was indicated. We sold the Yorba Linda house and moved into a swank apartment in Encino, which was near my doctors, both for heart and general practice, my son's office, two hospitals, and a very short drive to the studio. Dorothy, always the researcher, got cook books on salt-free diets and bulletins from the heart association to make sure that I stayed on a salt-free, fat-free, low-cholesterol diet, though the surgeons said that my veins were so free from sludge they were good for another seventy years. At the same time, they predicted that I could not live for more than a year. Even if they believed it and were not simply insuring themselves from any suit for malpractice, which I had assured them would never be forthcoming from my lawyer son, who was strong on legal ethics and gave me his word he would not bring suit against two fine doctors who had done their level best, they did not change their prognosis that I could not long survive. I did not agree with their findings, but I babied myself physically.

I worked harder than ever on the biography of Walt. I interviewed all the old employees at the studio and was proud that I had got the full story of Ub Iwerks before he died. After researching Walt's plans for Disney World om Florida, I felt almost ashamed of myself that I had not tried to be the producer he wanted me to be, if only to help him out. It seemed well-nigh impossible that one man had accomplished so much. Though chainsmoking cigarettes had given him lung cancer, the heart failure that killed him was certainly caused by the strain of supervising the myriad responsibilities he had assumed.

At last the biography was finished and I turned it in. I was sure the general public would like it, and I thought I had done a good job in answering Schickel. It wasn't all Schickel's fault, for Walt hadn't liked him as a biographer and barred him from access to documents he needed. So, whether he knew it or not, Schickel said to himself, "I'll get even with you," and pictured Walt as a crafty guy who was interested in making money. Unable to interview regulars at the studio, he talked to the guys Walt had fired, the ones who organized the strike against the studio and were bitter. By contrast, the old-time cartoonists loved to tell me everything they remembered about Walt, the bad with the good. Like the cruel way Walt had humiliated in front of them a man to whom he owed a lot. When that cartoonist was going great he had introduced a new character of his own creation that had become one of the most successful in the whole Disney gallery of animal portraits. The artist's wife had died and he fell apart and hit the bottle. Walt probably thought he was being cruel to bring the weakling to his senses, but he'd have been a lot kinder to fire him with a pension. Instead he just dropped him. None of the men liked that heartless streak in Walt. But they knew I wouldn't use a story like that in my book for pure sensationalism; and the guy who brought it up was soon telling me ten others that showed his unbounded admiration for Walt's genius, and his deep affection for the crazy, contradictory things Walt did that kept them on their toes, and highly entertained. Walt without his fellow workers would just be a stick; telling the story of Walt and his studio made him a human being. He seldom swore, but no day passed in which he didn't say *shit*. Nothing else expressed his disgust quite so well. He would never use it in front of a female employee. I didn't mention that either. He was not a foul-mouthed man, but he was anything but the highly moral, upright man the advertising men wanted church groups to think him to push the Disney product. Furthermore, Walt wanted to make money for one purpose only: to try out some seemingly wild scheme that nobody else had ever dreamed of. One day Roy reminded Walt that before he did anything else the stockholders had to be paid. "Hell," said Walt, "what could they do to have as much fun with that money as I could?" His idea of fun would not be to relax on a beach or play golf but to experiment with outer space. I'm sure that after Epcot that would have been next.

I waited a long time before I heard from the studio about my book, which was to be expected, for it was a complete study, and I was sure that at least eight or ten people would be involved in discussing it. At last I received a telephone call from Bill Anderson, who said that everyone who had read it said that it was just *not* Walt Disney. One, whom I guessed was Card Walker, now transmuted by his lofty managerial position into E. Cardon Walker, had recommended that I simply be paid what money was still owed me by contract without even the civility of an accompanying letter. Bill said he was against that. He thought I at least deserved this telephone call, for he knew how hard I had worked to bring it off. Knowing that Bill, like God, was always on the side of the heaviest battalion, I didn't embarrass him by asking what *he* thought of it, for I had always liked Bill and still do.

For years, I lamented that the managerial group who were now trying to replace Walt Disney were failing miserably at the job. Walt was a born gambler, always wanting to try something new. They had far less imagination than stockbrokers; they always wanted to play it safe; they tried to guess what Walt would do, and since they had no tiny spark of genius among them, they always guessed wrong. Walt had one aim in life, to make money to let him experiment; they had one idea in life, to make money and more money and more money. They could merchandise his good name, but they were even bad at that, they were so shoddy themselves. They didn't know a good artist; they had no idea what a story was all about; they squeezed out all such people little by little. I never looked at a Disney movie any more. My daughter told me that when one of the recently made movies was playing, the kids ran up and down the theater aisles, but when an old one was showing, no matter how many times it had been rereleased, the kids sat still and watched it.

Another thing these packagers did: they saw to it that anybody quoting Walt cut out anything that even bordered on indelicacy. They made him a demigod and people got sick of it. I had been guilty of that myself in a very small way, but the management which refused my book wouldn't have objected to that. I was sure of one thing: nobody reading my biography of Walt could complain that I hadn't made him a human being. Maybe they thought there was too much of me in it, but I was sure that I had not ever low-rated Walt to glorify myself. To tell it from your own point of view gave it immediacy, and I did not write in a coldly objective manner when I described his early struggles or even the later ones in which I had no part. It would be Frank Thomas or some such artist standing in for me, or maybe a dozen such for *Snow White* or *Dumbo* or *Bambi* or *Pinocchio* and that marvelous artist and planner John Hench for the later stuff. Maybe *that* was it; maybe they expected me to imply that Walt had done it all single-handed. I could hardly believe that. Walt was constantly saying to me, as he did to dozens of others outside the studio: "If there's anything I'm proud of it's the organization I built up. What could I have done without my artists?" Again he would say, "I was so lucky to get a hold of those guys when times were bad and they needed work. I could never have afforded them otherwise."

Once he dropped into my office and said that a friend of mine that he met in Grand Central Station said he knew that I worked for him. "He wanted me to draw him a Mickey Mouse. I had to tell him no, and if he writes you, I wish you'd explain."

"Was his name Mattimore?"

"I didn't catch his name."

"Was he on the heavy side with a kind of fat face, and probably drunk?"

"He could have been."

"Then I should apologize to you. He's a very nice guy until he has a few drinks in him; then he's a pain in the ass. I'm sorry he bothered you."

"Well, if he writes you, you tell him that I wasn't above drawing a Mickey Mouse for him. But I haven't drawn anything for so long I'd be ashamed to. I stopped drawing when I saw how much better my artists could do it. Those guys are terrific—all of them—just terrific!"

So that wasn't it. But it was. It's January 1981 and it was late in 1980 when by accident I noticed an advertisement for a book called *You Must Remember This*, oral reminiscences about the "real Hollywood." It mentioned that Marty Rackin's no-holds-barred interview was worth the price of the book. I have always thought Marty Rackin one of the funniest men who ever lived, so I bought the book. I read his essay first and thought it was superb. I noticed that the one which followed was Ward Kimball's "The Wonderful World of Walt Disney." I had interviewed Ward along with other old timers at the studio ten years before when I was writing my biography of Walt. When I read it through I found that Ward had given almost exactly the same brief explanation of Walt's character and manner of working that I had in my longer biography, but I didn't get it from Ward. What Ward told me was that Disney was anything but the prude the pious people like Senator Whetmore wanted to label him, that he would talk about turds and the outhouse they had at Marceline for half an hour, and was hipped on shit. Ward also said, "Don't put that in your book; I've still got some Disney stock." I said I had no intention of mentioning Walt's use of the term *shit*. I didn't think it important. I recall that I was riding up in the elevator with Disney and another guy one morning, and that they were discussing inspiration. I broke in to ask them if they had heard H.L. Mencken's definition of inspiration.

Mencken said it usually resulted from a barrel of mineral oil. Walt was delighted. He turned to the other guy and said, "That's what I told you. Everybody is full of shit!"

Reading on, I concluded that Ward had sold his stock, for he told the brutal truth about the present-day management, saying that the people who run the place have no personal relationship with the creative people, "because to me they're Chevrolet salesmen, high-priced messenger boys, who sit around in their offices, trying to second-guess how Walt would have done it. The artistic people are slowly being forced out...replaced with guys who operate computers. It's kind of frightening. ... So it's boring."

Ward even had something to say about Mrs. Disney: "She certainly didn't waste any time getting remarried after Walt died." I met the new husband once. It was not a case of Hyperion to a satyr, but the Lady and the cypher.

Amen, Brother Kimball. Let us all remember that a place run by advertising men rests upon pillars of froth, or have we forgotten so soon the backgrounds of the men who ran the Nixon administration? But I would make one exception: Walt's son-in-law Ron Miller had a mighty poor training for a man destined to take over for Walt, but he probably is doing no worse than any other football player would do in the same position. His last movie, an expensive disaster, failed because he did not follow his father-in-law's cardinal principle: "Spectacle alone will never make a hit. Never start making a movie until you have a sound story." But Ron is a decent guy. And you would have to work mighty hard to dislike him.

On the last page of the interview Ward Kimball gave me the answer I had been looking for. And it was news to me:

> There was a book written under the name of one: of Walt's daughters [Diane]. In it she gave credit to all the people who helped Walt up the ladder. About five minutes after Walt died, the guys running the studio ordered the book rewritten. All the people who'd done their share in making the studio successful were scrubbed out of it. I think that was a dirty trick. Walt was a giant, but he didn't do it all by himself. That's the unmistakable impression the new book conveyed. The book, which is still around and is still selling, is life rearranging history.

At last I had my answer. If in a book written by his daughter which Walt himself approved, the hucksters peddling Disney could not permit so much as a footnote to those who had made his name luminous, what possible chance did my book have? I had kept the spotlight on the conductor but had continually cut away to shots of the whole orchestra which he so brilliantly directed. They wanted the public to believe that Walt had composed all the music, orchestrated it, then brought it forth out of thin air without any musicians—possibly using the music of the spheres.

In 1973 they got the book they wanted, primarily a huge picture book with hundreds of illustrations. The text by Christopher Finch seems almost of secondary importance, but in general I'd call it first rate. Finch had been one of the curators on the Walker Art Center in Minneapolis. He had written books on pop art and on contemporary English painting. At the end of the book is a study by city planner and architect Peter Blake, which is better than anything that goes before. It's entitled "The Lessons of the Parks" and based upon an article Blake wrote in 1972 for the *Architectural Forum*. If you are interested in Walt Disney, this shows a side of him that I tried to bring out at the end of my biography, but couldn't do it half so well, a side of Walt that is little known: his engineering ability. It shows what a man of vision might do in coaxing American industry to achieve a well-nigh perfect city-state, a utopia. It gives you enough examples of the wonders that Walt Disney had already built to make you hope that the ungifted people now controlling the place will go on and complete the plans that Walt left in the hands of his best and most capable men, and not just turn it into a gigantic but conventional real-estate development. If they ever do bring his dream to life, I'll take back any of the harsh words I have used about them.

By the way, Finch does not hesitate to mention the old artists who worked with Disney, but he also implies that Walt had his eye on everything and worked closely to bend it to his desire. That is quite true with the early masterpieces, on which Finch spends an inordinate amount of time, but he applies it to everything and mentions how closely Walt worked with pictures where I know he did not. He neither credits artists for their characters nor producers like Bill Walsh for their originality, nor inventors for their inventions. Even if he names them, their contribution is glossed over. On the other hand, he does an outstanding job with Albert Hurter and at the same time gives Walt the credit he richly deserves for letting Hurter go his own way. This highly educated Swiss artist, possessed of a surrealistic imagination which took in everything, from classical gods and goddesses to medieval chivalry to birds and flowers and cats and candles and eyes and fingers and giants and witches and dragons and clowns and pigs, had worked in animation studios and even taught it, but was too valuable to be tied down to a single story. Walt had the foresight to let this man come to the studio from early morning until five o'clock each day and in pleasant surroundings draw and paint whatever he pleased. He was an artist's artist. Once he finished a drawing he had no interest in keeping it and would give it to anyone who admired it. Walt made sure that his other artists saw Hurter's work, which influenced so many productions thereafter and stimulated his fellow workmen. Ted Sears, Hurter's special friend, got together 700 of his inspirational drawings and the company published them in a delightful book. I have a copy and it's one of my most prized possessions. They say there are practically no Hurter originals left in the files. The other artists stole them, but they "loaned" Ted enough to organize the book, which should be reprinted.

Walt deserves similar credit for taking Ub Iwerks back into the fold, for he knew what Ub could and would do. Ub wanted only to be left alone long enough to create his marvels. He, like Hurter, no longer dreamed of fame and fortune—only a place to accomplish his ideas and the money to make them work. I don't think Fince knew Ub's story, but it's in my despised biography. Maybe some grandchild of Walt will be curious about it one day and dig it up.

40

Dot and I went to Stockton to retire—though a writer never actually does so—because of Miss Mills, the English teacher at Westlake School for Girls in Los Angeles which my daughters attended. Before Westlake I remember telling my older daughter that her punctuation was wrong, but she said that was the way her teacher said to do it. I didn't know more than her teacher, did I? I couldn't say yes, about a thousand times more, for that might make Maggie a target for vindictiveness; so I told her to go along with the teacher, who, I believe, based punctuation on breathing not grammar. But Miss Mills knew a restrictive relative clause from an inhalation of the breath, and I could rest easy. Miss Mills was a name often heard mentioned in parent meetings. At a Christmas party I was sitting beside a famous producer, who leaned across in front of me and said proudly to Fred MacMurray on the other side, "Miss Mills gave me a B-minus on Betty's last theme." I think she knew when parents had "helped." But on this occasion, every child taking part in the program pledged that the poem she recited was her own composition. Our daughter Anne was very young then, but being a straight-A student, she was chosen to take part. She walked up to the footlights and fired her verse:

> Star in the east, star in the west
> the star in the east
> is the biggest and the best.
> It shineth o'er a manger
> where a baby doth lay,
> now Jesus Christ is here to stay.

It brought down the house, but because it was plain from her demeanor that she thought the last line deeply religious, parents choked back their laughter and applauded vigorously. Anne was a lovely little kid. Engraved on my mind is the expression she wore returning from the country on a London subway. She had secreted a tiny flower in her left hand and was keeping it alive by placing its stem end in a diminutive globule of spit.

Miss Mills had graduated from Wellesley and loved the place. She never mentioned it to a student she didn't think would do more than roll a hoop, but she proselyted Anne. I heartily approved of Westlake, but I said to Dot, "Well, we can say goodby to our little girl. She'll meet a Harvard student who will have a business in Boston or New York City, and we'll be lucky to see her twice a year." She met the Harvard men; she was besieged by them, for she was beautiful, athletic, highly intelligent, and not easily impressed. She refused in her freshman year the aristocratic son of an enormously wealthy Venezuelan importer and fell in love in her sophomore year with a boy from Stockton, California, whom she eventually married. In visiting them we looked around for lots and houses, where we might abide. Stockton was a small city which didn't want to grow. It was halfway between LA where my son practiced law, and Boise, Idaho, where Maggie and her husband lived. Anne, being the youngest, had the youngest children, whom Dot thought would be most easily seduced by her cookie jar to visit us. We found a sizable condominium in the process of construction which was the time to shape it toward our needs. We gave good excess furniture and china and silverware and bric-a-brac to our children, and added cement patios so that Dot would have to keep her rose garden small enough to be cared for easily when we decided we had to have another look at London or the Balearic Islands or Copenhagen. I still had that sentence of early death hanging over me, so I visited both the heart specialists and a family doctor. The latter beat on me to get out and walk, walk, walk. If I thought I had overdone either the work or the exercise I rushed back for another checkup, which he swore was more perfect every time I came in. "Quit worrying about your heart. Let me worry about it. I'll tell you if it's acting up. Stick to your diet and walk. Rest when you're tired, but don't dope around. Your blood pressure and pulse is fine; your lungs are clear as a bell. Come back again in two months."

When I returned, it was the same story and soon I did forget about my heart. As I got older I had glaucoma, but medication kept it within bounds. I was troubled too by skin cancers, the result of too much sun years ago. Some had to be cut out, some frozen. I also survived a prostate operation with little difficulty, but the desire to travel grew less. I worried about Dot, who had developed a passion for needlework. I begged her to take walks with me, but she wouldn't. I think she knew she had high blood pressure but refused to go to the doctor to find out. She sat, engrossed in that needlework; several of the pieces became framed works of art, but I hated them for they cost her her life.

One day after a nap she fell beside the bed and I couldn't get her up. I called my daughter, only a few blocks away, who came in a hurry and together we lifted her to the bed. Dot couldn't speak. We called the doctor, got an ambulance, and rushed her to the hospital, where a team of doctors worked with her a long time. She had suffered a massive stroke, which meant a blood clot on the left side of the brain, paralyzing everything on her right side. Medical science may sometime be able to dissolve such clots, but not yet. She stayed in that hospital more than two weeks and slowly gained strength, but not her speech. The hospital therapist went through the motions of exercising her good leg and arm and even trying to get her to speak, but like most of those who dealt with stroke patients, he didn't know his job. As soon as it was decided that she was out of danger, all doctors assured us that she must go to a convalescent hospital, where they understood strokes. We tried the three most recommended. They all advertised rehabilitation of every patient, but I am not exaggerating when I say that all convalescent hospitals all over America are beneath contempt. I believe that there is one rehabilitation center in southern California staffed with competent people, but no doctor ever mentioned that. I believe there was another one, but Governor Reagan with his genius for doing the wrong thing closed that.

Convalescent hospitals perform only one service: when a stroke patient still lives on but has reached vegetable status, unable to do anything for him or herself, comprehending nothing, staring into space, the convalescent hospital puts them in a secluded back room and keeps them alive, treating them as well as could be expected under such circumstances. But it does nothing to help or in any way rehabilitate the patient who is only half disabled. Unless there is a husband or wife or responsible relative who visits and checks on the care being dispensed, the patient will be shamefully neglected. A brisk office force appears to be all efficiency, and so does a genial manager, strong on statuary and beautiful flowerbeds near the lounge rooms or patio where gay sun umbrellas surmount a few outside tables. You will be shown the "gym" with one set of parallel walking bars and maybe a small wrestling mat on the floor. The gym is usually locked and the therapist, a real pro, has just stepped out. The kitchens are usually clean and the food tolerable unless the management gets a cut-rate deal on a load of sugar beets, and then, by God, you'll eat beets until the juice is running out of your ears. You pass by a long row of old women in wheel chairs. You see only their backs. They sit facing a picture window, looking at the beds of beautiful flowers. Actually, they have been thoroughly doped—the euphemism is mildly tranquillized—and most of them have been left there so long they are peeing their pants. There is usually one registered trained nurse at the one central station. She is chair bound, so goddamn lazy she can just stay awake to tell her assistant that it's time for Ellie in 24C to have her medicine (Valium). If Ellie is properly doped, she won't cause any trouble, which means that one nurse can take care of fifteen patients or more, when she should never be taking care of more than half that number.

Nurses are desperate before they'll take a job in one of these places, so the turnover is tremendous. Some of the nurses do their level best, but it's humanly impossible to care for so many. Another drifter is hired. Promotions for good work are unheard of. You always work for scale. Otherwise the absentee owners can't reap a profit. Management usually is tipped off that an inspector is coming. So they hire ten extra nurses for a week and fire them when the government snoop has left town.

On your tour, some pathetic old woman may suddenly grab your arm and ask you, "Will you tell my son to come visit me? He's a butcher and I know he doesn't work evenings. He hasn't been over to see me since Christmas."

The manager gently but firmly detaches the hand of the poor old derelict from my arm, cooing, "Now Mary, you be a good girl. Your son is devoted to you. You just forget, that's all." She signals to a nurse.

I have an idea that the butcher is not devoted. He put his mother in here, in this swell joint, where she is getting tender, loving care that costs a pretty penny. Had to raise the price of hamburger last week to cover it. The doc tells him his old lady is in great shape.

How would the doctor know? The doctor slips into a side room once a week or so with a secretary, and goes over the files that management lets him see. He makes out the bills from the files, not from visiting the patient, not even for the cheery greeting he reserves for Medicare patients in the big hospital: "Well, how are we today? Getting a little color back. Let's feel that pulse. Strong, good! You'll be out of here in no time!"

Dot was in one of these big hospitals until they admitted they could do nothing more for her. Management suggested a convalescent hospital, so awful that I figured they must own a piece of it to recommend such a hole. Here the poor, overworked therapist, who did nothing as far as I could see, treated himself to a week's holiday, but in order to lose no salary he left one simple thing for each patient to do during the week that lay ahead. Dot's stint was to have the nurse drop the supports that held her feet off the floor, face her chair against a hand-grip built into the wall beside her door, lock the chair, then direct her to reach forward with her good left hand and pull herself to a standing position on her good left foot, sit back again, and repeat the exercise. He assured me that a nurse would be standing over her at all times. The nurse started her doing it. I walked up the hallway as if to depart, walked around the corner, then peeked back. The nurse had departed. I went back to Dot, calmed her down because she feared to perform the exercise without supervision. Then I went into Dot's room and looked at my watch. After some ten or fifteen minutes the nurse returned and told Dot she had done enough. She wheeled Dot back into her room. I asked the nurse if she would like to accompany me to the admissions office. She said no, and she didn't care what I said; she didn't have time to do her work and the therapist's, too. I went to the office, asked to use the phone, called the doctor my regular doctor had recommended as the authority on stroke patients. He handled most of the strokes cases in town. I asked him to suggest another hospital. He did, told me to get Dot in an ambulance and he would have a bed ready. He didn't think too much of that place either. So I paid the bill for the part of a week Dot had been there with no word of protest for my high-handed behavior. I think they feared that I might sue them, and I most certainly would have done so if they had let out a peep. The new set-up was better in some ways. Dot couldn't talk and the other patient (there were always two to a room and sometimes three) had been there for years. That patient didn't care to look at or speak to the newcomer.

The new hospital was huge. As usual the head nurse was a lazy moron; the therapist was also a moron, but a well-meaning one. He tried very hard to teach Dot how to walk by dragging her bad right foot and depending on her four-pronged crutch. By supporting her on the right side he managed to get her to take ten steps. That he said was as far as she could ever walk. She had peaked, as he put it.

The overworked nurses tried harder here, and there wasn't as much confusion, for here all patients were heavily sedated with Valium. I didn't know about it then, except that I sensed something was wrong. Dot was apathetic and wanted me with her every minute. I spent all morning and all afternoon with her, but my eyes were failing somewhat and I didn't dare drive after dark. I bought Dot a big color TV with a remote-control switch for the evenings. My daughter Anne had a growing family, but she visited Dot whenever she could in the evenings. Of all the hundred or so patients in that hospital, I and a big, gaunt, long-legged man who worked nights and was too poor to own a car, and another handsome young couple in their early thirties who visited the young man's mother twice a day, were the only relatives or friends who came regularly, if at all. The young couple had set out to teach the mother to walk, one on each side. They were magnificent. The mother herself was tall and beautiful with deep-set eyes. The man told me, "The secret of restoring a stroke victim is to have infinite patience." I admired them for their smiling good nature. I was testy myself, but I tried like hell to control myself.

There is nothing more infuriating than someone who has had a stroke. I could understand why relatives dump their responsibilities in a convalescent hospital, but there were only four of us who had any conscience about leaving these utterly helpless people to shift for themselves. The more I learned the angrier I became, and I made myself thoroughly hated by the greedy phonies who ran these places. When Dot had to go to the toilet I was supposed to call a nurse, but we always had to wait so long that I started the nursing myself. When I noticed that she had developed a bad rash in both groins and armpits I complained. The head nurse said that all old ladies had the same problem; they simply couldn't hold their water, so they were always wet. I said Dot had never been incontinent and wasn't now. She said I didn't know what I was talking about. I asked her if she had ever looked at Dot's rash. She said that wasn't her job; that was up to the nurses. Besides, she simply wet herself. No, she didn't; it was a matter of simple neglect, and she was the one responsible. She said they would put on a certain ointment. I had talked to a nurse about it, who said that the ointment had never cured a patient to her knowledge, and was almost impossible to remove. I told the nurse that if Dot were kept dry by using powder or cornstarch and using cloths that didn't let the infected parts touch each other, the rash would disappear. That was silly talk. What did I know about nursing? More than you do. You can't learn anything about patients sitting in that chair all day. I repeated that Dot was not incontinent. She lifted the phone and called the doctor. He backed her up. He said of course she was incontinent. What the hell does he know about it? He'd never looked at her. All he reads are your stupid charts. "Look," I said, "if I were nursing her, I could cure that rash up in less than a week."

"Then why don't you take her home?" she said.

"I will, today!"

I did. I used cornstarch and kept her dry and put her on the bedpan whenever she needed it. Anne spelled me, and in a few days, the rash was gone. We found another convalescent hospital nearer home, where they did much better, but I had a hell of a fight to keep them from making her sleep on a rubber mat under the sheet, which made her so hot she was sweating. A rule was a rule. Every stroke patient was so different that no rule should ever apply to them all. The only good thing about that hospital was that I could get Dot a private room.

My daughter Maggie came down to see her mother. She had four boys and it was hard to get away. When she arrived, she said, "There is nobody in Stockton that can do anything for her. I'm going to make the Elks Rehabilitation Center take her in. They can cure anybody. They're simply amazing." Maggie seldom asserted herself; she was too good-natured, but when she knew she was right she was a tiger. I needed a rest, too. The Elks wouldn't even let me in to see her except evenings; she'd be too busy and happy getting well. They can't teach her to speak, but we can communicate with her, and that's where she's going! It was against the rules, but if we both lived with Maggie, she knew her doctor had enough influence to get Dot admitted.

I entered the Elks Rehabilitation Hospital with the greatest doubt. I had associated the Elks with the lowest form of American yokelry, but when I entered that hospital, had a brief talk with the social worker, who took us around, I decided that this was the most sophisticated hospital I had ever seen. The gymnasium was no small dark hole, but as big as a basketball gym with every sort of exercise machine known to man. Nurses were busy and happy like their patients, some of whom were eighteen-year-old boys who had been in car or motorcycle accidents. Every patient was responding to the therapists, who knew exactly what they were doing. I could not see Dot until after supper from seven to nine, when I could wheel her around the grounds in the cool of the evening. On weekends, we could take her for drives, and she could get her hair done. One or two nurses out of the good of their hearts would devote some part of their weekends to dressing hair. Within a week Dorothy was full of hope and pride in the little she had already achieved. They had taken her off all medication. Her eyes were bright again with excitement.

She stayed a little over a month, and in that time they taught her how to use her wheelchair so that she could move it forward skillfully and back it into the narrowest sort of space. She could almost dress and undress herself. At night, she got into her wheelchair without calling her nurse, wheeled down the hall to the bathroom, got on the toilet unaided, using the built-in hand grips, wiped, returned to bed, and went back to sleep. All I had to do when we got home was to buy a commode with side rails, put it near the bed, and I would never have my own sleep disturbed. They threw away her cumbersome four-pronged crutch, got her a Lofstrand crutch, a special pair of shoes which could be replaced in any medical store, and made a plastic brace for her useless right leg. It fastened well above the calf. The plastic heel and half-foot mold fitted inside the shoe. When the shoe was laced, she could now move the thigh enough to walk stiff-legged with her right foot, normally with the left. Supported only by her crutch, she could walk all over the hospital. A nurse walked alongside but never touched her. If she stumbled and fell, and she never did in that hospital, the nurse would have thrown her body down so that Dot would have fallen on her. She was not to overdo the walking, but should do it twice a day for exercise. An expert masseuse put her on a high bed and went through a series in which both took part. I watched for three days and wrote down every move the nurse made so that I could give them in the same way. I would hire practical nurses when we returned to Stockton, but never again put Dot in a convalescent hospital. The Indians who left the decrepit behind to die were kinder.

More to show the Stockton stroke authority what could be done than to ask for aid, I drove Dorothy back to the doctor, who studied the plastic brace with astonishment. He had never seen such a device. I told him that Morton's surgical store, which furnished my trusses, made such braces right here in Stockton. What that doctor didn't know about his job would have filled a large book. He insisted on writing out a prescription for Dot. I insisted on knowing what it was. He was loathe to admit it was Valium. I asked him to look it up in his AMA manual. When he did so I believe that it mentioned it as a very strong tranquilizer, probably habit forming. I stopped going to him and asked my general practice doctor to take Dorothy as a patient, telling him that the expert on strokes was an utter igno-ramus, who should not be allowed to practice. He of course would never agree that any local doctor was inept, but he did take Dot on.

For a while all went well. Then tests showed that Dot was defi-cient in iron and the doctor had a hard time finding any way to have her system absorb it. I brought her in so many times that he was reluctant to have me bring her in again, but I insisted. He found that I was right. She damn near died from loss of blood. We got her into the hospital and got plasma into her veins just in time. Further tests revealed an abdominal ulcer, which was bleeding her white. Stockton has one first-class doctor, a surgeon named Arismendi. His patients healed in record time, with no complications. So it was when he operated on Dot's ulcer. After that she enjoyed a period of good health, considering all things, though mine deteriorated. Nurses are drifters. It makes no difference whether they are good or bad. In the time I took care of Dorothy at home, roughly four years, we had at least a dozen different nurses, only two of whom I fired for settling themselves down in another room and expecting me to see what Dot wanted when she called. One was a Far East Indian who spent her day looking at movie magazines of sloe-eyed movie stars. She didn't mind. She had already purchased a ticket for Bombay before she signed on with me, and would be leaving in two weeks. She came highly recommended by the employment office, as did her fat black successor, who complained that she had diabetes, should be pensioned by the government, was too ill to get Dot's lunch or her own, but ate like a horse and begged for a second giant sandwich with a slab of baked ham and bread and butter and mustard and several cups of strong coffee to stay her diabetic stomach.

When she had me working for her full time and I had tired of hearing about all the famous people she had enchanted, I reacted like a cruel slave owner and sold her down the river with a week's salary for her two days of labor. I called the employment office and said please, no more.

I then heard about a lady who ran a practical nursing school, who kept her eye out for a woman of stability and common sense, for I had exhausted all the fly-by-nights who had been beaten up by jealous husbands, or wanted to earn a little Christmas money, or heard of a better job in Alaska, or went to Hollywood to be discovered. She sent me three excellent ones, but the first fell sick, the second left town when her husband's company promoted him, and the third one stayed. That woman was middle aged, had four small sons she had to supervise, but she had never got a diploma for anything, she said, and she wanted to prove to herself that she could do something besides being a good wife and taking care of her young hellions while her husband, a chief petty officer almost always away at sea, finished his twenty-year tour of duty. The head of the school said she thought this woman would be the perfect nurse for Dot. The only trouble was she could only work while the kids were in school. She arrived at 9:30 or 10 and left at 1:00, but when Dot saw her coming while finishing her breakfast at the kitchen table, her face lighted up and my troubles were over until one o'clock. Dot loved that woman, and Dolores loved her.

A stroke patient can put anyone on edge in about five minutes. Their own frustrations are so great and their apprehensions so manifold that Dot would have me in a state of helpless fury, all the more maddening because I knew I couldn't argue with her. We had always debated everything, but the moment I got too heated, Dot would say something to make me feel silly and apologetic, for she was calmness personified. I once collected all her academic college pins and rings, Phi Beta Kappa and all the rest, had them attached to a charm bracelet, and gave it to her with the injunction to shake it at me whenever

I lost my temper and called her a moron. She never worried about my bad temper. She knew I loved her and that I would be apologizing if I went too far. Now it was different. I simply couldn't yell at her and if I did I felt like a heel.

Most of our nurses had their flare-ups, too, but not Dolores. After they learned about each other, they were talking like two gossipy women. Dot could say only one word, "No," but she jabbered and pointed and somehow managed to make herself understood. Dolores found that Dot was tremendously interested in the four boys and in the trials and defeats and triumphs Dolores went through in getting a swimming pool built for her kids. Also, they were both interested in clothes. I was always getting Dot a new blouse or slacks and a great deal of time went into the matter of what combination of colors she should wear and what ring went best with her outfit, or even what Dot wanted for lunch. After Dolores had to go, I gave Dot her lunch; then she took a nap.

Dot had her day to go to the hairdressers, where she got a shampoo and a set or a permanent or a restyling, or if she wanted to go shopping, I would take her out for a drive in the country or to a new part of town, or to an adjacent park or to another town. There were beautiful orchards of cherries, pears, peaches, almonds, oranges, and vineyards, and there were rides along rivers. She knew exactly where she wanted to go, and always begged for more. When she was in the car, she was quiet and content to be alive in a beautiful world. At Christmas time she was excited over every light or tree she could spot, just as she had been over flowers or boats on a river. One lady on a side street had the most beautiful display of flowers usually confined to a private patio, but hers were all out front, and at least twice a week we would drive down that street and park and feast our eyes. The lady would watch for us and come out and talk to Dot. Dot knew and loved every exotic bloom in the lady's yard; she would point and when the lady named a blossom, Dot would nod excitedly, then point to me and to herself and make a motion for digging with a trowel and it would spark my memory that she wanted me to explain about the house in Virginia or Los Angeles or Newport Beach when she had grown that plant. I think the lady was as pleased as Dot was. It's simply amazing how much people can say if one is incapable of uttering a syllable.

Of course Dot was a brilliant woman, and now with only half a brain she had more recall and basic intelligence than the average dolt. At first I had depended upon a six-page notebook with heavy sheets of paper 9 x 11 on which I had printed in large letters all the meats, PORK, LAMB, BEEF, CHICKEN, TURKEY, ROAST, STEAK, CHOPS, EGGS, FRIED, SCRAMBLED, OMELET, then drink: WATER, MILK, SANKA, ORANGE JUICE, GRAPE JUICE, V-8, etc., then the vegetables: SQUASH, ZUCCHINI, ACORN, YELLOW, TURNIPS, TOMATOES, PEAS, ONIONS, MUSHROOMS, etc., then desserts: PIES, CAKES, ICE CREAM, etc. I had a page that dealt with amounts, with time, with lengths, numbers, sizes. There was a part page saying: DOCTOR, NURSE, MEDICINE, KLEENEX, EYEDROPS, BANDAIDS, MAKEUP, FINGER NAILS, SCISSORS, SALVE. One page was devoted to ordinary things: TV, RECORD PLAYER, LOUDER, SOFTER, SHUT IT OFF, GO FOR A WALK, RIDE, WHEELCHAIR, CRUTCH, SPECTACLES, MAGNIFYING GLASS, SOLITAIRE, SHUFFLE THE CARDS, PENCIL, GIN RUMMY. We could play gin rummy as before, and we kept honest score, and sometimes Dot beat me. I piled up a barricade of books where she could lay out her cards so that I couldn't see them. Otherwise, I would be inclined to cheat to let her win, and she couldn't abide that. But after a while that book was discarded. She could scrawl a few words left handed and could sign her name, but usually pointing or playing twenty questions to narrow it down or a lucky guess or knowing her regimen made it easy to understand her.

Dolores was even better at it than I. She came Saturdays, and at 11 am on a certain radio station there was an hour of opera. Dot would try to hum along. She pointed to one of her books and would find the opera and ask Dolores to read the synopsis out loud. When the opera was approaching one of the great passages such as "Woman is fickle, false altogether," or "Swear in this hour," Dot would point to mention of it on the page. It appears that Dolores' husband, the chief, knew good music, and when we had tickets to a symphony in town, Dolores knew the chief would want to go, so she accepted the tickets gladly. She once told me, "Mr. Watkin, you have no idea how much I have learned from that woman." I told her how much we owed her. She sighed and said, "I have broken the very first rule of nursing: never get emotionally involved with your patient." I just said, "Thank God."

As the years went by, my eyes got so much worse that we began having car accidents, not always my fault, but though my vision passed the driver-test standards, I eventually grounded myself and got another part-time nurse. Actually, she was only a chauffeur for Dot and came back each day more resentful than before because Dot knew all the roads and insisted on where she wanted to be driven. I had to take the girl aside and try to make her understand what those rides meant to Dot. She was getting a big fee for driving a fine automobile through pleasant scenery, and if she didn't like it she was free to look for a better job. She didn't. She knew what real nursing entailed.

We lived from crisis to crisis.

Returning home one afternoon after a rainstorm, we were almost to our door when Dot's foot slipped on the slick cement, which the cement contractor was supposed to leave with roughened surface but found it cheaper not to bother. I had hold of her bad arm but couldn't support her when her full weight suddenly yanked down. She broke her hip. A surgeon put a ball joint in that hip which worked perfectly, but it slowed her down again. Then when she was completely recovered, I broke my leg after fixing the faulty alignment on the forms for extension of a back patio. When you have glaucoma, you stumble a lot, for your depth perception is affected. That meant another nurse until I could get a cast off. The cement man was supposed to pour the following day, but by the time he got around to it the bone had almost completely knitted again. When the concrete was finally poured, he swore that the drainage would be perfect. It looked fine, but after the first rain we found that he had left a depression about two feet wide where water stood until the sun dried it up. Among all inept and deceitful workmen you will have to search long and hard to find anyone who can beat a good old California cement contractor.

As 1979 came in, everything appeared to be going fine for both of us at last. The eye specialist found that my glaucoma was responding so well to medication that the pressure stayed down and for typing I didn't even need reading glasses. Dot was fine and had adjusted well to her problems. But by early summer she began having headaches. Spectacles helped. Then she had tiny heart problems and was fitted for a pacemaker. She was adjusting to that when without out warning at breakfast on July 3 she had the final seizure. I lived in a sort of daze, unable to think, but on July 8 pulled myself together sufficiently to write the following letter to our many friends throughout the country:

> July 8, 1979
>
> Dear Friends,
>
> Because I'll not be sending Christmas cards this year, I'm writing a Xeroxed letter instead. It's likely that I may be on the island with Phil and Anne for the holidays. To forestall the embarrassment of cheerful messages to Dot, it's my painful duty to inform you that she died in the evening of July 5, 1979. On the morning of July 3, she was apparently

very much her old self, but while I was at the stove pouring coffee she had a seizure that left her so rigid I couldn't get any restorative between her locked teeth. Anne, a neighbor lady, the paramedics, and the doctor who has been caring for her all arrived quickly and had her ready for the ambulance that took her to the hospital. She was in the intensive care unit in short order, but she never regained consciousness.

Two weeks previously she was listless, and had low blood pressure and a fluttery pulse. She also complained of pain around her eyes. Her heart responded to a pacemaker the surgeon installed; drops were helping an eye infection, and new spectacles helped temporarily.

This second stroke, which hit the still unaffected side of her brain, was so devastating that if she had lived, there would have been no comprehension left. The prognosis was to be locked away in the lunatic ward of whatever convalescent hospital would take her. Death saved her that final humiliation and put an end to her pain and frustration. Following her wishes, she will be cremated here and her ashes sent to a vault in Los Angeles, for that's where she asked to be buried. I would have been happy to have her back under any circumstances, for there isn't much else that has occupied my mind since she had that first stroke in 1974. She was by far the brightest, kindest, most tolerant person I've ever met. For something to do I'm going to stay right here and pound that typewriter for a long time. I couldn't care less if anything comes out worth publishing, but I'm going to give it my best shot.

There will be no service for Dot anywhere. The only people she knew and loved are either dead or too far away to attend, and to go through the motions for a group of good-hearted semi strangers would be a strain on everybody concerned. So many people have asked to send flowers that this is a more meaningful substitute: though it isn't at all necessary, a few dollars would be greatly appreciated by the Dorothy Watkin Memorial Fund, Elks Rehabilitation Hospital, 204 Fort Street, Boise, Idaho 83702. In thirty days those people did more for her than all the specialists who have worked on her since.

I'm fine. Our children are giving me more support than one lonely old man has any right to expect.

41

For weeks and months thereafter I found it impossible to adjust to life without Dorothy. I visited my three children as long as I could without disrupting their lives. I hated our comfortable condominium, for I saw Dot everywhere in it. We had a pair of beautiful four-poster beds, but I couldn't sleep in mine with the one beside it unoccupied. It helped when I gave them to my recently married grandson and bought a big new one to thrash around in. I sold my car. Fortunately, a supermarket, bank, drug store, and the like were within easy walking distance, and I had need to walk, though I saw very little point in living. I seriously considered suicide. Several things kept me from it then and now: my curiosity about the world and what may happen next, not to me but to the world at large, my children and grandchildren, and the lack of guts to do the deed. I enjoy the brief occasional visits I have with my relatives, and have been able to help one child slightly, but none needs me. I have written one good thing since Dot had her first stroke: the effect of Nixon's duplicity on a college boy, but it was finished at a time when people had tired of the Watergate mess. I sent it to what had been a highly respected Hollywood agency, which is now in its dotage. They lose everything and have never kept me informed. I don't much care. If I wrote the smash hit of all time, it would mean nothing to me now. Pounding the typewriter is a habit and keeps me occupied, but I am grounded here by the great amounts of medication I must take to stay alive, my restricted diet, and need to be within hailing distance of those who know what to do for me in case of emergency.

If I were a healthy old man, I know exactly how I could give pleasure to myself and to others: travel. I would take each of the eleven grandchildren in turn, or by couples if they were married, and show them the places in the world I know best, starting always with London. With that goal in the back of my mind, I took a trial flight to visit my sister and her husband in their winter home in Florida. Anne and her family were on the same plane with me as far as Atlanta, where they changed planes for their island off the coast of Georgia. I was to join them after Christmas. I didn't have to get off the plane until it reached Orlando, where Glenevieve and Gus met me. They had made great plans, but I fell sick with a severe cold. I couldn't get warm, no matter how heavily I was clothed. They took me to the doctor, who prescribed some placebo, and they overheated their house, but I knew it was more severe than they could cope with, and there was no hospital nearby, so I flew to LA where my son took me to my former doctor, who took a lung X-ray and hurried me into the Encino hospital to cure me of pneumonia. I spent nearly a month there. Dr. Hertz suspected that the amount of quinidine sulphate I was taking was now excessive. He took one blood test after another, cut the eight pills a day I had been taking since 1970 down to four. What had been right for the early years after my heart surgery was excessive now. He wrote my doctor in Stockton to give me a blood test two weeks after my return home to check out the new dosage. He did so and found that four pills a day was now perfect. Dr. Hertz knew what he was talking about. That put an end to travel.

I may visit LA again, briefly, but doubt I'd last a week in London, unable to walk the distances necessary to view Kew Gardens, forgetting what the pubsters wanted to see across the Thames in the old Prospect of Whitby, or falling down the stairs trying to climb to the top of a red bus and ending up in the London Clinic, where my despairing grandchild could visit me.

But in 1980 I did have an enjoyable two weeks. Twenty years ago I had written a screenplay for Mark Catesby, about Colonial Williamsburg. He makes the occasional film for their tourists. Currently he had tried to get a script from a New York TV writer, but the screenplay was a total disaster.

Art Smith was sure that I was the only one who could turn it into something they could shoot, and sent me a copy to be doctored. I explained why it would have to be discarded. He asked me to do a whole new play. I said I couldn't. I could write a new enveloping story, but not the rest, since it dealt with a traveling lecturer on 18th century science, even astronomy, of which I was completely ignorant. He told me that if I would write a new story to make the lecturer likable, replacing the wooden Indian of the present screenplay, he would persuade the researcher, Jane Carson, to come out of retirement and work with me, and indeed write all the parts dealing with the scientific demonstrations. Because I could not travel to Williamsburg, she would come to Stockton, check in at the nearest hotel, and taxi to my house every day for two weeks to work in all the parts dealing with astronomy, electricity, objects falling in a vacuum, and the like.

Art knew that I could not refuse such an offer. To work in close proximity with Jane Carson is the aim of every person with the

A-brain who ever met her. She is such a delightful combination of wit and knowledge, of scorn for the phony, of quick recall for almost everything worth knowing, and of great good nature that the only words to portray her are those used by Steele to describe Lady Mary Wortley Montagu, "To know her is to love her, and to love her is a liberal education."

She put up at a motel within walking distance, which was near to a restaurant that was sufficient for her breakfasts. She walked the rest of the way, arriving always at 10 am. For lunch, she would eat only one dish of her own devising. The nearby supermart had six different varieties of fresh lettuce. She could get only one or two kinds in Williamsburg, and so she munched lettuces as if they were the rarest delicacies. I took her out to some fine restaurants, but I think she preferred the lettuce, which, however disguised, I choked down for health reasons as so much grass. Since my habits were nocturnal, I had written a good many scenes for her to read the next morning. I'd have stayed up all night to get a chuckle from her and begged for adverse criticism. The little I got was useful, and she was always ready to be a sounding board. I hated to see her depart in the allotted time, taking a copy of my script with her. She still had an exhausting task ahead, and it took all her tact to persuade the two scientists from William and Mary who had perpetrated the original page-long scientifically correct but hopelessly un-dramatic speeches for the lecturer that they were not screen writers who had composed imperishable prose. I doubt if anyone else could have done it. Art is shooting it now. Not only did he pay me a most generous fee but collaborated with Jane to send me a gift which I cherish. The letter announcing it is a keepsake, too, a reminder of a fortnight that will not come again, but which let me have fun while writing as in the good old days. Her letter was dated November 16, 1980:

> Dear Larry,
>
> Any day now you'll get a package, which needs some explaining. It's from Art Smith and me, an un-birthday present—too late for a guest-to-host gift or for All Saints' Day, too early for Thanksgiving or Christmas or your birthday. And it has a history.
>
> Search for a Nineteenth-Century gentleman's Malacca covered the Tidewater, The Valley, the Carolinas and Pennsylvania. Then Art found this bone one in New Hampshire in his brother Merrill's possession. It originally belonged to a prominent Bostonian—Dr. Hitchcock, a heart surgeon and ladies'

man who visited New Hampshire each October and often played bridge with the Smith brothers. Art's memory supplies these details about "Doc" Hitchcock:

He drove a Volkswagen at great speeds around the countryside, and his appearance was distinguished in part by use of only one glove on cold evenings—because only one of his hands was ever cold. His warm heart was appreciated by his lady patients and some of them complained to his wife that she should step aside on their behalf. Before Mrs. Hitchcock finally decided to go to heaven, she auctioned some of her belongings and Art and Peg Smith acquired her large turkey platter, which ever since has supported the Smith Thanksgiving turkey.

Before leaving New Hampshire Dr. Hitchcock gave his favorite cane to Merrill Smith as a memento of many pleasant evenings. Then he accepted the company of one of his favorite young ladies and headed for Pennsylvania, where he still resides at the age of ninety-three.

We hope you'll enjoy his walking stick.

Yours,

Jane

I do enjoy it and use it daily on my hike over to the Village Square as the shopping district is called. Once it saved my life. At the end of the street I must keep within the wide-lined paths set aside for pedestrians. No California driver ever stops entirely to abide by the law giving a pedestrian the right of way, nor does he set his brakes. Rather he makes a bow and inches on to get the jump on the drivers about to turn left or right into his path. Sometimes he is completely across my right-of-way lane, while one or the other of his antagonists thinks I am far enough over so that he can make the turn around me into the main road. They all but shave my heels in doing so. Some young drivers don't stop at all, but make me wait, even honking at me to get out of the way if I can't walk fast enough to please them. I have often thought that a plain-clothes policeman could get some illuminating pictures of what an elderly pedestrian is up against at a four-way stop which has no stop-and-go lights.

About the cane. I had waited until all four turns were relatively free of cars before I started across. I carried a heavy package of groceries in my left hand which made me even more plodding. The one car at the stop on the wide street started to turn left toward me. I hurried on, but he made a big sweep and bore straight down on me. He was coming closer when I could see that he wasn't looking at me. I began to shout, for I couldn't spring forward or back up nimbly enough to escape him, but his windows were closed. I waved my cane frantically and he slammed on his brakes stopping his car only inches from my body. He was a man of fifty or so driving a new and very expensive car. He wasn't drunk. He was so scared he could hardly get out the words of apology, which were more or less as follows: "It's a good thing you waved that cane. I was thinking and I just didn't see you."

I thought I knew what he was thinking about and had this speech on the tip of my tongue, "Yeah, you were thinking about all that beautiful money you were going to make now that Reagan's in. Well, let me tell you something: if you had hit me, my son, who's a lawyer, would have sued you for every dirty penny. So after this, watch where you're going, you dumb shit!"

He was shaking so hard I just turned away, saying nothing. A week later a very small boy with his bike ran into me from behind and bruised my leg.

It never occurred to me that I might die on a street. Until Dot had her stroke, I gave little if any thought to death, but now that thought intrudes. When my time comes, I hope that if I am conscious I will accept death with good grace. I have cheated it so often that like my novel I have long been living on borrowed time. The defeated wolf presents his throat to be torn; a ploy that usually saves his life, for his victorious antagonist seeks only an admission of his superiority. I will not expect such forbearance and hope that my mind is clear enough not to let me whimper. I trust that no well-meaning relative or friend will expect a deathbed conversion. I have never been able to believe in a personal god in our vast, impersonal universe. I know how comforting it must be to believe in a life after death, and neither stubbornness nor conceit holds me back. Rather, I would think myself presumptuous and conceited to believe. The laws of nature are inexorable and neither cruel nor kind. When frost comes, the leaf falls to make a mulch to nourish the sprouting bud. And so, we say, we live again in our children, but that is our immortality. Nature does not watch the sparrow's fall, or the dropping of a leaf, or the passing of an old man like me. The resistless force that slowly created all the plants and animals, including man, set up the self-perpetuating laws that govern the universe, and in that universe, I am of no more importance than the leaf.

I do not express such thoughts to influence those who love me, for you are either a believer or you're not. I once asked Coons, "Hannibal, what do you believe?" He asked me in turn, "What've you got?"

If you are religious, your creed makes no possible difference as long as you accept religion quietly to make yourself a better individual. If, like my father, your religion or philosophy had as its basic tenet the Golden Rule, it would make you and everyone you knew the better for it. But I hope that any grandchild of mine will have enough skepticism to renounce all evangelists such as Billy Graham, a money-lover, and lesser or greater gurus who care not a fig for your soul but only as a follower to be used for their selfish purposes, whether power or money. The same applies to such organizations as the Moral Majority who band together for political ends to force their followers to whatever bigotry they hold dear. Religion should never use you. If it does, shun it as you would any other poison.

That about wraps it up.

42

Not long ago I heard a young couple say they wouldn't think of bringing a child into such a stinking world as we were living in now. When we were their age we thought our world was just as bad, but that didn't stop Dorothy. I said I was sorry she had had such a rough time. She felt the whole experience had been sublime.

"It's a lovely secret feeling," she said. "You're scared, then you feel that little kick and you know it's alive inside you. Then you have it and you don't care how much you're torn up. It's the most wonderful feeling you ever had in your life. Your insides have created something that never was before. Your purpose in life is to create life, and you did it. You feel you're floating above all the little small things in the world."

When I set out to write this book, I had no other thought than to relate with good humor what my experience had been in dealing with other human beings, both great and small. Then I lost my balance wheel and without her ran the risk of becoming an embittered old man. To keep my perspective and avoid becoming a carping old bore, I find that I need only stop and listen to what Dorothy might say by remembering things she actually said. She did not defend wrongdoers or quote proverbial wisdom to excuse human frailty. But if I let my hot temper get out of control, she had a quiet way of telling me that mindless vituperation brought me down to the level of the object I scorned.

Sometimes when I am conscious that I deserve a mild rebuke, I can see her tolerant smile, which is as eloquent as any words, remembered or imagined. Such people never die. As long as I live she will live, too, and I will be the better for it.

Lawrence Watkin died on December 16, 1981, at the age of 80.

AFTERWORD

Larry Watkin and Walt Disney

Despite his many other accomplishments, Larry Watkin is, perhaps, best remembered as a long-time screenwriter for many classic Disney films, such as *Treasure Island*, *The Story of Robin Hood and His Merrie Men*, *The Great Locomotive Chase*, and *Darby O'Gill and the Little People*. But long before Larry Watkin came to Hollywood—before he worked for Sam Goldwyn and later Walt Disney—he had a career as a college English professor and a literary novelist. In his early years, he wrote five novels, including *Marty Markham*, the story of a rich boy who finds his humanity at a summer boys camp. This novel was made into a long-running Disney TV serial, *Spin and Marty*, a semi-regular segment on *The Mickey Mouse Club*. But Watkin's first novel, *On Borrowed Time* (1937), was his best known and most celebrated.

On Borrowed Time won a National Book Award, was later made into a Broadway play, adapted for the big screen, and finally condensed for TV. The story focuses on an elderly man, named Grampa Northrup, who trapped the mythical character of Death in an enchanted apple tree. As long as Death was trapped, Grampa Northrup would continue to live, along with all of humanity. The removal of death from the world caused endless problems for insurance men and writers of murder mysteries. It forced doctors to rethink their practices. For others, mostly the elderly, it meant endless illness and suffering, without the possibility of a final release. Reviewers called the novel "thrilling," a rare work that made magical events utterly "convincing," a "delightful fantasy" focused on the meaning of life and the importance of it being understood as a cycle. Not only did *On Borrowed Time* establish Watkin's career as a novelist, it also brought him, a decade later, to the Disney studio, where his reputation in Hollywood blossomed as the writer (and sometimes producer) for a series of successful live-action films.

After WWII, Walt Disney faced a serious problem: the British government, hoping to revive motion-picture productions in the UK, insisted that 45% of films shown there be made in England. Moreover, they impounded ticket receipts from American films shown in the UK, requiring that the funds be spent there as well. The Disney studio, which had always enjoyed strong international interest in their pictures, looked for ways to overcome this problem: how could they best spend the mountain of money accumulated in their British accounts? The solution, as far as Walt was concerned, was to create a picture (or pictures) in England, under the Disney name, using British directors, cameramen, crew, and (largely) actors. But if the films were shot in England, far from his daily oversight, Walt wanted the scripts to be drafted at the Burbank studio, hoping that strong pre-production materials would ensure that the finished film held the cinematic values of a Disney project.

In 1947, after seeing a revival presentation of *On Borrowed Time* at a local theater, Walt asked an assistant to contact the author about a possible assignment at the Disney studio. Walt was impressed with the play, particularly how the author had created believable fantasy elements inside of a realistic world. He thought that, possibly, an author who could place the compelling figure of Death beside a fully realized grandfather might also be able to adapt the fantasy stories of Herminie Templeton Kavanagh into a unified script. The stories, collected mostly in the book *Darby O'Gill and the Good People*, presented a series of humorous tales about wee Irish fairies—leprechauns who were playful, spiteful, vengeful, and who had recently captured a human inside their underground city. When Watkin met him at his office, Walt explained that the film would mix live action and animation—specifically, the fairies would be animated.

Watkin, somewhat stymied with his previous attempts as a screenwriter, accepted the offer: he would receive an impressive salary of $500 a week, his own secretary, and a plush office on the third floor of the Animation Building (not far from Walt's office).

For weeks, he struggled with the Kavanagh stories. The stories, he later wrote, "had no basic plot. There was no real conflict; Darby was under no constraint to prove anything." To make a unified movie, Watkin would need to add these elements. He produced a first screen treatment—then a second. Watkin didn't think much of either effort. But Walt saw the strength of his work, even if it was raw.

Though Watkin had previously worked for other studios, he had been kept in the writers' wings. Walt thought that Watkin's work might improve if he was better exposed to the process of making a film at the Disney studio: he invited Watkin out to see movies being shot (primarily *So Dear to My Heart*); he allowed Watkin to watch the dailies with the production crew; he led Watkin into bays where editors were trimming and assembling a film into its final form.

This early admiration worked both ways: in Watkin, Walt saw a young man, one touched with literary sensibilities, who might blossom into a successful screenwriter, something the studio needed, especially as it was considering expansion into live action, both at the Burbank studio and possibly overseas. But Watkin, Walt believed, needed a stronger connection to the Darby O'Gill material to write a successful script.

One summer afternoon, Walt entered Watkin's office and asked if he would like to take an extended research trip to South Ireland, to get a better feel for stories about the little people. If so, he should leave as soon as possible, Walt said. "And take Mrs. Watkin along." The trip would include a first-class passage on a trans-atlantic ship. By the end of the trip, Watkin had a deeper vision for the Darby O'Gill project. He'd also met many people with whom he would correspond for the rest of his life. But the Darby O'Gill project was shelved—at least for a few years—while Watkin worked on other assignments.

In 1947 and 1948, Watkin briefly engaged *Alice in Wonderland*. Like the Kavanagh stories about the Irish fairies, the Alice material was essentially a series of isolated episodes about Alice's experiences in Wonderland. Watkin's job, as before, was to find a way to both preserve the flavors of the original material yet arrive at an overarching arc to connect the tales into a unified narrative. But once again, Watkin was moved onto a new project, leaving Alice to story artists focused on animation and Darby to a shelf of unfinished scripts. The new project, however, would establish Watkin's name at the studio.

In 1948, Walt again approached the problem of impounded British theater receipts, with his gaze now settled on a live-action adaptation of *Treasure Island*. In ways, *Treasure Island* better fit the Disney model: to create a feature presentation of a well-known children's story, much in the fashion of *Snow White and the Seven Dwarfs*, *Cinderella*, and *Pinocchio*. The name "Treasure Island" would also ensure immediate audience recognition due to the popularity of the classic Robert Louis Stevenson novel. But to minimize Disney's financial exposure to live action—a new form for the studio— Walt entered into a deal with its distributor, RKO (who also had impounded funds in England), to share both the costs and profits for a British production of a Walt Disney feature.

One afternoon Walt came into Watkin's office and laid out his plans to adapt *Treasure Island*. As with the previous projects, Watkin saw his job as unifying a literary property in such a way that would fit the narrative space of a Hollywood film. In the days that followed, he worked the Stevenson material into a treatment that he believed would flow well on the screen. When he showed it to his boss, however, Walt said that Watkin had misunderstood the assignment: "*Treasure Island* is a classic," Walt complained. "You can't change a classic that much."

But Watkin argued that the novel, in terms of creating a continuous story on screen, was "full of holes" and contained illogical jumps that might be managed in a written narrative with its emphasis on character and voice, but would be problematic in film with its emphasis on plot. If they adapted the novel scene-for-scene, the shortcomings in the story would be obvious. "People would blame us," Watkin said, "not Stevenson."

To demonstrate the problems with the Stevenson plot as a film property, Watkin returned to his office and created a chart: on one side, he listed the plot elements, metered out scene by scene, from the Stevenson novel; on the other, he listed the ways that his proposed script would correct them. "For example, I related that the captain, who should have known better, stupidly goes ashore leaving his ship under insufficient guard."

Walt looked over Watkin's chart then he re-read the Stevenson novel, noticing the differences. After considering the matter, with a note of apology in his voice, he said, "We'll do it your way." He explained that he wanted to bring in Perce Pearce as producer to oversee development. Pearce was a Disney artist whose career at the studio extended back to *Snow White*. "But stick to what you showed me," Walt added. "When you have the screenplay, let me read it."

These early discussions on *Treasure Island* moved Watkin into a central role at the studio, in that Walt saw Watkin could be trusted to create a script that would read well on screen and also that he would help protect the studio's image as it began a feature production that would be filmed overseas.

Treasure Island proved a financial success, bringing in $4.8 million against $1.8 million in negative costs. Production costs had depleted Disney's impounded funds, but the film proved so profitable that both Disney and RKO were interested in co-producing other British-made films. Beyond this, *Treasure Island* established a team of artists that would, in large part, comprise a second production unit for the Disney studio through the 1950s, one primarily focused on historical dramas. Watkin, of course, would be part of this team, as would Perce Pearce.

Joining them would be individuals like composer Clifton Parker and matte painter Peter Ellenshaw. The British production also allowed Disney to hire talented English technicians wishing to make stronger connections with Hollywood, such as cinematographer Freddie Young who would later shoot *Doctor Zhivago* and *Lawrence of Arabia*.

Richard Todd, who starred in a number of the British productions (*The Story of Robin Hood*, *Rob Roy*, and *The Sword and the Rose*) recalled that the overseas Disney team developed strong bonds. "There was a special quality [of working on a Disney film]," Todd said, "quite unlike the atmosphere on any other production. There was very much a family ambiance, a feeling of harmony partly engendered by Perce Pearce's avuncular presence, partly arising from the fact that most of us had worked together and knew each other well—but mostly perhaps due to the smoothness with which the schedule rolled along as a result of the careful pre-planning of previous weeks."

With the success of *Treasure Island*, Watkin found that other studios were interested in hiring him and increasing his salary. But he decided to stay at Disney's, a small studio in the Hollywood community, as he now believed that Walt "possessed a synthesizing genius—possibly a higher form of creativity." To put it simply, he liked spending time with the big boss. Walt was more approachable than other producers. And beyond this, Watkin liked the material he was assigned.

After *Treasure Island*, he returned to the Darby O'Gill stories and completed a full draft of a screenplay. He also gave the project a new name: *Three Wishes*. In July 1950, the studio announced that the leprechaun project would "combine animation and live action" and that "the live-action sequences [would] be filmed in Ireland" next year. But again the fantasy project was put aside so Watkin could focus on live-action historical dramas.

As these pictures progressed, Watkin was slowly ushered into Walt's inner circle, a position where he helped Walt shape and create films. In previous writing assignments, Watkin had been valued for his literary depth and his complex, realistic characters. At times, Watkin would find that these literary skills were valued at the Disney studio as well. But Walt was idiosyncratic—occasionally drawn to films destined to win awards and occasionally drawn to films that satisfied middle-American appetites for wholesome entertainment. Watkin found that his work at Disney's stretched him: it forced him to look beyond narrative as it was defined inside of novels and classrooms.

As Watkin moved from script to script, he came to understand Walt's tastes: the comic characters were "innocently resourceful and tinged with malice" and the villains were "terrifying but not loathsome." Examples of both can be found in *Treasure Island*. Jim Hawkins, the hero, was innocent and mischievous; Long John Silver, its villain, was calculating, mutinous, and power-hungry but still had a soft spot for the young Jim.

As the Disney/RKO British films were released, Watkin came to believe that Walt had the ability to understand the desires of middle America, impressions that he couldn't always articulate. "Sometimes he was unable," Watkin said, "to explain why he felt as he did." But his impressions were usually right.

Watkin also came to believe that his own strengths (largely literary and academic) were balanced by those that Walt possessed (largely intuitive and narrative). At times Walt dismissed formal education by saying, "Education is too important to be left to educators." But Watkin knew that Walt would "have given his eye teeth for a college education." He was an avid reader, always interested in talking to new people and understanding their perspectives.

Watkin's role at the studio extended far beyond that of a mere writer. For *The Sword and the Rose,* he accompanied Pearce and director Ken Annakin on a trip to Paris to cast actors and actresses for French characters included in the film. At times, he worked as a lyricist, with songs in three pictures. In the mid-1950s, when Walt asked him to produce *The Great Locomotive Chase*, Watkin explained that he would have no authority on the set as he had no experience as a producer. "Not if you pick the director," Walt countered. If Watkin hired the director, the director would see Watkin as his supervisor. "Go out and pick one," Walt added.

According to Fess Parker, star of *The Great Locomotive Chase,* Walt often promoted people into positions slightly outside their reach as a way of maintaining control at the studio, as less-experienced individuals would naturally defer to him. "[Walt] wanted the last word," Parker said. "He didn't want anybody to challenge him. When we did *The Great Locomotive Chase*, he put a producer in place who had never produced, Larry Watkin." The goal, according to Parker, was for Walt to have control in the editing room, to give a project its final narrative shape. But even in this, Watkin understood Walt's motivation: "It was in the cutting room that old-time producers like Disney were truly great," Watkin said. "They could cut, splice, turn whole sequences around in the most amazing fashion, often telling a slightly different story with the material at hand."

The Great Locomotive Chase was Watkin's first and only experience as a producer. After that, he returned to the familiar role of writer where he remained until he left the studio.

For the next three years he worked on historical dramas that explored American history, such as *The Light in the Forest* (which tells the story of a young white man who, in the 1760s, was raised by American Indians) and *Ten Who Dared* (which tells the story of John Powell's 1868 expedition down the Colorado River and through the Grand Canyon). He also saw his own novel *On Borrowed Time* adapted once more, this time for TV.

During a lull at the studio, his attention was drawn back to his first assignment, the Darby O'Gill material, which now flew under yet another title: *The Three Wishes of Darby O'Gill*. After putting the material aside for eleven years, he now believed he saw a way to unify the script—based in part on a short story he had published in *Colliers* magazine years earlier. In it, a night watchman was fired when he turned sixty-five years old. Unable to tell his wife, he returned to work each night to accompany the new watchman and hopefully prove his worth. This plot structure, Watkin knew, could establish the frame narrative for the Darby O'Gill material: Darby would be an elderly caretaker of a large Irish estate about to lose his job to a younger man. The concept would make Darby immediately sympathetic (having just lost his job due to his age) and would give the story an overriding quest (for Darby to prove himself valuable and retain his position). As he worked through the material, he added more dramatic elements, such as a love story between Darby's daughter and the man destined to replace him. He also arranged the sections with the "little people" to solve both Darby's job problems and those his daughter faced in romance.

When Watkin showed his story treatment to his boss, Walt immediately saw its potential, an imaginative work focused on romance, rivalries, and of course, self-worth. "Write it up," he said. "We'll shoot it."

In the weeks that followed, Watkin worked through the story many times, understanding that Walt would likely support such a film with a generous budget. The original idea to animate the leprechauns was now replaced with a plan to build massive sets and miniaturize human actors to appear as little people, using a set of expensive optical tricks. Watkin included everything he had learned, a decade earlier, about Irish folk culture, including the banshee and the death coach. The finished script presented not only the story of an individual man, but the story of an entire culture— or rather of an entire culture slowly passing away.

With the script approved, a team from Disney went to England to hire top-rate actors, including a young Sean Connery, a few years before he became a Hollywood icon as the big screen's first James Bond. Caroll Clark visually designed the film. Emile Kuri created massive sets, beautifully dressed at the Burbank studio as production was now slotted for California, not the UK. And Watkin's old friend Peter Ellenshaw painted glass mattes to place backlot sets into the Irish countryside and to bring the world of the leprechauns to life. Lastly, the film was given a new title—and this time it stuck: *Darby O'Gill and the Little People.*

To make the Watkin's script a photorealistic presentation, a team of Disney artists and technicians arranged a series of special-effects shots, bringing Darby into the world of the leprechauns. Forced perspective was used to create the illusion that human actors portraying leprechauns were only two feet tall when standing beside Albert Sharpe, the actor who played Darby, with Sharpe in the foreground and the other actors far behind. Mirrors—with part of the reflective backing scraped off—were used to blend images of leprechauns with Darby. Giant props (such as shoes, jugs, and chairs) were placed beside the leprechauns. Lifelike leprechaun puppets (with their backs to the camera) were used in the fore- or midground to better blend the human characters with the leprechaun actors filmed at a distance. Because of the oversized props and the stage space required for forced-perspective shots, the set required tremendous illumination: at times the technicians would oversee nearly 650 lights. "[It] was a very hot set," said visual-effects artist Peter Ellenshaw. "And many times we'd have to close down because it became too hot." The lights drew so much power that, at one point, nearby neighborhoods experienced a brownout.

Darby O'Gill proved a crowning achievement for Watkin's career. The *Los Angeles Times* called it "as physically perfect a job as can be had: the Technicolor, the camera work, the special effects, the Irish music and all are a rich feast for anyone's eye and ear." As for Watkin's contributions, the reviewer wrote, "There is a rather ingeniously arranged surprise ending which we'll not spoil for you." The *New York Times* praised it as an "overpoweringly charming concoction" in which "Mr. Disney [and] Lawrence E. Watkin have given us...more fairy folk legends and brogue than are heard on any soft summer's night at the Abbey Theatre or a Third Avenue saloon."

That summer Watkin accompanied Walt to the film's premiere in Ireland. He helped arrange publicity, including scripting an hour-long show on the film's creation. But during these same months, trouble began to build in Hollywood, with the Writers' and Actors' Guilds threatening to go on strike. At issue was residual compensation for older works as they appeared on TV, with millions of dollars at stake. Everyone in Hollywood understood that this would largely shut down the industry for months, with over 500 writers affected by the action. Television production would go down first, followed by theatrical production, once studios finished filming completed scripts. For writers, the strike would last twenty weeks, nearly half a year.

Shortly before the strike, Walt made Watkin an offer. In one version of the story (related in his memoir), he asked if Watkin would like to be a producer. In a slightly different version (that Watkin related elsewhere), Walt asked if he'd like to be an *assistant* producer. Regardless, either role would've saved him from the coming labor troubles and also given him more authority as the studio looked to expand its production schedule. "I knew that in offering me a producership," Watkin would later explain, "he was paying me the greatest compliment he knew how to give, but I knew it'd be no good, for my heart wasn't in it."

During the strike, Walt began to drift away from movies. His attention was more focused on his theme park in Anaheim and developing a new resort somewhere on the East Coast, perhaps near Miami. When the strike was over and Watkin returned to the studio, Walt called him in for a meeting. Watkin knew immediately that he was being dismissed. "We just don't have anything for you to do," Walt said. He complimented Watkin's work at the studio, particularly the last two British pictures. But in Watkin's estimation, his boss looked embarrassed, especially as they had worked together for over a decade. He also thought that Walt was still upset "because I had refused to be a producer," though Walt may have seen the situation from a different perspective. Perhaps Watkin was being let go because he had refused to adapt in ways the studio needed. As Walt began to focus on expanding his theme park efforts to the East Coast, he needed reliable people to help take over the role of producing Disney stories for film and TV.

When it became clear that Watkin wasn't going to put up a fight, Walt softened his tone, like he did in the old days, and said, "I'm sure you'll make just as much money as a freelance writer as you will working for me." Unsure of what to do—or how to end the conversation gracefully—Walt picked up a script and began to read it, signaling that the writer probably should leave, thereby concluding one of the most successful collaborations Walt had experienced with anyone outside of his circle of top animators.

In the months after Watkin left, resentment followed him, a sense that he had been wronged, that Walt hadn't honored all the work he'd given to the studio. As a freelancer, he wrote for TV, only to find he didn't much care for the medium. Instead he returned to teaching. Five years after Walt died, Watkin returned to the studio to write one final script, *The Biscuit Eater*, for producer and friend Bill Anderson.

By then the bitterness had been washed from his mouth. With distance, he could see that his time with Walt formed one of the most important experiences in his life. He found himself telling stories of the man, stories touched with notes of warmth, stories that, at times, he worked out into a list. There was the time that someone called Walt an "old sonofabitch." The following day, Walt said, "Hell, I've often been called a sonofabitch, but he had no right to call me old."

Of course Watkin's life and his memoir are much more than just an account of his relatively short time at Disney. It's a fascinating document of early Hollywood, originally written in the late 1970s, a look into that fabled wonderland, when a small group of enthusiastic men and women, most without formal screen training, could make fabulous pictures that would be presented around the world.

T.J. Pierce